MW00990892

BIGGS

on

FINANCE, ECONOMICS,

and the

STOCK MARKET

BIGGS

on

FINANCE, ECONOMICS,

and the

STOCK MARKET

*Barton's Market Chronicles
from the Morgan Stanley Years*

BARTON BIGGS

WILEY

Cover image: © iStockphoto.com/nicoolay & © iStockphoto.com/Ursula Alter
Cover design: Wiley

Copyright © 2014 by Barton Biggs. All rights reserved.

Published by John Wiley & Sons, Inc., Hoboken, New Jersey.
Published simultaneously in Canada.

No part of this publication may be reproduced, stored in a retrieval system, or transmitted in any form or by
any means, electronic, mechanical, photocopying, recording, scanning, or otherwise, except as permitted under
Section 107 or 108 of the 1976 United States Copyright Act, without either the prior written permission of
the Publisher, or authorization through payment of the appropriate per-copy fee to the Copyright Clearance
Center, Inc., 222 Rosewood Drive, Danvers, MA 01923, (978) 750-8400, fax (978) 646-8600, or on the Web
at www.copyright.com. Requests to the Publisher for permission should be addressed to the Permissions
Department, John Wiley & Sons, Inc., 111 River Street, Hoboken, NJ 07030, (201) 748-6011, fax (201)
748-6008, or online at http://www.wiley.com/go/permissions.

Limit of Liability/Disclaimer of Warranty: While the publisher and author have used their best efforts in
preparing this book, they make no representations or warranties with respect to the accuracy or completeness
of the contents of this book and specifically disclaim any implied warranties of merchantability or fitness for
a particular purpose. No warranty may be created or extended by sales representatives or written sales
materials. The advice and strategies contained herein may not be suitable for your situation. You should
consult with a professional where appropriate. Neither the publisher nor author shall be liable for any loss of
profit or any other commercial damages, including but not limited to special, incidental, consequential, or
other damages.

For general information on our other products and services or for technical support, please contact our
Customer Care Department within the United States at (800) 762-2974, outside the United States at (317)
572-3993 or fax (317) 572-4002.

Wiley publishes in a variety of print and electronic formats and by print-on-demand. Some material included
with standard print versions of this book may not be included in e-books or in print-on-demand. If this book
refers to media such as a CD or DVD that is not included in the version you purchased, you may download this
material at http://booksupport.wiley.com. For more information about Wiley products, visit www.wiley.com.

Library of Congress Cataloging-in-Publication Data:

ISBN 978-1-118-5723-06 (Hardcover)
ISBN 978-1-118-6546-68 (ePDF)
ISBN 978-1-118-6548-66 (ePub)

Printed in the United States of America

10 9 8 7 6 5 4 3 2 1

Contents

Introduction

The untimely passing of Barton Biggs in 2012 created a void for many who never wanted to imagine a world devoid of his uniquely illuminating voice. It was a loss widely felt, and we were inundated with requests for old essays. Seekers would rarely recall dates or titles but would easily refer to a phrase like "the one where he is overfed and maximum bullish." Our team would happily search through the (mostly paper) archives, losing themselves in the guilty pleasure of reading Barton's lucid and often prescient prose of one of Wall Street's truly wise men.

Biggs was a world apart from the cacophony of 21st century infotainment pundits of the twenty-first century; now shouting at us via every medium. The commentaries in this collection span the roughly two decades between 1980–2000 that corresponded with a great bull market in stocks. It was a market that made people rich on paper through their IRAs and 401(k)s; it also broke their hearts. This was a cycle that Barton knew well. He understood that knowledge of human psychology and philosophy was more essential than any quantitative numbers crunching to truly insightful analysis. He was fond of personifying "Mr. Market" as an ingenious sadist or a manic-depressive. Like a therapist, Biggs sought to understand and accept his seemingly irrational companion instead of futilely attempting to change or control him. Along the way, he helped us discover that "the market" is really a mirror into the self and ultimately a foil that could lead to great personal growth beyond mere monetary gain for those courageous enough to do the work.

Biggs was the product of a superb education and insatiable intellectual curiosity that he cultivated throughout his life. His interests were wide-ranging and he read vociferously. He once, in a single paragraph, inventoried some 27 newspapers, periodicals, and commentaries that he consumed on a regular basis. This erudition contributed to a vivid and often beautiful prose style. He would enlighten his readers with a quote from the philosopher John Locke to illustrate the importance of informed judgment in successful investing, and draw upon verses from the poets W.H. Auden to elucidate equity markets psychology, or W.B. Yeats to describe the panic of 1987: "The blood dimmed tide is loosed." Instead of single-mindedly studying charts and quantitative models, Biggs suggested keeping an investment diary and examining our own biases and temperament. "Know thyself and know thy foibles. Study the history of your emotions and your actions," he would write.

This was a man who devoured life. Whether climbing Kilimanjaro, raging against the corrupting economics of college football, or studying the global impacts of government policy, Biggs felt that hard work and discipline were the qualities that mattered. He cheekily poked fun at the idea-of-the-month club with his satirical characters, including Jim the Trigger and his (fictional) Plumber. And his predictions were notable in both their prescience and transcendent views.

In the early 1980s Biggs correctly believed the end of inflation was at hand which would lead to a mighty economic boom. All the while his contemporaries decried the end of the American economy itself. In 1989, he called the Japanese market downturn even as market observers-and broad popular culture-accepted Japan's future of world economic dominance as a foregone conclusion.

Biggs was also a keen student of bubbles and panics, dissecting the historical underpinnings and discovering their commonalities. "It is fascinating," he wrote, "to be reminded of how little human nature has changed and how the pattern of events repeats itself over and over." He called the "dot-bust" in 1997—a couple of years early perhaps but right on the mark in terms of magnitude and impact. "The most dangerous phrase in the investment business," he wrote, "is 'this time it's different'." At heart, Biggs believed in fundamental intrinsic value-both personally and professionally. He believed equally in the value of a contrarian stance in a world where "hordes of investors routinely plunge together off the cliff of financial destruction."

Reading through his work, it is remarkable how far ahead of the moment his mind operated. Biggs was one of the first true global strategists during a time when prevailing thought was locked in a binary us-versus-them world model dominated by the US-USSR Cold War standoff. He identified global flashpoints like Afghanistan and the growing threat of radical Islam decades before 9/11. In 1989 he wrote about the "Greening of Portfolios" and the coming trend toward environmental activism. In that same year, he predicted the skyrocketing costs of healthcare and a broken system we're struggling with today.

He was also a driving force behind the creation of "Emerging Markets" as an asset class. He had his own "boots on the ground" in countries like Kuwait, Singapore, Thailand, India, Brazil, and Argentina before most Wall Streeters could find them on a map.

In some sense, Biggs may have been too far ahead of his time. When taking the long view, inevitable macro-trends can play out over decades despite wild market gyrations over minutes and seconds. Or in the famous words attributed to John Maynard Keynes: "The markets can remain irrational far longer than you or I can remain solvent." All of which makes a compendium of Biggs' forward thinking that much more compelling today now that the world has had a chance to catch up.

James P. Gorman
Chairman and CEO
Morgan Stanley

"We forget that Mr. Market is an ingenious sadist, and that he delights in torturing us in different ways."

– Barton Biggs

With the passing of our friend and colleague
Barton Biggs, the world seems a
little less colorful, insightful and eloquent.
He will be missed.

Morgan Stanley

© 2012 Morgan Stanley & Co. LLC. Member SIPC.

Section 1

WHAT'S OLD IS NEW AGAIN

Back across the ages, bear markets follow bulls as famine follows feast, and 3,000 years ago Joseph proved that anticipation of the inflection point can make tremendous difference in your life-style.

—Barton Biggs, April 1, 1996

Reading through over two decades of Barton's chronicles, it's hard to argue with one of his favorite adages, "history doesn't repeat itself, but it rhymes." Biggs believed that a deep and thorough understanding of the past was important—nay, absolutely necessary—to preparing for the future. Like a symphony orchestra, the music may change and evolve, but ultimately the players behind the instruments remain the same. "The present always seems different from the past, but human nature doesn't change, and the patterns of fear and greed repeat."

Biggs was fascinated with the mechanics of bubbles and panics and devoted numerous weekly missives to the topic. He read narrative accounts of past market crashes and assembled lists of dozens of "stock market breaks and deaths" from around the world—most unknown to the U.S. investor—which convinced him that the boom-bust cycle was not a rare occurrence, but an integral aspect of the market. Manias and panics are simply a phenomenon to be expected, understood, and planned for like any naturally occurring and ultimately unstoppable event such as a hurricane. Or as Biggs would say more succinctly, "As long as there are markets and people, there will be panics, manias, and crashes, and the more you know about them, the better your chances of not getting killed in one."

He also believed strongly in the reversion to the mean. While extremes do exist in nature, conditions moderate back to the normal over time, just as sunshine follows rain. "The course of events in markets really don't change much from century to century, because the two great constants in the stock market are human emotion and prices. Patterns tend to repeat themselves."

If there was ever an investor living at the polar opposite of today's high-speed, black-box trader, it was Barton Biggs. Biggs didn't just study markets over weeks, months, and years. He launched himself into geosynchronous orbit to view economic cycles on the scale of decades and centuries. He concluded that despite the ups and downs, stocks were the place to be in the long run. "History supports the cult of the equity, providing you can hang on through the air pockets," albeit with a tempering caveat: "They really do generate the real returns, but not the double-digit ones some people now anticipate."

Fundamentally, history is the study of past human actions. Whether the scene is the trading floor, battlefield, or political podium, Biggs saw commonalities. He studied the full gamut of history and came to his own startlingly prescient conclusions for our future.

For one, Biggs foresaw Islamic extremism as a long-term market risk years before 9/11 brought the concept front and center in the mindshare of America. He saw a future with "random acts of terrorism" that would someday "degenerate into a real shooting war."

He was also a voice of reason among doomsayers amid skyrocketing oil prices during an existential standoff between Eastern Communism and Western Democracy. While heavyweight pundits decried the decline of the West, Biggs dismissed the catastrophization as nonsense, not because of wishful thinking or pathological denial, but because of the astute observation that events throughout history do not happen in a vacuum. Actions beget reactions, and human beings have a remarkable ability to adapt and cope—often in unexpected ways. As Biggs noted, quoting Barbara Tuchman, "You cannot extrapolate any series in which the human element intrudes; history, that is, the human narrative, never follows, and will always fool, the scientific curve."

Some of his most captivating and unique work came in the form of diary entries, where Biggs provided readers a hypothetical inside glimpse of the innermost thoughts of world leaders and despots in the midst of historic events like Tiananmen Square and the fall of the Berlin Wall. The creative approach serves as a memorial to the Cold War–era mind-set, along with the unknown consequences of our current involvement in Iraq and Afghanistan.

While Biggs's occasional articles with a historical bent are hardly a comprehensive treatment of world events, an investor could do worse. Together, the pieces constitute a powerful foundation for understanding the long view of a true financial luminary through three decades of dramatic change and tectonic world shifts.

Section 1A:
Market History and the Long View

In Search of History and a Word Processor That Works

April 23, 1985

Last week, I said I would write this week about the crucial allocation between stocks and bonds that is on everybody's mind. After spending three hours or so writing on this subject on Sunday, the ultimate word processor nightmare occurred, and, on the print command, my entire text was erased. It's too late to attempt to rewrite this week what was lost so, instead, let me summarize some conclusions.

In making asset allocation decisions, I use both mathematical tools and subjective judgment. Nunzio Tartaglia's Analytical Systems Group has developed a variety of quantitative models for comparing stocks, bonds, and short-term investments, and I use a Present Value Model and the Ford Dividend Discount Model. In addition, straight risk/reward analysis of stocks, bonds, and bills is helpful. Next week, I will report on the status of each of these systems, all of which, incidentally, say that bonds are more attractive than stocks right now.

However, I place more emphasis on judgment considerations, because valuation models are just snapshots of the present's relative value relationships. These models have no predictive powers. Yet, financial asset prices have a lot of the future in them; in other words, they incorporate discounting mechanisms. Valuation models are like X-rays; they do not in and of themselves evaluate a patient's future health, but they help the doctor to do so.

It may sound corny, but I believe the investor should heed the lessons of history, because the past replays, and one ignores its lessons at one's peril. The present always seems different from the past, but human nature doesn't change, and the patterns of fear and greed repeat. The cycles of economic history, particularly the ebb and flow of inflation, and the pattern of the relative performance of asset categories recurs. I am convinced that the past really is the key to the future.

We have done a great deal of work in collecting and ordering statistics. We found that it is very difficult to determine the exact year (much less the quarter) in which a particular era began or ended, and it is often difficult to fairly represent the performance of different assets. Messing around in the yellowing, dry pages of old manuals trying to reconstruct the past into an orderly framework is a good way to learn that even economic history is extremely complicated.

I think our work indicates that you want to be in bonds and commercial paper in deflationary times and in stocks in periods of price stability, disinflation, and moderate inflation. In times of rapid or accelerating inflation, real estate, precious metals, and equities provide positive real returns. But generalizations must be viewed with caution because performance varies considerably relative to the initial valuation of the asset in question. In other words, if the asset entered the period overvalued, its relative performance suffered. A recent example is equities in the latest inflationary era. After a long bull market, stocks were overpriced by all historical and psychological benchmarks as inflation began to accelerate; thus they failed as an inflation hedge. Knowing the record of history is not enough. The investor must be able to determine the present valuation of each asset relative to other assets and to its own valuation cycle.

Kondratieff and the Long Cycle

June 25, 1985

I believe that although knowledge increases, the world progresses, and technology advances, human behavior unfortunately remains the same. This is certainly true in the cycles of emotion in the stock market, and it has always seemed to me that it also should be valid in economic patterns. Thus I have been intrigued with the idea of a long cycle in human events that in general terms recurs. History does not have to repeat itself, but because people don't change, it does.

Economics is really mostly about cycles. Economists like Wesley Mitchell, Simon Kuznets, and Joseph Schumpeter have written about both the conventional business cycle and longer, 10- or even 20-year Juglar cycles. I have been fascinated for years, however, with the supercycles described by a Russian government economist named Nikolai Kondratieff, who created the first five-year plan for Russian agriculture in 1920. In 1922, Kondratieff published "The Long Waves in Economic Life," which describes a recurring 50- to 60-year economic cycle driven by the ebb and flow of innovation and capital investment, and that had social implications. In many ways, Kondratieff's writings are an explanation of history.

The commissars were not amused, however, when they realized that their agricultural economist's theory argued that the downturns in capitalist economies were not attributable to inherent defects within the system but were self-correcting. He was put on trial and sentenced to Siberia, where he spent the rest of his life breaking big stones into little ones. It is believed he died in the 1930s. His papers were generally ignored until the last decade or so, when the work of Professor Jay Forrester of the Sloane School at MIT attracted attention.

The idea of long cycles in human economic history goes back to biblical times. The Old Testament tells of 50-year jubilees, in which slaves were freed and debts were forgiven. Gibbon's *Decline and Fall of the Roman Empire* gives evidence of a 50-year cycle of war and inflation, and a 54-year cycle can be found in the history of agricultural prices going as far back as the Mayans in Central America in 1260. Even primitive economies seemed to become overextended in a regular, more or less half-century cycle. Wealth in terms of land, slaves, and debt would become concentrated, and a purge to revitalize was almost part of the order of nature.

Each cycle, as the accompanying chart shows, is characterized by four distinct phases. First there is a long growth era (27 years on average) culminating in an inflationary peak. Then comes a 1- or 2-year primary depression, which is followed by a plateau of 5 to 10 years. The last phase is a secondary depression and 15 or more years of stagnation. The precise timing of each cycle is different, but the broad outline is eerily similar.

Kondratieff identified three 54-year cycles: 1790 to 1843, 1843 to 1896, and 1896 to the early 1940s. His charts and papers, which relate to England, the United States, and France, analyze commodity prices, interest rates, and wages. Actually, Kondratieff identified rather than analyzed. Professor Forrester and his Systems Dynamics Group believe the waves can be explained by capital investment. During growth phases, demand is imposed on the capital goods industries by both the consumer goods area

Kondratieff's Long Wave

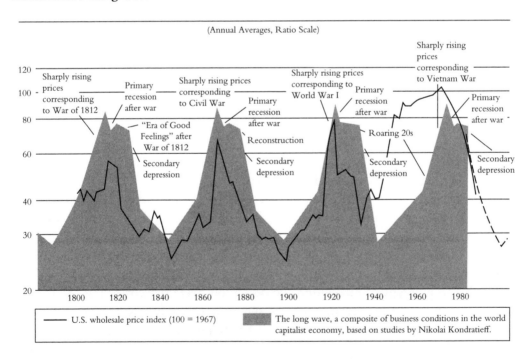

SOURCE: Richardson & Snyder, Publisher, NY/Paragraphics.

and the capital goods sector itself. At the peak, a labor shortage drives wages up and encourages capital-intensive production, which puts even greater stress on the capital goods area. During the plateau phase, the capacity created during the growth period is not exploited, while a relative fall in labor costs encourages a shift back to greater use of labor, which further diminishes the need for new capital equipment. The stagnant phase is marked by a secondary depression and a rapid collapse of the capital goods sector. Accumulating physical depreciation then sets the stage for the next growth phase. In effect, as Forrester says, a major depression rebalances the economy, liquidates debt, and clears away accumulated excesses.

Anyone who wants to get really immersed in the theory should contact Professor Forrester or, for the lighter version, buy *The Long Wave Cycle* by Julian Snyder, published by Richardson & Snyder, 25 Broad Street, New York. Another excellent article on the social and historical aspects of the Kondratieff cycle, including trough wars and peak wars, by Ronald Kaiser was published in the May–June 1979 issue of *The Financial Analysts Journal*. I think Forrester puts too much emphasis on innovation and capital investment and not enough on the human factor. Kaiser is more eclectic and even points out that every U.S. war has occurred either at the peak or the trough of a growth phase.

In any case, whichever way you look at it, the "primary depression" was either in 1974 or in 1980 when, just as in 1920, the prices of commodities, land, and real assets reached incredible peaks. We are now in the plateau phase where the world, thinking the worst is past, enjoys a false, Indian-summer prosperity. Economic growth is slow. Deflationary pressures in commodity prices and real assets offset inflationary monetary and fiscal policies. Stock prices rise, speculation surges, and a financial panic and stock market bust usually terminate the phase.

I am very struck by the similarities between the plateau stages of the past, and particularly the 1920s, with conditions today. For example, previous plateaus always began with major political scandal (the demise of the Federalist Party, the attempt to impeach President Andrew Johnson, the Teapot Dome–Harding scandal, and, this time, Watergate). Invariably, real estate and, particularly, land prices peak early in the plateau and then begin to decline (1820, 1875, and 1925). This time, farmland prices peaked right on schedule in 1980. Women's rights movements are strong (Susan B. Anthony's suffragette movement in 1890–1900, women's suffrage in the 1920s, and the attempt to ratify the ERA today). Other characteristics include a political shift to the right and more stable, traditional behavior by the younger generation after a surge of political and social liberalism in the last decade of the growth phase.

Financially, plateaus tend to be characterized by protectionism, usually in the form of tariffs (the 1816 tariffs, the Smoot-Hawley tariffs), a massive debt overhang (Germany's war debt then and the LDC debt today), and increasing use of leverage and margin for speculation in financial asset bull markets. The very low margin requirements of the 1920s were certainly a factor in the Crash of 1929. I think the growing acceptance of options and even the Fed's talk of eliminating margin requirements are very ominous signs, because plateaus often end with financial panics that precede the secondary depression and stagnation.

Most economists deride the "long wave" theory as being in a league with astrology and argue that advances in economic theory, the much greater role of government in the economy, and international cooperation in the past half-century make the economic cycle much more controllable today. I devoutly hope they are right, but the similarities between past cycles and the present bother me a lot. I worry that we really are in a period comparable to the mid-1920s—maybe even as late as 1926 or 1927. We investors will see one more powerful bull market characterized by massive speculation that will end badly (the panic of 1819, the panic and bear market of 1873–1879, the Crash of 1929). Most cycles in the past were not as severe as that of the 1930s, but they were depressions nevertheless. Some of the social and political aspects were not pleasant, including a trend toward witch-hunting, prejudice, and authoritarian government in other countries.

The similarities of the Kondratieff cycle to the present may just be fascinating coincidences, but the historical record is compelling, and, as I said at the beginning, human nature doesn't change much. Don't become obsessed with the precise timing, but as events unfold over the next few years, be open-minded, and keep Dr. Kondratieff's long-wave pattern in mind.

The Phony War

January 2, 1991

The present stalemate in the equity markets around the world reminds me of the time 50 years ago called the "phony war." After the blitzkrieg in the spring and summer of 1939, when Hitler and his Panzers overran Eastern Europe, the Germans stopped and consolidated on the Western front. From September 1939 until May 1940, there were skirmishes at sea and in Scandinavia, but nothing much happened. A false calm, a tranquility, lulled many people into thinking that it was just one more border war in Europe, that it wasn't different this time. They knew something threatening and savage, a product of past evils, was ranging loose in the world, but they still felt that, somehow, things would work out, that a world war could be avoided and that their lives wouldn't change. W. H. Auden caught the mood best in his great poem, "September 1, 1939."

Today, it is not so much physical death (although that could happen in the Gulf), but a lingering financial death that offends our night. To me there are, for the United States in particular, no credible reflationary levers left to reignite growth. The markets with their jaundiced, skeptical eye can't be fooled by the old stimulative tricks of the Fed and the Treasury. Debt rather than savings has financed growth, and now the United States is at record levels of public and private debt relative to GNP. The piper must be paid. The movie of the 1980s must be run backwards. But I find people still think we are in just another cyclical correction in the economy, real estate, the banking system, the art market, and the financial services industry.

One of the ancient and iron rules of forecasting is that events always take much longer to develop than expected, but once they begin, they occur much faster and go much farther than anticipated. So it was in the spring and summer of 1940, as Winston Churchill wrote in *Their Finest Hour*:

> Now at last, the slowly gathered, long pent-up fury of the storm broke upon us. Within a week the front in France, behind which we had been accustomed to dwell through the long years of the former war and the opening phase of this, was to be irretrievably broken. Within three weeks the long-famed French Army was to collapse in rout and ruin, and the British Army to be hurled into the sea with all its equipment lost. Within six weeks we were to find ourselves alone, almost disarmed with triumphant Germany and Italy at our throats, with the whole of Europe in Hitler's power, and Japan glowering on the other side of the globe.

I pray to God nothing like that happens to us, but, to me, the world, the markets now seem somewhat as they were then. It's not just the deadline in the Gulf. It's the banking system, real estate, and the Soviet Union, too. I can't prove it, but I feel it's the end of a supercycle of growth induced by debt, leverage, and asset inflation. At the same time, for years now, balance sheet liquidity has been declining. *The Bank Credit Analyst* expressed it well in its year-end review, which is well worth reading but which won't make you sleep any better: "The ultimate implication of the supercycle is a decline in living standards. It can occur in an orderly or disorderly way, through deflation or inflation."

House prices, art, salaries, bonuses, stocks can't keep going up forever. The average price of a home in California has risen from $24,680 in 1970 to $99,760 in 1980 and to $196,521 by the end of 1989. Charles Biderman, writing in *Barron's*, points out that the mortgage payment required to pay debt service on the usual California new home amounts to 80 percent of the average income of a California family. As he puts it, all Californians believe they have inherited a divine right to make a killing in California real estate and are leveraged up to do it. The only trouble is that even home prices don't go up forever. In the United Kingdom, for example, home prices peaked after the Napoleonic War in 1815 and then fell for a hundred years. Even in the United States in this century, they declined in real terms for 30 years in one stretch.

Speaking of real estate and its condition, the best, most dispassionate analysis I have seen is Salomon's December 1990 "Real Estate Market Review." The writers anticipate that the Russell-NCREIF Index will report total returns of 2 percent in 1990 and minus 2 percent in 1991. After 1991, they believe returns will be dismal for a while because they assume that writedowns will be spread over "at least the next several years." They expect that before this cycle is over, the capitalization rate for commodity real estate will trade through mortgage rates and that rates for trophy/franchise real estate will increase from 5–7 percent to 7–9 percent. They argue that there is a secular imbalance in the office, retail, and hotel sectors that will be exacerbated by the current recession and estimate that the United States has a 10-year visible supply of office space. Hotel occupancy rates, they say, will fall again in 1991. The industrial and apartment sectors will do relatively better because they are overbuilt only on a cyclical basis. The institutions that have lent billions in mortgages and home equity loans collateralized by high percentages of the current market value of residential real estate may be in for a financial blitzkrieg if job layoffs and falling house prices result in homeowners walking.

As you might have guessed by now, I think stocks are still in a bear market. My asset allocation remains 20 percent cash, 40 percent equities, and 40 percent bonds. It's not the end of the world. The good guys won 50 years ago, and they will win again. It just may take a while.

Ancient History

August 12, 1996

The hedge fund guys are the elite, the Green Berets of the investment business. To mix a metaphor and engage in the hyperbole that is a staple of our trade, the guys who run the big successful ones have the glamour of professional sports superstars but have a lot more money. Even Joe Montana and Michael Jordan don't have their own G-3s.

Hedge funds should be the perfect investment vehicles for all seasons. Because they can pay big money, the smartest talent flocks to them, their trading volume gets them the first and best call, and the managers' own money is usually in the pool with the clients', which minimizes conflicts of interest. There is no other job in the business where you can accumulate serious wealth faster than being a successful hedge fund manager. And then there is the psychic satisfaction of making central bank chairmen whimper.

Success breeds imitation. A large number of smart young people want to be hedge fund managers, and most think they can, that they have the touch for macro, if only they could get some money to run. New funds sprout like weeds, and it seems everyone's no-good brother-in-law who got laid off and then failed at venture capital is starting one. It's frightening! Van Hedge Fund Advisors of Nashville, Tennessee, says there are 4,700 hedge funds, up from 1,400 in 1988. This same source, which does research with the Owen Graduate School of Management at Vanderbilt University, reports that actively managed hedge funds worldwide now have $300 billion of assets, which is a lot of high-powered money. It's hard to tell what the underlying equity investment is, but Van says the 2,000 funds in their performance database (which presumably are the principal ones) have equity of about $100 billion.

In theory, hedge funds have the weapons to protect their capital in a bear market and even make money. It hasn't worked that way. I recently was sent a page from the May 1971 *Fortune* about what happened to hedge funds in the 1970 bear market. It was just one page, but it brought back very bad memories of cold sweats and sleepless nights.

The first hedge fund, A. W. Jones & Company, was started in the mid-1950s by Alfred W. Jones, a Time Inc. journalist who never ran money himself but had the idea of using leverage while maximizing stock selection by hedging some portion of the long position with shorts. A. W. Jones & Co. put up big numbers, and by the mid-60s its offspring were proliferating, with many newcomers, including yours truly, posting spectacular returns by using leverage and buying the speculative highfliers of the time. New money poured in. As usual, a bull market was confused with genius, and euphoria reigned.

Unfortunately, in December 1968 the Dow peaked at 985, and by the end of May 1970 had fallen 36 percent. By then, the hot stocks (a motley crew but probably no worse than the current crop) had been destroyed. For example, Itek fell from 172 to 17, Leasco from 57 to 7, National Student Marketing from 143 to 3, Litton from 104 to 15, LTV from 135 to 4, and University Computing from 186 to 13, to name just a few. This was when I learned that in a secular bear market, junk gravitates toward 3.

By September 30, 1970, when *Fortune* (using SEC figures) made its calculations, the Dow had rallied 8 percent from the May low, but the surviving hedge funds had recovered even more. For example, our hedge fund, Fairfield Partners, after falling 40 percent in the fiscal year ending May 30, 1970, was up 29 percent by September 30. Nevertheless, as the table (excerpted from *Fortune*) shows, the devastation from portfolio losses and limited partner withdrawals was immense despite the recovery.

	Total Assets ($ millions)		Percent Change (decline)
	12/31/68	9/30/70	
A. W. Jones & Co.	$220.2	$30.7	(86%)
City Associates	106.6	18.2	(78%)
Fleschner Becker Associates	75.1	15.0	(80%)
Fairfield Partners	63.1	27.6	(56%)
Cerberus Associates	50.5	23.0	(55%)
Steinhardt Fine Berkowitz & Co.	47.3	49.7	5%
Strand & Co.	37.4	12.5	(67%)
Lincoln Partners	33.5	33.1	(1%)
Hawthorn Partners	29.4	8.0	(73%)
Boxwood Associates	26.7	12.4	(54%)
Whitehall Associates	26.0	5.9	(77%)
Woodpark Associates	23.9	—	(100%)
Guarente Harrington Associates	19.8	5.3	(73%)
Scruggs & Co.	19.4	6.7	(66%)
Broad Street Partners	18.2	6.5	(64%)
Berger Kent Associates	17.4	1.0	(94%)
Tamarack Associates	14.7	1.0	(93%)
Hartwell & Associates	13.3	1.7	(87%)
Buttonwood & Associates	12.5	—	(100%)

SOURCE: *Fortune.*

Although some hedge funds like ours and A. W. Jones had June fiscal years and had already felt the full impact of withdrawals by September 30, others didn't and suffered further withdrawals at the end of 1970. Buffett is not on the list, because he wisely closed his hedge fund at the end of 1969. Soros was small and offshore and did not have to report to the SEC.

The psychological impact of these ravages on the superstars of the time was considerable, especially since many had considerably enhanced their lifestyle. One well-known hedge-fund manager, who had bought a big stone house in Greenwich and was famous for his jolly disposition, in the midst of the carnage went to bed and simply stayed there. His wife begged him to get up, his associates warned him of the effect on his limited partners, but to no avail. Finally, his wife sold everything for him including the house, closed the fund, and they moved to Wyoming and presumably lived unhappily ever after.

Bear in mind that this was just the first stage of the secular bear market. The Dow rallied 66 percent from the May 1970 bottom to its high on January 11, 1973, and then fell 45 percent to the bear market low of 577 on December 6, 1974. This was when the Nifty-Fifty got crushed, and the hedge funds did relatively better because they were generally short these stocks. Nevertheless, by 1975 most of the hedge funds listed in the table were out of business, with their principals so demoralized they virtually disappeared. Steinhardt Fine & Berkowitz went on to fame and fortune, as did Bill Berger, Ron LeBow, Carl Jones, and John Hartwell. As far as I know, none of the funds on the list survive today now that Michael Steinhardt has retired.

The fury of the second half of the bear was felt by U.S. Trust, Bankers Trust, and Morgan Guaranty, the institutional stars of that era. All three were into the so-called one-decision growth stocks, and their commingled equity funds for employee benefit accounts each lost around 50 percent of their value in 1973 and 1974. This was child's play compared to what happened to the hot mutual funds. The No. 1 performing fund in 1968 was the Mates Investment Fund, which ended the year with an NAV per share of $15.51. At the end of 1974, its NAV was $1.12. The Neuwirth Fund, the No. 2 1968 finisher, did better, only losing 59 percent, but the NAV of No. 5, Pennsylvania Mutual, collapsed from $11.92 to $1.09.

Hedge funds didn't do worse than the aggressive mutual funds or the top institutional managers. But they didn't preserve capital or make money the way they were supposed to. Are things different now? Will hedge funds as a class make money in the next bear market? I don't know, but I doubt it. So far, the results don't seem very encouraging.

Everyone struggled in 1994, a difficult year, but many hedge funds ended with losses, some with big losses. In other words, even with their ability to do macro and short index futures, they couldn't deal with a bad environment. July 1996 was also tough, and a fellow who invests big money in a portfolio of hedge funds showed me his list. Out of 53 funds, 7 were unchanged or up 1 percent or less, and the rest were down. The average decline was around 7 percent, but there were eight that lost over 10 percent.

My friend who studies hedge funds and their techniques closely doesn't think even the best can preserve capital in steep, violent declines. He suspects that they probably could deal with a long-drawn-out bear market. The problem, he says, is that they tend to be momentum players and their bias is to be long and leveraged. I agree, but it's the limited partners who are so performance-oriented that push the managers to take risk.

The other difficulty is that markets are not accommodating. The 1973–1974 decline was not a panic bear market that had a waterfall decline, but it was relentless. It was very difficult to get an uptick, and it sounds silly, but the Nifty-Fifty stocks we were short (and which basically were great companies that were just drastically overpriced) declined so rapidly that everyone made the mistake of covering them way too soon.

Some of the statistics in this piece come from Marc Faber's new report *The Beginning of the End*. I think Marc is too bearish, but his essay, as always, is well worth reading.

History, Market Deaths, and the Cult of the Equity

April 21, 1997

D espite all the volatility in markets, I think we are still on track for an important move up in U.S. bond prices, a simultaneous reflex rally in U.S. stocks (particularly the interest-sensitive ones and the New Nifty Fifty) up toward and maybe through the old highs. I also expect a rally in technology and continuation of the outperformance of emerging markets. My read is that the U.S. economy is slowing a little; pricing power is weak, which eventually will result in disappointing profits; commodity prices are flat; the economic news from Europe and Asia is still mixed; and it looks as though the dollar still needs to go higher. Japan's economy and equities remain enigmas to me, but its bond market does not. It's outrageously overpriced.

Going from the short term to the cosmic, Britt Harris of GTE Investment Management recently sent me a fascinating unpublished article by two professors[1] about long-term returns from equities in different markets around the world. It's relevant because deep in the American psyche, along with motherhood, apple pie, and the flag, is the belief that stocks are fabulous investments and that if you hold them long enough you can't lose. Surveys show that 75 percent of mutual fund owners expect the future to be as rewarding as the past five years—that is, a nominal annual return of over 15 percent, a real return of over 12 percent, no correction of more than 10 percent.

Although I would argue that stocks in most parts of the world are currently very expensive, it's hard to argue with these strategies based on the performance of U.S.

---

[1] "A Century of Global Stock Markets," by William N. Goetzmann, Yale School of Management, and Philippe Jorion, University of California at Irvine.

equities over the long run and since the Second World War. However, to me the issue is whether the happy American experience of progress and political stability over the last 200 years is sustainable, and whether it is the model of what will happen in the rest of the world. If so, then the world indeed is moving onto "a broad, sunlit upland," and the exalted current valuation of equities is justified.

The study focuses on the 21 countries for which the professors could find good stock market and inflation data back to 1921. Of these, only six (the U.S., Canada, the U.K., New Zealand, Sweden, and Switzerland) experienced no interruption in trading in that 75-year period. Eight experienced a break in trading that lasted at least six months, and seven suffered a long-term closure lasting years related to war, invasion, or revolution. In three-quarters of a century, there were 11 occurrences of permanent breaks, or what the authors call "a death," in which the stock market in question never restarted in its existing form. The German stock market has actually been shut down twice: The first time from July 1931 to April 1932, because of a credit crisis; the second for five years beginning in August 1944. Argentina was closed for 10 years in its time of trouble.

The history of this century has been that stock markets do get closed from time to time because of external events, with devastating effects on both liquidity and wealth, as shown in the accompanying table. This reckoning doesn't take into account what happened to the Russian stock market in 1916.

Well, you say, no wonder. The first half of this century was one of war and revolution. But that has been the history of the world, and the past 50 years are the exception rather than the norm. Maybe the human race has progressed and changed for the better, and there will be no more evil empires or dictators, no expropriations, no pogroms, just unbridled happy capitalism. Today's record-high stock market valuations suggest investors believe that this is the case. The refugee mentality of the dispossessed from the first half of the century has virtually disappeared.

The other interesting part of the paper is the return calculations. The compound annual real (inflation-adjusted) price return for the United States over that 75-year period was 4.73 percent before dividends. Remember that U.S. stocks in 1921 had just fallen 46 percent in 18 months and were about to begin an incredible run, which is why their number is higher than the one based on our own data, which begin in 1910. In any case, the United States was the best market by a considerable margin.

The median compound real price return for the 14 countries with long histories back to the 1920s was 2.13 percent, and the median return for all 39 countries was 1.5 percent. A major flaw in this paper is that apparently reinvesting dividends was an impossible calculation, so there are no total return numbers. The authors use the MSCI 1970–1995 yield calculations and assume that the average dividend yield for the 39 countries over the period was around 4.25 percent, which would bring the real total return to over 6 percent for the 14 countries with long histories and to 5.75 percent for all countries. The U.S. dividend return is assumed to be 4.14 percent, implying a total real return of almost 9 percent, which seems high to me even coming off the low base of 1921.

Stock Market Breaks and Deaths

Country	Break Date	Previous Year Return*	Series Restart Date	Comment
Hungary	7/31	−22.2%	9/32	Financial crisis, country in default
Germany	7/31	−31.6	4/32	Credit crisis
Greece	10/31	−09.9	12/32	Financial crisis, drought
Spain	7/36	−11.3	3/40	Civil War starts
Austria	4/38	−17.9	12/46	Annexation by Germany
Czechoslovakia	10/38	−20.5	1/40	Cession of land to Germany
Poland	7/39	−16.9		Invaded by Germany (Sep 1)
Finland	12/39	−19.2	3/40	Invaded by Soviets (Nov 30)
China	12/39	N/A		Invaded by Japan
Denmark	4/40	−32.8	6/40	Invaded by Germany (Apr 9)
Norway	4/40	−27.4	6/40	Invaded by Germany (Apr 11)
Netherlands	5/40	−23.1	9/40	Invaded by Germany (May 10)
Belgium	5/40	−26.7	12/40	Invaded by Germany (May 10)
Switzerland	5/40	−19.3	7/40	Mobilization
France	6/40	−12.2	4/41	Invaded by Germany (Jun 14)
Greece	10/40	−24.9		Invaded by Germany (Oct 28)
Romania	7/41	−39.6		Enters war
Hong Kong	12/41	N/A		Occupation by Japan
Singapore	12/41	N/A		Occupation by Japan
Philippines	1/42	N/A		Invaded by Japan
Czechoslovakia**	7/43	−14.1		War ending
Japan**	6/44	−21.1		War ending
Hungary**	7/44	−49.1		War turmoil?
Belgium**	8/44	−16.1	6/45	War turmoil?
Germany**	8/44	−01.3		Invaded by Allies (Sep 15)
Egypt	10/62	−12.6		Arab socialism
Argentina	8/65	−69.2	7/75	Widespread unrest
Chile	4/71	−54.3		State takes control of economy
Portugal	4/74	−11.2	3/77	Takeover by junta (Apr 27)

For Portugal, the index was observed right after the break, but does not continue thereafter.
*Deflated by WPI.
**Equities were effectively subject to price controls.
SOURCE: "A Century of Global Stock Markets"; Morgan Stanley Research.

This raises an interesting issue. In most markets, around two-thirds of the return came from dividends, although in the United States it was only about half. With the yield on the MSCI World Equity Index at 2 percent currently, or less than half of the normal yield, can we realistically expect the same kind of total returns in the next decade? I say no, but the markets say yes.

The other point is that the price return ex-dividends for the 39 countries is a thin 1.5 percent. If you were a wealthy Argentine or German, assuming you could be a buy-and-hold investor, would you have done better to have your wealth in real estate, in business, or in equities? There is no way of knowing. A diversified portfolio of equities obviously would be less risky.

These calculations do not take into account the years when equity markets were closed. For example, for Germany from 1924 to 1944 the annual real return was 1.65 percent. During World War II, dealing in shares in Germany and the occupied countries was subject to strict controls by the Nazis, ranging from taxes on capital gains to the rationing of purchases. No German could sell shares without first offering them to the Reichsbank, which had the option of buying them at December 1941 prices, in exchange for bonds that remained in the bank's possession. Then, from 1944 to 1950 there was no German stock market whatsoever. Hershey bars, Lucky Strikes, and lumps of coal were the favored medium of exchange. Then in 1950 to 1995 German shares compounded at a nominal annual rate of 8.27 percent and real rate of 5.74 percent. For the 67-year period the market was open, it compounded at a real rate of 4.46 percent, but for the entire 72 years it compounded at 4.15 percent.

The authors calculated the price effect of market interruptions and arbitrarily assigned a charge of 50 percent of the value of equities to a permanent series interruption. They also point out that there is a company survivorship bias in all the indexes, particularly in countries that experienced wrenching change. It would be interesting to know how well the 10 biggest stocks in Germany in 1921 did over the next 75 years, if one could have held them all that time.

The paper shows, not surprisingly, that the returns from 1950 to 1995 are much higher than those from 1921 to 1950. Communism, the Third Reich, and the Second World War wreaked havoc. Japan is another example. The real return from 1921 to 1944 was a negative 0.34 percent per annum, but the real return since 1950 has been 5.8 percent before dividends. Italy, Spain, and Belgium have been the worst, with real total returns around 2 percent.

There were two surprises in this paper for me. The first was that so many stock markets were shut down, either for years or months. It shows how chaotic the world of equity investing has been and how lucky we have been in the United States. Second, I am astounded at how high the real total returns from equities around the world have been across this span of years, particularly since the value effect of interruptions and market deaths was very severe. It is incredible that the real returns from German equities have been somewhere in excess of 8 percent per annum over a period that includes Hitler, war, two hyperinflations, and the total devastation of the economy. Germany and Japan both had higher real returns for the entire period than most of the countries that had continuous markets. This suggests either that you should invest in aggressive, warlike countries or that it pays to lose a war to the United States.

So history supports the cult of the equity, providing you can hang on through the air pockets. They really do generate the real returns, but not the double-digit ones some people now anticipate. I still believe in reversion to the mean.

Section 1B: Fire and Ice

The Fire and Ice Debate

April 3, 1997

Fire: You Ice guys, with your bet on low inflation and falling interest rates, will be lucky if you get a light frost. The latest batch of economic statistics shows the U.S. economy is heating up, wage gains are accelerating, the European economies are improving, and even Japan is doing better.

Ice: The Ice case was never based on economic growth slowing. We think inflation will stay low because at the margin, there is an oversupply of low-cost labor, manufacturing, and services capacity in the world. In the new global economy, there is competition almost everywhere, putting pressure on prices and wages. In the United States, financial services, health care, hospitals, retail, and fast food all have excess capacity. As result, in a relatively strong economic environment, many companies in very different businesses are reporting loss of pricing power. Obviously, this is a broad generality, and there are important exceptions. The price of gold continues to drift lower, and commodity prices are flat to down. We think that when the next recession comes, there will be even more downward pressure on prices, and for a time the CPI may actually be negative.

F: You are missing the point. There has been disinflation, but it is ending. Haven't you guys ever heard of the Phillips Curve? In a modern industrialized economy, there is a point (in the United States, it is 2.2 percent) above which faster growth always generates higher inflation, particularly wage inflation. This is the history of the last 30 years. It's a proven fact. Now the world is on the verge of a synchronized economic expansion that will lead to overheating, rising wages, more inflation, and higher interest rates, which will sink stock markets.

I: First, we doubt the synchronized growth surge. Sure, Europe is improving, but Japan is stumbling, the rest of Asia is struggling, and in the United States the expansion is long in the tooth, debt growth is slowing, and credit stress, particularly in the consumer sector, is rising. Even if the world economies stay healthy, there should be no serious overheating. Admittedly, industrial commodity prices will rise cyclically, but we don't see wage rates rising much. The industrialization and urbanization of the developing countries is resulting in huge numbers of people who are willing to work harder for less money. Second, the concept of an inflationary flash point is not a law of nature like gravity. It is a recent development, but the world changes, and economies change. Are you guys just econometric historians?

F: Recall that "He who does not remember the past is condemned to repeat it." Our econometric models forecast the future based on what has happened rather than your fanciful theories. Besides, even if growth does not generate inflation, governments will because they need to get reelected. Democracies, particularly weak coalition ones, are inherently inflationary. Politicians used to say, "tax and tax, spend and spend, elect and elect." Now they have dropped the tax part, and it's just spend and elect. This creates an inflationary bias in the system.

I: It is myth that the world has an inflationary bias and that growth is always accompanied by inflation. Peter Bernstein recently pointed out that inflation is only a recent phenomenon in America, and the *Economist* has shown that until World War II the price level in England was stable for several centuries. In the United States and Europe, the nineteenth century was a time of rapid growth and rising nominal and real wages, yet it was a deflationary century. For example, in the United States the price index fell from 140 in 1800 to 91 in 1900. Of course, there were bouts of inflation after the Civil War here and the Napoleonic Wars in Europe, but they were only episodes. As for the politicians, the voters now understand that inflation doesn't solve problems, it just masks them for a while and in the long run causes higher interest rates, more unemployment, and stagnation. The old scams don't work as well anymore, and the politicians have to respond to the voters. Furthermore, the huge spending on technology further reduces costs.

F: Nevertheless, despite years of prosperity, all the industrial countries are running large public-sector deficits; they have huge amounts of debt and unfunded social security and pension liabilities that are far bigger than their economies. The only politically palatable solution to these problems is for governments to depreciate their currencies.

I: The unfunded pension liabilities are a serious problem and in the longer run may result in some inflation. But in the meantime, for one reason or another, countries are stumbling toward fiscal balance. In the United States, debt growth is slowing, the deficit is falling, and there is surprising support for balancing the budget. Also, revising the CPI calculation for Social Security payments—although sidetracked for the time being—has bipartisan backing. In Europe, the EMU treaty as it reads will compel at least some fiscal discipline. In the long run, nobody knows if it will last, but over the next couple of years, it will be a force for austerity.

F: What about Japan? Although it's had a deflationary episode, Japan's budget deficit is the biggest of any major country as percent of GDP, unfunded pension liabilities are 150 percent of GDP, and there is a huge bad loan problem. The Japanese have no rational recourse but to try to inflate their way out.

I: We agree. Japan should be the exception, as inflation may be an important solution to its problems. However, instead of following stimulative monetary and fiscal policies, the Japanese are doing the opposite, particularly on the fiscal side with tax increases and spending reductions. They seem obsessed with the fear of becoming the "Italy of Asia." If by temporizing they allow their banking crisis to get out of control, bank failures with all their secondary effects will be very deflationary.

Incidentally, we believe that what happened in Japan between 1990 and today is a fair model for what happens when a stock market bubble infects an economy. As stocks and real estate collapsed, the economy was severely affected, and there were periodic episodes of deflation. Mutual funds suffered very heavy redemptions. Bonds, however, were superb, with the 10-year rate falling from 8 percent to 2.2 percent, but it is fascinating that falling interest rates did not revive the stock market. A less extreme but still very unpleasant version of this liquidity trap scenario could happen in the United States.

F: You guys keep babbling about pricing power diminishing, but as the world economy continues to grow, shortages will develop, and prices will rise as they always have.

I: Maybe, but there is an oversupply of so many things, from fast-food restaurants to sneakers, TV sets, and electronic chips, which means competition and price cutting. There is also an oversupply of labor. As people in the developing world move from farms to cities, they join the industrial labor force. When a poor country becomes richer and moves up the wage scale, manufacturing capacity migrates to another country with lower labor costs. If the first country uses its new wealth to educate its labor force, it can begin to compete on more sophisticated products. In the industrial countries, the bull markets in stocks have resulted indirectly in capital spending booms that have meant more capacity and more competition.

F: Nevertheless, faster growth will mean higher wage costs because workers still want more money, and as shortages of labor develop, they will be able to get it. Do you realize that new unemployment claims as a percentage of total employment are at the lowest level since 1969, and wages in February rose 4 percent year-over-year?

I: So wages are rising 4 percent. Productivity is improving at 1.5 to 2 percent, so unit labor costs are increasing 2 to 2.5 percent. Let's say wage increases escalate to 5 percent, so unit labor costs rise at over 3 percent; so what? This is hardly a terrifying inflation threat at the top of the cycle. However, we doubt it will come to that, since many workers are in industries that have foreign competition or are employed by companies that can build products, process credit cards, or write software someplace else in the world, so they have little bargaining power. Globalization is basically disinflationary, maybe even deflationary in bad times.

F: We think the world is still in an inflationary cycle, and as economic growth accelerates, so will inflation. The Fed and other central banks will raise interest rates again and again. Bond prices will fall, and the 30-year Treasury rate should reach 8.0–8.5 percent. As a result, we are bearish on stocks, not because of earnings but because multiples will decline as bond yields go up. You can't fight the Fed.

I: By contrast, we think there is more than a 50 percent chance that the United States and the world are entering a new cycle of generally stable price levels, with cyclical swings up into low inflation and probably shorter cyclical swings down into low deflation. In the short run, over the next couple of years, the world's economic system will have to adapt itself to this change, and it will be painful for profits. Much slower top-line growth will wreak havoc on companies that are leveraged both operationally and financially. Besides, corporate profits, particularly in the United States, have been overstated by accounting artifices such as awarding options in lieu of cash compensation, nonrecurring charges, and one-time restructuring benefits. As interest rates decline in the United States, for a while stocks will do well because everyone is conditioned to believe lower interest rates mean higher stock prices. Then, as profit margins are squeezed by higher wages and no pricing power, profits will prove very disappointing, and there will be a bear market.

F: How do you square this thesis with the fact that the greatest watchdog of inflation, the Bundesbank, is now a wimp because it is so worried about unemployment in Germany? The Bundesbank is intentionally depreciating the strongest, best currency in the world, the mark, to export the Federal Republic's deflation and unemployment to the United States. As countries have problems, the tendency in a linked world economy is to depreciate your currency, improve your terms of trade, and export your deflation. Competitive devaluations are inflationary. If the EMU fails, this will exacerbate this trend.

I: Look, we concede there is a chance we are wrong about the secular trend toward low inflation. However, we do feel fairly confident that the cyclical trend is for "freezing rain" at least, and we will just have to see what happens over the longer term. As Keynes said, in the long run, we are all dead. The risk/reward ratio on U.S bonds is incredibly favorable, everyone is light bonds and record-heavy stocks, and real interest rates are very high. High-quality, not low-grade, bonds are where the value is.

F: It's obvious the Federal Reserve, Alan Greenspan, and the bond market agree with us and not you.

I: Central bankers, like generals, are admirable and get a lot of honorary degrees, but they are always preparing to fight the last war instead of the next one.

Ice Creeps On

August 18, 1997

I still believe the Ice scenario is playing out, and as a result, the present uncertainty and volatility in the stock market is not about the direction of interest rates but about Ice and slush and its heavy effect on earnings.

Whether the decline last week was just a brief correction or the beginning of something more serious will depend on what happens in the next few weeks. If the weakness continues, I expect there to be heavy carnage in some of the emerging markets like Russia, Hong Kong, and Mexico that are still up on stilts.

Many people seem unconcerned about equity prices falling much further because, as they point out, a bear market has never begun with interest rates stable or falling. It is as though they believe it was ordained by God that stocks and bonds are forever linked and perfectly correlated.

I say: Beware the conditioned response because it could be wrong this time. Yes, stocks and bonds have been correlated in the United States for almost 40 years, but it is also true that over the long run, the coefficient of correlation between stocks and bonds is only 0.2, in other words, mildly positive. Furthermore, when inflation is around zero, history shows stocks and bonds have had an inverse relationship. In Japan recently, a secular bear market in stocks began just as the greatest bull market in bonds was commencing because the country was going from inflation to deflation.

As I have discussed previously, the evidence is quite conclusive that above some innocuous level of inflation, probably around 1.5 percent, stock and bond prices are closely correlated. It makes sense because in a world plagued by inflation, the primary fear of investors is not of recession and falling earnings but of rising prices and wages and higher interest rates. In this environment, which has prevailed in most of the world since the early 1960s, good news is bad news. Strong economic news is bad for both bonds and stocks. Investors want a Goldilocks economy.

But below 1.5 percent inflation, it's a different story. The analogy used is that this is the sound barrier, where the controls reverse. It is completely rational. As an economy gets close to price stability, investors aren't as concerned about inflation as they are about the loss of pricing power and falling profits, so news of a stronger economy suggests some pricing power and higher profits and is therefore bullish for stocks—but, of course not good for bonds. Conversely, weaker economic news suggests more price cutting, declining profits, and even the dreaded deflation, which is wonderful for high-quality bonds but horrible for equities and equity-like securities.

I could go on and on about this subject, but I have already written about it on several occasions. An excellent treatise on the subject was the interview in *Barron's* on July 27 with James Paulsen, chief investment officer of Norwest Investment Management. It is well worth reading. Peter Bernstein also wrote an interesting piece on this subject recently.

I have always envisioned Ice as another round of gradual disinflation in spite of continuing economic growth, with brief episodes of deflation during recessions. Ice is a loss of pricing power and a world where prices are as likely to go down as up. Ice is an erosion of profits. Ice is excess capacity. Ice is developing countries with low-cost factories and huge new labor forces. Ice is creative price destruction from technology. Bursting stock market bubbles cause Ice. Although Robert Frost's poem is melodramatic, my Ice creeps.

Ice historically has been a very favorable environment for stocks, as long as they weren't overvalued to begin with. Theoretically, a period of price stability (but not deflation, which is bad) is a time of peace and prosperity, which should be very good for long-term financial assets. Ice means slower nominal sales and earnings growth for companies, but higher valuations of those earnings. Companies that can grow earnings and dividends in an ice age should be prized. In the 1950s and early 1960s with stable price levels, slow steady growth sold at 40 times earnings. The problem is that making the transition from one environment to the other can be very disruptive and painful for the companies that are structured for the previous one.

Ice is also about competitive devaluations, as countries try to export their unemployment and lack of growth. The new factor in the Ice equation is the epidemic of devaluations in Asia. The spiral is gaining momentum, and it is not only disinflationary but antigrowth. Currency volatility is bad. It raises the risk premium on commerce and investment. There probably won't be much growth in non-Japan Asia, formerly the fastest-growing part of the world, for the next couple of years as these economies adjust.

The wild card is China. As I have noted, China's exports are bigger than those of Thailand, Malaysia, Indonesia, and the Philippines combined and have been growing much faster. I believe China has very severe economic and social problems and desperately needs to maintain and grow its export markets. It must keep its factories running to keep its population employed. Now suddenly its competitors have, in effect, cut prices 20 percent or so by depreciating their currencies, and my guess is that China will have to react. It can't depreciate its currency because of its huge trade and capital account surpluses, so its only choice is to cut the prices of the products it exports. This would not be a minor event.

With the U.S. economy still robust and close to effective full employment, wage pressure should increase. Steve Roach is right that labor has been a loser to profits for years now and that it may be payback time. The issue is whether, in a disinflationary world environment, U.S. labor can get very much. This was what the UPS strike was all about. It is interesting that in Europe labor for the first time is making concessions. Inevitably, the rate of increase in wage rates in the developing world seems sure to slow dramatically.

My guess is that wage increases in the United States will continue at about 2 to 3 percent annually until the next recession. Higher wage costs won't be inflationary because companies will be generally unable to pass them on in the form of price increases, so they will come out of profit margins.

One thing is for sure, with Europe and Asia now depreciating their currencies versus the dollar, somewhere out there the United States is going to experience growth and unemployment problems.

I think stocks are dangerous here and still like U.S. Treasury bonds and bills best of all. Spreads on emerging market debt and U.S. high yield are way too skinny to make them an attractive alternative. They are markets where excesses have been compounded on excesses.

The other important thing to remember is that the system itself may be flawed. George Gould, a wise man and under secretary of the treasury at the time of the 1987 crash, remarked to me last week that the problem then was that the portfolio insurance strategies assumed the ability to execute in a continuous market. I suspect that many of the derivative hedges assume the same. And don't forget that we are in a market environment where the tail (the futures) wags the dog (the cash market), and the short sellers of futures contracts don't need an uptick.

In times like these, it has been suggested to me that poetry is better than finance:

Fire and Ice

Some say the world will end in fire;
Some say in ice.
From what I've tasted of desire
I hold with those who favor fire.
But if had to perish twice,
I think I know enough of hate
To know that for destruction ice
Is also great
And would suffice

—*Robert Frost*

A World Lit Only by Fire?

September 22, 1997

I believe in Ice, but what could make Fire happen? A synchronized worldwide expansion, that's what.

Synchronized worldwide economic growth in 1998 would drain off excess liquidity from the financial markets to the real economies. It would cause wage costs to rise, prices of manufactured goods to firm, inflation to stop falling and begin rising almost everywhere, interest rates to rise, and stock prices in most, but not all, markets to fall.

It could happen, although I think it's unlikely. The Fire advocates say that Europe led by Germany is even now beginning to grow at a stronger pace as domestic demand revives across the continent. Exports will strengthen further in the months to come because of the lagged effect of the fall in European currencies against the dollar in the last two years, and the booming stock markets have buoyed business and consumer confidence. Already, there are signs of faster money growth and rising wholesale prices. It's not an old-fashioned boom, but the stagnation seems to be over. Europe, they argue, will have five consecutive quarters of 3 percent real GDP growth beginning with 4Q1997.

Unemployment is still sky-high across Europe, so governments and central banks in the face of this recovery will be gentle, both for political reasons and because of the approach of the EMU deadlines. The European establishment wants the EMU to occur on time, and better economic growth makes meeting the Maastricht criteria less painful. Growth will also make it easier for the fringe countries to qualify, so the result will be a broader EMU, which may be good or bad, depending on your point of view.

However, in a world lit only by Fire, by early next year the Bundesbank will be worrying about inflation, and so German short-term rates will be nudged higher. This

29

will hurt bonds, and they will drag down with them the other European bond markets. Short- and long-term interest rates in Europe could rise 150 to 200 basis points in the next year, and the bourses could fall 20 percent.

Higher European interest rates and America's huge trade deficit will spell the end of the dollar bull market. A weaker dollar, huge wealth gains from the stock market, and the incredible balance, diversity, and resilience of the U.S. economy will keep America's growth humming as well.

Again, no boom, but another year of solid 3.5 percent real growth. This pace will begin to create imbalances in labor and commodity markets, and who knows what effect El Niño will have? By next year, labor will be much more aggressive, the Fire believers say, and wage rates will be rising 4–5 percent. Pricing power will improve but not that much, so profit margins will come under pressure. The U.S. inflation won't by any means surge but by midyear will be through 3.5 percent and looking higher. The weak dollar obviously won't help.

As all this unfolds, Chairman Greenspan will change his tune and speak of the menace of inflation. The Fed will raise rates a number of times next year, and the bond market will fall. Long-term interest rates in the United States will drift up to the 7–7.5 percent range, and it will turn out that Buffett never bought any zeros after all. There will be talk that Steve Roach should succeed Greenspan as chairman of the Fed. U.S. stocks will decline 20–30 percent. The Latin American economies will continue to grow briskly, but their stock markets will suffer, too.

As for Japan, although everyone has become very bearish about the economy and cites record low JGB yields for confirmation, the Fire case holds that, against the odds, the Japanese economy should revive, too. Quarterly Japanese real GDP numbers have always been very volatile. Some serious people argue that if you take out the distortions from the consumption tax increase, real final demand in Japan has continued to grow at a trend-line rate of around 3 percent a year, or even little more. Automobile sales rose 5.1 percent in July and August compared to the second quarter, and business investment seems to be picking up again. There must be a lot of deferred demand furtively stored away in the inner sanctums of Japan after so long an economic contraction.

With the rest of the world healthy, Japanese exports will continue strong, further propping up the recovery. As deflation ends, the real estate markets will revive, and the confidence of both consumers and businessmen will improve, possibly dramatically. The Tokyo stock market will boom even as JGB yields rise to 4 percent or even higher.

But the big beneficiary of Fire would be non-Japan Asia, which is now flat on its back. A healthy world economy and weaker dollar, combined with the repricing of exports from the devaluations, mean that the ravaged Tigers will jump back on their feet much faster than anyone now thinks. Trade account deficits will suddenly become surpluses, with all the resulting virtuous circle effects. Dr. Mahathir will retire, and the ravaged stock markets of places like Thailand, Malaysia, Indonesia, and the Philippines will come roaring back.

As for China, its true financial condition will remain an enigma, but despite its excesses, domestic demand will revive, its trade surplus will expand, and growth will continue at 8 percent, or so the government says. The other big emerging-market economies like India, Russia, Brazil, and Mexico also remain healthy, as do their stock markets.

This is not an extreme Fire scenario; inflation doesn't set the roof ablaze anywhere. However, it sure would make my investment strategy wrong, based as it is on a cyclical version of Ice. In particular, I could own too many U.S. government bonds.

If this Fire scenario comes true, an equity portfolio that owns Japan, non-Japan Asia, certain other emerging markets (Russia, India, and Brazil), and the right cyclical sectors in the United States and Europe should do okay. Not great, because liquidity will be contracting, but okay. High-grade bonds everywhere will get killed, especially JGBs. On the other hand, if you believe a more extreme Fire scenario could happen, both stocks and bonds will get slaughtered.

As for me, I believe in Ice, and as I said at the beginning, a world lit only by Fire is unlikely. But I do worry about it.

Section 1C: Bubbles and Panics

Manias, Panics, Crashes

November 30, 1981

Not that I think we are going to have a panic or a crash again soon, but human nature being what it is, one certitude is that we will have both again in our investment lifetimes. Fortune favors the prepared mind, as they say, so it's worthwhile to study the anatomy of financial distress at leisure rather than in the eye of the storm. The definitive work on this subject, *Manias, Panics, and Crashes*, was published in 1978 by the well-regarded economic historian, Charles P. Kindleberger, and is now available in paperback from Palgrave Macmillan. Another good study of American crashes is *Panic on Wall Street* by Robert Sobel.

Walter Bagehot, first editor of *The Economist*, described the explosive combination of people and money as well as anyone in his essay on Edward Gibbon when he said:

> Much has been written about panics and manias, much more than with the most outstretched intellect we are able to follow or conceive; but one thing is certain, that at particular times a great deal of stupid people have a great deal of stupid money. . . . At intervals, from causes which are not to the present purpose, the money of these people—the blind capital, as we call it, of the country—is particularly large and craving; it seeks for someone to devour

it, and there is a "plethora"; it finds someone, and there is "speculation"; it is devoured, and there is "panic."

Kindleberger's book is full of the fascinating details of manias, panics, and crashes, but it is a serious analytical work and not meant to entertain as is Charles Mackay's epic *Extraordinary Popular Delusions and the Madness of Crowds*. Kindleberger emphasizes the important role of the fallacy of composition (in which the whole differs from the sum of its parts) in inflaming mob psychology. In other words, each individual is acting rationally when, for example, he sells his stocks, or would be, were it not for the fact that others are doing the same thing. Each participant, by rationally trying to save himself, contributes to the ruin of all. Related to this is the so-called cobweb effect in which demand and supply are not linked simultaneously, as in an auction market that clears at each moment of time, but instead are connected with a lag. A destabilizing exogenous shock occurs that radically alters expectations, but otherwise-rational expectations fail to take into account the effect of similar responses by others. In other words, buying a scarce commodity in response to a shortage is rational on an individual basis but excessive when many do the same. The participant in financial markets must understand and compensate for cobwebs and for the "chain letter" aspect of successful investing. We are buying stocks, not companies, which is a crucial distinction.

Kindleberger relates how the history of manias and panics is full of cases of rational men who sensed an engulfing madness, sold out, and then were sucked back in and ruined by the speculative atmosphere. The great Master of the Mint and epitome of the rational scientist, Isaac Newton, said in the spring of 1720 in the midst of the South Sea Company bubble: "I can calculate the motions of the heavenly bodies but not the madness of people" and sold his shares in the South Sea Company at a solid 100 percent profit. But as the stock continued to climb, infectious speculative enthusiasm overcame him, he rebought, and was wiped out in the crash. Apparently, so bitter was his loss that for the rest of his life he could never bear to hear the name "South Sea."

It is also fascinating to be reminded of how little human nature has changed and how the pattern of events repeats itself over and over. The objects of speculation change from cycle to cycle, but greed and fear are always there. In previous centuries, successful speculators bought country houses during the latter stages of bull markets, just as they did in the 1960s and 1970s. Anyone with a memory and discipline who reads and thinks about the chronology of events and the signs of forthcoming trouble that Kindleberger lays out has no excuse for getting caught in the next wave of euphoria.

Kindleberger makes the case that, to have a really significant crisis, two or more objects of speculation have to be in play—a bad harvest coming at a time of a railroad mania, for example, or an orgy of land speculation. The two markets are usually interconnected by excessive money creation, and in the case of truly serious panics, almost invariably they tend to become international, either running parallel from country to country or spreading from the centers where they originate to other countries.

In another interesting section, Kindleberger argues the historical case that when circumstances change—in his words "a displacement event" occurs—the investor must sell immediately. It may seem to be rational and resolute to hang on and not panic in the hope of some improvement, but it usually is the wrong thing to do. Kindleberger cites a whole series of past events where individuals and institutions, from Jay Cooke & Company to the Hamburg banks, were ruined by hanging in there. In other words, if you're riding an irrational, speculative animal, at the first change of direction, get off fast.

Kindleberger also cautions that a common failing of many intelligent people is to have a rational model in mind, but the wrong one. He calls this "Maginot Line psychology." "When man's vision is fixed on one thing," said Ponzi, "he might as well be blind." A good point because it happens to all of us from time to time.

Kindleberger also makes the argument that speculative manias gather speed through expansion of money and credit or even get started because of an excessive expansion of money and credit. He states that throughout history, the market, in its ingenuity, has created new forms of money in periods of boom to get around the currency regulations of the authorities. Certainly, we have seen this in the last few years. This subject leads Kindleberger into a rather tiresome couple of chapters on the need for a lender of last resort. He also describes the many methods that the promoters and authorities have used in an attempt to avert disaster once a panic has begun. Frankly, the discussion seemed rather useless to me as no strategy does anything more than delay the inevitable, which is all the more reason to sell quickly at the first sign of serious trouble.

As long as there are markets and people, there will be panics, manias, and crashes, and the more you know about them, the better your chances are of not getting killed in one.

Tulipomania

November 18, 1982

The news last week of tumbling prices in the Hong Kong real estate market and the collapse during the last few months of the over-the-counter Kuwait stock market reminds me again how human nature never changes. Over the centuries and despite different cultures, excessive speculation is invariably followed by panic and collapse. In this regard, the most incredible episode of all occurred over 300 years ago when "tulipomania" engulfed the normally stolid, conservative Dutch nation. My understanding of this strange mania is based on *Tulipomania* by Wilfrid Blunt, onetime art master at Eton College; Charles Mackay's epic *Extraordinary Popular Delusions and the Madness of Crowds*; and the novel *The Black Tulip* by Alexandre Dumas.

Tulips—so named, it is said, from the Turkish word signifying turban—were introduced into Western Europe from Turkey around 1550. The tulip becomes most beautiful when intensively cultivated and bred. But the more exquisite it becomes, the weaker and more fragile it grows, so that only with great skill and most careful handling can it be cultivated. By the seventeenth century, tulips had become the fashion of the wealthy, especially in Germany and Holland. Prizes of increasingly large sums of money were given at competitions for the most beautiful bulbs. The winning bulbs could then be sold for cross breeding.

By 1630 the Dutch people in particular were becoming obsessed with the growing and trading of tulips. Amateur growers began to bid up the price of certain species that were especially popular or that had the potential of winning prizes, and by 1634 an adjunct to the Amsterdam stock exchange had been set up for the trading of tulips. The rage to own tulips became such that "persons were known to invest a fortune of 100,000 florins in the purchase of forty roots." Soon, everyone who had a few square yards of back garden was growing bulbs, and at first all were winners as the price of bulbs kept rising. Stories of common people cultivating rare bulbs and suddenly becoming rich abounded, and working men began to quit their jobs in order to have more time to grow and trade tulips.

As the new wealth swelled the money supply, the price of everything else began to rise also. In addition, money from England and other parts of Europe poured into Holland, and the Dutch imagined the passion for tulips would last forever and that the wealthy from every part of the world would buy Dutch tulips because they were uniquely beautiful. In the early days of the mania, sales took place between the end of June, when the bulbs were taken out of the ground, and September, when they were replanted. But, as the fever increased, trading continued all year with delivery promised for the summer. As Wilfrid Blunt describes it:

> Thus a speculator often offered and paid large sums for a root which he never received, and never wished to receive. Another sold roots which he never possessed or delivered. Oft did a nobleman purchase of a chimney-sweep tulips to the amount of two-thousand florins, and sell them at the same time to a farmer; and neither the nobleman, chimney-sweep or farmer had roots in their possession, or wished to possess them. Before the tulip season was over, more roots were sold and purchased, bespoke and promised to be delivered, than in all probability were to be found in the gardens of Holland.

The height of tulipomania was between 1634 and 1637. The price of prime bulbs soared to the present equivalent of $100,000. As the mania expanded, the fabric of society began to unravel. Farmers sold their livestock to raise capital to speculate in tulips, and houses and estates were mortgaged. No man's garden was safe from thieves, and in *The Black Tulip* there are tales of greed and depravity as the passions of the people became inflamed. Some growers only cultivated secret plots at night so rivals would not know of their stock. Visitors to Holland were astounded, and MacKay recounts the story of an ignorant English sailor off a visiting ship in Rotterdam happening to eat a tulip bulb from a garden, thinking it was an onion. Its owner turned out a lynch mob, and the sailor was committed to debtors' prison for 10 years. The craze spread to France and England by 1635, but most of the trading activity and wild speculation was centered in Holland.

In 1636 various coolheaded people warned of impending disaster and tried to restore the country's balance. One Evard Forstius, Professor of Botany at Leyden, could not see a tulip without attacking it with his walking stick. Eventually because of his antitulip harangues and attacks, he was judged criminally insane and committed to the dungeons at Loewstein where Dumas's hero languished. Other notables cautioned of the consequences, but were mocked and derided.

The operations of the tulip trade became so intense and intricate that it was found necessary to create an entire infrastructure of notaries, clerks, and dealers. Tulip exchanges were established in many towns across the country. Normal trade and manufacture were neglected, and except for tulips, Dutch exports declined. But as long as prices stayed high, it didn't matter, and in fact the Dutch people had never been so prosperous.

But the false prosperity couldn't last, even though prices swept higher throughout 1635 and 1636. Suddenly, early in the spring of 1637 the crash came. Neither Mackay, Blunt, nor Dumas describes any trigger event that suddenly disrupted the psychology of the market. At first only a few people wanted to sell in order to convert their tulip holdings into other forms of wealth. No one wanted to buy. Prices declined 25 percent, and more sellers entered the market. In vain the dealers and exchanges resorted to such devices as mock auctions to build confidence, and new larger prizes were announced in the hope they would restore prices. Nothing worked, and suddenly prices really collapsed as sellers panicked. The value of prime bulbs such as Semper Augustus, General Bol, and Admiral van Hoorn fell in a few weeks from 6,000 florins to 400 or 500 florins as it dawned on people that what they owned was bulbs and not real assets. As MacKay describes it:

> Hundreds who a few months previously had begun to doubt that there was such a thing as poverty in the land suddenly found themselves the possessors of a few bulbs which nobody would buy, even though they offered them at one quarter of the sums they had paid for them. The cry of distress sounded everywhere, and each man accused his neighbour. The few who had contrived to enrich themselves hid their wealth from the knowledge of their fellow citizens, and invested it in the English or other funds. Many who for a brief season had emerged from the humbler walks of life were cast back into their original obscurity. Substantial merchants were reduced almost to beggary, and many a representative of a noble line saw the fortunes of his house ruined beyond redemption.

Eventually, there were so many lawsuits filed that the courts could not handle them, and in April of 1637 the Court of Holland intervened in an effort to stabilize the social situation of the country. However, the court's complicated rulings were to no avail, and the sharp contraction of the wealth and money supply of the country caused a depression that lasted for some years. However, in spite of the carnage, the Dutch have retained a great partiality for tulips.

Anarchy

On or about October 23, 1987

Turning and turning in the widening gyre
The falcon cannot hear the falconer;
Things fall apart; the centre cannot hold
Mere anarchy is loosed upon the world,
The blood-dimmed tide is loosed; and everywhere
The ceremony of innocence is drowned;
The best lack all conviction, while the worst
Are full of passionate intensity.
　　　　　　　—*William Butler Yeats*

Of all the words babbled about last week, Louis Rukeyser quoting Adlai Stevenson put it best on Friday night: "I'm too old to cry but it hurts too much to laugh." The world financial system, shaken by the blood-dimmed tide and the anarchy of the markets, will hold together, will prevail. Many now say that it won't, but to bet against it, you have to assume an unlikely convergence of bad luck and mismanagement. The system has great resilience, and everyone, except for the short sellers, will be working very hard to maintain it. It's not 1929 nor is it 1927. It's 1987, which will have its own profile.

I am almost but not quite amused by the avalanche of venom and doom poured on the Reagan administration, stocks, supply-side economics, and Wall Street in general by professors, the liberal press, and a lot of people who should know better. "Close down the casino and string up the money changers." I read today that after last week another Republican president and the August high in the Dow will not be seen for 20 years. The total demise of the New York condominium and Greenwich real estate markets is gleefully anticipated, and all the vicious MBA yuppies and the fat cats with their

39

Porsches will disappear into a pool of distilled greed. The politics and dialectic of envy are overwhelming. However, although there will be distress, I doubt Wall Street will be transformed into a wasteland.

Last week, we had a real, honest-to-goodness, old-time financial panic. A panic is really psychological in nature, and, as I count it, this is the ninth in American history. The best book on the subject is *Panic on Wall Street* by Robert Sobel.

Each panic has to be different from its predecessors—otherwise it wouldn't be terrifying—but each has the same general psychological background and characteristics. Last week's panic had all the usual ingredients of optimism, speculation, leverage, greed, and stupidity being transformed into fear, uncertainty, and despair, but it was the biggest, most intense financial panic of all time.

History shows that panics do not necessarily lead to recessions. The stock market's bark is worse than its economic bite. Recession or depression did not follow the panics of 1869, 1901, 1914, or 1962, and even the 1929 crash did not cause the Great Depression. Every post–World War II recession except that in 1980 has been preceded by a falling stock market, according to Geoffrey Moore of the Center for International Business Cycle Research. He points out, however, that numerous other market declines were not followed by recessions. The stock market has predicted eight out of the past five recessions. It's still very early to guess, but my hunch is that although there may be some weakness in consumer spending this winter, the combination of lower interest rates and surging liquidity will offset the negative wealth and confidence effects of the panic, and 1988 will be a year of moderate economic growth. Unless the governments bungle things, a depression is not in the cards.

So far, the governments and central banks are doing a fair job of counteracting the panic. Walter Bagehot, who lived through several English panics, said: "The best palliative to a panic is a confidence in the adequate amount of the bank reserve and in the efficient use of that reserve." I know that Alan Greenspan believes that also, but the central banks must provide liquidity. A U.S. budget compromise is essential also, and time is running out.

The history of panics also shows that sometimes their stock market impact fades quickly, as in the Northern Pacific Corner panic of 1901 and the panic of 1792, while on other occasions the aftereffects lingered for years. My feeling is that because of the severity of the damage and the shock of seeing blue-chip stocks fall 35 percent in a week, the effects of this panic will be with us for a long time. For example, the specialist system, the derivative markets, and program trading may be materially changed.

Also, equities have been discredited and proven to be much more volatile than anyone thought. A higher risk premium will be demanded. My guess is that fiduciaries will want lower equity ratios for years to come. Bonds and probably income-producing properties that are not quoted will have enhanced appeal. The structure of the money management business is bound to be affected. Clients don't like round trips.

Are we still in a secular bull market, or are we now in a bear market? Or, have we already had most of the bear market? I don't know, because I think we have to see

Major World Equity Markets
Comparative Absolute Valuations

Country	Current Absolute Valuation[a]				Historical Average[b]				Current/Historical			
	Price/ Cash Flow	Price/ Earnings	Price/Book Value	Yield	Price/ Cash Flow	Price/ Earnings	Price/ Book Value	Yield	Price/ Cash Flow	Price/ Earnings	Price/ Book Value	Yield
Austria	7.1	29.6	1.86	2.3	7.27	73.9	1.33	3.1	0.98	0.40	1.40	0.73
Australia	8.8	13.3	1.77	3.6	6.93	11.5	1.25	4.5	1.27	1.16	1.41	0.81
Belgium	5.1	11.5	1.69	6.3	3.66	11.1	0.96	11.3	1.39	1.04	1.76	0.56
Canada	8.9	22.1	1.60	3.0	6.66	15.2	1.40	3.9	1.34	1.46	1.14	0.77
Denmark	5.6	27.0	1.12	2.4	5.53	9.9	0.99	4.1	1.01	2.74	1.13	0.59
EAFE	8.6	26.2	2.76	1.7	5.73	14.7	1.55	3.5	1.50	1.78	1.78	0.49
France	5.2	13.5	1.67	3.1	3.65	15.5	1.07	5.6	1.42	0.87	1.55	0.56
Germany	4.7	13.6	2.03	3.3	4.02	11.5	1.62	4.6	1.17	1.19	1.25	0.71
Hong Kong	14.4	16.0	3.07	2.7	10.62	13.3	1.88	4.4	1.36	1.22	1.63	0.62
Italy	4.8	16.4	1.92	2.4	7.71	23.9	1.28	2.6	0.62	0.69	1.50	0.92
Japan	16.8	59.4	4.55	0.5	8.43	24.8	2.41	1.6	1.99	2.40	1.89	0.31
Netherlands	4.4	10.3	1.08	4.6	3.08	6.5	0.79	6.2	1.43	1.59	1.36	0.75
Norway	6.0	21.8	1.93	2.3	3.71	10.8	1.34	4.3	1.62	2.02	1.44	0.53
Singapore/Malaysia	14.7	28.9	1.85	1.6	15.73	22.8	2.15	2.4	0.93	1.27	0.86	0.68
Spain	4.6	19.0	1.14	3.5	3.55	11.9	0.53	10.3	1.30	1.60	2.15	0.34
Sweden	8.5	14.8	2.15	2.1	4.93	10.1	1.22	4.1	1.73	1.46	1.76	0.51
Switzerland	7.9	18.1	1.52	2.0	5.38	11.9	1.12	2.8	1.47	1.52	1.36	0.72
United Kingdom	7.8	13.2	1.87	3.9	5.74	9.6	1.24	5.3	1.36	1.37	1.51	0.74
United States	7.2	15.5	1.76	3.6	5.80	10.4	1.39	4.9	1.24	1.49	1.26	0.73
World	8.1	20.9	2.27	2.5	5.80	12.1	1.47	4.3	1.40	1.73	1.54	0.58

[a]As of October 22, 1987.
[b]Last 10 years except P/E for Austria (since October 1981), P/E for Italy (April 1984), P/E for Spain (January 1980), and P/CF for Switzerland (January 1980).
SOURCE: *Morgan Stanley Research.*

what happens in the next few weeks. Thus, I believe strategic planning about country and group leadership is premature. Supply versus demand and panic versus value—that's the battle for now. My hunch is that a big rally is coming. There's too much bearishness, with too many futures contracts sold and too much portfolio insurance written. I am not selling anything now and would be a buyer with our 10 percent cash position if the beast broke again to last week's lows. After the smoke of battle clears, we will have to take another look at strategy. The accompanying table shows comparative country valuation levels as of the end of last week.

Life on the Good Ship Swine

June 25, 1990

I n the 1980s, investors bought properties and started businesses not because of the underlying earning power or free cash flow but because they were convinced the property could be sold at a higher price to someone else. Come to think of it, maybe by definition they weren't investors but speculators because investors are in the cash flow business, while these people were in the asset appreciation game. But, at the margin, the financial buyers set asset prices, and soaring private market values were the stuff of dreams.

Money makes the mare go. Now, with expansion in every monetary aggregate from bank reserves to M4 declining, one asset class after another falls into the cold bath of economic reality. With excess liquidity dissipating, suddenly cash flow matters again. Everybody knows about real estate, but the story in last Friday's *New York Times* about the demise of *Manhattan inc* highlighted the fact that the magazine caper is now over.

In the 1980s at the height of the mania, magazines were started or bought by publishing conglomerates without regard to profitability. There was always a buyer out there willing to pay a fancy price for a niche magazine. There were too many magazines chasing too few readers, and most of them were not making any money. Suddenly the music stopped, and there were no buyers. In New York *Seven Days* disappeared from the scene without a ripple or a bid, and there apparently were no buyers for *Manhattan inc*, which after all had a famous editor, Clay Felker, and was a sophisticated, readable monthly, not just some rag. I remember a couple of years ago when the magazine market was hot; Larry Tisch sold CBS's magazines for something like $600 million, and people criticized him because six months later maybe he could have

43

gotten $50 million more. That sale looks pretty good now. To Tisch the investor, the properties simply could not measure up on the operating numbers, and eventually, inevitably, prices came tumbling down.

The same applies to so many assets, from baseball cards to radio stations and hotels. When some proud Morgan Stanley father tells me how he bought his 10-year-old a mint-condition Mickey Mantle for $800 and it's now worth $1,500, so he's got it in the safety-deposit box, I figure the kid is about to have his first investment lesson. I speak from experience. In 1974 the Treasury auctioned off its inventory of Morgan silver dollars mounted in plastic boxes, with the American eagle on one side and some inspirational words from Richard Nixon on the other. I bought a bunch for something like $200 a shiny copy and gave them to my children and some nieces, counseling safe-keeping and forecasting massive appreciation. Today they trade at $25. The offspring like to remind me what a great inflation hedge they've been and wonder whether I will buy them back at cost.

The economics of the Plaza Hotel have been mentioned a lot. With room rates of over $350 a night including taxes and assuming reasonable occupancy, the hotel can earn $25 million pretax. The building is old, so there really is no excess cash flow from depreciation. What should you pay for a $25 million pretax earner that grows in line with inflation? The Plaza has a magnificent location and a beautiful, historic building that lifts the spirit on a spring morning, but those attributes are already in that fancy room rate. I hear Trump would take $350 million, which is well below what he and the banks have in it, but, at over 13 times pretax earnings, the price doesn't sound cheap to me. Of course, when he bought it and the banks lent him the money, they assumed some crazy would pay a billion dollars for it because it's a trophy.

I don't know. Asset prices are coming down, the loans aren't going to be repaid, wealth is being extinguished. Can the good old stock market escape the holocaust? Michael Thomas, whose *New York Observer* column is marvelous but disquieting reading, thinks not. "Whose heart does not sing at the prospect that the *Good Ship Swine*, and all who sailed in it, are—like, before them, the crew of Melville's *Pequod*—being drawn finally and inexorably toward a giant, downsucking vortex, in this case caused by the flushing of a monstrous financial toilet rather than the animosity of an enraged white whale." I can see it now. Morgan Stanley going down like the doomed *Titanic* in the movie *A Night to Remember* with the staff in the lifeboats singing "Nearer My God to Thee" and the brave managing directors at attention lining the rails, the band playing a medley of Princeton football songs, and our "Prince of Swine," his bronzed hand gripping the lifeless helm, resolute on the bridge.

On the other hand, the stock market is nowhere near as outrageously overpriced as a lot of other things. In fact, stocks look downright cheap compared with the Plaza. And as money flees the carnage, why won't it run to high-quality bonds and equities? It has to go somewhere, and if money begins to worry seriously about the safety of banks and money market funds, the shares of real growth companies with global franchises may look as good as anything. And maybe some of the scared money runs to gold, although gold certainly doesn't behave as if it's at the receiving end of the hose.

All this asset deflation makes me very uneasy, particularly after eight up years in stocks. I own lots of growth stocks and government bonds, and think they are going to work out fine in the long run. But I worry that the stock market toilet, to extend Thomas's analogy, may get flushed once first. Take two aspirins before retiring.

The New New Thing

November 29, 1999

The technology, Internet, and telecommunications craze has gone parabolic in what is one of the great, if not the greatest, manias of all time. There is no question that the Internet and the communications revolution are transforming events; the issue is profitability and what stock prices have already discounted. To better understand what is going on, it is important to read Michael Lewis's new book, *The New New Thing: A Silicon Valley Story*. I also recommend the article in *Fortune* entitled "Nice Work If You Can Get It."

We live and invest in a momentum-following world, but in my view rational investors should begin gradually to reduce their holdings in these three areas, with a plan to get at least half-weighted in technology and telecommunications over the next three months. Tech is 18 percent and telecom is 11 percent of world market capitalization, so this is a big bet that will make or break performance next year.

European and Asian incumbent telecom stocks seem particularly vulnerable to me. Earnings disappointments are starting to occur, and the group is plagued by intense competition, deregulation, new entrants, and severe rate-cutting. But price momentum is strong, and these elderly giants are viewed as Internet plays, so selling should be measured.

The history of manias is that they have almost always been solidly based on revolutionary developments that *eventually* change the world. Without fail, the bubble stage of these crazes ends in tears and massive wealth destruction.

There are two major delusions operative. First, many of the ordinary people who buy Internet-related equities don't understand the difference between fundamentals and stock prices. They want to own technology, Internet, and telecommunications stocks because they correctly believe these businesses have bright futures. What they don't get is that owning the shares of a company is not the same as owning the company itself, because the share prices have valuations and expectations embedded in them.

Second, many of the professional investors involved in these areas know that what is going on today is madness. However, they argue that the right tactic is to stay invested as long as the price momentum is up. When momentum begins to ebb, they will sell their positions and escape the carnage. Since they have very large positions and since they all follow the same momentum, I suspect they are deluded in thinking they will be able to get out in time, because all the other momentum investors will be doing the same thing.

Michael Lewis has done some great business writing, and his prose is in a class with Gerry Goodman's, which is world-class stuff. The book centers on Jim Clark, the guy who created Netscape and perhaps the epic technology entrepreneur. Clark is an eccentric and fascinating character, but Lewis treats him sympathetically. Economic growth comes from new innovations, and any society that wants to become richer must encourage the traits, however bizarre, that lead people to create new recipes. In other words, a certain tolerance for nonconformism is critical to the process. Qualities that might have been viewed in the past as antisocial or even criminal will now be rewarded, honored, and emulated, says Lewis. The Prime Mover of Wealth is no longer a great industrialist or a Wall Street tycoon but a geek holed up in his basement all weekend discovering new ways to change the world with his computer. To Lewis, Jim Clark was "the disorganization man, a mixture of intelligence and testosterone, who in addition had an amazing over-the-horizon radar."

The book helps you understand that historically, it hasn't been uncommon for great, admired technology companies to fail over time because they must believe to the very end that their products are the best and their technology will win. Understandably, they have trouble entertaining the thought that they are doomed because a couple of guys in a garage have come up with a better sewing machine. It is essentially the same insight that Clayton Christensen explains in *The Innovator's Dilemma* but more dramatically expounded. You see, Jim Clark's first big hit was Silicon Graphics, which eventually fell on hard times.

As Lewis puts it: "The genealogy chart of Silicon Valley companies that decorated the walls of every office . . . Shockley spawned Fairchild, Fairchild spawned Intel, Intel spawned . . . was a cheery face on a violent truth." New companies put old ones out of business, the young were forever eating the old, the Valley was a speeded-up Oedipal drama. In this drama, technology played the dominant role. It was the murder weapon.

If the technology entrepreneurs are paranoid, shouldn't investors be paranoid, too? The book makes me very conscious of the risk inherent in investing in technology, particularly now. As huge amounts of new money flow to venture capitalists (VCs) and are dispersed increasingly mindlessly at an ever more frantic pace, the speed of the life cycle accelerates. Innovation is disruptive, and an era in which money is available to fund anything is even more disruptive. Technology makes "anarchy respectable." A tech mania may be great for innovation and for the country, but it may be awful for the incumbent stocks.

And money is available. The book shows how most of the old rules of capitalism and venture capital fell away after the success of Netscape; now they have really been suspended.

For instance, it had long been a rule of thumb with the Silicon Valley venture capitalists that they didn't peddle a new company to the investing public until it had had at least four consecutive profitable quarters. No longer did you need to show profits; you need to show rapid growth. Never mind that you weren't making money—there would be a time for that later, assuming someone eventually figured out how to make money from the Internet. Having a past actually counted against a company, for a past was a record and a record was a sign of a company's limitations. You had to show that you were a company not of the present but of the future. The most appealing companies became those in a state of pure possibility.

The *Fortune* article recounts with awe what is going on in the VC world. VCs are hounded by people who want to be VCs, too, and connect to the gravy train. VCs are showing gains of 100 percent, and run-of-the-mill VC partners are making $20 million annually, at least on paper. Startups can now get money in weeks instead of months, because there is no risk. "What risk?" one VC asked *Fortune.* "If the company doesn't work out, we'll sell it for $150 million. If [it] kind of works out, we'll sell it for $500 million, and if it really works out, it'll be worth between $2 billion and $10 billion. Tell me how that's risk?"

The VCs are raising huge new funds faster than ever before, but the competition for deals is brutal. VCs have to prove their worth with startups, *Fortune* writes: "Will you recruit, make calls on [the startup's] behalf . . . have breakfast at Bucks with strategic partners at 7 A.M., and answer your home phone when it rings at 10 P.M.? If yes, then maybe you can invest. Maybe." You can imagine what a supplicant environment like this does for deal pricing.

Investors, said Clark, and the investment bankers, too, must close their eyes and imagine a new world. Look to the future. The future is bright. The belief was partially self-fulfilling, as belief often is. An up stock was like the golden boy in his senior year, headed toward some indefinable great height. Moreover, it now costs almost nothing to start new companies. The venture capitalists will hurl money at any new venture that has a visionary and some engineers. As a result, the investors got less and the visionary and the engineers got more. Often the visionary has some vague idea, gets money, and then hires the engineers to see if it works. The failure rate rises exponentially. As Lewis says:

All you needed was an idea, some excellent engineering talent, and a pair of big brass balls to execute that idea. You didn't need to raise millions to build your product and in the process whittle your stake down to almost nothing. You found the concept, you wrote the software to exploit the concept, and you sold the company to the public . . . because the American public was willing to take a flying leap into the future on whatever . . . entrepreneurs were willing to take a flying leap on at ten times the price.

These vignettes and the two pasted-together, abridged paragraphs tell the story of what is happening. The final event is that the engineers, the geeks who can babble tech talk, flock to the startups because that is where they have a shot at the big financial hit. Of course, as a result, if the technology falters, these new new companies cannot withstand pessimism because then the engineers all desert ship. As for the venture capitalists, they have gone to business school, speak the jargon, understand nothing, and flock like wildebeests.

When?

January 4, 2000

The incredible momentum of the New Economy stocks around the world dazzles us all, and every day it gathers more innocents into its warm and luxurious embrace as they hurtle down the road toward El Dorado. (In case you don't know, El Dorado is a legendary place associated with gold rushes and synonymous with fabulous wealth where everyone lives happily ever after.)

Meanwhile, we misanthropic professionals are obsessed with guessing when it will all come to a bad end. Incidentally, anyone who doesn't think the tech bubble is a world-encompassing event should observe the accompanying chart, which shows the Osaka High-Tech Index, or look at the charts of emerging markets telecom stocks. What we may be missing is that the road to El Dorado is, as always, paved with credit creation and leverage as well as promise and potential.

My inclination, derived from a stern, Puritan investment upbringing, is to expect righteous retribution in the form of a crash or at least a sharp break, but history actually suggests otherwise. With the exception of the late 1920s, parabolic technology runs in the 1950s, early 1960s, early 1970s, and from 1981 to 1983 tended to erode rather than explode in terms of relative returns, even though they almost always went vertical just before the fade stage. This is not to say that there couldn't be a sharp, short correction at any time, but a total free-fall collapse is relatively unlikely if you believe in history. I don't believe that the break in the first few days of the new year is the end. I think that comes later and probably higher.

However, 1929 proves that if some bolt from the blue, psychological or real, devastates the mood of the entire market, the New Economy stocks will make rocks look buoyant. Furthermore, the erosion tends to last a long time—like 5 to 10 years. We also looked at speculative manias that ended in vertical ascents in other equity markets and found that crashes tended to be rare. Everyone knows about 1929, and after a

Rocket–Osaka High-Tech Index (through December 30, 1999)

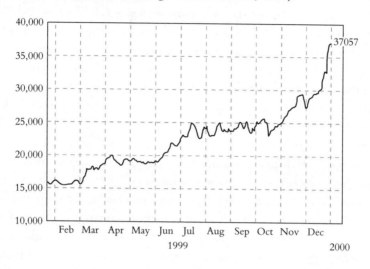

SOURCE: Reuters.

1000 percent run in three and a half years, Hong Kong did collapse 90 percent in 1973, and U.S. biotech stocks fell 60 percent in 1992, but these are exceptions rather than the rule. As for short-term timing, I am an amateur. Momentum studies by Ned Davis and others suggest that after a "good" bottom like last October, a leadership momentum group should outperform for at least 12 to 13 weeks. This suggests danger in the second half of January.

I am convinced that the huge increases in M3 around the world since the fall of 1998 and the tremendous acceleration in the creation of unregulated credit *outside the banking system* are major factors feeding the speculative fires. The Internet and the new technologies are clearly for real, and so they also have fanned the flames. You probably couldn't have one without the other—or at least, without the money surge, the bull market in tech would be more muted. Money makes the mare go, and in the last three months, M3 and credit have literally exploded to the upside. Together with the total ascendancy of greed over fear, they are the fuel that has powered the fourth-quarter surges in tech around the world.

In the last three months in the United States, M3 has soared at an annual rate of 16 percent, and similar trends are evident in both Europe and Japan. Whether this most recent burst is Y2K-related is irrelevant. It is the raw liquidity that has to go some-where, and some part of it is pouring, rushing into New Economy stocks. The inno-cents are buying them because their prices have gone up. It's a feeding frenzy straight out of Tulipomania. Does anybody know what Qualcomm really does?

But there is more to the story. Doug Noland of David W. Tice & Associates in Dallas recently gave a fascinating interview to Kate Welling (editor, publisher of Welling@Weeden). He argues that most economists are missing the boat on credit excesses. They focus on the narrow money supply, he asserts, and don't understand that credit is also being created by the GSEs (Fannie Mae, Freddie Mac, the Home Loan Bank), the finance arms of major companies (the GE Credits and GMACs), and a whole slew of companies Wall Street created to lend money in the subprime area in everything from credit cards to home equity loans. The GSEs are unregulated, have an implied government guarantee, and have no reserve requirements. Furthermore, they borrow short and lend long. Noland points out that over the last 21 months, the three GSEs have expanded their assets by $521 billion, while the Fed's own assets have grown by only about $70 billion.

The interview is complex and needs to be read in full. I don't pretend to have anything more than a rudimentary understanding of the complexities of credit creation in a modern economy, but I think I understand the general principles. Noland's point is that massive and unprecedented credit creation is inflating the asset bubbles in the stock market and real estate that are hugely distorting the financial system, the economy, and the market-pricing mechanism itself. "Down the road," he says, "when this credit bubble is pierced, we'll be left with an economy that's so maladjusted it'll probably take decades to set it right." As a caveat, it should be noted that Noland's firm runs the Prudent Bear Fund, which hasn't exactly shot the lights out recently.

Nonetheless, this line of thinking hearkens back to the Austrian School economists, of whom Joseph Schumpeter, who coined "creative destruction," is the most famous. Their theory is that any credit creation beyond savings is credit inflation, which will manifest itself in one of three ways: asset price inflation, trade deficits, or consumer price inflation. Of the three, CPI inflation is the least dangerous because all the central bank has to do is tighten to slow things down.

However, asset price inflation and a trade deficit are deadly because over time they lead to a stock market bubble, spurring even more consumption, which then distorts the investment cycle and leads to a massive trade deficit. This combination eventually jeopardizes the entire economy and financial system because it results in a crash and a dysfunctional economy with little ability to repay its foreign debts. Noland thinks there will be a dollar crisis that will be compounded by foreigners selling their leveraged tech holdings. In fairness, it must be said that Noland makes no prediction as to when the chickens will come to roost, only that someday they will. Thus the crucial question of "When?" remains unanswered.

We should all scan the story of the early 1970s, Adam Smith's *Money Game*, one more time, not because it will tell us when but because it will remind us that it has all happened before and that there are always *whens* waiting out there in the sunshine for us. In one section, the narrator is talking to Harry, a hot money manager who has turned cold in the midst of the craziness.

"No," Harry said. "The worst thing isn't the money. The worst thing is that I don't believe myself. I don't know what makes stocks go up any more. Things that used to be true, aren't true. Everything has turned to paper." "The woods are deep and dark and full of tigers," Harry said, and the tigers Harry was thinking of are twenty-eight and have fire in their bellies and a Bill Graham–like conviction of what is to transpire next year. All of them expect to be zillionaires, but

the Witch of Wall Street is capricious, and by the rules of the game some of them must end up on a barstool with a slip of adding machine tape in their slightly fraying $300 pockets saying 00.00, Do Not Pass Go.

Ah, you say, gamblers must expect this. Did not Lord Keynes, himself a successful speculator, say, "The game of professional investment is intolerably boring and overexacting to anyone who is entirely exempt from the gambling instinct; whilst he who has it must pay to this propensity the appropriate toll." Is this not the toll? But Harry was not really a gambler. You can tell those with the propensity: If the stocks are not moving they will play backgammon, and if not backgammon, they will be laying off on football games, and if all else fails there is the gamble of which raindrop will make it first down the window. But they know themselves, and their identities are not in any one raindrop . . . but when the machine says 00.00 there should be no one there at all because that identity has been extinguished, and the trouble is that sometimes when the adding machine tape says 00.00 there is still a man there to read it.

Section 1D:
Wars and Rumors of War

The Last Supper

January 21, 1980

With the bond market in disarray, questions arising about the restrictiveness of Fed policy, and with market analyst John Mendelson maximum bearish from a technical viewpoint, the stock market's rally is at a crossroads. If the market reacts in its usual way to higher interest rates, prices should fade. But if the market is now being driven by the "profitable stagflation," store-of-value psychology I discussed last week, then prices could work higher, confounding those who think the market pattern doesn't change. My guess continues to be that prices are going higher.

Meanwhile, a bizarre story that is making the rounds in London and the Middle East, if true, could explain the crude brutality of Russia's sudden move into Afghanistan. One of the sources of this tale is the same one that accurately described to us the dimensions of the attack before the true story appeared in the Western press. Anyway, it is known that in early December the Russians sent Lieutenant-General Victor Paputin to Kabul. Paputin, age 52, was first deputy chief of the Ministry of Internal Affairs and a candidate member of the Central Committee of the Communist Party. He was considered a real star by the Politburo and was Russia's premier political-secret police operative, which means he was their main man when high-level arm twisting (and breaking) was required.

His mission in Afghanistan was to persuade President Amin to formally invite the Russian forces to intervene. He and his 90-member staff were working with only moderate success toward this end when they were invited to a dinner at the presidential palace outside of Kabul on the evening of December 26. It is doubtful that anyone who attended that dinner is still alive, but apparently Paputin and his staff during the meal and afterwards put heavy pressure on Amin to invite Russian forces into the country. Amin refused, Paputin threatened, and violent argument resulted between the two men and their advisers. In the midst of the shouting, one of the Afghanistan aides grabbed a gun from a guard and shot and killed Paputin. In the ensuing gun battle, most of the Russians were killed or wounded, but apparently a few escaped capture and got back to the Russian compound, where they presumably reported the massacre to Moscow. Within hours, a major attack by Russian aircraft and tanks was launched against the palace, and by the morning of the 27th the Russian invasion of Afghanistan had begun. The Afghanistan guard company defending the palace fought fiercely, and it was not until late on the 27th that the Russians were able to storm the palace, which by then had been reduced to rubble, and recover the body of Paputin. Amin was killed by the Russians in the attack on the palace, not, as has been reported officially, by an Afghanistan firing squad after he had been tried for treason by a people's court.

The surmise from all this is that the Russian leadership launched the attack on Afghanistan in "hot blood" over the murder of their colleague. It was a furious, emotional reaction and not a carefully considered move. The brutality of the action has aroused widespread criticism from even their allies such as Cuba, appalled the nonaligned nations, and awakened the United States to its weak defense posture. As I have discussed previously, the Russian economy is too sick and not big enough anyway to match our expenditure levels (except at high social cost) if we materially increase our defense spending as is now being proposed. Furthermore, the summer Olympics are now in jeopardy. Thus, it could be argued that the Russians will now try to undo some of the damage their invasion has done by beginning a peace offensive and even perhaps by making a token withdrawal of some troops. The Russians, of course, will not change their long-term strategy of moving to gain control of Middle East oil, but they may wave the olive branch for a while. Unfortunately, we may be dumb enough to fall for it and get deflected from rebuilding our defense establishment. Such a peace offensive would be short-term bullish for equity prices, although not for defense stocks. The price of gold would probably decline sharply.

On the other hand, the Russians may reason that although their emotional and heavy-handed lunge into Afghanistan was in retrospect unfortunate, the damage to world opinion has been done and they might as well go for the oil and the warm water ports now while the United States is still weak. In any case, it is now certain Victor Paputin is dead. His official obituary published in *Pravda* succinctly reported that he met "an untimely end." There are worse jobs than being an investment manager.

Speaking of gold, Alan Greenspan points out that the surge in gold this time is different, because with the exception of silver, other commodities have not followed, as has invariably occurred in the past when there was a flight from currencies. Thus, there has been a significant drop in the price of commodities defined in units of gold. Greenspan suggests an alternative explanation for the recent phenomenon. He argues that the evidence suggests we are seeing a run from store-of-value claims that require an intermediary (a bank, a government, a financial institution, etc.) to the most readily negotiable store-of-value claim—gold—which governments cannot freeze, devalue, or easily confiscate. Also, a special premium in recent months has surfaced for the preservation of wealth with anonymity.

If this is the case, Greenspan argues, then much of the recent gold buying must be coming from the Middle East. The fall of the Shah, the unrest in Saudi Arabia, the freezing of Iranian bank deposits, and the invasion of Afghanistan are all contributing to this new insecurity of the very rich in the Middle East, who every day get richer and more scared. The big oil price increases of 1979 created new surplus accumulations in the Middle East kingdoms, which could well be the source of the cash being converted to gold. So they are frantically paying up for gold.

Meanwhile, last week I talked with several bankers from the Midwest. All across middle America, the people are lining up day after day to sell their gold and silver objects. The lines stretch around the block, and the people stand quietly and patiently. They are not scared. Midwestern America always has had superb instinctive timing at both the tops and bottoms of the stock market cycle and an inherent sense of value, and my guess is that the people out there are going to be right again. Every mania comes to a bad end, and gold is just as hard to value as tulips or old masters. I'll bet gold's a lot lower than 850 by year-end.

The following charts from *Public Opinion* seem to summarize the mood of the American people and the political dilemma of the Carter administration. Inflation is

Inflation Is Here to Stay and Government's Most to Blame

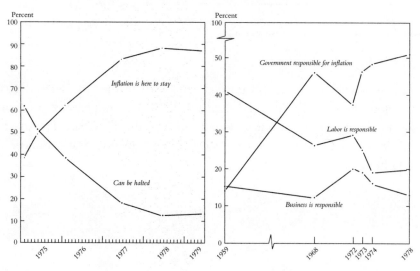

Increase Defense Spending ...

Question: Would you like to see federal defense expenditures increased, decreased, or remain where they are now? (1971) President Carter has asked Congress to increase federal spending on defense by 3 percent. Do you favor increasing the defense budget of the United States, decreasing that budget, or keeping it the same as it is now? (1979)

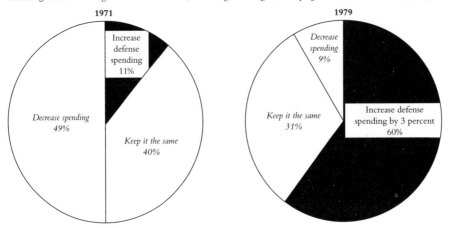

SOURCE: Surveys by Louis Harris and Associates, 1971; ABC News/Louis Harris and Associates, September 26–October 1, 1979.

... But Support for Controls at Five-Year High

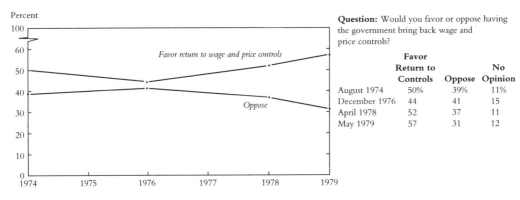

Question: Would you favor or oppose having the government bring back wage and price controls?

	Favor Return to Controls	Oppose	No Opinion
August 1974	50%	39%	11%
December 1976	44	41	15
April 1978	52	37	11
May 1979	57	31	12

SOURCE: Survey by the Gallup Organization, latest that of May 4–7, 1979.

here to stay, says the first chart, and government is to blame (the second chart). The country has now dramatically reversed itself on defense spending, and wage and price controls are becoming more popular (as indicated in the third and fourth charts). In other words, it will be good politics to boost defense spending and impose controls. Carter is a politician.

The Beam That Broke the Camel's Back

August 6, 1990

The events of last week, the new Saddam factor in the global equation, are bad for world tranquility, growth, and the price of long financial assets. America's power and credibility have been diminished, but what's really bearish is that the richest oil reserves in the world are coming under the control of a fanatic with an entirely different agenda from that of the conservative, pro-Western Gulf Arabs who have owned them. Consequently, I think the risk premium on financial assets has risen, and the odds of a cyclical bear market have increased. Cash is king.

In my view, last week signaled the beginning of the new post–cold war era. I suspect the new era will be one of shifting alliances, commercial disturbances, regional wars for economic advantage, and religious fanaticism and terrorism. Saddam is only the first of the opportunistic regional bullies who will want to extend their reach. Unfortunately, when one bully gets away with aggression, you can be sure that he and others will try again. The United States has looked foolish and ineffective, and Kuwait will not be the last incident. A world with only one great power, and an aging one at that, may be inherently less stable, and it is discouraging that the United States cannot project its military power to defend its friends. Why do we spend hundreds of billions on carrier task forces if we are afraid to use them?

I am not at all optimistic that Kuwait will be put back together again. The deafening silence from the rest of the Arab world indicates that Saddam—with his belligerence to Israel, his military power, and his socialist tendencies—has struck a popular chord. The Arab masses see him as a new Nasser; even King Hussein of Jordan speaks of Saddam as the leader of the Arab people. Of course, the fact that there are two regiments of the Iraqi Army in Jordan may have affected his tongue.

Unless Saddam is sent packing back to Baghdad with his tail between his legs, isn't it just a matter of time until the house of Saud in Saudi Arabia is overthrown under one pretext or another? The small sheikhdoms of Bahrain and Abu Dhabi and the other Emirates will be easy pickings. Thus, there is an excellent chance that within a few years Iraq will control the entire Gulf and its oil production. With 45 percent of the globe's oil reserves under his belt, Saddam will then be one of the most powerful men in the world—unless we discipline him now, which seems unlikely. This is what I mean by the risk premium going up.

Meanwhile, at home our leveraged economy is staggering toward recession, as I suspected. Higher oil prices and interest rates aren't going to help. I think the great popularity run of George Bush is over and that his 81 percent approval rating will sink like a stone. Saddam; Bush's son Neil; lip reading; the economy—the president's luck has run out. Now he has staked his international credibility on expelling Iraq from Kuwait. Even as the S&L bailout swells, say good-bye to the peace dividend; rising oil prices have further undermined the basis of a budget compromise. I don't see anything good happening to George Bush for a while, and the equity markets will also be disquieted by this factor.

Now, if by some chance the Western democracies, the Arab world, and the Soviet Union got together and forced Saddam from Kuwait, that would be a different story. The risk premium would go down. But good luck on that one. I want to believe George Bush when he talks tough, but don't see what his options are. There will be no standing up to Saddam; instead, we'll get just the usual dose of UN-speak and some trade sanctions (which most nations including Japan will ignore), and there will be more bullying somewhere else soon.

I was cautious before the events of last week, and if anything I am more cautious now. The U.S. economy is slipping fast, and stocks still aren't cheap. Nevertheless, if prices keep falling, I will become a buyer. What is happening in the Gulf is not the end of the world, just the end of post–cold war euphoria.

Bioterrorism and the Case for Higher P/E Ratios?

September 7, 1999

R ecently I spent some time speaking with William S. Cohen, the Secretary of Defense. What he had to say frightened me. A lean, almost ascetic-looking man with intense eyes, Cohen is not flamboyant or given to hyperbole; in fact, he almost radiates intelligence and control. Before being appointed secretary in January 1997, Cohen served three terms in the House and three in the Senate representing Maine. For years he has been an influential voice on defense and international security matters, and it is generally acknowledged that he and Bob Rubin have been Clinton's two best Cabinet appointments.

William Cohen is a serious man and by no means an alarmist, but his concerns about America's vulnerability to bio or germ terrorism are scary. He has no axe to grind. "Welcome to the grave new world of terrorism," he said, "a world in which traditional notions of deterrence and counterresponse no longer apply."

America remains unquestionably the world's superpower, Cohen began. Our ability to project conventional force is unsurpassed. The air war in Kosovo was probably the most successful military campaign ever fought. The U.S. Air Force flew over 10,000 combat missions, often in abysmal weather, with the loss of only two planes and no pilots, and inflicted tremendous damage with pinpoint accuracy.

But the United States now faces something of a "superpower paradox," he said. Our conventional supremacy makes a direct challenge fruitless, so our enemies seek unconventional, asymmetric means to hurt us. Terrorism through weapons of mass destruction both atomic and biological is the weapon of choice, and in many ways, bioterrorism is the best in the sense that germs are easier to create and deliver.

The old Soviet Union had a huge germ warfare research program known as Biopreparat, or "The System," in Western Siberia at a sprawling, clandestine virology center code-named "Vector." With the disintegration of the Soviet Union in 1989, most of the Vector bioweapon scientists with the formulas memorized hightailed it to countries that would pay up for their black skills. The diaspora headed for such friends of America as Iran, Iraq, North Korea, Libya, and Syria (must have been a nice bunch of guys at Vector).

Cohen told me at least 25 countries have biological weapons or are developing them. It's almost certain these weapons will fall into the hands of fanatical terrorists and religious zealots who are willing, even eager, to undertake suicide missions. The Arab terrorist bin Laden is known to be working on germ packages, and I am sure it was no accident the pharmaceutical plant in the Sudan got taken out.

Cohen thinks bioterrorism is, in many ways, the most dangerous threat America faces because our open society makes us so vulnerable. Anthrax, Ebola, and smallpox are three of the most deadly agents. Vector scientists may have developed a combination of Ebola and smallpox nicknamed "blackpox," which combines the massive hemorrhages and mortality of Ebola with the lethal contagiousness of smallpox. A rogue state or terrorists could make ancient scourges become monstrous modern plagues.

Anthrax is easy to produce with little space, inexpensive equipment, and relatively rudimentary chemistry. Nevertheless, it's not something to try in your garage, because the anthrax must be totally isolated or the manufacturers may end up killing themselves. Just a flask of culture can produce pounds of anthrax bacteria in four days. One gram contains enough doses to infect a million people. To kill, anthrax needs to be inhaled, which means gently dispersing it as a mist at ground level. A crop-dusting plane would be the ideal delivery vehicle, and a small bag sprinkled from a single-engine plane could infect a major American city.

In the case of smallpox or "blackpox," the biological agent would sink into the respiratory and nervous systems of the afflicted, infecting unsuspecting thousands, who would in turn communicate the virus to whomever they touched. Smallpox can be transmitted through the tiny droplets of saliva from a cough, which can infect someone 10 feet away. The speed and scope of modern air travel could carry the invisible contagion across the world in hours. Smallpox is explosively contagious, and 200 million people died of it in this century alone before it was declared eradicated in 1979. Today no one is even vaccinated against it. If the stricken were taken to hospitals, the nurses and doctors would be immediately infected. A smallpox plague could begin with a suitcase left in a public place. I will never feel the same about Grand Central Station.

In the summer of 1998, North Korea fired a test ballistic missile over Japan and the missile fell into the sea. The Koreans have old grudges, and it is believed that the missile could have been designed to carry a smallpox *Variola major* warhead. Japan has almost no smallpox vaccine and is totally unprepared to deal with a germ warfare attack. If such a Korean missile had landed in Japan, a widening chain of infection could have wiped out half the population. A defector from Vector now known as Ken Alibek says the old Soviet Union had stockpiled liquid smallpox for loading on biowarheads targeted at American cities.

These agents are very dangerous. In 1979 an accident at the Soviet biological warfare plant allowed perhaps at most a gram of anthrax spores to escape from the facility. Some 96 people died who were downwind of the plant, some of them inside with doors and windows closed, and the contaminated plume killed sheep 30 miles away. Anthrax, unlike smallpox, is not contagious, but its spores can persist for decades and make land permanently uninhabitable.

In another terrifying incident, a Soviet scientist at Vector, Nikolai Ustinov, who was in a sealed chamber injecting guinea pigs with Marburg virus (a cousin of Ebola), accidentally pricked himself with his needle. Although every effort was made to save him, he died about two weeks later. The Soviets recorded his horrible agonies as he sweated blood from his pores and wept. This incident is recounted in the March 9, 1998, issue of the *New Yorker* in "The Bioweaponeers," by Richard Preston, who has also written superb but very scary articles about smallpox.

Cohen pointed out that in 1995 the Japanese cult Aum Shinrikyo used sarin gas for a terror attack on Tokyo subways and also planned to unleash anthrax against U.S. forces in Japan. The World Trade Center terrorists were gathering the ingredients for chemical weapons when they were apprehended. In February 1998, two men were arrested by the FBI outside Las Vegas with what turned out to be a nonlethal form of anthrax in the trunk of their car, and the charges (later dropped) alleged that one of them had plotted an attack on the New York City subways.

Bioterrorists are particularly difficult to combat. They leave no postmarks or return addresses. There are no telltale signs of a missile launch, no TNT residue or rental truck receipts to be traced. In fact, bioengineering often proceeds under the guise of pharmaceutical research. As Cohen put it: "Penicillin for the poor or Ebola for the enemy? Who is to say, and with what deterrent is America left?"

Cohen described what he thinks America must do. Preparation itself is a deterrent, and by minimizing the death and destruction terrorists hope to spawn, we reduce the likelihood they will even try. Although we are beginning to get organized, we are far from prepared, however. As things stand today, I wouldn't place much faith in our ability to cope with a serious biological catastrophe. As panic spreads, the "run for the hills" factor would be very high. The nation would be paralyzed by fear.

Merely managing the consequences of an attack is not sufficient, Cohen argues: "We must be vigilant in seeking to interdict and defeat the efforts of those who seek to inflict mass destruction on us. This will require greater international cooperation, intelligence collection abroad, and information gathering by law enforcement agencies at home. Information is clearly power, and greater access to information will require the American people and their elected officials to find the proper balance between privacy and protection." Intelligence agencies must be able to use the power of the computer and the Internet without being blocked by privacy codes, Cohen argues. Just as in time of war citizens must sacrifice some civil rights, citizens today must be willing to give up some privacy rights in order to ensure protection from terrorism.

Although he was not specific, Cohen suggested that we had already defeated a number of planned attacks on American cities. But unless we become more vigilant and change our ways, he worries that some future attack would succeed with God-only-knows what consequences. It would be tragic if America had to suffer the biological equivalent of Pearl Harbor before we developed the will to mobilize.

Only the bad guys have bioweapons. The United States and the rest of NATO destroyed our arsenals in 1969 and ceased all development. What else would you expect? But James Glassman of *Dow 36,000* fame says in the brave new world, equities should sell at 100 times earnings.

Section 1E: Geopolitics

Popcorn and the Decline of the West

June 30, 1980

Walter Levy is an eminent, elderly guru, and *Foreign Affairs* is the heavyweight American intellectual magazine. Mere publication of an article in its gray, ponderous cover means many will take very seriously the messages delivered. Thus, it is not surprising that the press and others are reacting with handwringing and deep sighs to Levy's lead article in the new issue of *Foreign Affairs* with the dire title of "Oil and the Decline of the West."

Actually, the title tells it all, and there really isn't anything new in the 16 pages of gloomy text. It's just another in a long line of "Decline of the West" essays, with oil, weakness, and self-indulgence the culprits this time. Levy outlines the inevitability of the world's inability to find enough oil to replace what is being used up in what is a fairly classic extrapolation analysis that makes very little allowance for the impact of price or technology on either supply or demand. He is very pessimistic about the political stability of the Middle East and seems to make the assumption that social and political change inevitably means monstrous supply stoppages. My view is that there will be social change in the Gulf nations, but the supply interruptions will be short and not necessarily synchronized because governments in the area need massive oil revenues to meet the rising aspirations of their people. For example, I suspect Iran's production of oil soon will be increasing rather than declining further.

As far as the petrodollar recycling problem is concerned, Levy states flatly that "the jig is up," and he discusses other "structural" dangers. The essay concludes with this cheery paragraph:

> Instead, we will probably be confronted by a series of major oil crises which might take any or all of several forms: fighting for control over oil resources among importing countries or between the superpowers; an economic-financial crisis in importing countries; regional conflicts affecting the oil-producing area; or internal revolutions or other upheavals in the Middle East. At best, it would appear that a series of future emergencies centering around oil will set back world progress for many, many years. And the world, as we know it now, will probably not be able to maintain its cohesion, nor be able to provide for the continued economic progress of its people against the onslaught of future oil shocks—with all that this might imply for the political stability of the West, its free institutions, and its internal and external security.

In my view, this is traditional doomsayers' nonsense. Barbara Tuchman put it exquisitely: "The doomsayers work by extrapolation; they take a trend and extend it, forgetting that the doom factor, sooner or later, generates a coping mechanism. You cannot extrapolate any series in which the human element intrudes; history, that is, the human narrative, never follows, and will always fool, the scientific curve."

Time and again in the past, doomsayers have convincingly forecast the decline of Western man. Their arguments are always rational and compelling extrapolations of past trends into the future without allowance for man's ingenuity when confronted with challenge and opportunity. Inevitably, they fall into the oldest trap of all in the prognostication game, which is to underestimate everyone else's intelligence but their own.

For example, almost 200 years ago, the British economist Thomas Malthus predicted that the imbalance between population growth and food production increases would shortly cause the world to starve to death. He and the eminent (most doomsayers have great eminence at the time of their pronouncements) David Ricardo were very pessimistic about agricultural productivity because of the then-diminishing returns of investment in agriculture. The experts called the theory "Malthus's iron law." As things turned out, it was neither a law nor iron because Malthus, Ricardo, and most of the other famous intellectuals of the time were incapable of imagining that out of the Industrial Revolution would come farm machinery and that from the green revolution would spring fertilizers and seeds that would compound agricultural productivity a thousandfold and lead to an era of surplus and price supports.

A second example is W. S. Jevrons in the 1860s. Jevrons extrapolated the then 3.5 percent current annual rate of energy consumption growth and concluded that there was simply not enough coal in England or the world and that inevitably "our motion must be laid to rest." Europe and England had cut their timber, and whales were being slaughtered at a rate that would lead to extinction in 20 years, said Jevrons, and so there was no hope from alternative energy sources. Of course, he couldn't have been expected to foresee the discovery of oil in Pennsylvania, but maybe he should have at least allowed for "the coping mechanism."

Another classic example was the study made for the New York City Council in the late nineteenth century that correctly forecast rising living standards and the magnitude of the population growth the city would experience. The experts postulated that, by 1960, nearly 100,000 men would be employed just in the removal of horse manure from the streets of New York and that the volume of traffic would be such that, in an average day, a foot of manure would be deposited on the streets of Manhattan by the multitude of horses.

More recently, after the Second World War, when food and materials prices continued to rise relative to those of industrial products, everyone got worried, and the president created a Materials Policy Commission (otherwise called the Paley Commission) to study the world's diminishing natural resources. Fortunately, the commission's work was so ponderous that the trends that caused its formation reversed before the report was issued, and its authors avoided serious embarrassment. Much the same can be said for Dennis Meadows and his *The Limits of Growth*. In fact, a recent article I read by some of the Club of Rome–Meadows team seemed to suggest they now recognize that incremental technology and price belied the inevitability of their assumption of an apocalyptic crisis. Walt Rostow put it well when he wrote: "Behind their anxiety were projections of geometric increases in demand set off against absolutely limited or arithmetically expanding supplies, shadowed by diminishing returns."

Herman Kahn has an article in the latest *Fortune* entitled "Why OPEC is Vulnerable," and I'm sure the precise, very optimistic scenario he outlines also will be wrong. "The universe is full of magical things patiently waiting for our wits to grow sharper," and I believe "the coping mechanism" will work again the way it always has in the past. To paraphrase William Faulkner, Western man will not just endure; he will prevail. Reports of his imminent demise are greatly exaggerated.

What Could Be Worse?

Last week, so the story goes, three executives were talking about how bad things were. The first told how orders were down 50 percent, his plants were running at 30 percent of capacity, his company was running at a loss, and his sales manager had quit to go to work in a less cyclical industry. "What could be worse?" he asked.

"That's nothing," said the second. "There's no orders at all. I've had to shut down two of my three mills, we eliminated our dividend, we're close to bankruptcy, my wife has run away with the executive vice president, and the board is talking about firing me for not anticipating the recession. What could be worse?"

"July," said the third.

In spite of this kind of talk, many Wall Street economists and institutional investors think the worst of the recession is over and that the next change of perception will be that a recovery has begun. They point to the firming of sensitive spot industrial commodity prices, the strength in gold, and the rise in interest rates as early indicators. Also, new unemployment applications appear to have peaked several weeks ago. They argue that the jump in the money supply last week and specific talk of a tax cut suggest monetary and fiscal stimulus will follow soon. Also, there are some suggestions of a bottoming in demand for housing and automobiles, and Walter Loeb points out that retail sales for the time being seem to have firmed. In fact, Erich Heinemann discussed these trends in last week's *Weekly Federal Reserve Report*.

Stocks and bonds were acting last week as though the buyers believed the recession was nearly over. My view is that the evidence is fragmentary and speculative, and it is too soon to be confident that business activity has stabilized or that the economy may not trace a *W* pattern. We continue to be fully invested, with the emphasis on energy, technological growth, the old Nifty Fifty, and the athletes. We own very few cyclicals. In other words, our commitment is to quality stocks rather than to an economic scenario.

Diary of
Mikhail S. Gorbachev—
Sunday, May 4, 1986

May 5, 1986

'm beginning to wonder if I want to be premier. Everything is going wrong, and although it's not my fault, our failures may be used against me in the Politburo. Incompetence everywhere.

Our economy is sick and getting sicker. The IMF report was right. Real GNP was down again in 1985, and the standard of living has been falling for five years. Life expectancy is declining, infant mortality and alcoholism are rising, and the people are sullen but not mutinous—yet. Even the hard-liners admit after a few vodkas that the pure Lenin model doesn't work and that we need the discipline of prices and profits. What a mess! My program for productivity and less drinking has had little impact on my cynical countrymen.

I am also depressed about our defense effort. We are spending more than the Americans but getting less, and defense is three times as heavy a burden relative to GNP for us as it is for them because our economy is so much smaller. Worse still, we put all our best people into the defense effort instead of industry, but they become bureaucrats—not inventors or entrepreneurs.

Afghanistan is our Vietnam, and this Libyan episode is only the latest fiasco. After the Bekaa Valley turkey shoot four years ago, when the Israelis, using American electronic equipment, paralyzed our missiles and shot down 88 new MIGs in a few hours, we spent billions designing a new guidance system that would work against the Hawkeye. Libya was a test under battle conditions of the latest equipment on both sides. We had 3,000 Russians there on the scopes, and we knew they were coming. But their electronic countermeasures gear is still a generation ahead of ours, and when our people turned on the missile guidance radar, they could immediately see that they were jammed and that the U.S. missiles could home in on our radar. Sensibly, they turned off the radar and went to the basement. The foolish Libyans fired the missiles blind and hit nothing but their own city. Incidentally, what the hell was Qaddafi doing sleeping in a tent on such a night?

So now all the money we have spent on electronics was for nothing. How can we sell arms in the Middle East or anywhere else when they are obsolete? We are a supplier of inferior weapons and thus an unreliable ally. Already, the Syrians seem uneasy. And speaking of technology, there is simply no way we can duplicate the Americans' Star Wars effort. Even if we spent the money and further impoverished our economy, our system wouldn't work properly anyway.

Chernobyl could turn me into an alcoholic, too. We didn't tell the world about it because we wanted to buy grain futures before the markets knew, like last time, but the fire occurred on Saturday, and the world found out before we could buy. Incompetence compounded by bad luck. Shutting down 20 percent of our electricity production is going to further complicate the economy and give everyone an excuse for more production failures.

If the Urals' grain crop and soil are truly contaminated not only for this year but also for years to come, we are going to have to buy grain in the West. If so, we are in deep trouble. As the IMF said, we are running huge balance-of-trade deficits in spite of overcharging the Eastern Europeans for oil and everything else, and our foreign exchange reserves are gone. The oil markets are depressed to begin with, and if we dump oil and gold, it will lower inflation in the West so interest rates will decline further and their stupid stock markets will go up more. Agricultural commodity prices are already rising, and it enrages me that this will help that lucky old man in the elections this year in America. If crop prices rise significantly, the Republicans might even hold the Senate and gain seats in the House, which would be unprecedented in a second-term, off-year election. Lenin only knows what damage Reagan could do to us with that kind of mandate.

However, there is a way out of this quagmire. As Stalin said, the capitalists are so foolish and greedy that they will sell us the rope with which we will hang them. Now we will persuade them to lend us the money to buy the rope. Dobrinyn tells me that the bull market in stocks and bonds has enabled corporations to refinance themselves, so the demand for bank credit is weak. With the proper atmosphere and a fat spread over LIBOR, why shouldn't the Western banks, whose managements care only about present earnings to make their stock options worth something, lend us huge amounts of money so we can buy the grain and technology we need from the West? After all, we are an LDC if there ever was one. And didn't that Walter Wriston fellow say there was no risk in sovereign credit lending because a country can always print money? Of course, like the other LDCs, we will never pay the loans back. Each year we will pay the interest with new borrowings but make sure they always give us more money than we return to them.

It also should be possible to raise billions in the world's capital markets. Every member of the proletariat deserves to have some Russian junk bonds in his portfolio, and each year we'll borrow more to pay the interest. That fellow Ponzi had a good idea. We'll ask the big investment banking firms to come to Moscow for a bake-off. They will fall all over themselves preparing elaborate presentations and forming syndicates to be the lead underwriter for the mighty Soviet Union. But to get this financing, I've got to be a lot nicer. We must change the atmosphere of distrust and suspicion. I must be all charm and go to the summit this year with Reagan. We must stop the arms race because the Americans are winning, and it is bankrupting us. We also must change our image. From now on, it is Russia, not the cold-sounding Soviet Union, and when possible we should refer to "Mother Russia." The world loves mothers. We must seem to be open and kindly and speak of human rights. We will let all the dissident Jews go, as it is crucial to get the liberals around the world off our case. We must make the West feel sorry for us and even guilty about us, as then they will lend us or even give us money. It will not be easy, but it can be done because they have short memories and are greedy.

And if all this doesn't work, Raisa and I will defect to the West where I will write a book called *Power and Glory in the Kremlin*. If Stockman can get several million for his boring reminiscences, the publishers will give me tens of millions, or at least enough to support us in the style to which we have become accustomed. Then I could go on the lecture circuit or form a consulting firm the way Kissinger did.

Close-Up

1986

Last week, I attended a White House briefing and lunch arranged by Lew Lehrman for the founders of Citizens for America. I'm not a founder or even a big contributor, but Lew had an extra slot at the last minute. Citizens for America is a conservative, nationwide political action group. The original idea was President Reagan's; he persuaded Lehrman to raise the money, create an organization, and run it. Lehrman has done a superb job, and this day was the president's way of rewarding Lew and his core supporters.

There were about 40 or 50 of us in a small briefing room. I sat about 10 feet from the speakers. Since I wasn't legit, I shut up and listened. Also I've learned from experience that you don't hear anything at these briefings you couldn't read in the press, but it is valuable to see the big hitters up close and get a feel for their mood. For example, a White House briefing I went to in 1978 clearly revealed a disorganized, leaderless administration.

I'm not a conservative; in fact, I've voted for more Democrats than Republicans for president. I have voted for Reagan twice, so take this for what's it worth. The impression I got last week was of a confident, vigorous president and administration that are gaining strength and momentum rather than losing it. The president, Don Regan, and Mitch Daniels all talked about "1986 as a vintage year" for the restoration of American patriotism and the Reagan revolution in tax, budget, and monetary policy.

First up was Daniels, Assistant to the President for Political Affairs. He is young (36), a former presidential scholar, and obviously very bright. He made the point that even Reagan's critics now concede that he has restored the power and prestige of the presidency. Every second-term president in this century has suffered a 12 to 24 percentage-point decline in popularity by this time, but this president is at a new all-time high. "Some lame duck." Like Roosevelt, Reagan is disparaged as an intellectual lightweight by the press and the intelligentsia, but both presidents effected a genuine revolution. Reagan is a political phenomenon, and there is no telling what he can accomplish in the next three years.

The Director of the Office of Management and Budget, Jim Miller, was next. Miller looks and talks like a back-country Georgia farmer. He is pleasant and shrewd, and I liked the way, at lunch (I sat at his table), he listened to what people had to say to him. Unfortunately, I didn't think he was credible on the budget agenda. He said that the strategy was to focus the Congress on the "national compact of budget reduction" and broad themes rather than specifics. "The administration will hang tough on Gramm-Rudman," he said. Miller didn't seem to know the specifics of the effect of changes in the variables like interest rates and economic growth on the deficit, which was disconcerting. I was not encouraged by what he had to say.

Then came Don Regan. He looked a little weary, but after all he was coming down with a cold. I was impressed with his range and depth. He speaks fluently and handled some foolish questions well. Perhaps instead of losses in the midterm elections, he said, the Republicans—with the president, peace, and prosperity going for them—could hold the Senate against all odds and gain seats in the House. He wants a tax-reform bill that doesn't increase corporate taxes on investment too much or violate fairness for the lower income groups. He talked sensibly about world economic growth, but the most significant point he made was that the G-5 meetings would be talking about monetary reform.

The Secretary of Defense followed. Up close he seemed tired and very pale. Most of the CFA people responded warmly to Weinberger, but I didn't. He was too hard-line in his opposition to any cuts in the defense budget, and he said any arms control agreement would be "just a treaty which benefits the Russians as they won't agree to anything else." Waste in defense spending is minor and is a distraction. Defense spending is much less as a percentage of GNP now than it was 20 years ago. My impression was that Weinberger is a sincere fanatic who sees himself as the keeper of the sacred flame. He will never yield on the defense budget or support a treaty unless the president gives him a direct order.

Ed Meese followed. He looks ruddy and healthy and was the biggest surprise to me, as my impression from the press was of a political animal with a poor memory. Instead, he spoke eloquently and with force and clarity. He had good answers to some tough questions. He said the primary goal of the Justice Department is to reduce drug traffic in the United States by cutting off the supply and reducing demand. He went on to say that excessive litigiousness and its effect on insurance coverage is a major problem in American society and one that he is going to deal with.

Then we went to the State dining room for lunch with the president and the Cabinet officers. This was the third time I had seen the president up close, and he looks even better in person than he does in pictures or on TV. He is completely natural and at ease, and I was amazed again at how little security there seemed to be around him. After dessert, two waiters rolled up a microphone, and he immediately got up and moved toward it. Lehrman apologetically intervened, saying that the schedule called for him to thank a few people first. The President grinned. "You know," he said, "I'm just like a trained monkey. They bring up a microphone and I instinctively head for it." Later he spoke of the impact CFA as his "grassroots lobby" was having and then of the need to cut marginal tax rates and reduce the size of government.

Standing under the portrait of Lincoln over the fireplace, he talked of the changes in young people's attitudes ("when I was governor, they'd throw things at me when I went to a campus") and cracked a few somewhat corny jokes. They were nothing you hadn't heard before, but they seemed funnier when he told them. In the question-and-answer period that followed, you could see that, although he might not know the specific numbers on everything, his mind worked conceptually off a consistent model.

When it was over, each one of us had a few moments with him as a photographer took the traditional picture. You had time for about one zinger. A well-known money manager in front of me gave the president a "thank you for all you've done for us," which got a big grin. I decided to go with "Please don't let them talk you into raising taxes, sir." "You bet," said the President genially, moving me right along, "the Lord willing and if the creek don't rise."

Diary of
Mikhail Gorbachev,
May 1987

May 27, 1987

Well, events finally caught up with Ronald Reagan. He got cocky with Daniloff and was unprepared at Reykjavík, and now the Teflon legend is a thing of the past. But you know, I really like the old guy. Some evening I'd like to do some vodka drinking with him and Margaret Thatcher. She would probably put us both under the table.

Raisa got very jealous of Margaret at our Moscow meeting this spring. She knew right away why the meetings were lasting longer than the schedule. Thatcher is both formidable and attractive, and that upper-class English accent is very sexy. I wonder if she would go for a summit for two at my dacha. We'll send Raisa shopping in London with whatever his name is. However, Margaret's so damned smart I might end up like those Marine guards at the U.S. Embassy.

Meanwhile, if I do say so myself, I have orchestrated the disarmament negotiations brilliantly. My offer to remove all medium- and short-range arms from Europe has created what the *Wall Street Journal* calls "ideological chaos" in the West. The American hard-core conservatives are lining up with European socialists in support of it, and the liberal Democrats have joined the West German conservatives in opposition. Everyone is so confused that the press can't tell the hawks from the doves. Kissinger snipes at Perle, Adelman and Aspin have reversed positions, and the Europeans suddenly are realizing they may have to defend themselves with conventional arms, which will cost them a lot of money. For years, the nuclear standoff between us and the Americans has permitted Europe to skimp on defense and get rich instead. Well, if I manage this right, their respite is over. The Russian people are tired of bureaucrats and armies and are sick of what George Orwell, in *1984*, called "the sour, oily taste of Victory Gin."

I think I can get a major disarmament treaty in the next year. Certainly, Reagan wants and needs it to restore the sheen to his presidency and alleviate his budget-deficit problems. I need it even more. We're spending as much on defense as the Americans are and getting even less, and it's three times as heavy a burden relative to GNP for us as it is for them because our economy is so much smaller. Worse still, we have to put all our best people into the defense effort where they become bureaucrats instead of entrepreneurs. We must concentrate on butter rather than guns, or Russia, the Eastern European satellites, and old-style communism will be on the scrap heap of history.

Dick Nixon told me when he was here a few months ago that if Reagan left office without a disarmament treaty, that wife of his would never forgive me and that if I tried to make a deal with the next president, she would get Reagan to fight it. Nixon said that as a popular, retired president, Reagan would be formidable adversary. I certainly wouldn't want to spend a weekend disarming at a dacha with her.

In spite of glasnost, the Russian economy still stinks. People are drinking less because they can't get the vodka, but without incentives, it's almost impossible to make them work harder. The wheat crop this year is poor, and Afghanistan is still a quagmire. Central planning simply doesn't work, but eliminating it threatens the jobs of the party hierarchy. The trouble is that if we don't restructure soon, we will be the last true communists in the world and the poorest. The people are sullen but not mutinous, yet.

Both the Americans and the Soviets are spending far too much on defense, and it's impoverishing us even as Japan and the Europeans get richer. A strategic arms treaty will force the Europeans to spend more on conventional arms, but I must figure out some way to get the Japanese to waste some serious money. But we must make sure that it's only on defensive weapons. Conventional forces today are almost as worthless as strategic arms. Look at how pathetic the great Red Army is in Afghanistan against a ragtag bunch of partisans. And the *Stark* incident was another farce. The Americans are spending money and lives to keep the Gulf open so the Japanese can keep getting their cheap oil. That frigate must have been made out of tinfoil because the Iraqis have never seriously damaged anything before. How could the ship be in a war zone and not have its defensive systems on? It sounds like something our military would do.

If Reagan and I surprised the world and negotiated arms reduction for Russia and the United States, it should mean a lower budget deficit in the United States and bigger deficits in Europe, as defense spending there would rise. The dollar should firm, and American interest rates should decline. Maybe we could make some money in the U.S. stock market with that kind of inside information. A higher dollar would help us, too, since our exports, particularly oil, are sold for dollars.

The old guard in the party continues to be the disloyal opposition because I am reducing their power and privileges with glasnost and reforms. I have made some serious enemies there. If I don't make progress soon, I will end up like Khrushchev at best or, worse, Beria. Yegor Ligachev, who has spoken for the old ways, has got to go, as does that old Brezhnevite, Vladimir Shcherbitsky. But I don't have much time.

Things are not great at home, either. The old guard made a secret movie about Raisa's shopping habits. The KGB must have filmed it, which is disconcerting. The story line was that she was going to make a run at Imelda Marcos's world record for shoes. So now I've taken away her American Express card, and, of course, she's furious. I'll bet Margaret doesn't care about shoes. If she loses her election, I'll invite her to Russia, and maybe we can have some time together without those secret service busybodies.

The Diary of Deng Xiaoping: Wistful and Wishful Musings

June 20, 1989

May 10 Here I am, an old man in a dry month not being read to by a boy but irritated by students. The demonstrations in Tiananmen Square are becoming tiresome. At first I thought it was the usual spring madness of students trying to avoid classes and exams, but it persists. They say they want more democracy, faster economic progress, and less corruption. They are impatient naive children. We have grown China's economy at a 10 percent rate and artfully encouraged foreign investment. Of course, there is some corruption, but much less than there used to be. Soon they will tire of this prank and go home. But I still don't like it. All revolutions in China have begun in libraries.

May 14 I saw videotapes today of the students in Tiananmen. They are a scruffy, dirty crew with long hair. When I was young, we never looked so unkempt. The security people tell me that Tiananmen stinks of garbage and urine, that the students spend all day playing loud music, and that there is much promiscuity. They have been joined by the unemployed and the riffraff of the city. Now the students have started a hunger strike to embarrass us just as that troublemaking Gorbachev who began all this foolishness arrives. The whole thing is a disgrace. What those students need is to make a Long March like we did, and then they would appreciate the progress in the standard of living that we have made for them. They don't realize that this kind of rebellion against the state will discourage the foreign investment we need to continue our growth. Investors want order, not disorder.

May 20 Gorbachev and his preening, camera-mad wife who makes Nancy Reagan look natural have left. The students humiliated us, the rightful leaders of China, by forcing us to greet the Russians at the airport instead of in Tiananmen, while the world laughed at our impotence. Well, we shall see who is running China. Today we will declare martial law as a first warning. This demonstration is becoming serious and almost seems to be aimed at overthrowing us. Mao was correct when he said "political power grows out of the barrel of a gun" and that "those who wield pens must be controlled." However, the foreign investors are important to our economic growth, and I don't want to alarm them unduly.

May 23 Zhao Ziyang, my protégé, my personal choice to succeed me, without even asking me went to Tiananmen and attempted to persuade the students to leave. He must have been trying to upstage me and take power. And he failed to convince the students. Now they think we are weak. However, I still believe they will tire of this escapade, and the horribly unsanitary conditions in Tiananmen will force them to leave. Then we can arrest the leaders, some of whom are not students but well-known agitators. As for Zhao, he will spend the rest of his life making big stones into little ones.

June 3 Enough is enough. Just when I thought the students were giving up, they have erected this Statue of Liberty and taken to carrying signs saying, "Of the people, by the people, for the people." We, not they, are of the people. They act as though we are oppressing them like the old warlords. We who made the Long March for them, so they could be free. No rightful government can indefinitely permit social and economic disruption and rebellion by a small segment of the population. This has nothing to do with our commitment to free markets, economic growth, and foreign investment. Mao wrote a poem, "Cold Eyed I Contemplate the World"; I have followed his example and ordered the army of the north to clear the square using whatever force is necessary. We can afford to shed a little blood, and if we strike them hard the first time, we will not have to hit them again, as they will have learned their lesson.

June 5 Clearing the square was a bloody business as both the students and the soldiers overreacted. The world is screaming, and the foreign businessmen are running home, which is not good. I am shocked at the fall in the Hong Kong stock market and have ordered our banks there to buy. In China we must restore order and keep the economy healthy. Otherwise, we could have a real revolution of hungry people on our hands.

June 6 We are being portrayed as barbarians, which is ridiculous. For 2,000 years governments have been putting down student rebellions with troops, and inevitably people get killed. We are gentle compared with the Koreans, and after all, American troops killed American students at Kent State. The only difference is that in Tiananmen there were far more troops and students and so more got killed. The British and the Europeans murder each other in hundreds at football games. Perhaps a few thousand demonstrators died, many of whom were probably thugs. On the Long March, we lost more men a hundred times fighting to cross some forgotten river. But appearances count, and the economic system cannot be permitted to break down.

June 8 I am working hard to restore internal stability and confidence in China, but we had to arrest the leaders of the rebellion. Otherwise these provocateurs would cause new disturbances. A few of the worst criminals who burned trains and killed soldiers will be shot as an example. No student leaders will be executed because that would create martyrs. Life is returning to normal, but we cannot let the economy falter, or we will have more than just a few million students challenging us.

June 10 The foreign aid, businessmen, and investors we so desperately need must be coaxed back with soothing words and deeds. In fact, the Japanese are already returning. Hong Kong is the linchpin now and later. The barometer of the world's confidence in China is the Hong Kong stock market, which is really our stock market. We must act to reassure that market and get it back up. Investors and businessmen like stability; they are basically indifferent to how democratic the process that creates the order is. They care about profits, not politics or morality. We will give them what they want because we must have their knowledge and their money. It is not a question of liberal or conservative communism, but of our party's survival. Maybe I will buy some Hong Kong stocks myself.

Hang Seng Index: Chronology of Events in China

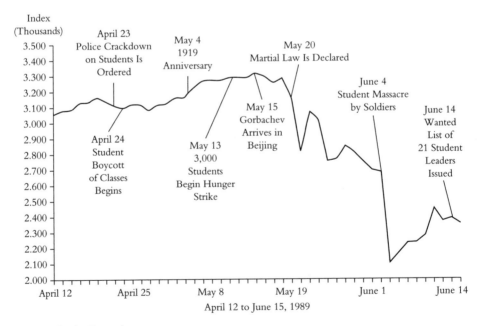

SOURCE: Morgan Stanley Research.

Bottomless Pits and Nuts with Missiles

May 29, 1990

Had we heard about the dyslexic, agnostic insomniac who lay awake all night wondering if there was a dog? Well, said the composite wise old man who once was secretary of state, he lay awake wondering about the bottomless money pit that was Eastern Europe. Last year was the annus mirabilis, the *Wunderjahr*. Expectations had run, no, soared beyond reality, and there were disappointments and turbulence ahead. Maybe he was getting old, he said, but he had this uneasy sense the world had become unhinged and was becoming more, not less, unstable.

He didn't believe there was going to be an economic miracle in Eastern Europe anytime soon. Impoverished, developing countries need strong governments with a clear vision capable of making bold and difficult economic decisions. For a country to bootstrap itself up to the takeoff stage, the people, the workers had to be "persuaded" to make sacrifices. Coalition democracy was a lousy, inefficient way to run a developing country. Furthermore, the Eastern European countries almost without exception had no experience with self-rule or the democratic process, and so the learning phase was bound to be disorderly.

I think he's right about developing countries and democracy. In many ways, a benevolent, enlightened dictatorship like Singapore or Taiwan is best for a developing country, but even a harsh dictatorship can work, as it did for so long in Korea. Of course, eventually the piper has to be paid. But Hong Kong, Malaysia, Indonesia, and Thailand are not true democracies, either.

The old man went on. Everyone seemed to think that all Eastern Europe and the Soviet Union had to do was to declare capitalism and free markets and their troubles

81

were over. The money needed to modernize their economies and restore the environment was staggering. It reminded him of the heady days of the 1950s, when the received wisdom was that the switch from colonial status to nationhood would miraculously unshackle the economies of Africa and eliminate poverty. Capitalism didn't seem to be working too well in South America, either.

As for East Germany, the one state in Europe that could have been a quick, shining success story, for political reasons West German Chancellor Kohl had botched that one by setting the D-Mark/Ost Mark exchange rate too low. As a result, East German wage rates at over $5.00 an hour were too high in relation to West German wages and productivity—and compared with countries like Portugal and Turkey. He suspected East Germany would remain a backward and relatively impoverished part of Germany, just as southern Italy languished compared with northern Italy.

Eastern Europe and the Soviet Union were now falling into an inflationary depression, he said. People were losing their jobs and incomes at a time when prices of essentials were soaring. This was a recipe for riot and revolution. The Soviet Union could break apart with perhaps the military assuming control in some of the republics. Certain of these new, unstable regimes would have the capability to deliver nuclear weapons. The Balkanization of Russia was destabilizing for the entire world.

All this chaos made the old man very nervous. History teaches that decaying empires are often dangerous, he said. The dying Ottoman Empire dragged Europe into 11 wars in the nineteenth century. The great power of the time, Britain, lost nearly 20,000 men in the Crimean War trying to stop Russian expansion into Ottoman territory. And the First World War began as a result of the collapsing Austro-Hungarian Empire. In fact, the next 20 years might resemble the last decade of the nineteenth century and the first of the twentieth. That period was characterized by shifting alliances, commercial disturbances, and regional wars.

A world with only one superpower, and a fading one at that, may be less stable, he said. The next 20 years might be the era of the regional bully. Two prime candidates in his mind were Iraq and India, but he admitted to a bias against the Indians from his own past. He did not believe there would be a peace dividend. The United States will be involved in all the regional conflicts because the Soviet Union will not be. We will need conventional forces to project power, but we will also need strategic defenses. In the past, the anti-American Third World countries were armed with Kalashnikov machine guns, but in the years to come, many of the maniacs will have nuclear-tipped missiles.

The rise of a new strain of militant, fanatical religious terrorism is also very dangerous. Kashmir is only the latest flash point, but it could disintegrate into a regional nuclear conflict.

He didn't want to sound too gloomy, the old man concluded. Eastern Europe would eventually emerge, and there was more international cooperation than ever before. But all this talk now about the end of history and how on a clear day you can see forever was baloney. What was my reaction? The earlier euphoria was overdone, and then disillusionment follows, which will become excessive also. Reality will be investable.

Diary of Saddam Hussein

June 18, 1991

Despite all the dire predictions and desires of Beorge Gush (I mispronounce his name, just as he does mine), Mubarak, and the sheiks of Araby, I have survived the war. My power in Iraq is as absolute as ever, and the only thing I have lost besides a few hundred thousand men and some worthless Russian tanks is weight. My favorite gun belt sags on my hips now as though I were a Western cowboy. But I am much more fit than that arrogant, overweight General Schwarzkopf who scoffed at my military leadership at his obnoxious press conference.

I will admit that toward the end of the war I did get depressed and lost my appetite from being in my bunker for so long, but I'm feeling much better now. My dreams of leading the Muslim world on a jihad have been delayed, but after all I am only 50 years old, and the Arabs in the street still revere me for standing up to the sheiks and the Great Powers. Besides, I have a couple of nuclear warheads hidden in Samarra. I still cherish the idea of one of my sons marrying a daughter of the King of Jordan, creating a royal Hashemite and Hussein family dynasty that could rule a greater Iraq and the Middle East for centuries.

Brutalizing the rebel Kurds and Shiites with helicopter gunships revived my appetite. It made the army feel much better, too. Also I know it was a relief for the Turks, although they will never admit it, and of course the crushing of the Shiites is welcome to the Kuwaitis and the Saudis. Here in Baghdad, I had to hang some of the so-called intelligentsia who had the nerve to say I should step down so that the sanctions could be removed. I shot a few generals, too; after all, someone had to take the blame for the defeat. I'll bet Schwarzkopf has never shot anyone at close range in his life.

I read with disgust that Schwarzkopf has received several million dollars as an advance on his memoirs. I'm sure I could get much more. Can you imagine what those New York publishers would pay for my life story, with personal anecdotes like when I strapped that traitorous son-in-law of mine to the nose cone of a Scud and fired them both at Israel? Or the true story of why my son Uday killed a bodyguard with a crowbar in a dispute over my mistress of the time? (She was nose-coned to Saudi Arabia.) We all have our problems. Beorge Gush has his son Neil, and I have Uday, but what's killing a few people compared with squandering half a billion dollars? I also have some wonderful family snapshots I could include in the book.

The soldiers who returned from Kuwait are a potential source of trouble. There is much bitterness, particularly from the families of those who died. Every dead hero has a mother who is resentful. For the time being, the Iraqi people are still frightened of me; they are sullen, but not mutinous . . . yet. Public beheadings are a fine deterrent. Still, some are saying that the invasions of Iran and Kuwait were disasters that have set Iraq's development back 30 years, and that I should be overthrown.

The allied bombing has seriously damaged our electric power system and economy. Before my next adventures against Israel and the sheiks, I must give the Iraqi people a higher standard of living. For that, I must have foreign money, and a lot of it. The Americans will always rebuild any country they defeat in a war, but Iraq cannot get any money from them because I am still in power.

This is a serious source of danger to my continuing rule. No matter how I frighten them, the Iraqi people eventually will choose the money and a better way of life over me. That could be unpleasant. When King Faisal was overthrown, he and his entire family were stripped, beaten, and dragged through the streets of Baghdad before being beheaded, mercifully.

There may be a way that I can stay in power and get all the money I need. I have read of the huge amounts of capital that have gone to Mexico and the emerging markets in Asia, such as Thailand and Korea. Iraq must become the next emerging market for the world's investors, and when it does, the money—equity money, with no cost attached to it—will pour in.

After all, Iraq is a good stock market story. We have a population of 18 million that is growing at over 3 percent a year, the second-largest oil reserves in the world, and per capita income of more than $2,000, which is higher than those of Mexico or Thailand and about comparable to Malaysia's. Because of 10 years of war, there is immense pent-up demand for consumer goods. I can imagine IPOs for hot new companies producing exports like the official Iraqi Army running shoes and a Republican Guard line of riot-control equipment. We can use our poison gas capability to start a global insecticide company. After all, the world knows that our gas works.

I will stun the world by renouncing Baathist socialism. Many investors believe dictators are better for emerging markets in their takeoff stage, which was the case in Korea, Singapore, and Taiwan. We will invite the World Bank and the investment banking firms to come to Baghdad, and I will sweet-talk them. Quickly they will be begging us to let them raise money for us (they will do anything for a fee). First, we will authorize them to do a series of closed-end country funds. The funds will go to premiums, and if I keep our stock market closed to direct foreign investment, there is no reason we can't keep issuing new ones. It should be just like Korea: the funds sell at premiums, and then individual companies can do convertible offerings with low coupons and huge conversion premiums. Then, we will privatize our telephone company, our electric power system, and finally our industrial companies by selling shares to the foreigners. After I have charmed them, the oil companies will pay big money for drilling concessions. Iraq will receive billions of dollars and sell at 30 times earnings.

The wonderful thing is that we won't have to pay the foreign investors interest, and they will have nothing but pieces of paper. When Iraq is rich, rebuilt, and powerful again, I can with one edict confiscate the infidels' holdings and nationalize again the oil the companies have paid us to find. Will the United States fight another war to protect the rights of Wall Street, the City of London, and Big Oil? Of course not. And the Japanese have no ability to fight anyone at any distance from their islands. Well, enough of this musing. I must see to the grand reopening of our stock exchange (which has been shut for 30 years).

I might even travel to the West for some of the road shows. In New York this year, people paid $10,000 a head to have lunch with Margaret Thatcher; I would be an even bigger draw. I will suggest a $2,000-a-plate benefit for the Orphans of Iraq, catered by Glorious Food at the Temple of Dendur with all of the beautiful people. Inshallah.

Islamic Fundamentalism

June 12, 1995

The big risk in investing in emerging markets as an asset class in my view is that the basic thesis that they are where the growth is is flawed. The story could fall apart for any of several reasons. First, free market capitalism as the way to run an economy could prove to be a failure; second, the Mexican model, where early success spoiled, could turn out to be the rule rather than the exception; and finally, Islamic fundamentalism could infect and wreck many of the developing economies.

If this Islamic Jihad reason proves to be the case, then for emerging markets investors to prosper, they must avoid the countries with an Islamic risk factor, which today would include (to greater or lesser degree) Turkey, Indonesia, Pakistan, the Philippines, Morocco, Egypt, and Malaysia, and maybe Russia and India. The loss of these big actual or potential emerging market stories would materially diminish the appeal of emerging markets as an asset class.

The Muslim religion is a great and good religion. I have read a lot about both it and Islamic fundamentalism and have often discussed the subject with Muslims, but only once with a real, live fanatic fundamentalist. He pointed out to me that the Islamic fundamentalist movement is diverse, with some sects advocating violence while others do not. At its best, it is a force for good, offering the disenfranchised a moral way of life free of crime, drugs, and alcohol. There are a couple of great novels on the subject, particularly John Buchan's classic *Greenmantle* and John le Carré's *The Little Drummer Girl*. The Foreign Policy Association has published several good pamphlets on the rise of religious fundamentalism, and there are a number of worthwhile books.[2]

---

[2]Others are *Inside the Arab World* by Michael Field (Harvard University Press); *The Arab Mind* by Raphael Patai (Scribners); and *Allah O Akbar* by Abbas (Phaidon Press), which I have not read.

I don't believe fundamentalism will wreck the Muslim world, although it may impede progress in some countries just as it already has in Iran and threatens to in Algeria. Fundamentalists make up a small minority of Muslims, and most experts are convinced fundamentalism is spawned by ignorance, poverty, corruption, and the wide gap between rich and poor in many Muslim countries. As for the threat to the developed world, fundamentalist excesses are far more threatening to their Islamic brethren than to us.

However, this is not to say that militant Islamic fundamentalism is a trivial risk for the world. It is not just random acts of terrorism, and some day it may degenerate into a real shooting war. Since fundamentalists believe death in battle ensures salvation, they can be formidable adversaries. The Iraqi Army in the Gulf War was not a fundamentalist army, so its poor performance is not indicative. A better example of the raw courage of the fundamentalists in battle might be the human wave assaults across the marshland at Basra by the Iranians during the Iran-Iraq war.

Some informed people are taking the fundamentalist threat very seriously. In February, the general secretary of NATO said it was "the gravest threat to Western security" since the end of the Cold War, and Newt Gingrich called on the U.S. military as a first priority to devise a strategy against "Islamic totalitarianism." If fundamentalists destabilized the Gulf and particularly Saudi Arabia, which is not beyond conception, the consequences could be very grave.

Wherever fundamentalism flourishes, its disciples curse both Western values and our economic system with equal fervor. It is essentially an extremist and revolutionary cause that wants to change the way the world lives and works. But it is not all bad, and I don't agree with those who predict a grand clash of civilizations, pitting the Christian West against the Islamic East. Remember, one man's terrorist is another man's freedom fighter.

In the world today, fanatical fundamentalists are causing lot of trouble. Islamic Algeria is in the midst of a brutal civil war in which thousands have died, and this vicious fight to the death—in which the issue is still very much in doubt—is absolutely crucial for the future of the Middle East. If Algeria falls, Tunisia and Morocco are in danger, and Egypt will be next. Some Arabs I have talked with recently are very pessimistic. They worry that the brutality and atrocities of Algerian government forces, though understandable, will create thousands of future terrorists who will plague the Middle East for a generation. Terrorism has destroyed the tourist industry in Egypt, and there have been fundamentalist-inspired uprisings in the Gulf. Iran, the most powerful country in the Middle East, has been ravaged by fundamentalism but continues to export the deadly virus even though its own economy is collapsing.

In Asia, the Islamic fundamentalists have a gentler face but still represent a threat. Malaysia has been particularly effective in containing it without undue repression. Of course, economic growth has been strong, and the prime minister has been wise. Indonesia, with the world's largest Muslim population, could have a problem, although liberal Muslims are the vast majority. The moderate head of the largest Muslim organization there has warned that the government is making too many concessions to the militant movement, whose leader decries both the influence of the "Zionist lobby" and of Chinese businessmen. He actually told a French newspaper in March that Indonesia could become another Algeria in 10 years. I trust this was said for effect, but don't forget there was a pogrom in Indonesia only 25 years ago. Nevertheless, I am bullish on Indonesia because the standard of living is steadily rising, which does not make fertile soil for fundamentalism.

Elsewhere in Asia, in the southern Philippines there is a serious fundamentalist insurgency in Mindanao, which the government claims is supported by international Islamic terrorist organizations. Pakistan, particularly Karachi, is a mess, the epicenter for three civil wars (Afghanistan, Tajikistan, and Kashmir) in which fundamentalism is a major factor. India, with 150 million Muslims, also has a sensitive problem. And of course there is Turkey, the bastion of secular Islam since Ataturk but now showing scary signs of backtracking.

So why am I reasonably optimistic that fundamentalism will not wreck these countries? Because if they can deliver a rising standard of living, fundamentalism will die out. A prominent Turk recently pointed out that his country would be better able to stand up to its fundamentalists if it could demonstrate the economic benefits of its Western connection by closer ties to the European Union. "In the Islamic world, by and large, the ruling elites have failed to deliver the goods to the people, and the end of the Cold War has only stripped off the veil," says Khalid Ahmed, a Pakistani writer on Islam. "The growing gap between rich and poor, runaway inflation, massive corruption, and widespread disillusionment with the mainstream parties and their leaders are the core issues in the Islamic world."

In countries with a strong central government and where wealth has trickled down, radical fundamentalism has not been nearly as severe a problem. An occasional dose of severity doesn't hurt, either. Malaysia and Indonesia are good examples. A delegation from the Palestinian extremist organization Hamas was received very coldly in Indonesia last year, even in the two most staunchly Islamic provinces. Permission to open a Jakarta branch of Hamas was politely but absolutely denied. Radical fundamentalism really has its roots in the Middle East, where there are still kings and emirs and the wealth disparity is most extreme. It has far fewer converts in Southeast Asia, where there have been economic miracles.

Another potentially beneficial factor is that radical fundamentalism is not popular with women throughout the Muslim world. It's the young women and the mothers versus the mullahs. The mullahs bar women from public office, force them to wear the chador, compel absolute obedience to their husbands, restrict their activities, even forbid them from having wealth in their own name. And even suicidal terrorists have mothers who mourn them.

The feminist movement is too strong throughout the world for this oppression to go on, and in many countries from Iran to Saudi Arabia, women are leading the opposition to fundamentalism. I wouldn't bet against this force.

Finally, radical Islam doesn't have an economic answer. It is essentially a negative, destructive force that almost seems to advocate poverty as way of life. It intentionally drives away foreign investment and tourists. It promotes terrorism as evidenced by its call, still not formally revoked, for Muslims to kill Salman Rushdie.

Some optimists like the *Economist* argue Islam is not like communism, something to be resisted tooth and nail. The magazine wrote recently that "it may be more like socialism, an ism with many facets, some entirely compatible with liberal democracy, some more hostile to it, some perhaps wholly at odds with it. Living with Islam involves discrimination, as well as vigilance."

It is a force in the developing world we are watching very closely.

Section 2

ECONOMICS
AND INVESTING

The highest concentration of pretense and disinformation in the investment world is probably at a lunch of twenty money managers. Listening to the babble, everybody else is a genius, your portfolio is full of leaks, and before you know it, the roast beef tastes like salmon. The only rule I've learned is that the more confidently someone pontificates, the more likely he is to be wrong.

—Barton Biggs, 1984

I t's easy to forget how far and fast the financial markets have evolved over the past few decades until you pull up some of the first typewritten pages from Barton Biggs's initial Morgan Stanley dispatches from the early 1980s. Not only was he years away from a word processor that worked, he was decades from a cell phone, the Internet, online chart, or stock screening tool. An 11MB disk drive cost as much as a car, and traders cherished their cutting-edge HP12C calculators to price options using the revolutionary Black-Scholes model.

During his ensuing 30-plus-year career, Biggs witnessed the wholesale invasion and occupation of Wall Street—not by protesters but by statistical methods, quantitative models, technical analysis, and computerized trading. While his contemporaries tried to leverage powerful technologies to calculate future events through mathematical formulas, Barton Biggs was decidedly carbon-based in his approach to economics and investing.

Biggs understood that economics is actually the science of human behavior, based not on the immutable laws of Newtonian physics, but on the more visceral patterns of individual habits, biases, and emotions. "Just as a stock doesn't know or care that you own it, the market doesn't know you've written an equation for it" summarized his attitude toward those seeking to learn sociology through a careful application of calculus.

Instead of a trick to be gamed, Biggs believed in the discipline of investing as a vehicle for personal growth. Markets can provide a mirror into the self and a counter-acting force for overcoming our own self-defeating urges. Ever-changing conditions and interrelated events become a mental gymnasium for constant growth, adaptation, and flexibility of thought that keeps the mind nimble.

He also believed that a certain rare human talent could indeed consistently outperform passive market indexes over time. Great money managers are not "just the random winners of a national coin-flipping contest," he said, rebutting a popular statistical thought exercise. "Instead, they must have some special magic with the markets that enables them almost intuitively to do the right thing, buy the right stock far more often than ordinary investors." The key to that success, Biggs believed, lay in contrarian behavior.

As social animals, we feel safe when our opinions, beliefs, and behaviors are validated by those around us no matter how irrational. But while safety in numbers may be a survival tactic on the wide open plains of the Serengeti, the opposite is true in the financial markets where hordes of investors routinely plunge together off the cliff of financial destruction. "The financial crowd is transported from rationality by the beguiling contagious image of 'instant wealth,'" wrote Biggs. "Thus it pays to invest against rather than with the fads and extremes of the crowd."

Biggs also recognized that a large central government manhandling the fiscal rudder has both direct and less obvious impacts on our economy. While clearly on the side of free markets and limited government, Biggs's tone was even, objective, and measured throughout his career. He was a keen observer and a thoughtful synthesizer of the economic and political events transpiring around him, a refreshing contrast to today's fanatical demagogues seeking to out-shout their competition in a vain quest for info-tainment market share.

In the early 1980s—as today—the U.S. economy was struggling under the weight of recession and high unemployment. Barton Biggs saw a nation "moving toward a state of affairs where the earnings of the workers are attached to the support of the needy, the nonworkers, and the elderly." Politicians were unable to make needed cuts to grotesquely unsustainable government programs. "They always hope for last-minute tax increases and more revenues, because it is the act of spending from which they derive their power," he wrote in 1985.

Biggs's chronicles provide a clear view into the empirical formula for successful economic recovery, yet he repeatedly found that our financially illiterate leaders and so-called experts continue to cling to superstition and false dogma in the name of John Maynard Keynes—a doctrine Biggs labeled a "bloated and false priesthood." By contrast, Biggs believed that the supply-side neoconservative creed championed by Ronald Reagan was "the most important socioeconomic idea of this generation."

Lowering taxes in the face of a recession and increasing government spending both result in deficits—but with markedly different results. Tax cuts free the private sector to create economic worth by incentivizing work and investments in profitable, value-building ventures. Government spending is invariably misdirected by political, rather than economic, incentives, resulting in erosion of productive work. In short, "the one sure effect of raising tax rates is always, everywhere, every time, slower economic growth than what otherwise would have been," wrote Biggs.

Along the way, Barton wove his wide-ranging knowledge, clear thinking, and astute observations together with his own set of principles into a remarkable string of accurate predictions. In 1980, he advocated buying stocks in the face of 17 percent money market rates. When the equity markets rallied slightly, then slumped in 1982, he advised his readers to resist their inner urge to sell. Those who heeded his advice rode one of the biggest bull markets in history fed by the decidedly non-Keynesian engine of Reaganomics.

While the world was preparing for the Japanization of the globe in the late 1980s and marveling at the powerhouse that had catapulted from a fifth-place also-ran to the earth's second-largest economy in less than two decades, Biggs foresaw an end to that country's hyperbolic growth. Sure enough, since its apex in 1989, the Nikkei index plummeted over 60 percent and is still recovering.

Biggs finally secured his mantle as a market sage when he famously called the 2000 dot-com bust labeling it among the largest bubbles in the history of the world. His prophetic warnings spawned harsh backlash among the true believers of the new economy. At one point, he was unexpectedly accosted at the train station by a complete stranger who insisted, "It really is different this time"—an event Biggs called "so un-Grand Centralish."

In the end, it seemed that Barton Biggs genuinely enjoyed the process of investing and the opportunity for continual learning that it presented. Like an athlete playing for love of the sport, he wrote (quoting Warren Buffett), "The wonderful thing about being a rational investor is that you are the batter in a game in which there are no called strikes. Day after day the pitches keep coming, but you don't have to swing."

And the game continues today under the same sun as yesterday. Heed the sage and pick your shots wisely.

Section 2A:
Economics and Policy

The Evolution
of the Supply Side

January 5, 1981

I believe the supply-side, neoconservative creed is the most important socioeconomic idea of this generation. Neoconservatism should be, if given the chance, the salvation and redemption of both capitalism and democracy. It could turn the world and reverse the trend toward stagflation and socialism, just as Keynesian demand economics and the New Deal swung the West away from depression, deflation, and totalitarianism a half century ago.

However, as an economic theory, acceptance of the supply-side creed has been retarded by a lack of intellectual respectability. One of the movement's seminal thinkers, Robert Mundell, has had problems. Another, the irrepressible Art Laffer, arouses skepticism among his fellow economists, mostly because they think he is too glib, too witty to be profound. Their Boswell, the deeply committed Jude Wanniski, is disparaged as being "just a journalist," and Jack Kemp is dismissed as a "shallow jock." The establishment Keynesian economists with their PhDs and pipes can't believe this motley assortment of two disreputable professors, a journalist, and an old quarterback can have created a new economic religion.

Little of this contempt should be taken seriously, nor is it surprising. Last week in reading about John Maynard Keynes in Ronald Steel's fine new biography of Walter Lippman, I was struck by the outrage and hostility Keynes's ideas evoked in the early 1930s among establishment thinkers. What is now the conventional liberal economic wisdom about deficits, government spending, demand, and the gold standard was then heresy. In terms of economic and social problems, existing conventional wisdom, and proposed radical solutions, the early 1930s were almost a precise mirror image of today, like the past reflected backwards into the present. The political leader then, Roosevelt, instinctively understood and grasped an opportunity. I hope the same for Reagan.

It is also fascinating to read of the bitter personal attacks on Keynes as a man of diverse tastes, which ranged, as Steel says, "from the collection of abstract paintings to that of His Majesty's guardsmen." Keynes was not an economist but a mathematician and a stock market speculator, said the establishment thinkers with their educated but orthodox and unexpandable minds. The point is that this conventional breed always reacts with personal and professional scorn to the apostles of a radical new philosophy that would obsolete them overnight.

The Way the World Works was the first important book to explain the supply-side economic and social model, but it is flawed by Wanniski's occasional extremism. The supply-siders were derided as fanatics, and one joke had it that if the news came that Russia had fired its strategic missiles and we had two hours to do something, the supply-siders would advise the president to cut taxes. One famous Keynesian economist shouted at me at a dinner that the book was "trash" yet under questioning admitted he had never read it.

However, the core neoconservatives stuck to the basic Laffer curve thesis that taxes should be cut and that there was no need to reduce government spending or the federal deficit because tax revenues would rise quickly as the economy surged. The people were skeptical, although Reagan made a Kemp-Roth tax cut a vital part of his electoral platform.

Then, in recent months, men like Congressman David Stockman and my friend Lewis Lehrman began to come to the fore, arguing that taxes must be cut but government spending simultaneously reduced and controlled. And now a serious, intellectual heavyweight, George Gilder, has written a major book that both extends Wanniski's concepts and is an articulate and profound manifesto of the supply-side creed. The book, *Wealth and Poverty*, has just been published by Basic Books but already has attracted considerable acclaim. Wanniski, a generous spirit if there ever was one, is full of praise for it, and Stockman says he is going to give a copy of *Wealth and Poverty* to every member of Reagan's cabinet. I will discuss the book next week, but the importance to the movement of the circulation of this kind of worldly and messianic manifesto should not be underestimated.

Keynes argued that, in a time of depression, deflation, and inadequate demand, government spending must be increased in spite of government deficits to restore the economy to health. On April 18, 1933, when Walter Lippman wrote a column suggesting that this policy be followed and the gold standard abandoned, the stock market soared, and a major bull move in equities began. If Reagan did almost exactly the opposite and proposed that in a time of stagflation, inflation, and inadequate supply, government spending must be reduced and taxes cut in spite of the deficit, stocks again would soar, in my opinion. I'm still not sure about gold.

The Tax Cut Misconception

May 18, 1981

O n another subject, the principal opposition to the administration's tax cut proposals now seems to center on the point that the tax cuts for the lower income
brackets will be spent rather than saved. The Keynesians scoffed, but ridicule is
the most effective weapon, and the much quoted Doonesbury cartoon mocked the idea
that the average taxpayer would invest his tax reduction in a steel mill. Last week, the
New York Times quoted Senator Russell Long as follows:

> "Here's the weak point on 10-10-10," Senator Long said today, voicing a view
> held by many in Congress. "There's no real assurance those people are going to
> invest that money in plant and equipment."

The point is that supply-side theory has never maintained that tax reduction would
stimulate savings in the lower income brackets. The confusion began when in the very
early going, an inadequately briefed Secretary of the Treasury Regan predicted that a
very high percentage of tax reduction would be saved, and, of course, the Old Guard
economists leaped upon his misstatement with joy.

In fact, supply-side theory argues that savings and investment are stimulated by
reducing most the taxes on the wealthy who have the big money to invest. The purpose of the cuts, to quote George Gilder, "is to expand the tax base"—to make the
rich pay more taxes by inducing them to consume less and to work and invest more.
Not only does the bigger tax reduction for the rich stimulate investment but also it
increases taxable entrepreneurial activity and tax revenue. The way to soak the rich is
to lower their tax rates so they are not diverted into tax shelters. The elimination of the
distinction between earned and unearned income now being proposed is an important
step in this direction.

The supply-siders believe that a reduction in personal income taxes in the lower brackets leads not to savings but to a rise in labor force participation and work effort, thereby increasing the supply of labor to produce more goods and services. As a result of higher maximum capacity, the inflationary pressures of shortages and bottlenecks diminish, in time thereby reducing the rate of inflation. Also, since wage bargaining is based at least in part on the level of after-tax income, lower personal income taxes lead to smaller wage gains. So, the argument goes, lower tax rates cause a reduction in inflation because the gap between actual and maximum potential GNP rises; productivity increases because workers are willing to work more, thereby lowering unit labor costs; wage rates rise more slowly; and since the U.S. relative position improves versus the rest of the world, the dollar strengthens, causing less imported inflation and so on. As Gilder tersely put it: "Taxes are costs and when costs rise, profits fall, marginal suppliers fail, output declines, demand continues, and prices rise for the remaining supplies." Eventually, the increase in the after-tax return on personal savings caused by the reduction in rates raises the incentives of individuals to save, but this is a secondary effect.

A recent American Enterprise Institute study by Edgar Browning and William Johnson demonstrates the debilitating effects on initiative of high *marginal* tax rates. This study offers evidence that the average American worker now encounters tax rates of more than 50 percent on earnings above his current income because of the combined effect of federal, state, local, and Social Security taxes. The people choose leisure, home improvement, or barter not because of moral weakness but because they are paid to do so. This has the effect of reducing the tax base and increasing inefficiency in the economic system because the division of labor and productive specialization is diminished. The skilled are performing unskilled personal tasks because of higher marginal tax rates. The concept of the impact on the willingness to work not of the overall tax rate but of the marginal tax rate is essential in understanding the leveraged benefits of tax rate reductions in terms of motivation and expanding the tax base.

The essential point is that the supply-side program attacks stagflation on two fronts: investment and work incentives. It is a growth-oriented program. The marginal tax rate of the rich is reduced to foster investment; the tax rates of the lower brackets are reduced to create work motivation and spending. Unless the people spend, the investment of the rich in new production is of limited value. To be opposed to the tax cuts on the lower brackets because the people will not put the additional income into savings completely misses the point.

Running the Movie of the Seventies Backward

November 29, 1982

F or Paul Volcker, the most powerful man in the world at this moment, this must be a time of considerable uncertainty about the force of economic expansion in 1983 and what the proper fiscal and monetary responses should be.

Last week, the Fed cut the discount rate, but long-term interest rates rose, the price of gold climbed, the Fed funds rate declined, and commodity prices drifted lower. Spot crude prices fell sharply, and the dollar weakened slightly against the major currencies with the exception of the pound and the guilder, which, interestingly enough, are oil sensitive. Except for automobiles and housing, the economy is stagnant. The unsatisfactory outcome of the GATT talks suggests protectionism is not diminishing, and a back-page, one-paragraph item in Saturday's *New York Times* reported that the largest bank in Venezuela in terms of deposits was unable to meet its clearinghouse obligations.

Volcker has probably read the interesting interview with Helmut Schmidt that appeared recently. My impression is that Schmidt, among major political figures, is in a class by himself as an economic thinker, and he says now that he is no longer the chancellor, he feels able to express himself more openly. In the article, he remarked that he fears another surge in unemployment next year in Europe, the United States, and even Japan.

> I am deeply troubled. I have the feeling that we are now in the second phase of world depression. I don't want to forecast any mischievous dramas or tragedies, but I very clearly see dramatic developments as being possible.

I would think all this must make Volcker quite nervous. The environment and sensitive prices are hardly suggesting that there is too much money in the world system. No one wants to preside over the "second depression of this century," in Schmidt's words. More discount rate cuts seem likely.

Yet, in spite of all these signs, many politicians continue to call for the cancellation of the third stage of the Reagan tax cuts. Next year, in the midst of a serious and persistent recession, Social Security taxes will rise, a gasoline tax will in all probability be levied, and almost inevitably state and local tax rates will increase. How is it that politicians on both sides of the aisle can demand higher taxes on working people?

The more I think about it, the more I come to the sad conclusion that the answer is that many politicians think raising taxes is good politics. All the talk about the size of the deficit is mostly smoke screen. There are now 36 million people receiving social security benefits, 22 million people getting food stamps, and 16 million public employees with highly organized unions. This is a huge political constituency that exercises its power as a voting bloc. These people receive tax dollars and have a stake in continued government spending growth, and naturally they think of their own self-interest.

Thus, as a nation we are moving toward a state of affairs where the earnings of the workers are attached to support the needy, the nonworkers, and the elderly. Most people don't quarrel with a rich country like ours aiding the truly needy, but it is a question of the level of support and whether that level is so high it reduces incentive. The *Wall Street Journal* calculates that a family of four in New York State eligible for a basic welfare grant, shelter allowance, food stamps, and Medicaid has an earned-income equivalent that puts the head of the household 45.4 percent over the minimum wage level. Clearly, this individual has no financial incentive to trade leisure for basic work.

The danger in this situation is that a kind of political and economic polarization could develop. The very high level of social security benefits that were not earned is a transfer of real earned wealth from the young to the old. Looked at another way, there are the beneficiaries of federal transfers on one side and the donors on the other. Unfortunately, the beneficiaries are much better organized and have more time for political activity.

The present economic stagnation intensifies the stress of these transfers because the standard of living of the workers is no longer rising and they know it. Higher tax rates and inflation have actually reduced real wages in the last decade. This is the stuff of revolutions. The workers may be growing tired of a conventional political consensus approach to economic problem solving. They sense that government spending must be reined in, including the defense budget, and that tax rates must be reduced significantly to provide once more the incentive to work and to get the economy growing. Reaganomics, for all the early talk, has failed to accomplish either because it wasn't true to itself. It has not been a supply-side, growth-oriented program. Only through economic growth can we get people to work again and reduce the deficit.

The most encouraging thing is that some very astute observers of both political persuasions are starting to sense a change in the mood of working people. Writing in the *New York Times* earlier this month, Patrick Caddell, who has been the principal pollster for the Democrats and who accurately warned President Carter he would lose, made the following comments:

> Two elections, above all, raise doubts about the easy theory that the public has signaled a desire for moderate political consensus on economic problems—the Michigan and New York gubernatorial races. In both cases, radical GOP renegades, way out of the political mainstream—if one considers Mr. Reagan part of the mainstream—ran close to Democratic opponents expected to win by wide margins, and did far better than "acceptable" Republicans in similar races in nearby states. Both GOP challengers did particularly well in areas hardest hit by the recession, and in both cases they emphasized radical change and purist ideological solutions.
>
> In depression-riddled Michigan, Richard Headlee rejected Mr. Reagan as an economic compromiser and did particularly well in the devastated northern industrial cities. In New York, Lewis Lehrman also campaigned on a purist's platform. When challenged as an architect of Reaganomics, he answered that Mr. Reagan had not been true to his program and that its principles had to be pushed further. Mr. Lehrman garnered a surprising 48 percent of the vote against Mario Cuomo. As Mr. Cuomo's pollster, I can testify that the race was never secure—not even when he built sizable leads. Mr. Lehrman swept upstate, where the economy was the only major issue—as Mr. Cuomo was increasingly viewed as the establishment candidate and natural successor to the unpopular Hugh Carey. Mr. Lehrman flatly rejected Mr. Reagan and boldly offered an even more radical plan of change—large-scale income tax reductions and a return to the gold standard. Had Mr. Cuomo faced a more mainstream or conventional Reagan supporter, he might have won a much handier victory.

I still have the strong sense that some invisible economic and political hand up there is running the movie of the Seventies backwards.

The Piper Must Still Be Paid

October 1983

A World That Has Lived beyond Its Means

The world today to me is an enigma, with a glossy veneer of progress, emerging prosperity, and soaring financial asset prices in the industrialized economies contrasting starkly against the dark side of unrest and depression in the developing countries. The $900 billion of debt owed by one to the other, and swelling in the night through interest, is like some great, bloated, prehistoric, two-headed python threatening to consume prosperity in both worlds. Meanwhile, high government deficits, particularly in the United States, keep interest rates at choking levels.

The basic problem is that for more than a decade the world has been living beyond its means. Excessive debt creation and inflation of the money supply have financed a false prosperity. This is the age-old cycle of capitalist economies, and now some of the debt must be liquidated to restore the system to equilibrium. Unfortunately, this will be at the expense of economic growth and consumption. In other words, someone's standard of living has to decline. One man's debt repayment is another man's unsold merchandise, and the same iron formula applies to countries as well.

My conviction that the world cannot generate a strong, sustained economic recovery until this excessive debt burden has been dealt with is fundamental to my investment strategy. I believe governments and central banks understand at last that to try once more to lighten the debt load by fiscal or monetary reflating merely creates additional pain and forestalls the cure. The financial markets, the foreign exchange markets, and people everywhere are cynical. They believe only what the authorities do, not

103

what they say. Keynesian reflationary policies immediately result in higher interest rates, less economic growth, and more inflation. There is no trade-off of growth for inflation anymore. The markets, not the politicians or the central bankers, are in control.

Thus, there is no way out other than disinflation and debt liquidation. In the industrialized economies, government spending has outrun revenues, and huge deficits have resulted. In the United States, the politicians told the people they could have guns and butter, and we lived beyond our means for a while. But eventually the piper has to be paid. However, governments, being political animals, have great difficulty arresting the spending momentum of the welfare state because the standard of living of certain groups has to suffer when spending is cut or taxes are raised. Special interest groups have disproportionate blocking power. The emerging sociopolitical conflict that will radically change party affiliations in the next decade will be between workers who pay taxes and the beneficiaries of government spending (including government itself) who get the money. But smaller deficits and less government spending in the transitional short run mean less income for someone and are thus disinflationary. In the long term, they mean lower taxes, declining interest rates, and faster growth.

In the developing countries, the issue is similar. Debt financed growth both in the form of capital infrastructure and, unfortunately, in consumption. The international banks were eager to make the loans because of their exceptional profitability, and there was "no risk" in sovereign credit lending. However, excessive debt and the high interest rate on that debt, which now preempts an average 40 percent of the LDCs' total export earnings, led inevitably to the present crisis. As George Soros says, sovereign credits don't go bankrupt, but they can stop paying. These countries also have to accept a standard of living reduction from a level that, although higher than a decade ago, is still relatively low. People quickly accept as their due better living, and a reversal causes not only misery but also political discontent. Mexico's population is growing 3 percent annually, and as long as real GNP was advancing at a 7 percent clip, the standard of living was rising 4 percent yearly. But with real GNP declining 4 percent or so this year, the standard of living will be down a brutal 7 percent. When you add unequal sharing of the pain and a heavy dose of corruption, you have an explosive mixture from which revolutions are brewed. The developing country politicians and the aristocracy understand this, and their survival is at stake.

This is the principal reason I expect debt moratoriums and unilateral interest rate reductions from many of the heavily indebted developing countries. For the banks, a highly profitable short-term loan then becomes at best a marginally profitable long-term asset. This will result in slower earnings and capital growth for the international banks, which in turn will reduce their ability to increase their loan portfolios. Less loan growth means slower economic growth. Already, net new lending to the developing countries is declining, which is in large part why the economic revival outside America is so weak.

More than 30 countries are now under the none-too-tender ministrations of the IMF, which imposes a disinflationary austerity program that entails devaluing the currency, slashing welfare spending, reducing imports, and increasing exports in order to run a balance of trade surplus and restore economic equilibrium. Many other countries, including the wealthy members of OPEC, are following similar policies on their own initiative. (This is a classic case of the fallacy of composition. What is perfectly logical for one, like running for the exit when someone screams fire in a crowded theater, can lead to disaster when all do it simultaneously.) Thus, import demand everywhere is relatively weak, world trade is sickly, and protectionism is rampant. All this is a depressant on growth. The circular effect here is vicious, as sluggish trade and stagnant economic growth result in relatively depressed commodity prices, which also hurt the developing countries.

This "debt problem" also affects interest rates. The many who still believe long-run salvation will be through reflation demand a higher rent for investment money. In the industrial nations, deficit phobia and the sticky residue of monetarism keep interest rates high. Legislative gridlock on spending control in the face of special interest group tyranny is a contributing perception. With inflation low, high interest rates are doubly punishing in real terms, as Figure 1 indicates, and restrain long-term capital spending, the wellspring of lasting economic growth. The vicious linkage continues in that slow growth and the resulting high unemployment and political instability have caused the dollar to be bid up as the safe haven currency. This overvalued dollar complicates the rest of the world's return to economic health.

But all is not bleak by any means. Inflation is quiescent, the people continue to tug the politicians toward a neoconservative order, and the locomotive economy, the United States, has once again demonstrated its enormous self-regenerating vitality. In fact, our economy should be the healthiest in an anemic world for a while. I believe there is a good chance disinflation will be not just cyclical but secular as well. Figure 2 shows the pattern of descending peaks and troughs in world inflation, and the decline

Figure 1   Real Interest Rates Are Brutal

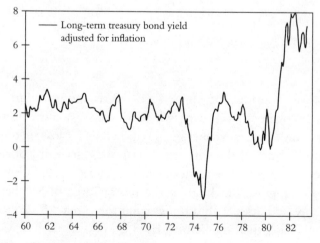

SOURCE: Data Resources, Inc.; Morgan Stanley Research.

Figure 2   Classic Decline in World Consumer Prices (Year-over-Year Monthly Percent Change)

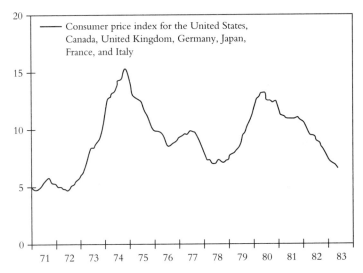

SOURCE: Data Resources, Inc.; Morgan Stanley Research.

Figure 3   The Ebbing of Wage Inflation Looks Secular (Year-over-Year Monthly Percent Change)

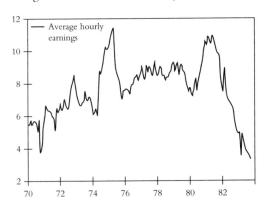

SOURCE: Data Resources, Inc.; Morgan Stanley Research.

in the rate of wage increases, shown in Figure 3, is stunning but hardly surprising, given record unemployment levels everywhere. But this is where disinflation comes in, as one employer's wage or cost reduction is another man's lost income. Productivity is bound to improve because of the entrepreneurial surge, so unit labor cost analysis supports somewhere around 4 to 5 percent endemic inflation in the United States.

I find it hard to anguish much about the recent surge of M1 here and in Europe. There are too many definitional adjustments, and the other Ms do not confirm excessive money growth. Also, the huge, unregulated Eurodollar money pool is growing little if at all after 15 years of 20 percent-plus growth. This is an important and neglected factor in the decline of the rate of growth of world liquidity. Equally compelling, the prices of industrial commodities and gold are not telling us there is too much money in the world.

If disinflation truly is upon us, and if the relative price of oil declines slowly as I believe it will, the cancer of the Seventies that eventually would have destroyed the capitalist West has been beaten for decade. This is profoundly bullish for long-term financial assets. In time, interest rates will also decline. I have pointed out in the past that our work shows bond buyers have long memories, as the correlation between interest rates and a five-year moving average of inflation shows (Figure 4). I think a year from now, the long government rate should be around 9.5 percent.

The political equation is heartening. As Figure 5 indicates, total local, state, and federal government employment in the United States has begun to decline after a rise

Figure 4   Inflation and Long-Term Interest Rates

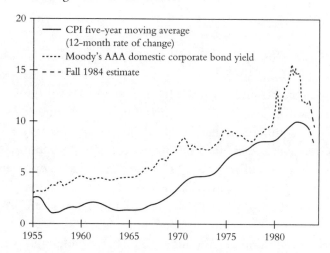

SOURCE: Data Resources, Inc.; Morgan Stanley Research.

Figure 5   A Secular Reversal in Total Government Employment (Millions)

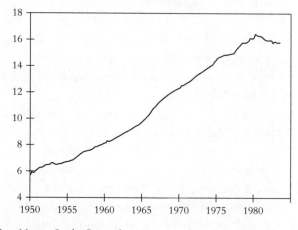

SOURCE: Data Resources, Inc.; Morgan Stanley Research.

Figure 6   The Lines Cross

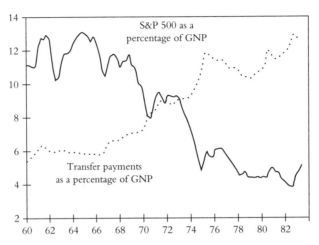

SOURCE: Data Resources, Inc.; Morgan Stanley Research.

that began almost 50 years ago. The old Keynesian ways of tax and spend and elect have been thoroughly discredited. But, as noted previously, the financial and currency markets, not the politicians, are in control. In fact, "the market is the Fed." The sensitivity of the stock market to a welfare economy is shown in Figure 6. As social spending gained share of GNP, equities lost share. Will the lines ever cross again?

Although a new, broad-based constituency composed of those who work and pay taxes is building, it is still so young it doesn't know its own strength. Moreover, the resolution of the spending impasse in a special-interest-ridden political process is agonizingly slow. But these tides have substantial momentum, and the politicians in Washington are always the last to understand.

Despite the Korean airliner interlude, a bilateral reduction of strategic arms spending between Russia and the United States seems possible next spring because it is imperative in both an economic and political sense. Otherwise, the two super-powers will exhaust themselves with defense spending, leaving Germany and Japan to inherit the world. It would be ironic if the disarmament process was begun by a hawk American president and a former KGB official.

And also far from bleak is the U.S. economy's recent performance. However, as Figures 7 and 8 indicate, the main engine of expansion, the consumer, is not in shape to sustain the recent pace of GNP growth.

The savings rate is at a record low, and debt levels are still uncomfortably high. The recent rise in interest rates will dampen housing, autos, and durables spending, now that some of the deferred demand has been fulfilled. Real interest rates are still too high to induce much capital spending except for fast-payback technology items. With the dollar strong, exports are in a depression. Thus, the expansion lacks balance and is fragile.

I anticipate the next change in the consensus opinion will be that the U.S. economy is slowing and that real growth will be at an annual rate of 4 percent or less in the first half of next year. The rate of increase in wages and inflation will be in the

Figure 7 The Savings Rate Has Plummeted

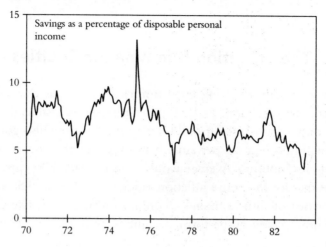

SOURCE: Data Resources, Inc.; Morgan Stanley Research.

Figure 8 Debt Levels Still High

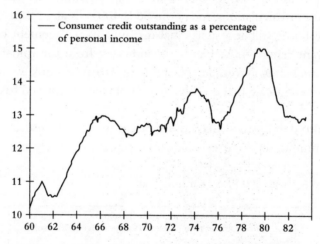

SOURCE: Data Resources, Inc.; Morgan Stanley Research.

4 to 5 percent range, interest rates will painstakingly slowly work lower, the dollar will soften a little, then steady, and Europe's economic renaissance will strengthen.

But disinflation and slow growth will still be the linked characteristics of this economic cycle for a world that has lived beyond its means. The piper must be paid. Disinflation inevitably induces slow growth, so it must be understood as a very mixed blessing. Until the balance sheets of the industrial nations, the developing countries, and the people themselves are restored to health by extinguishing the excess debt, economic growth will be sluggish. Sustained growth cannot occur until business can sell goods and services its customers can afford to buy. Although disinflation is painful, it is far more desirable than reflation, which would cause not only even slower growth but also more inflation.

The Valuation Dilemma for Equities

Stocks are still very cheap in a long-term historical sense. For example, the S&P 500 today is still at only 60 percent of its 1969 purchasing-power value. In the past, equities have always not only regained the ground lost to inflation but also gone on to provide a total return roughly 6 percent per annum in excess of the rise in the general price level. The Dow Jones Industrial Average would have to reach 2000 just to restore parity. And don't forget that for the entire inflation-ridden decade of the Seventies, stocks and bonds were the worst of all investments: illiquid, esoteric objects like Chinese ceramics and antique furniture vastly outperformed equities, and gold and Florida condominiums buried them.

Price/earnings ratios are still very modest as well. Figure 9 shows that on the basis of both real and reported earnings, price/earnings ratios are only around the middle of their postwar range. On the basis of both replacement cost and stated book value, stocks, although obviously not rock-bottom cheap anymore, are still reasonably valued. According to our calculations, today the S&P 400 sells at a 50 percent premium to stated book value but is still at a substantial discount to replacement cost book, which is the more relevant criterion. As Figure 10 indicates, from the mid-Fifties to the late Sixties, the S&P traded at a considerable premium to true book value. Certainly it is hard to make a coherent case that equities as a whole are overpriced based on traditional valuation tools.

Past studies also demonstrate that equity prices move with real earnings. In a disinflationary environment, reported earnings increases are relatively modest, but with the

Figure 9   Standard & Poor's 500 Price/Earnings Ratio

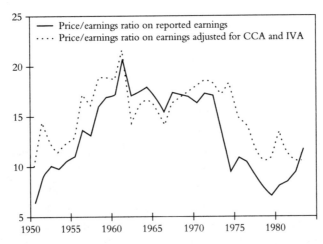

SOURCE: Data Resources, Inc.; Morgan Stanley Research.

Figure 10   Replacement Cost Book Value and the Stock Market

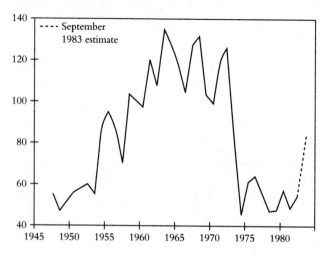

SOURCE: Data Resources, Inc.; Morgan Stanley Research.

Figure 11   Real Earnings and the Stock Market

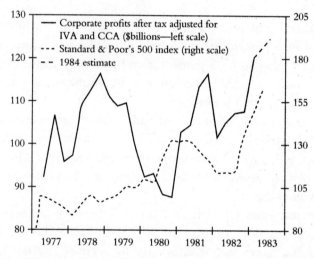

SOURCE: Data Resources, Inc.; Morgan Stanley Research.

inventory and depreciation adjustment, true profits should surge, and shouldn't equities follow as Figure 11 suggests?

Our valuation studies indicate there is a strong correlation between price/earnings ratios and inflation. A quick way to determine what multiple levels are appropriate is to use the "Rule of Twenty," which says stocks should sell at P/E ratio equal to 20 minus the inflation rate. This formula was discovered in the late Seventies, and, as usually happens, retrospectively it worked perfectly. Prospectively, it was flawed because

Figure 12   Dividend Discount Model Price/Value Ratio and the Stock Market

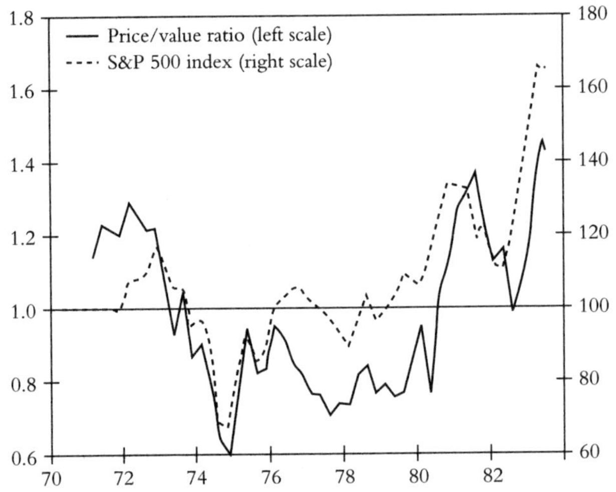

NOTE: Current price divided by intrinsic value.
SOURCE: Ford Investor Services.

it assumed normal real interest rates of 200 to 300 basis points. In other words, today, with inflation at 4 or 5 percent, stocks should sell at 14 to 15 times earnings, but the long government rate should be 7 percent, not 12 percent. Equities can't sell at teenage multiples and compete with 12 percent bonds. Double-digit interest rates truly do mean single-digit price/earnings ratios.

Thus, the inevitable conclusion is that today stocks are overvalued based on any standard dividend discount or valuation model that is driven by a risk-free interest rate assumption. In fact, as Figure 12 shows, our Dividend Discount Model indicates equities are some 40 percent above intrinsic value and at a level at which in the past the market has been vulnerable.

With real interest rates so high and the risk-free government rate at 12 percent, stocks simply are not competitive with high-grade bonds. Either the stock market has to go down, or interest rates have to decline. The tricky part is that the equity market is a discounting mechanism and will anticipate future interest rates. My dilemma is that at present levels the market already seems to be discounting a 200-basis-point decline in the government rate. I think we will get a 200- to 300-basis-point drop over the next year, but, even so, stocks already reflect two-thirds of it, and supposing I'm wrong and the inflationists are right and interest rates go higher instead of lower?

However, the equity market is not monolithic, and there are always major valuation discrepancies and earnings momentum opportunities that can be exploited by the group and stock picker. As I have discussed so often and as is summarized by Figures 13 and 14, our work indicates the shares of high-quality, substantial companies are very cheap compared with stocks of lesser quality, smaller companies. I anticipate an equity

Figure 13 Capitalization and Relative Value (Equally Weighted Averages)

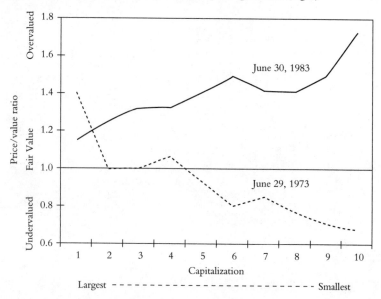

SOURCE: Ford Investor Services.

Figure 14 Quality Rating and Relative Value (Equally Weighted Averages)

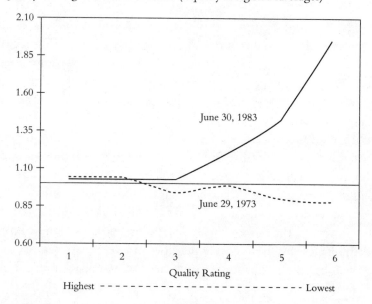

SOURCE: Ford Investor Services.

market environment more price/earnings ratio- than earnings-driven than has been the case for the last decade.

I also want to concentrate on investments in companies that, as processors of commodities into consumer products, were the victims of inflation and are now the beneficiaries of disinflation. This occurs in an era in which consumer prices rise more than wholesale prices instead of vice versa. In this kind of slow-growth, disinflation

Figure 15   Market Leadership Groups

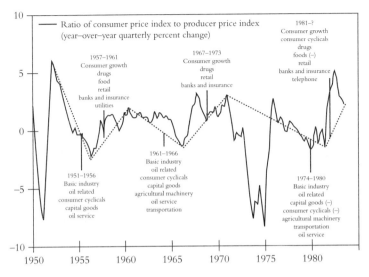

SOURCE: Data Resources, Inc.; Morgan Stanley Research.

environment, characterized by the loss of preemptive pricing power, it is essential to have some unit growth capability. Groups that would be included in this category include autos, retail, electrical equipment, tires and rubber goods, auto parts, consumer durables, and apparel, and in general any company that buys raw materials and then converts and bolts them together. Other growth cyclicals include truckers, airlines, railroads, newspapers, and broadcasting.

As Figure 15 indicates, I believe these soft cyclicals and the consumer groups will be the enduring leadership of this bull market. Energy commodity products, capital goods—the traditional basic industries—will not be persistent leadership sectors. However, in almost every case, the quality companies in each industry will be the best performers, both in the market and in terms of earnings. In a disinflationary environment, having the least leverage, the lowest breakeven point, and the highest profitability will be significant advantages, just as they were penalties in inflationary times. Quality will pay again. The best will be able to finance, expand capacity, and prosper, while the worst will falter and sometimes fail.

All things considered, for an endowment or pension fund, I would have an asset allocation as shown in the accompanying table. In the volatility and liquidity ratings, 1 is best and 5 is worst, assuming that less volatile is better than more.

Note that I am unusually heavy in bonds. I am very light on real property. Observe Figure 16. An era is over. Why should an individual invest in illiquid real estate (tax and leverage considerations aside) when he can get over 10 percent tax-free in high-grade tax-exempt bonds? If inflation remains at 4 to 5 percent, he will almost double the

Asset Allocation Model

Asset Class	Historical Annual Real Return	Volatility	Liquidity	Allocation Range	Present Allocation
Short-term investments	0.6%	1	1	0%–30%	4
Equities	7.1	4	2	20–70	44
Emerging growth stocks	9.8	5	4	5–25	6
Venture capital	15.0	5	5	2–10	4
Bonds	2.0	3	2	10–50	35
Real property	4.8	3	4	5–30	7
Gold	3.0	4	2	0–15	0

Figure 16   Single-Family Homes Sold

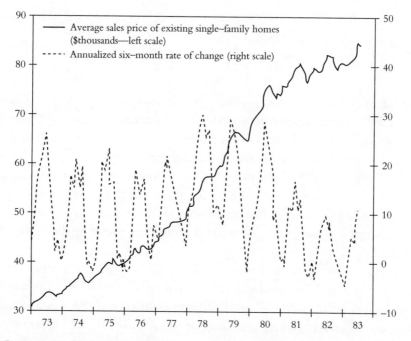

SOURCE: Data Resources, Inc.; Morgan Stanley Research.

purchasing power of his capital in a decade. For a tax-exempt institution, governments and high-grade corporates are just as compelling.

It is late in the performance cycle in the two high-return categories—emerging growth stocks and venture capital—both on a valuation and a sociological basis, as we have discussed elsewhere in recent months. Substantial, high-quality, long-term financial assets are the place to be for these times. But, remember, if bonds do as well as I think, stocks will do even better.

The Old President with the Right Intuitions

August 6, 1985

Early last week President Reagan showed us again how tough he is and how straight he thinks. The congressional leadership came up with the idea of a $5-a-barrel tax on imported oil as the keystone of a budget compromise. All the politicians from Dole to Tip were for it; the *Washington Post* and the *New York Times* endorsed it; the secretary of the Treasury and the vice president were quietly enthusiastic; Reagan's chosen columnist Safire liked it; and there were even suggestions that Don Regan was favorably disposed. The entire LibGovWashNY establishment insisted the president had to endorse it to get the budget process going and warned ominously that if he didn't, he was inflexible, senile, and sick.

But the old president, minus some stomach, with a spot on his nose, and a worrying wife, never wavered. He instinctively, immediately rejected the oil-import tax so fast that there was no question of deals or compromises. And he was absolutely right. As a nation we will never reduce spending or the relative size of government by raising taxes. Only by reducing the revenues of government and creating the tension of deficits do the people hold the feet of the whining politicians to the fire and eventually force them to cut spending.

This summer the politicians have showed us how hard it is for them to cut. They always hope for last-minute tax increases and more revenues, because it is the act of spending from which they derive their power. It is no coincidence that only after the president made it unequivocally clear he would not tolerate any tax boost that some progress on spending cuts was made.

The oil-import tax was a particularly dangerous device because it could masquerade as a tax on OPEC and a strategic necessity when actually it was both a tax increase and a tariff. Tariffs are terrible for trade, prosperity, and the world. Tariffs will cause depressions faster than anything else will. Tariffs could make me bearish overnight. For the United States, the leading industrial nation in the world, the imposition of tariffs would be a giant step toward global economic disaster. And that applies to tariffs on Japan as well.

If we posted an import tax making American oil more expensive than world market crude, it would not be long before American industries that were disadvantaged versus their international competitors because of higher energy costs demanded protection, too. After all, it wouldn't be their fault that they had to pay more for oil. So this is the vicious circle of protectionism, and this is the way the world ends, not with a whimper but with a tariff. Adam Smith in *Wealth of Nations* in 1776 said it so well.

> . . . it is the highest impertinence of kings and ministers, to pretend to watch over the economy of private people and to restrain their expense, either by sumptuary laws, or by prohibiting the importation of foreign luxuries. They are themselves always, and without any exception, the greatest spend-thrifts in the society. Let them look well after their own expense, and they may safely trust private people with theirs. If their own extravagance does not ruin the state, that of their subjects never will.
>
> To give the monopoly of the home market to the produce of domestic industry . . . must in all cases be either useless or a hurtful regulation. If the produce of domestic industry can be bought there as cheap as that of foreign industry, the regulation is evidently useless. If it cannot it must be hurtful.
>
> It is the maxim of every prudent master of a family never to attempt to make at home what it will cost him more to make than to buy. The tailor does not attempt to make his own shoes, but buys them of a shoemaker. The shoemaker does not attempt to make his own clothes, but employs a tailor; the farmer attempts to make neither the one nor the other but employs those artificers. All of them find it in their interests to employ their whole industry in a way in which they will have some advantage over their neighbors, and to purchase with a part of its produce, or what is the same thing, with the price of part of it, whatever else they have occasion for. What is prudence in the conduct of every private family can scarce be folly in that of a great kingdom. . . .

Of course, deficits are bad, but they must be reduced by restraining spending, not by raising taxes, which increases the share of government and reduces the incentive of the people to work and save. I wish the president was tougher on defense spending, but I give him high marks for his performance last week whether it was instinctive or intellectual.

Also last week, A. B. Laffer Associates published a paper entitled "America's Great Opportunity: The Incredible Social Security Surplus," written by an expert on the

Social Security system. The study argues that the Social Security amendments of 1983 have changed the funding equation to such an extent that, beginning this year with an $8.6 billion surplus, the system is a cash cow which will generate a rising stream of surpluses that will reach at least $200 billion in 15 years. As the surplus rises inexorably in the next century, the annual cash flow will swamp the "on budget" deficit, resulting in decades of unified federal budget surpluses. If Social Security funds are invested only in Treasury securities as the law now prescribes, then the system will own all of them by 2016, thus in effect retiring the national debt. There will be a $1.9 trillion public surplus by 2025. The paper considers various alternatives, such as cutting Social Security tax rates, creating a national pension system, or increasing benefits.

This is a stunning new idea. The prospect of decades of federal budget surpluses is completely contrary to the conventional wisdom of huge unified deficits into the indefinite future. I hope it's right, and we are going to try to verify it.

What Kind of People Are We?

October 7, 1986

This diatribe is strictly personal. It has nothing to do with investing or asset allocation. I think it has something to do with America.

I like to watch pro football. It's a tough, hard, commercial world with lots of intensity but very little sentiment—like the stock market and Wall Street. It's professional and the participants get busted up, but they do get paid. In contrast, college football is phony and, in my opinion, is a deadly poison that pollutes American society, perverts our youth, and degrades great universities. Let me make clear at the outset that I'm talking about big-time college football, not the amateur variety played in the Ivy League or at the thousands of colleges that are below the first division. The former is a national disgrace of which we should all be ashamed.

Strong words—but I believe them. The college sports business works something like this. The big sports (football and basketball) generate huge revenues through ticket sales, concession income, and TV contracts. These monies pay a lot of salaries for a lot of people on the athletic staff, university administration, and faculty. They probably buy some libraries and dormitories, too, but mostly they support the vested infrastructure. Teams that win a lot mean sold-out stadiums, extra money from play-off and bowl games, and richer TV contracts. A winning team is great advertising for a university, and it attracts alumni giving, new students, and even faculty. A study done by two Clemson economists found that from 1971 to 1984, schools with winning football records had more applicants and rising SAT scores for entering freshmen. To cite one example, after Boston College had a championship season and a Heisman Trophy winner named Doug Flutie in 1984, freshmen applications jumped from 12,500 to 16,000 the next year.

Big-time college football is a commercial venture. "You have to realize that you have a product on the field, a TV product and a corporate sponsorship product," says Michael McGee, the University of Southern California's athletic director. The coaches, of courses, are professionals, and their salaries are doubled or tripled by outside contracts and booster club contributions. If they don't win, they get fired. They must be dispassionate, cold-blooded users of hired athletic meat. Although they may be ruthless and preach violence, however, they are not the villains.

To win, a university must attract athletes. While scholarships and spending money are legal, booster clubs can illegally slip the really serious money to a boy or his family. Competition for athletes is intense, and the colleges bid for superstars like racehorses. These hired hands attend universities in name only, and it is made clear they are there to perform rather than to learn.

In fact, for many, there are no academics, either in high school or college. Recently, one famous halfback could not even read his professional contract in court, and the *New York Times* has written about college football players with "the capabilities of a fourth or fifth grader." In the court case involving an instructor at the University of Georgia who was fired for complaining about being forced to give phony grades to football players, the university's lawyer actually argued that if an illiterate jock learned to read at Georgia and became a mail clerk instead of a garbage man, the university was doing its job. Educators, coaches, and boosters continually and without hesitation break the academic and financial rules.

They also violate the rules of humanity. Players are forced one way or another to play with or to inflict injuries. Even worse is the pressure to use strength-building steroids that have personality-altering side effects. Every coach in the country will deny that he encourages pill popping, but the drugs are made available, and there is job and peer pressure to use them. Too many college football players end up with maimed bodies, brains, and dispositions. The drugs also raise the level of brutality on the field.

Jesse Jackson said recently in talking about the exploitation of black athletes, that blacks who are recruited "as appendages to the university to fill up stadiums" should get a share of the proceeds, and some of the money should go toward really educating them and other minority students. He's on target on this one. He singled out Ohio State University, calling it the "Ohio State plantation."

There are other evil side effects that pervert our society. The system encourages many talented kids, especially those from the inner city, to concentrate on sports rather than book learning for a free trip to college. Beyond that comes the big pot of gold of professional sports. However, the odds are stacked against them, and the risk of injury is great. Out of 10,000 high school football players, only 100 play at the college level, and only a few of these make it to the pros. The rest are discarded when their eligibility expires, or they're injured or fail with nothing to show for their bumps and limps but a fancy letter jacket.

The use of drugs on the fields inevitably leads to "recreational" consumption. The rash of athlete drug deaths is no coincidence. Even more appalling was the recent

Maryland cover-up attempt that was overlooked or ignored—you pick the word—by the university administration. How can kids be expected to respect authority or the "system" when they see their coaches, the business executives who are the fans, and the university itself all cheating to create a winning team? The recent stories about hooliganism, petty crimes, and disrespect for authority on the University of Miami's squad indicates how far out of control socially many players are.

I particularly object to the pious phoniness of most university presidents. They pretend not to see or know, but it's really "praise the Lord and pass the ammunition." The end of winning and money justifies any means. Of course, when you come right down to it, the real villain is all of us Americans. We are the ones who watch college football, pay for it, demand it. Do we really identify with the employees on the field who aren't even students? Are we really elated when the gang of thugs in our college's uniform brutalizes the hired guns from the school in the next state? Is that what it's all about? Is that why we want to send our children to one educational institution rather than another? I thought sports were supposed to be recreational and to teach values. What kind of people are we, anyway?

Emerging Markets Are Only for the Brave

August 5, 1991

Throughout the "second" and "third" worlds, the real jihad is for privatization, free markets, tax reduction, and supply-side economics. No politician or political party dares oppose bull markets. As I have said before, emerging markets as an asset category are here to stay. Major institutions around the world are not only investing in public and private funds for individual countries but are also assigning money to specific managers who specialize in emerging markets to invest at their discretion. Timing entrances and exits is always crucial in investing, but nowhere more so than when playing emerging markets.

Our studies indicate emerging market investments have delivered a return of around 18 percent per annum in the post–World War II era. Last year was a bad one because two of the biggest emerging markets, Taiwan and Korea, had large declines. So far this year, results are mixed. Through the end of July, the Morgan Stanley Capital International Emerging Markets Global Index of 14 countries is up 27.8 percent but remains 25 percent below its high (the southern European markets are particular laggards). The MSCI Far East Emerging Markets Index has gained 12.2 percent in 1991, but is 42 percent from its peak. The star performer has been Latin America, where the MSCI index is up 99 percent this year.

Intrigued with such strong results—on the order of venture capital returns—and with the inverse correlation with developed markets, certain consultants are suggesting allocating up to 5 percent of a large, diversified portfolio to emerging markets. In my model balanced portfolio, I currently have an allocation of 3 percent, within a range of zero to 5 percent. I am convinced diversification is especially essential here because of the volatility and illiquidity. Anyone investing in this area must be prepared for scandals, coups, assassinations, and horrendous natural disasters. Remember when Rajiv Gandhi was assassinated two months ago and the country funds fell 20 percent in the first hour of trading, or the day there was a military coup in Thailand. Emerging markets are not for sissies.

The "Emerging Market Life Cycle" diagram (prepared by Eugene Chung) tells more than you may want to know about the emerging markets we follow. Actually, it is a gold mine of information. The life-cycle diagram depicts some of the same information in a different way. At the moment, some country funds for the partially open markets are selling at substantial premiums, so direct investment seems more attractive. Others, however, are at hefty discounts. Buying a country fund in an attractive market at a discount is by far the best way to participate.

The Asian emerging markets seem moderately attractive. I agree with Marc Faber that because of their dependence on exports, the developing Asian economies are like warrants on the U.S. economy. If the United States does well, Asia will do even better; as Marc put it, Thailand is like an option on a warrant. I don't expect any great things from the U.S. economy, but on the other hand it shouldn't fall apart, either. Most of the Asian emerging markets are well below where they were a year ago, so valuations are reasonable.

The bears argue that if economic progress and trade stop, these leveraged economies and markets will be devastated, particularly in real estate. This is true, but although

The Emerging Market Life Cycle

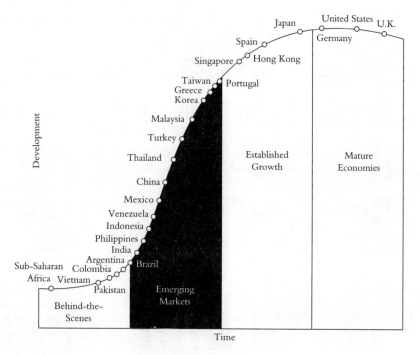

Major World Equity Markets
Comparative Absolute Valuations

Country	Current Absolute Valuation[a]					Historical Average[b]					Current/Historical				
	Price/ Cash Flow	Price/ Earnings	Price/ Book Value	Equity Yield	Bond Yield	Price/ Cash Flow	Price/ Earnings	Price/ Book Value	Equity Yield	Bond Yield	Price/ Cash Flow	Price/ Earnings	Price/ Book Value	Equity Yield	Bond Yield
Australia	8.4	13.6	1.43	4.8	11.0	7.41	12.0	1.33	4.6	13.64	1.13	1.13	1.07	1.05	0.81
Austria	5.4	29.9	2.09	1.7	8.1	7.98	59.5	1.75	2.5	7.96	0.68	0.50	1.20	0.69	1.02
Belgium	4.9	11.2	1.42	5.3	9.7	4.21	10.6	1.30	8.4	10.14	1.16	1.06	1.10	0.63	0.96
Canada	8.2	21.5	1.40	3.3	9.9	7.37	17.4	1.45	3.5	11.26	1.11	1.24	0.96	0.94	0.88
Denmark	9.0	NA	1.90	1.4	9.5	7.38	NA	1.42	2.3	13.02	1.22	NA	1.34	0.60	0.73
World ex U.S.	7.9	21.0	1.99	2.4	NA	7.13	18.5	2.03	2.7	NA	1.11	1.13	0.98	0.90	NA
Finland	6.1	61.7	0.73	2.7	11.7	NA	NA	NA	NA	NA	NA	NA	NA	NA	NA
France	5.4	11.8	1.48	3.6	9.3	4.67	15.8	1.46	4.3	11.53	1.16	0.74	1.02	0.85	0.81
Germany	4.9	15.3	1.91	3.5	8.7	4.50	13.7	1.87	3.9	7.42	1.09	1.12	1.02	0.90	1.17
Hong Kong	10.2	13.1	1.43	4.4	9.5	10.00	11.7	1.59	4.7	10.24	1.02	1.12	0.90	0.94	0.93
Italy	2.9	15.3	1.23	3.3	13.6	5.82	18.3	1.54	2.6	14.20	0.50	0.83	0.80	1.26	0.96
Japan	11.2	36.5	2.67	0.7	6.5	11.72	36.3	3.25	1.0	6.15	0.96	1.01	0.82	0.72	1.06
Netherlands	6.8	17.6	1.45	4.3	8.9	3.97	8.7	1.02	5.2	7.95	1.71	2.02	1.42	0.82	1.12
New Zealand	5.1	7.8	0.96	6.9	9.9	NA	NA	NA	NA	NA	NA	NA	NA	NA	NA
Norway	6.3	22.4	2.12	1.7	9.8	4.40	12.0	1.88	3.2	12.20	1.43	1.86	1.13	0.53	0.80
Singapore/Malaysia	12.6	19.4	1.85	1.8	4.7	15.25	23.6	1.94	2.0	5.03	0.83	0.82	0.95	0.91	0.93
Spain	4.6	10.4	1.11	4.8	12.0	3.92	12.6	0.79	7.3	13.80	1.17	0.83	1.40	0.65	0.87
Sweden	9.5	19.6	1.85	2.8	11.1	6.87	12.4	1.83	2.7	12.37	1.38	1.58	1.01	1.03	0.90
Switzerland	8.2	17.0	1.48	2.3	6.3	6.09	13.4	1.32	2.6	5.05	1.35	1.30	1.12	0.90	1.25
United Kingdom	8.4	14.3	1.95	4.9	10.2	6.80	11.3	1.54	4.8	10.16	1.23	1.26	1.27	1.02	1.00
United States	8.9	18.8	2.15	3.2	8.2	6.65	12.7	1.67	4.2	9.87	1.34	1.48	1.29	0.77	0.83
World	8.3	20.1	2.05	2.7	NA	6.88	15.6	1.87	3.3	NA	1.21	1.29	1.10	0.82	NA
World ex Japan	7.9	16.8	1.86	3.5	NA	NA	NA	NA	NA	NA	NA	NA	NA	NA	NA

[a]As of July 31, 1991.

[b]Last 10 years except PIE for Austria (since October 1981), PIE for Italy (April 1984), PIE for Spain (January 1980), PICF for Switzerland (January 1980), and bond yield for Spain (December 1982). Bond yield is long term except Hong Kong (prime rate), Singapore (three-month deposit).

Source: Morgan Stanley Research.

I expect growth to slow, I don't expect it to cease. I think Thailand, the Philippines, and Indonesia are all attractive for new money, and we can find cheap stocks in all of them. All three markets are well below their all-time highs. The First Philippine Fund ($7 7/8), which trades on the New York Stock Exchange, sells at more than a 20 percent discount to net asset value. I still wouldn't touch Taiwan, and Korea has already had a substantial rally. The NYSE funds for both countries sell at big premiums.

In the subcontinent, the Indian stock market set new highs again last week, but strategist Madhav Dhar remains bullish. The new prime minister has taken the country by the scruff of the neck, and the right things are finally being done. India could be on the verge of realizing its immense potential. The new budget proposes large reductions in both capital gains and dividend taxation and opens the economy to foreign investment. Another country just beginning to emerge is Pakistan. This is a big country with rich natural resources. The government is following free market policies and is committed to privatization and financial liberalization. The problem is extreme political instability. The stock market is at eight times prospective earnings and five times cash flow. If Pakistan could get its act together, it could be the next Thailand.

The emerging markets in southern Europe have languished this year after big moves in the late 1980s. When the wall came down, Eastern Europe stole the spotlight from countries like Portugal, Greece, and Turkey. Turkey seems the most attractive to me at this time. The stock market has declined 60 percent from its high, and valuations are reasonable. The country is still plagued by high interest rates and inflation, but growth is strong. In the short run, Turkey's courageous stand in the Gulf War has hurt the country economically, but in the longer term, if there is any justice in the EEC, it should help. Turgut Ozal is a big plus, too. Unfortunately, the Turkish Growth Fund ($8 1/4) on the NYSE sells at a fairly healthy premium to net asset value. Portugal is another interesting and neglected market, which has been almost cut in half since 1989. This is the time to be buying both equities and the funds. Greece and Jordan are small markets.

I believe there is a good chance (at least 50 percent) that in this decade South America is at long last going to have a breakout period. If so, all the south-of-the-border markets should do very well in the next five years. However, in the short run, both Mexico and Chile seem a little frothy, and I am inclined to wait for a better buying opportunity. On the other hand, Brazil and Argentina are still far below their previous highs, and I consider them buys even though the markets have been running in the last few months. Unfortunately, the Brazil Fund ($17 3/4) sells at a premium on the NYSE, and there is no easy way to play Argentina. The Venezuelan market has already had a big move, and again there is no fund. A country to watch is Colombia, where the new president appears to be making real progress.

For the next generation of action, the cognoscenti chatter about China, Vietnam, and Sri Lanka. On the assumption that governments everywhere will figure out that attracting equity money is good for their survival and their people's health. Africa and the Middle East also could be next. For that matter, Egypt, Kenya, Nigeria, Zimbabwe, and even Iraq could be names for the future.

Section 2B:
Investment Discipline & Tactics

Discipline and Reading

February 7, 1983

Amassive organizational problem with which the investment manager has to
contend is the reading material that he is deluged with daily. "No one can know
everything," said Horace, an investor as well as a poet in the days when P/Es
were low before Christ was born, but today most of us are compulsive readers, hoping
to find the touchstone fragment of information that will spark a great investment decision. We read because we think we are accumulating knowledge and information. Yet, so
much of what we read is repetitious, trivia, or random noise information.

As investment managers, we must realize we are not in the information or knowledge collection business but rather in the judgment business. In his great *Essay
Concerning Human Understanding*, however, John Locke wrote: "He that judges without
informing himself to the utmost that he is capable, cannot acquit himself of judging
amiss." But he went on to say that although knowledge is the treasure, judgment is the
treasurer of a wise man, and that "he that has more knowledge than judgment is made
for another man's use more than his own." Judgment, not knowledge or information, is
the final and only product of the investment manager.

Another facet of the problem is that we become obsessed with the housekeeping aspect of paper flow. Getting through a stack of reports and statements becomes an accomplishment in and of itself, which is, of course, ridiculous. In part, investment management is a job where there is no way to measure labor expended, and so there is a natural tendency toward any symbol of actually having accomplished something. The trouble is that the exercise of clearing your inbox or checking off a stack of material may not enhance the judgment process and, in fact, may actually detract from it because it consumes thinking time and may dangerously reinforce the conventional wisdom.

A very bad habit I have is setting aside reports and articles that I know I want to read carefully and think about, with the idea that I am first going to go through the junk quickly. What happens, unfortunately, is that the mass mail takes longer to get through than it should, and I end up carrying the good reports in my briefcase for a week or so because I simply haven't had time to read them. In other words, I've processed the junk and haven't read the important material.

The dilemma for the experienced investment manager who has read 100,000 reports and understands the critical variables of the major industries is that, although there is nothing to be derived from reading another long report about General Electric or the aluminum industry unless it has some new insight, there is no way of finding this out except to at least scan the report. And if you have the stock in your portfolio, you feel almost morally obliged to read the whole report. I now have decided the odds are so low of there being truly fresh insights in most brokerage research, business magazines, and company reports that you shouldn't read any of it unless you own the stock. Then you just scan it for signs of life. Long research reports are written by analysts for analysts. Business magazines are more interested in being cute than analytical. The only exception is when you see a report by one of the dozen or so analysts or writers that you know does really original work. We all pretty much know who they are, and some work for us, and some don't but should.

Maintenance information—in other words, how order rates are and what the next couple of quarters' earnings are going to be—has to be processed because you need to know what expectations are. I get this by reading our weekly *Investment Perspectives* publication and by scanning the cover page summaries of the weekly research reviews of three or four other firms. It is changes in business conditions and relative earnings momentum from expectations that move stocks in the short run, so it's important to know what analysts are reporting and what the market is discounting. But this kind of information is pure maintenance knowledge.

Although I don't do it, I am convinced that when on vacation not only should you read history, biographies, poetry, novels, anything but business, but also you should tell them back at the office to throw all the regular business mail away. You should start fresh when you come back, and I guarantee you will never notice what you supposedly missed. I do the worst thing of all, which is to have the office send me all the material. Again, I don't practice what I preach, but I believe that, like several of the great leaders in Nixon's new book, we all should commit half an hour each weekday and an hour each Saturday and Sunday to pleasure reading. As Nixon points out, this is not "escapist reading." It is mind-expanding reading that provides a sense of history and perspective and lifts one out of the morass of reports and short-term commentary that, as Nixon puts it, "so consumes a leader's time and assails his mind."

In *Leaders*, MacArthur comments that a commander's single most important function is to separate the 5 percent of intelligence that he receives that is crucial from the 95 percent that is not important. This is precisely the problem of the investment manager. A recurring theme of the book is that leaders need private time to contemplate. As George Soros says, a good investment manager must have time hanging heavily on his hands so he has nothing to do but chew on his portfolio. With all the distractions, such as meetings that must be attended, unless the investment manager disciplines his reading habits, he will become buried in paper and literally will not have time to think. Thus, I believe he should list, in a logical manner, his priority weekly reading material and always read it first and carefully before going on to secondary sources. He really should have his secretary do the sorting, and he must be very disciplined.

For what it's worth, in the morning on the train I read the *Wall Street Journal* and the *New York Times* carefully, and I read the *Financial Times* in the evening. I find the *FT* has a perspective that is uniquely international. We must be world investors. Its columnists, like Samuel Brittain, are every bit as good as the *Journal*'s. As far as magazines are concerned, I read *Time*, the *Economist*, and *BusinessWeek* from cover to cover for different reasons. The rest I scan. Each month I read *World Press, Institutional Investor, Discover, World Financial Markets*, the *Bank Credit Analyst*, and *Fortune*. I also go over Jude Wanniski's monthly summary of reading material. As for quarterlies, I look at *Public Opinion*, the *Public Interest, Foreign Affairs*, and the *Mideast Report*. I also read some weekly letters like *Petroleum Intelligence Weekly* and the *Economist's Financial Report*, both of which are first-rate primary sources. Then, of course, I study our research and look at the competition. I read carefully Hyman, Cooperman, Moltz, Farrell, Francis Kelly, Wenglowski, Laffer, and some others who don't come right to mind.

This doesn't sound like a lot of reading compared with what some people I know do. I find it very hard to get any serious reading done at the office, and even with two hours of commuting reading and at least two hours every night plus a lot on weekends, I am barely able to keep up. If I miss a couple of nights, I'm hopelessly behind.

How to Lose the
Winner's Game

January 14, 1986

As everyone now knows, most professional investment managers had difficulty matching the S&P 500's total return of 31.6 percent last year, with the average equity portfolio up around 28.5 percent. Furthermore, 1985 was the third straight year in which the median manager underperformed. In addition, for the second consecutive year, it was also tough to keep up with the Morgan Stanley Capital International World and EAFE Indexes. Fiduciaries, consultants, and the press are all happily disparaging professional investors as grossly overpaid underachievers, and indexing is again the cry. In fact, *Pensions & Investments Age* reports that the total of indexed assets leaped 70 percent in 1985 and projects another huge gain this year.

To add insult to injury, Charlie Ellis has written a new book (*Investment Policy: How to Win the Loser's Game*, published by Dow Jones Irwin) that is attracting a great deal of attention because it explains why managing money in an active fashion is "a loser's game." Charlie is an articulate, informed, and intelligent analyst of the investment business, but, in this case, I fault his timing and his perspective. He published his original Loser's Game article in the mid-seventies, right after the last bout of underperformance and in the midst of the previous wave of indexing. The timing was exquisitely wrong. I suspect it will be again.

In his new book, Ellis argues that, as the professionals play an increasingly important role in the market, they have in effect become the market. Thus, by definition, their diligence and hard work are self-defeating, and they can't significantly outperform the popular averages or each other. "Their efforts to beat the market are no longer the most important part of the solution; they are the most important part of the problem."

Furthermore, he points out that, while it is very difficult to beat the market, it is easy "while trying to do better, to do worse." The problem is compounded by size, which is the inevitable result of performance success; thus, it's a loser's game. He then goes on to discuss the crucial role of investment policy, and his thesis is sensible. It is a worthwhile book, and everyone involved in supervising or managing money should read it.

Still, I have a problem with Charlie's loser's game concept, and I think the trend toward investment socialism (which is what straight indexing is) in domestic and international equity portfolios is dead wrong. The anomalies in the indexes that have caused the professionals to fall short now will operate to produce superior relative performance by the majority of active portfolios, but that is another subject.

My point in this piece is that performance relative to the S&P 500 is cyclical and always has been. An owner of money pays a fee of 40 to 100 basis points to an investment manager to obtain over time an annual return that is a couple of hundred basis points higher than that provided by an index fund that costs 5 or 10 basis points. Compounding this extra return over long periods results in staggering wealth enhancements after payment of fees that are far greater than could be realized through mimicking the averages. Just as an example, over 31 years, John Templeton's shareholders have seen an investment of $10,000 grow into $632,469; a comparable commitment in the Dow would have been worth only $35,400. The results of some private investors are even more spectacular; for example, over 19 years, Pacific Partners achieved an average annual return of 32.9 percent overall—23.6 percent to the limited partners—versus 7.8 percent for the S&P. Over almost 16 years, Tweedy Browne's limited partners enjoyed a gain of 936 percent versus 238.5 percent for the S&P.

The fascinating thing, however, is that all of these superstars underperformed the S&P in 30 to 40 percent of the years studied. The only exception is Warren Buffett, whose partners had just one down year out of 11 when he retired from the fray in 1969. The New Horizons Fund, which admittedly has a good but not spectacular 25-year record, exceeded the S&P in only 13 of those years. Templeton underperformed about 40 percent of the time. None in the group always beat the S&P, probably because no one thought that was the primary objective. However, the underperformance in the down years was generally (but not always) small, and the positive differentials were large. Most of the lag occurred in years when the averages made big advances.

Furthermore, with only two exceptions, all of the great investors had long bouts (defined as three straight or three out of four consecutive years) of underperformance. Almost invariably, these bad periods were either preceded and/or followed by sustained bursts of spectacular returns. Obviously, to close your account after a cold spell would have been a costly mistake. By contrast, it would have been a better tactic to lighten up after four or five vintage years. Relative performance runs in three- to five-year cycles, probably related to the manager's style and the dominant themes of a particular market.

Some of the history is fascinating. An extreme example is Pacific Partners, which, after providing gains for investors of 120, 114, and 65 percent in the late sixties, had returns below those of the S&P for the next four years and in five out of six years in the early and mid-seventies. In 1976, it got back on track with a 127.8 percent rise. Charles Munger had a 5-year period in which he lagged in 4, but over a 13-year span, he achieved a compound return of 19.8 percent a year on his portfolio versus 5 percent for the index. Tweedy Browne had a spell in which it underperformed the S&P three out of four years. The Sequoia Fund lagged the S&P for its first three-and-a-half years but has provided an annual return more than eight percentage points higher than the S&P's over its 16-year history. Templeton has had two three-year underperformance cycles and one run of nine straight years outpacing the S&P. I discussed his ranking variations in last week's *Investment Perspectives*. The New Horizons Fund underperformed for its first four full years in existence.

The returns achieved by the superstars cannot be attained by us mortals. Also, there is no question that size becomes an impediment, although at different levels for different folks. I believe that, over a five- to seven-year cycle, the average manager can provide annual returns that are two to three percentage points above those of the index. Obviously, as is true with the superstars, these satisfactory results will not follow a smooth progression; there will be both cold periods and hot spells.

Shifting from an active manager to an index fund is similar to changing managers. In the assets we supervise, we never close an account because of a bout of underperformance by a previous achiever if we are convinced that the investment management firm involved has its head intact and has not been demoralized, has kept its core people, has stuck to its style, and has generally maintained its character. In moving from a good cold manager to a good hot one, there is the risk of being whipsawed twice. In fact, we would be inclined to give the cold guys more money. Similarly, I am convinced that switching from good active managers to index funds at this time is the way to lose at what is, over time, a winner's, not a loser's, game.

UK Price to Book Value Ratio, 1976–2002

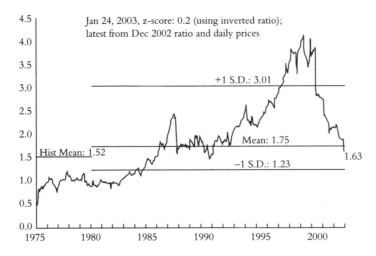

SOURCE: MSCI.

You Gotta Believe

January 27, 2003

W.H. Auden's "September 1, 1939" was written at another grave time for the world (September 1, 1939, was, of course, the date on which Hitler ordered the invasion of Poland and World War II began). For me, the poem captures the current *uncertain* and *afraid* mood of the equity markets: *Afraid* of war with all its unintended consequences; afraid of terrorism, the intifada, and feckless allies; afraid of recession, deflation, and the poison of the lingering hangover from the bubble. *Uncertain* whether this is the moment when truth and courage prevail, or we are at the precipice from which we plunge through the old lows to new depths. Look at the chart of price-to-book value of the UK stock market. The entire bubble has been expurgated, and the ratio is back to where it was 12 to 15 years ago.

Having endured one whipsaw after another, professional investors are bruised and uncertain. In the gloom, the investment consensus believes that there is no pricing power, that deflation is the real danger, that the American consumer is highly leveraged and spent out, and that the Anglo-Saxon housing bubble is about to burst. Furthermore, Japan is a hopeless case, Europe suffers from a severe case of rigor mortis, and the Chinese behemoth will eat all our lunches (and dinners, too, for that matter). Investment returns over the next decade for stocks and bonds will be mid-single digits, stocks are still too expensive to rally very far, and technology will be dead money for years to come. No one has much hope for meaningful dividend tax relief. All these assumptions should be questioned simply because they are so widely held.

The state of mind of the professional investor class is part of the problem. A long bear market and vicious whipsaws have sapped their natural optimism, and the fickle loyalty of their clients has hurt. No one can afford another big hit. As a result, the aggressive money is very conservatively invested, with hedge funds showing minimum net long exposure, and long-only managers clinging to their benchmarks. Equities have been down three years in a row, there are dark forces out there in the world, and everyone's confidence is at a low ebb, but clients still pay fees, there are conferences to go to in Florida and Colorado, and investment life goes on.

I am not so gloomy. I think it's not the beginning of the end but instead the beginning of a better, safer world that will emerge from the other side of this crisis. I am of the Thomas Friedman school, and I recommend the two-part piece he published in the *New York Times* on January 22 and 26. He argues the way to bring peace and prosperity to the Middle East is to bring about capitalist democracies where there is real economic hope for both men and women. Despair and poverty spawn terrorism. Removing Saddam and building a democratic Iraq would have a domino effect, causing progressive change in the Arab world and defusing anti-American anger. We can go it alone and win the war, he says, but we can't rehabilitate Iraq by ourselves.

That's opinion, however, and the facts are that the threat of war with Iraq has cast a pall on stock markets everywhere. MSCI Europe went to a new low last week. There is also increasing evidence that uncertainty has severely affected the U.S. and therefore the world economy. Consumer and business confidence measures have faltered, and the data clearly indicate that businesses are deferring capital spending, not rebuilding inventories, and delaying hiring. The pattern of this economic cycle is very different, partly because of the excesses of the previous boom, but also because of the geopolitical uncertainties that weigh on it.

Thus, a favorable resolution to the Iraqi crisis should result not only in a spurt in stock prices but also in a surge in the world economy. Under conceivable and not totally far-fetched circumstances, the U.S. economy could take off in the second and third quarters. Real GDP growth could be 5 percent or more as the dam breaks on capital spending, restocking inventories, and hiring; as the massive fiscal and monetary stimulus that has already been unleashed takes hold; and as oil prices decline. In fact, the surge could be so strong that inflation fears revive far sooner than most think possible. Incidentally, a new Fed report indicates that the median household owning stock really wasn't affected much by the bear market because it only owned $34,000 and had four times as much wealth tied up in its house. Furthermore, households aren't nearly as indebted as commonly believed. In 1998, the median family paid 18.1 percent of its after-tax income to service its debt. By last year, that figure had fallen to 16 percent, virtually the same as it was seven years earlier before the consumer supposedly went crazy.

So I am bullish on America, on our ability to dispose of Saddam quickly and cleanly, and on the intended consequences. The naysayers will come around quickly. As always, victory has a thousand fathers and defeat is an orphan. On Sunday, *Meet the Press* rebroadcast a January 1991 show with Senator Ted Kennedy arguing against attacking Saddam's huge army in Kuwait and saying that the majority of the American people were against going to war. And make no mistake. If I am right and there is a happy ending, you have to be invested before it's obvious because by then it would be too late.

Section 2C:
Market Psychology
and Investing Philosophy

Contrarianism

April 5, 1982

I n Europe last week, it seemed as though everyone was bearish about something. The Germans were downcast because of Eastern Europe and Helmut Schmidt's decline, the Arabs were depressed because of oil and Iraq, the French were bearish because of their government; only the British seemed a little upbeat, but that was before the Falkland Islands incident.

We continue to be virtually fully invested, and I feel uneasy, but I am still inclined to sweat it out with what I think are the right stocks. The world could be tottering on the brink of high interest rate deflation, which initially could be very painful to financial asset prices, but I think the odds are against it. However, I would like to see commodity prices firm as they did last week, gold stay above $300, and only a little more weakness in oil prices—without a sudden collapse in the price structure. Also, as the second quarter progresses, I would like to see the fiscal 1983 federal deficit reduced and some signs of economic recovery. Weakness in prices and profits is causing credit demand to remain relatively strong as cash flows crumble, and, combined with concern about the size of the federal deficit, is keeping interest rates high. Stabilizing prices and an improving economy would now lower interest rates and not vice versa. I think all these things will happen, but clearly at this point I am in the minority. I guess I'm a contrarian bull, which leads me to another subject.

For many years I have dabbled with the theory of contrary opinion, but only recently I happened to read two of the best, most lucid books on the subject that I have come across. They are *Contrarian Investment Strategy* by David Dreman, published in 1979 by Random House, and a little volume with the inauspicious title *Why You Win or Lose* by Fred C. Kelly, published first in 1920 and printed again recently by the Fraser Publishing Company of Burlington, Vermont.

Dreman is a successful investment counselor with his own firm in New York, and he writes for *Forbes*. I don't know the man, but judging from his profound book, he has done a lot of heavy research into psychology—particularly as it relates to crowd behavior, decision influencing, and the effects of uncertainty. I never had heard of Kelly before, but the foreword, with considerable charm, describes him as an "amateur psychologist, writer, traveller, breeder of dogs, all-around student of human nature, and successful speculator." It is apparent he was the type of rugged individualist who got up at the "crank" of dawn to make money. On credentials alone, both men appear more qualified to write original books on investing with some real wisdom in them than all the charlatans and pointy-headed professors who write "how to beat the market" books.

Dreman argues that an understanding of crowd psychology or group madness is essential to successful investing. Other prime sources on this topic are Charles MacKay's *Extraordinary Popular Delusions and the Madness of Crowds*, Gustave Le Bon's *The Crowd*, and W. Trotter's *Instincts of the Herd*. Le Bon says that an individual regresses in a crowd and "descends several rungs in the ladder of civilization. Isolated he may be a cultivated individual; in a crowd he is a barbarian." This is because the principal characteristic of a crowd is its great difficulty in separating the imagined from the real. Crowds are only capable of focusing on images and thus are only influenced by images. The financial crowd is transported from rationality by the beguiling, contagious image of instant wealth. Thus, it pays to invest against rather than with the fads and extremes of the crowd.

Trotter claims man is a gregarious animal who is very susceptible to suggestion and that the herd inclination is one of his four primary instincts. "Physical and intellectual loneliness will be a real terror, insurmountable by reason." In other words, he feels more comfortable running toward the financial cliff with the rest of the lemmings than going in the other direction alone.

Fred Kelly says much the same thing. His basic thesis is that "the game is old but the players are always new." The crowd always loses, he writes, because it is always wrong. It is wrong because it behaves normally, and "every natural human impulse seems to be a foe to success in stocks." To win, you must invariably do the opposite of what seems to be the sensible thing that everybody else is doing. One's chances for success are greatly enhanced by doing what seems to be illogical. Investors, like people, want to conform and congregate as a herd, and the mass media reinforces this tendency. "Be contrary but be cautious" is Kelly's motto.

Kelly doesn't claim contrary opinion investing is infallible, merely that one's chances for success are greatly enhanced by doing what is difficult, lonely, contrary, and seems illogical. For example, the easy, logical thing to do is to sell stocks that you own that have gone up and hold those that have gone down. Nothing could be more wrong. However, a big difference between Kelly and Dreman, which reflects the changed nature of the stock market in the last 40 years, is that the crowd Kelly wants to be contrary against is individual investors, while Dreman's crowd is the experts (e.g., market strategists like this poor soul) and institutional investors.

Dreman demonstrates, through various psychological experiments, the proposition that the vaguer and more complex a situation, the more we tend to rely on other people (so-called experts) whose intelligence and opinions we respect. Furthermore, the expert's support of a concept legitimizes it and locks it into place. People are often persuaded by a message not because of its compelling logic but because they consider the communicator an expert.

Dreman then proceeds to argue (again with considerable data) that experts in general don't make better judgments than intelligent people with no training, mostly because the expert is overloaded with information. Man is a highly effective processor of sequential data and can handle very complex and massive amounts of information reliably in a linear manner, that is, moving from one point to the next in a logical sequence, like building a ship model or a space station.

However, investment decision making is a configural or interactive process in which the decision maker's interpretation of any single piece of information changes, depending on how he evaluates many other inputs. The human mind is not well suited to configural analysis, and Dreman argues that the sophisticated analytical investment decision process is a configural system that even a one-in-a-million mind like Bobby Fischer's, that can sort a maze of contradictory implications, would have trouble with.

Furthermore, professional investors tend to overload themselves with information through obsessive reading and analysis, which does not improve their investment decisions but only makes them more confident and more vulnerable to serious errors, principally refusing to recognize and reverse wrong actions. Excessive information input overloads our mental tachometers, and we no longer process information reliably. The two main points I derived from this section of Dreman's book are, first, keep your thinking simple, and second, compulsive information insemination either through reading or meetings is counterproductive. I am convinced there is nothing like unstructured leisure thinking time as a prelude to good, clear, abstract reasoning and decision making. Sometimes you need time hanging heavily on your hands. Identify and focus on the big, simple concept of the period—be it energy, technology, consumer growth, or whatever—and stay with it, but always be open to change.

Dreman's contrary opinion theory is also anchored to his strong belief in the basic principle of regression to the mean. A good example of this principle is a professional baseball player who over 10 seasons has a lifetime average of .250 but in the first month of the new season bats .410. The odds are very high that as the season progresses, he will regress toward his career mean. In business, sports, and nature, the momentum is back toward the average.

The argument is that the greater the complexity of the uncertainty present in an investment situation, the less emphasis you should place on your appraisal and judgment, and the more you—like a good professional coach in baseball or football—should go with the historical probabilities. Ignore the latest popular experts who confidently predict rates of return for the market or individual stocks that deviate sharply from past norms based on an extrapolation of only the most recent past. Be contrary. Bet the regression to the mean probabilities. The long-term odds are with you.

Kelly approaches probabilities from a different angle. His studies and experience prove that it is far safer to average up in a stock than to average down. Cheapness alone is no reason to buy stock. You have to know whether it's cheap on the way up or cheap on the way down. He quotes Colonel Leonard P. Ayres, who put it this way: "The man who buys a stock solely because of its seemingly bargain price is like a farmer with a thermometer but no calendar, who thinks a hot day in autumn must be the time to plant crops."

Another point that Kelly makes repeatedly is that greed and impatience drive the crowd and are the mortal enemies of successful investors. Greed is the enemy of patience, he says. There are seldom more than two or three times in any one year when one should buy stocks and be fully invested, and the good investor must be patient and contrary. In other words, he must wait to buy stocks until most other people don't want them and then sell stocks when they do.

Kelly is a contrarian trader. Dreman is more of a contrarian investor. Basically, he believes in being contrary by "buying solid companies currently out of favor as measured by their price/earnings ratios," in other words, the lowest P/E stocks. Dreman argues that analysts can't forecast earnings or growth rates and that there really are no true growth companies for two reasons.

First, the more successful and bigger a company becomes, the more difficult it is to maintain growth momentum because of competition, government controls, size, and market saturation. Second, the law of regression to the mean applies here as well. As a source for this view, he quotes Benjamin Graham, the father of value investing and security analysis, whom I knew and who never made any big money except on one fling on a venture growth stock called Government Employees Insurance, which he never should have bought, he once told me, based on his value criteria.

I think Dreman's point about growth stocks maturing is in the long run indisputable. However, as Lord Keynes said, in the long run we are all dead, and it is the short and intermediate runs we care about. Dennis Sherva has collected very conclusive evidence that small companies not only grow faster but also are better, though more volatile, investments than big companies.

Anyway, Dreman says he uses the bottom 40 percent of stocks ranked from low to high by P/Es for selection and from that group buys those with strong financial positions, high sustainable yields, and higher past and projected earnings growth rates than the S&P 500. When the P/E of the stock approaches that of the overall market, no matter how favorable the outlook, he sells it. He gives a stock a two-year period to work out, although he might go as long as three years for cyclical companies. In his book, Dreman marshals a lot of historical data on the superior results of low-P/E-ratio stock portfolios. Basically, his contrary strategy is buying good-quality out-of-favor stocks—"the unloved," as Howard Stein of Dreyfus, a superb instinctive contrarian, would say.

Although he doesn't say so in the book, in a recent *Forbes* article, Dreman argues that price/earnings ratios are really nothing but barometers of current stock market fashions and measures of the prevailing consensus of opinion about a company. Thus a strategy of buying low P/E stocks is contrarian in that one is buying what is out of fashion.

Fred Kelly warns about the dangers of high P/Es, buying stocks "to put away in your box and forget," and change. He cites the high P/Es of canal stocks before their fall and the fact that 20 years earlier, 25 percent of all hardware goods sold in the United States had something to do with a horse, buggy, or wagon, and a buggy whip company was considered a blue chip equity. It is also intriguing that Kelly practiced the rule of selling a stock, no matter what, when it declined from its purchase price by a predetermined amount. As I have written previously, I am convinced this is a great discipline that keeps you from being hung up in losers.

As Robert Frost said about two roads diverging in a yellow wood, taking the less traveled road makes all the difference.

Electronic War Rooms and Lying in the Sun

August 9, 1983

In the City
They sell and buy,
And no-one ever asks them:
Why?
But since it contents them
To buy and sell,
God forgive them,
They might as well.

—Anonymous English

The financial markets in the United States seem hyperactive to me. As the ditty suggests, God may forgive us for overtrading, but the clients for certain will be less tolerant as the activity costs them performance in this trendless market.

The *New York Times* last week carried a story about online, computerized trading trend analysis, complete with flashing electronic war rooms, which provides real-time input on tape momentum tactics. Believe it or not, friends, considerable numbers of our professional investor brethren running other people's money actually react and trade on moment-to-moment, electronic analysis of how a stock or the market "acts." Even worse, your veteran correspondent recently succumbed to the siren song of electronic certainty and has been justly punished, so it is with firsthand bitterness that these words gush forth.

Particularly in fluctuating markets like the present, I think this kind of information for the true investor has all the relevance of the message of dogs barking idiotically in the distance through endless nights and the pattern of laundry hung out to dry in Harlem as seen through the grimy window of the commuter train. Or as H. L. Mencken once wrote about the quality of President Harding's oratory: "It drags itself out of the dark abyss [was about to write "abscess"] of pish, and crawls insanely up to the topmost pinnacle of posh. It is rumble and bumble. It is flap and doodle. It is balder and dash." It does not even have a "redeeming defect."

Gentle readers, there are those whom I inadvertently offend in these pages. Some who are not so gentle write unpleasant letters to the boss partner, which neither endears them to me nor me to the boss. So, no offense is meant to serious technicians, whom I revere as brothers in tripe. As they say, some of my best friends are technicians. I pay a great deal of attention to the work of "technical analysts" (as opposed to technicians) like our John Mendelson, Bob Farrell, and others because they are extraordinarily helpful in identifying trends and market turning points based on long-term relative strength and sentiment measures. As we all know, Mendelson has had a hot hand this cycle. Technical analysts clearly are not part of the scruffy electronic network disseminating this frenetic hour-to-hour noise that is actually disinformation for the investor because it dislocates his head into trading instead of investing.

In my view, the stock market is overpriced today when seven-year government bonds yield 12 percent-plus. The big, quality growth stocks are much less overvalued than the small junk, which is some consolation given our quality-loaded portfolios—some but not much, as our performance numbers this year are hardly exemplary. I think the government bond market from 7 to 30 years is very cheap. However, there is no reason to expect much performance from stocks until the bond market works its way through this spasm of residual monetarism and deficit phobia. I expect this to happen before the end of the year as the economic growth spurt slows and inflation remains dormant.

Meanwhile, I think it's a time for inactivity as the stock market rotates listlessly. Portfolios, like foreign policy, sometimes need a little benign neglect. We think of ourselves as active managers, so it's difficult to let a portfolio simmer. James Reston commented recently that Rudyard Kipling often recommended that the leaders of nations study the art of "judicious leaving alone," and the same advice is equally applicable to investors. If you believe you are generally properly positioned, doing very little is just as active as and a lot less expensive than responding to every shift in the investment breeze.

The course of events in markets really doesn't change that much even from century to century, because the two great constants in the stock market are human emotion and prices. Patterns tend to repeat themselves. Walter Bagehot, the great editor of the *Economist*, wrote that "over-activity is a very great evil." Much of the trouble in the world comes from man's being unable to sit still in a room. Bagehot believed man's inherent desire to be doing things came from his primitive past as a hunter and later as a farmer. Life was relatively simple. There was always something to do. Action was rewarded.

Writing over a century ago, Bagehot said: "But the issues of life are plain no longer. To act rightly in modern society requires a great deal of previous study, a great deal of assimilated information, a great deal of sharpened imagination . . . and much lying in the sun." August and September should be a good time for lying in the sun with your favorite portfolio.

God Is a Mathematician? The Fibonacci Numbers

February 19, 1986

Over the years I have been sent a multitude of weird and wonderful treatises on systems for forecasting the stock market, ranging from relative strength to astrology. Technical analysis does not intrigue me, and I ignore the occult. Kondratieff waves are about as metaphysical as I get, but for years I have been fascinated with the Fibonacci numbers and their possible application to the stock market in the Elliott Wave Theory. The recent market violence caused me to review the Fibonacci file.

Fibonacci was born in Italy in 1175. He was fascinated with numbers and must have been a mathematical genius. In 1202, he published a book, *Liber Abaci*, that introduced Arabic numerals to Europe. In this historic manuscript, Fibonacci created his mystic numbers by posing a problem.

> Someone placed a pair of rabbits in a certain place, enclosed on all sides by a wall, to find out how many pairs of rabbits will be born there in the course of one year, it being assumed that every month a pair of rabbits produces another pair, and that rabbits begin to bear young two months after their own birth. The answer is 1, 2, 3, 5, 8, 13, 21, 34, 55, 89, 144, 233.

Fibonacci went on to analyze these numbers and extend the series. The hundredth number in the sequence is 354,224,848,179,261,915,075. He found the sequence had many strange and intriguing characteristics. Among them are:

- The sum of any two consecutive numbers forms the next number in the sequence.
- The ratio of each number to the second below it is always 261.8 to 100, and the ratio to the next below is 161.8.

- Each number divided into the second above it goes twice with a remainder of the exact number below it.
- The square of a Fibonacci number less the square of the second number below it in the series is always a Fibonacci number.
- The sum of the squares of any consecutive series of Fibonacci numbers from 1 will always equal the last of the series chosen times the next higher number.

But most cosmic, if you divide a Fibonacci number by the next highest number, you will discover that it is precisely .618034 times as large as the number that follows. And .618034 is the magic number. The "golden proportion" of .618034 to 1 is the mathematic basis for the shape of the Parthenon, sunflowers, snail shells, Greek vases, the great spiral galaxies of outer space, and playing cards. It is the most pleasing shape, whether in rectangular or spiral form, in the universe.

The golden proportion has been and is everywhere. The Great Pyramid of Gizeh has an elevation to its base of 61.8 percent. The Egyptians used inches as the standard of measure, and the height of the Great Pyramid is 5,813 inches (5, 8, and 13 are Fibonacci numbers), and the circumference of a circle inscribing the pyramid is 36,524.2 inches. How could the Egyptians have known that the exact length of year is 365.242 days? The angle of the "Ascending Passage" in the Great Pyramid is 26° 18°. This pyramid is believed by many who are into the occult to be the residuary of the Divine Message of Revelation. The Revelation includes not only that of love and death but also of feast and famine. Sounds nuts, but such serious citizens as J. P. Morgan and Henry Ford, among others, were very big on pyramids and particularly the one at Gizeh because of that message.

The Greeks also were aware of .618034 and called it the "golden mean." They based much of their art and architecture on its dynamic symmetry, "whirling squares that seemed to vibrate with intense energy." They believed the navel was the golden mean of the body with golden proportions at the neck, eyes, legs, and arms. The secret was lost with the fall of Greece until Fibonacci discovered it again, and in the seventeenth century, Jakob Bernoulli transposed the golden rectangle into a golden spiral and linked it to nature.

Fibonacci numbers and both the golden rectangle and spiral are broadcast throughout nature. *Science* magazine has published several scholarly articles on the subject, and my summary is that the numbers are found in everything from daisy petals and sunflower spirals (55 counterclockwise and 89 clockwise) to phyllotaxis, which is the arrangement of leaves on the stalk of a plant. The golden spiral appears in horns, claws, teeth, shells, and even the web of a spider. Bacteria multiply at a Fibonacci sequence, and the examples go on and on as documented in these articles. The human body has five extremities, five fingers and five toes, and in music the octave has 13 keys with 8 white and 5 black. The musical chord that gives the greatest satisfaction is the major sixth, and the note E vibrates at a ratio of .625 to the note C. The ear itself is a golden spiral.

There are no really good explanations of why the sequence exists. One response is that God was a mathematician; others say it is all pure coincidence and the humbug of fevered minds. Some scientists argue that the Fibonacci sequence and the golden spiral are so widespread that they must be part of some recurring growth pattern. Others speculate that it is nature's way of building quantity without sacrificing quality.

As you would expect, attempts have been made to apply Fibonacci to the stock market, most notably by R. N. Elliott in the early 1930s. He seems to have worked from the wave patterns of light through a lens, which fall into a Fibonacci sequence of five waves up and three down. This cycle is then part of a supercycle, which also consists of five up and three down. In the 1960s, Hamilton Bolton and A. J. Frost of the *Bank Credit Analyst* wrote extensively on the Elliott Wave Theory. In any case, the Elliott Wave theorists have been saying for some time that the fourth supercycle wave ran from 1966 to 1982 and that U.S. equities are now in the fifth wave of the supercycle that will take prices to the mid-3000s on the Dow. A killer three-wave downer will follow. Maybe God is a technician.

Beware of Linear Thinkers: Chaos on the Upside

January 17, 1989

Chaos theory is the science of the global nature of systems, and it makes strong claims about the universal behavior of complexity. Systems, it says, are inherently turbulent, disorderly, and unstable and are extraordinarily difficult to forecast because they are not linear. Chaos is all about jagged fractal geometry and a world that displays a regular irregularity. It's very deep, heavy stuff that I can only fleetingly grasp, although I have pored over James Gleick's book *Chaos*, but intuitively it explains a lot that I have only vaguely sensed. Some even argue that this century's science will be remembered for three things: relativity, quantum mechanics, and chaos.

In the 1970s, scientists believed they could use massive computers to create a model that, with the right equations, would predict the weather. Weather forecasting would change from an art to a science. Anyway, what happened is a long story, but the massive effort failed miserably. In forecasting, tiny differences in input caused huge changes in output, a phenomenon called "sensitive dependence on initial conditions." In weather, this translates into what is now known as the Butterfly Effect, the notion that a random butterfly stirring the air today in Africa can transform storm systems next month in New York. As Gleick points out in his chapter on the Butterfly Effect, in science as in life, it is well known that a chain of events can have a point of crisis that could magnify small changes. Chaos theory says that such points are everywhere. The process of modeling flows on computers, even when the data are reasonably trustworthy and purely physical, as in weather forecasting, is incredibly fragile. Imagine how fragile stock market and economic modeling is. Chaos theory explains to me why no single indicator—not sentiment, not value—is infallible, why nothing always works.

Chaos theory says that, within systems, data and events form disorderly patterns. Some data patterns are orderly in space but disorderly in time; others, orderly in time but disorderly in space. Some are linear; some are fractal. But the system will almost always eventually confound those who try to forecast it as a linear progression. Thus, the "dynamic" asset allocators who last week sold stocks because their computers said they should, based on the last cycle's patterns, are naive. There are too many butterflies. To me, that approach is akin to navigating a sports car down a winding road at high speed by steering through the rearview mirror.

The market is only linear on a random basis. The asset allocators say interest rates must fall before stocks can rise, but the linkage may be just the opposite. As the stock market goes up or maybe even after it rises, the news gets better. The economy is healthy but not overheating. Last week, it was reported that retail sales were not as strong as expected in December. Automobile sales were a little sluggish in early January, and unemployment claims rose in late December. Meanwhile, inflation worries were assuaged as average hourly earnings rose at only a 3.6 percent annual rate in December. The growth in M2 continues to decelerate, and commodity prices are moderating.

As I sensed, the dollar is firm instead of weak, and there are some signs that interest rates may be in the process of peaking in the United States, Europe, and the United Kingdom. All these developments at the margin create a better environment for equities, and around the world stock markets are rallying. This makes life nerve-racking for those with large amounts of cash. After the run-up of the last month, global equity markets are a little extended, so a pullback would be natural before the next push. This is probably the most likely outcome, but there is perhaps one chance in three or four that instead the global equity system will stage a chaotic, disorderly blowout on the upside.

In any case, we may all be healthier if we turn off the computer. Just as a stock doesn't know or care that you own it, the market doesn't know you've written an equation for it.

How George Soros Makes Money: The Theory He Says Guides Him

July 5, 1994

A book with this title would be a best seller, because almost everyone agrees that George Soros is the best macro investor of modern times. There is no one else even close. In fact, you could say that Soros invented macro. Warren Buffett is a great stock picker, but that's different from what Soros does. It's ironic that although the investment hordes, obsessed with unraveling the mysteries of how to beat the market, react like lemmings to any Soros pronouncement, apocryphal or not, almost no one seems interested in what Soros says is the theory that has guided him, which he calls "reflexivity."

Reflexivity is for Soros the way the world works, and it applies not only to markets but also, he hints, to human history. Somehow I can't take it as seriously as he does, but that is probably because I don't fully understand the complexities of it, even though I have made a real effort. Soros is an intellectual, almost a philosopher, and I'm not. Even so, I think that even partially understanding his theory gives the investor a new framework with which to analyze investments.

Soros first discussed reflexivity in print in 1987 in his book *The Alchemy of Finance*, but not much attention was paid to the book or the theory, despite its intriguing subtitle: *Reading the Mind of the Market*. The book is being reissued in paperback version by John Wiley & Sons, but in the first version, the writing about reflexivity was, shall we say, dense. I never have been able to understand his "shoelace theory of history." In fact, reflexivity is still heavy going. If the publishers really want to sell some books, they should change the title to the one here, but I'm sure Soros wouldn't let them. I suspect he doesn't care at all about popular readership.

What he wants is for the intellectual elite to examine reflexivity critically and debate him on what he believes is an important new theory about the relationship between thinking and reality. Recently he said: "I am thrilled by the possibility that I may have reached a profound new insight, but I am also scared because such claims are usually made by insane people, and there are many more insane people in the world than there are people who have reached a profound new insight." And of course, the economists and philosophers are disdainful because he is in their view just an astute, instinctive trader who has made far too much money and now has come up with a theory to intellectualize those instincts. A couple of years ago, one wise guy even asked George to his face if reflexivity was about his reflexes. The guy went on to compare Soros to Michael Jordan, but Soros had no idea who Michael Jordan was.

Anyway, Soros in recent years has been complaining almost wistfully that his stock market pronouncements are taken too seriously but his decision-making process is ignored. He recently delivered a paper on reflexivity to the MIT Department of Economics in which he elaborates further on reflexivity and its application not only to markets but also to history and morality. This is a scholarly paper with references ranging from the Cretan philosopher Epimenides and the paradox of the liar to chaos theory and strange attractors. It has to be read, reread, thought about, and then applied to financial market analysis. Reflexivity is a way of thinking about the world, not a magic formula.

Soros rejects the conventional wisdom of efficient markets and modern portfolio theory that says markets discount the future and tend toward equilibrium. Instead, markets are inherently unstable and cannot possibly discount the future correctly, because they help shape it. "In certain circumstances," he says, "financial markets can affect the so-called fundamentals which they are supposed to reflect. When that happens markets enter into a state of disequilibrium and behave quite differently from what would be considered normal by the theory of efficient markets. Such boom/bust sequences do not arise very often, but when they do they can be very disruptive, exactly because they affect the fundamentals of the economy."

I am taking the liberty of discussing reflexivity as I understand it without Soros endorsing the effort or even saying if my explanation is valid. He is currently traveling in some dark, underprivileged part of the world.

Furthermore, to do justice to the theory, the MIT paper and *Alchemy* itself should be studied in their entirety. Reflexivity is far too complex and profound a theory to be summarized.

But let me try. Reflexivity, Soros says in the MIT paper, is a two-way feedback mechanism in which reality helps shape the participants' thinking and the participants' thinking helps shape reality in an unending process; thinking and reality may come to approach each other but can never become identical. Full knowledge implies a correspondence between statements and facts, thoughts and reality, which is not possible.

The key is the lack of correspondence, the inherent divergence between the participants' views and the actual state of affairs. It is this divergence, the "participant's bias," that provides the clue to understanding the course of events. Put another way, reflexivity is the feedback between investors and the impact of their perceptions and actions on the market and on each other. Soros says that "in certain cases, the participant's bias can change the fundamentals which are supposed to determine market prices."

Examples that Soros cites of this feedback at work are the conglomerate boom and bust of the late 1960s and the same phenomenon in real estate investment trusts in the early 1970s. In both cases, companies used excessive investor expectations to issue new stock at inflated prices to make acquisitions, and the resulting increase in earnings per share went a long way to validate those excessive expectations. The participant's bias involved an actual fallacy: the growth in earnings per share was treated as if it were independent of equity leveraging. In reflexivity, the process is initially self-reinforcing but is bound to become unsustainable in the long run—thus, its boom/bust cycle. In an investment environment in which many of the dominant players are trend-following, momentum investors, it seems to me that reflexivity may be particularly potent.

In the MIT paper, Soros also cites an example where no such fallacy is involved: "For instance, in a freely fluctuating currency market, a change in exchange rates has the capacity to affect the so-called fundamentals which are supposed to determine exchange rates, such as the rate of inflation in the countries concerned; so that any divergence from theoretical equilibrium has the capacity to validate itself. This self-validating capacity encourages trend-following speculation, and trend-following speculation generates divergences from whatever may be considered the theoretical equilibrium. The circular reasoning is complete. The outcome is that freely fluctuating currency markets tend to promote excessive fluctuations, and trend-following speculation tends to be justified."

It seems to me that this is what is happening today. The financial markets have no special insight into inflation or the pace of the recovery in 1995; they are not discounting the future—instead, they may be causing it. The weak dollar and rising interest rates will have definite effects on the real economies of the United States, Europe, and Japan. Reflexivity is a prism to understand and evaluate this circular effect. Soros says that "reflexivity occurs only intermittently." In fact, this is what makes it so significant. He writes that he has always been fascinated by booms and busts and that some of his greatest financial coups have come from identifying the inflection points of these "far-from-equilibrium conditions." However, I don't find where he relates how reflexivity sharpens his exquisite timing.

I haven't seen the new edition of the book, but I gather it isn't much different from the first one. Anyway, I recommend getting hold of the MIT speech and seeing what you can make of it. As I said at the beginning, Soros thinks reflexivity is the way the world works, and because no one has been as good as he has been in figuring out how the world works, you almost have to take his theory, dense as it is, very seriously.

The Horse Whisperers

October 28, 1996

I believe that when you come right down to it, there are maybe half a dozen "great" investors in the world, a number of "good" investors, and a multitude of what you might call "journeymen." The great ones are the superstars who consistently put up the big numbers, the good ones generally outperform and have long-term records above the indexes—which is no mean feat—and although the journeymen will have an occasional year when they light up the night sky, in the long run they are average performers. In other words, there are only a few fixed planets in the investment firmament but many shooting stars.

There is a lot of cynicism around about investment performance. A recent study by a "respected" consulting firm concluded that there was no correlation between the recent past performance of an investment manager and forthcoming future performance. In fact, the study claims, if you invest with a manager who has been in the top quintile for the last three years, the odds are you'll find that manager mired somewhere in the two bottom quintiles in the next three years. Reversion to the mean, it's called.

This doesn't mean investment journeymen are incompetent or bad people. In fact, they are usually bright, articulate, often charming, well dressed, and have a plausible line of investment patter. And you don't need to feel sorry for them. One of the ironies of the business is that professional investors who are unable to consistently beat their benchmark index are highly paid, but that's another story.

As for the superstars, there are conflicting views on the authenticity of their magic. I can't remember who, but someone made an imaginative but disparaging comparison between superstar investors and the finalists in a hypothetical national coin-flipping contest. It went like this. Suppose there were 250 million entrants in the All-America Coin Flip Tournament, and everyone put up $10 to enter, winner-take-all—with one flip-off each week to allow the drama to build. After about six months, there would be 32 contestants left in the tournament, each one of whom would have made 24 right calls and would have turned $10 into about $20 million if my math is right (it probably isn't).

At this point things would go crazy. Magazines would run features on the rags-to-riches stories of some of the contestants, and others would make appearances on talk shows at $50,000 a crack describing their unique flipping skills, ability to will a coin to reverse in midair, and their mystic reflexive vision as it was about to land. Several would be rushing out books with titles like *How to Make Millions Flipping* and *Why Jesus Helps Me Make Good Calls*. Probably by then Revlon and one of the contestants would be marketing a special fingernail enamel for better flipping.

Of course, shortly thereafter, bitter business school professors who had lost in the early rounds would be writing articles about efficient coin flipping, zero-sum games, and how the contest really was a random walk, and the contestants would be arguing that if it can't be done, how come there are 32 of us who have done it? In the weeks before the round of 16, the winners would be much in demand by the opposite sex, and you can imagine the excitement that would exist by the quarterfinals when winners would be checking out houses in Southampton and Aspen.

As I remember it, the point of this somewhat far-fetched analogy was that the great investment managers were similar to the finalists in the national coin-flipping contest. In other words, they were just consistently lucky in what was basically a random series of calls. How else, the author argued, can you explain the differences in performance when all the players are so similar?

The so-called great investors don't work any harder and don't have bigger staffs, higher SAT scores, or any other unique characteristic. The journeymen go to the same meetings, talk to the same analysts, and are generally just as intense, but man, boy, or woman, they just can't consistently or predictably outperform the S&P 500. It's not like Coke, where there is some secret 100-year-old formula that was invented by a half-mad chemist sealed in a safe-deposit box that is guarded night and day. There is no formula. The great ones, say the skeptics, aren't really great; they are just plain lucky.

I have a different theory. The great ones are like the horse whisperers of yore. On one of those interminable flights to Tokyo, I read this new novel, *The Horse Whisperer*, by Nicholas Evans.★ It's currently being sold at supermarket checkout counters and obviously was written for the soccer moms of America who yearn for romance. It's not great literature by any means, but it successfully consumed half of my flight to Tokyo.

The Horse Whisperer is like another version of the erogenous tearjerker, *The Bridges of Madison County*. It has the same tried-and-true formula: Two middle-aged married people from completely different backgrounds meet, feel this magnetic attraction, resist it because they are good people, finally succumb (described in erotic detail), and

---

★Nicholas Evans, *The Horse Whisperer* (New York: Delacorte Press, Bantam Doubleday Dell Publishing Group, 1995).

after an idyllic interlude of sensuality and communication, it ends tragically, bringing moisture to the eyes of soccer moms. In this book, the protagonists are a sophisticated English magazine editor from New York and a cowboy from Montana who is very, very good with horses and smells like unscented soap, leather saddles, and May mornings.

You see, throughout the ages as long as men have tried to tame horses so they could ride them, there has been a premium on strong, fast horses. The best horses, the strong, fast ones, tend to be wild, but always there have been few men who could soothe and saddle even the wildest horse. No one knew how they did it, and they would never explain it—maybe they couldn't. Did they have the bleached bones of frogs plucked from some moonlit stream in their back pockets, or was it a gift from God the way certain men can hit a baseball? Some who saw them work said it was magic; others said they were shamans and charlatans at best and witches at worst. Probably a few were burned at the stake in the Middle Ages.

In America there was an Irishman named Lynch who lived in Colorado and who could calm almost any horse. There was a wild, mean stallion named Lightning who loved to buck men off and then stomp them. His owner took him to country fairs, and if you paid a dollar you could win $500 if you mounted him and stayed on for one minute. Nobody ever could, but then one day Lynch went up to the horse talking softly, and Lightning seemed to listen, and then he put his hands on Lightning, all the time whispering in his ear, and then very slowly he climbed on and rode Lightning around the ring as the crowd cheered.

Later, there was John Rarey from Groveport, who was said to be the best in the world. In 1858 Queen Victoria sent for him to calm her favorite horse, who had gone crazy, and he whispered for a long time in the horse's ear as the queen watched and the horse nuzzled him and all the madness was gone. Then the queen could ride her wonderful, powerful horse again.

In England at that time, the fastest racehorse was a stallion named Cruiser, but he was so mean and wild that by the time Rarey became involved, no jockey could ride him. He had been fitted with an eight-pound iron muzzle to keep him from killing stable boys. Rarey went into Cruiser's stall, where no one else could go, and shut the door. Three hours later he emerged leading Cruiser without his iron muzzle "gentle as a lamb." The cowboy from Montana in the book is a "horse whisperer," too.

So my theory about the great money managers is that they are like horse whisperers. I don't believe for a second they are just the random winners of the national coin-flipping contest. Instead, they must have some special magic with the markets that enables them almost intuitively to do the right thing, buy the right stock, far more often than ordinary investors. They have what Churchill called the "seeing eye . . . that deep original instinct which peers through the surface of words and things—the vision which sees dimly but surely the other side of the brick wall or which follows the hunt to fields before the throng. Against this, industry, learning, scholarship, reputation, an ordered mind, plenty of pluck count for less than nothing."

Like the horse whisperer, they can tame the wild, dangerous market beast that can kill you and get the best ride of all. Does that mean that they will never have a bad year, never get bucked off? Of course not. Even they can't ride every horse, every day. But they are consistently successful.

How do they do it? Each one does it differently, and the market whisperers I know have no common characteristic, no similar style, except that they are intensely obsessed. They understand and love the market just as the horse whisperers understand and love horses. They have an intuitive sense. The active market whisperers I know are named Buffett, Cooperman, Druckenmiller, Robertson, Soros, Bacon, Marvin, Sarofim, and Day.

There are also some other promising horse whisperers around that seem to have a way with stocks and markets, but they haven't stood the test of time yet.

Incidentally, all the horse whisperer stuff is pure fiction.

Mr. Market Is a Manic-Depressive

November 1, 1999

I t was Benjamin Graham, the patron saint of value investors but unfamiliar to most of the *Dow 36,000* and Internet crowd, who advanced the proposition that living with the stock market was like having a manic-depressive partner. After October's mood swings, I have to respect Mr. Graham's description.

Clinically, the term *manic-depressive* pertains to an individual "having a mental disorder marked by cyclothymic manifestations of excitation and depression." In other words, the guy has extreme mood swings. Graham's theory was that although Mr. Market is a pleasant fellow who can have long periods of relatively sane behavior, underneath he is a functioning manic-depressive. Graham's theory was that when Mr. Market is giddy, euphoric, infatuated with the future, and willing to pay crazy prices for your shares, you sell to him. On the other hand, when he is tortured by gloom and despair and wants out at any price, you buy.

Obviously, investment life its own self is not that simple, but after observing Mr. Market's dementia for lo these many years, it strikes me that right now he is not just a good old manic-depressive on a high, but one whose illness verges on the psychotic. I think Mr. Market is on drugs, maybe even heroin. There is some serious craziness going on.

I went to a dinner last week put on by one of Warren Buffett's companies, and the great man answered questions with his legendary homespun charm. He said what he has said before, which goes something like this: "The wonderful thing about being a rational investor is that you are the batter in a game in which there are no called strikes. Day after day the pitches keep coming, but you don't have to swing. They

155

throw you XYZ at 60, but you let it go by because it's not juicy enough or you don't understand it. As long as you are patient, you can just stand there and wait for the perfect fat pitch. You may not hit even that one out of the park, but the odds are with you. It may get boring standing there with the bat on your shoulder day after day, and boredom limits the capacity of many investment managers, but it's the intelligent way to invest."

I thought about it afterwards, and the problem is that Buffett's game is not the game we professional investors are in. We have to play and swing every day because we are pitted against some benchmark, and the benchmark relentlessly competes every day. And against the benchmark, holding cash is not the same thing as standing there with the bat on your shoulder. You are swinging when you have cash, since it isn't in the index.

So even though this huge, wild, psychotic manic-depressive that is sniffing heroin scares the hell out of me, here are my views of the world economic environment (many of which are not shared by our economists):

- The base rate of inflation is about 1.5 percent in America, and there will be a whiff of deflation in the next recession.
- There is very little pricing power anywhere, and the Internet is disinflationary for the world.
- The U.S. economy is slowing and may even have a recession next year.
- Reported profits are overstated and will prove to be very disappointing in the quarters to come, because of low top-line growth and margin pressure.
- The European economies will continue to improve.
- Japan's economy will surprise next year by being stronger than expected.
- The developing economies will continue to recover.
- A severe U.S. recession or a financial accident would have serious ripple effects on the world economy.

As for the investment environment, it seems to me that the data released last week do set the stage for a rally in both stocks and bonds between now and year-end. My conclusions (and again, these are not the firm's official views as reflected in *The Macro Navigator*):

- U.S. bonds are going to be good, both for now and long term.
- Central bank rate hikes in the United States and Europe will be bullish for bonds.
- I want to be very underweight U.S. equities in a global portfolio, because although the S&P 500, the Dow, and technology may go higher, they are grossly overpriced and very dangerous.
- Internet stocks and the tech IPO market are huge bubbles that will end with massive wealth destruction.
- I would be overweight equities in Europe but underweight U.K. stocks.
- I am bullish on the euro.

- I am 30–40 percent overweight Japanese equities.
- I am very overweight Hong Kong and Singapore.
- I expect emerging market equities and debt to run into the new year.
- It is well to remember the nature of the maniac we are dealing with.

As for the IPO market, our Technology Research Team points out that of the 1,200-plus technology IPOs since the debut of the personal computer in 1980, a mere 5 percent have created 86 percent of the wealth. The 241 major Internet stocks have a combined value of $549 billion, with sales of only $24 billion and a combined loss of $7 billion. You have to kiss a lot of frogs before you find a handsome prince, which is why a whole hedge fund industry has sprung up that does nothing but short IPOs after they have popped.

The Internet bulls argue that although many Internet companies may flop, the winners will go up so much from here that the investor will still be far ahead. They may be right, but Tony Perkins's recent *Red Herring* letter points out that in the early 1980s, dozens of companies in the PC industry went public with soaring prices, only to see their prices crash in the great technology bust of 1983. And the bull market in tech didn't resume again until 1991.

Although the unit growth of PCs continued to compound at an annual rate greater than 25 percent for over a decade, only one company founded during the early PC boom, Apple Computer, survives today. Dell and Compaq, the two present major PC hardware companies, emerged only after the PC bubble had burst. Microsoft didn't go public until 1986. The nature of technology is "creative destruction."

As Buffett said, "If you are in a poker game and after half an hour you don't know who the patsy is, *you're the patsy.*"

Section 2D:
Alternative Investments

Filthy Lucre

March 28, 1989

Last week, a very rich, elegant man asked me to design a global portfolio for his family, using all the various real and financial asset alternatives, with the dollar as the currency of reference. His objective is to enhance the family's fortune at least four percentage points a year above inflation, which incidentally is no modest goal, since it means his real wealth doubles in 18 years. He added that he is interested in net returns after carrying costs and that although he is a long-term investor, risk in terms of both volatility and liquidity should be considered.

Is not art a better investment than real estate? he asked. What about venture capital and real estate in modern times? He has a bias toward holding some gold as insurance, he said, but what would be the opportunity cost? His questions, many of which I couldn't answer, sent me back to our database, and the table here shows the returns I came up with for the various asset categories in modern, post–World War II times. I excluded junk bonds and leveraged buyout funds because of lack of history. All return numbers are approximate orders of magnitude. For volatility and liquidity, 10 is best and 1 is worst. (Standard deviations were the benchmarks for volatility, but liquidity is a pure judgment call.) Transaction and market impact costs (10 is the cheapest, and 1 the most expensive) are not scientific either but attempt to take into account the expense of a $10 million commitment.

In piecing together the various returns, I could find no source that collects comprehensive, comparable data. The best single reference is *World Wealth: Market Values and Returns*, by Ibbotson, Siegel, and Love, but their statistics run only from 1960 to 1984 and do not include venture capital, timberland, emerging markets, or art. I also used data collected by Sprinkel and Genetski. The venture capital number came originally from General Electric and Venrock, adjusted to represent the approximate return to the investor. The figure for emerging markets equities is an index of returns from developing country markets before they are included in a hypothetical Morgan Stanley Capital International (MSCI) world index. In other words, Japan was an emerging market in the 1950s, as was Singapore in the early 1970s.

As for art, Jim Grant's *Interest Rate Observer*, that most literate, bearish, and provocative publication, pointed me toward an article in *Public Interest* entitled "Is Art Such a Good Investment?" by Bruno Frey and Werner Pommerehne. The writers argue that

Average Annual Total Returns in "Modern Times"

	Annual Return	Volatility	Liquidity	Transaction Cost
Short-term investments (Treasury bills, commercial paper)	5.6%	10	10	10
Major equities	10.1	4	7	7
Secondary equities (OTC and emerging growth)	11.8	3	5	5
Foreign equities	10.9	4	6	6
Emerging markets equities	16.0	3	2	1
U.S Government bonds	6.6	5	9	9
Corporate bonds	6.0	4	8	8
Foreign Bonds	7.7	4	7	8
Venture capital	19.0	1	1	10
Timberland	8.5	4	2	4
Residential real estate	8.1	9	3	3
Commercial properties	7.7	8	4	5
Farmland	9.4	4	2	2
Art	9.0	5	5	1
Gold	7.0	2	9	9
Inflation	4.0			

Certain asset return measuring periods do not overlap exactly.
SOURCE: Morgan Stanley Research.

collecting art is not as good an investment as buying bonds or stocks and that the prices of paintings are driven by random swings in fashion that cannot be predicted, even by experts. The piece is scholarly, although a little shrill, and it concludes that "predictions of high profits in the market for art—particularly for paintings—are mistaken."

The authors constructed an index of profits on paintings from 1950 to 1987, which produces a real rate of return of 1.6 percent annually. This is slightly higher than the 1.4 percent per annum real return achieved from 1635 to 1950. Their data (much of which is derived from Gerald Reitlinger's *The Economics of Taste*) are based on linked 20-year holding periods but take into account transaction costs of 10 percent at both ends. None of the other asset returns considers cost of acquisition or market impact. At the same time, the art index does not allow for the expenses of preserving the painting's value, such as temperature control and insurance. The writers point out that in the last decade art thefts have tripled but only 5 percent of stolen paintings are recovered. They also discovered that the returns are more volatile.

The Bull Market in Art: Mania or Magnificent Obsession?

March 22, 1988

I try to monitor the art market as an investment category. Since I am not an art lover or into collecting, I like to think my view is that of a dispassionate philistine, perhaps with a jaundiced eye. The art market presents a fascinating valuation dilemma, as, unlike any other wealth category except raw land, it has no intrinsic value or return benchmarks, and prices are driven by passion and fetish. Thus, the judgment of cheap or dear is uniquely difficult and intuitive.

For 30 years, art has been in a bull market that has had pauses, most notably in the early 1970s, but no major corrections. Index prices rose around 10 percent a year in the 1970s, 12 to 13 percent annually in the first half of the 1980s, but have surged in the last couple of years with a gain of 26 percent posted by the Sotheby's Index in 1987, as shown in the accompanying table. Other collectibles, with the exception of English and American furniture, have not been kissed as passionately by the bull. Continental and Chinese ceramics have been appreciating about 5 percent a year and old silver by about 10 percent.

The October stock market unpleasantness has had no perceptible effect on the market for blue-chip art. A few days after the crash, a Van Gogh sold at auction for a record $54 million, or well above the previous high of $36 million, also for a Van Gogh, six months earlier. Incidentally, that price was three times the old record, which gives you an idea of the escalation that has occurred in great paintings. In fact, there has been nothing like it in collectibles since a bunch of rich Dutchmen went stark raving

Sotheby's Art Index

Index Sectors	One-Year Change	Two-Year Change	Five-Year Change	Average Annual Change
Old Masters paintings	+13.4%	+28.6%	+82.0%	+12.7%
Nineteenth-Century European paintings	+15.8	+29.7	+75.5	+11.9
Impressionist & post-impressionist art	+47.6	+90.3	+170.8	+22.0
Modern paintings (1900–1950)	+47.9	+108.0	+209.0	+25.3
Contemporary art (1984 onward)	+10.5	+22.5	+78.1	+12.2
American paintings (1800–pre-World War II)	+24.8	+30.6	+93.6	+14.1
Aggregate index	+26.3	+49.4	+103.2	+15.5

SOURCE: Sotheby's.

mad over tulip bulbs in the seventeenth century. So far in 1988, new highs have been set for premier pictures by Degas, Picasso, and numerous American painters.

Demand and prices, however, have ebbed for secondary work, including lesser pictures by the great artists. At the same record-setting January auction, secondary pictures by Degas and Picasso either sold within estimate or remained unsold. New York dealers characterize the present market as "concentrated" and "lacking depth." The emergence of a two-tier, thin market reminds me of the signs I didn't pay attention to last summer in the stock market.

I am dazzled by the raw hubris of art market participants. No one admits to ever having made a bad buy. The dealers all seem to believe, as one put it, that "you make your living from buying and selling, but you make your fortune from not selling." Art is bought by individuals and corporations for its beauty but also for ego, because name pictures are the most striking and stylish tokens of wealth and status in the world. There's no scarcity of yachts and jets, but there are only a few Van Goghs and Renoirs. Art is acquired by the "power" collectors with new money, because nothing makes one respectable faster, but also because they are convinced they can't lose with good art and it's just a question of how much and how fast specific pictures appreciate.

In the last few years, Japanese buying has become the driving force in certain art markets. Registered imports of art into Japan rose 41 percent in 1986 over 1985 and in 1987 soared 85 percent over 1986. The Japanese always work through their own dealers and have very specific taste, almost never buying anything painted before 1870. They like impressionist, post-impressionist, and modern art done between 1900 and 1950. It is estimated they have acquired about 40 percent of the impressionist pictures sold at auction and from private collectors in the last two years. Japanese corporations and businessmen buy art for their offices, not their homes. Yasuda Insurance purchased Van Gogh's *Sunflowers* for its corporate museum, and it is said the current holder of the world price record, *Irises*, hangs on the office wall of a certain chairman in Tokyo. But the Japanese also are acquisitive. Mr. Seijiro Matsuoka, a property tycoon who presumably knows something about manias, says that once he has a beautiful picture, he loses interest. "I put them away in my storehouse."

The bull market in art has been stimulated by the dealers and auction houses who, with champagne and culture, fatten the innocents for the slaughter. Last November a famous Japanese dealer, Ikkan Sanada, brought 18 wealthy young Japanese entrepreneurs to the United States for an educational and buying tour. Most of the "beginner collectors," as he calls them, did not speak English, but at a subsequent auction of impressionist and modern art, Mr. Sanada's clients swept up 48 percent of the art for sale and 5 of the 10 most expensive pieces.

Some of the inflation in art prices has also been caused by museums attempting to enrich their collections by deliberately exaggerating, sometimes by threefold, the value of art owned by prospective donors so they could claim a larger tax deduction. The scandal involving the Getty museum's antiquities curator focused attention on this abuse.

As I pointed out in a previous piece, the history of art prices is one of changing styles and extreme price swings. For example, great British eighteenth-century portrait painters like Reynolds, Romney, and Gainsborough worked for the equivalent of $100,000 a picture. But a generation later, after the death of the subjects and the painters, no one wanted to pay much for pictures of someone else's overweight ancestors, so prices fell to 10 percent of what they had been. Then, in the first third of the twentieth century, with a flamboyant dealer, Joseph Duveen, cultivating the market, prices for eighteenth-century portraits soared to $4–7 million in current terms, mostly because new American millionaires wanted ancestors to go with their baronial mansions.

Portrait prices held up well in the early 1930s, despite the Depression. Then, at a Christie's auction in 1934, a Romney attracted no real buyers and sold for one-10th of what had been paid for it five years earlier. Abruptly, the psychology of the market changed, and the prices of all types of art collapsed. By the 1940s, most eighteenth-century portraits were selling for 5 percent of their 1920 highs, and Duveen was knocked to the sidewalk in front of Claridge's and scratched by two angry American "collectors." Incidentally, the present art boom has neglected English portraits, and, although their prices have risen, most have never reached their 1920 highs even in depreciated present dollars.

This pattern is not the exception. Western art, which was very hot in the 1970s when everyone in the Southwest was oil-rich and wanted a remembrance of their mythical cowboy past, now sells for 20 percent of what it did a decade ago. Isn't it possible that if the Japanese and the new breed of LBO-rich suffer diminishment of liquidity, the same thing could happen someday to the impressionists and moderns? The Japanese favor bright, voluptuous art. Some future generation of buyers may have very different tastes.

Magnificent obsession or mania? Looks like the latter to me.

Jewelry Is a Girl's Best Friend

June 18, 1990

Shown here is our wealth model, with arrows indicating the direction of changes since it was last published, February 12. At that time, because of the steep decline in long-term financial asset prices that occurred in January, I was considerably less cautious on U.S. and European equities than I am today. Other than farmland and emerging growth stocks, there is not much I want to buy aggressively. With a few exceptions, almost every category of wealth over the last five years has appreciated about twice as fast as its total return in "modem times," and I am convinced the central and powerful tendency over the long run is for returns to gravitate back toward the mean.

One exception to these excesses is antique jewelry, which I have upgraded a little frivolously and nervously to "buy." Frivolously in the sense that we have not been able to develop much hard data on the appreciation rate of jewelry; nervously because it's probably going to cost me some money at home with the madam. I focused on jewelry because recently the patriarch of a very wealthy Hong Kong Chinese family told me of the difficulties of preserving wealth in Asia over a century of wars, depressions, inflations, and revolutions. He said that, in his opinion, quality jewelry was as good a storehouse of value, a disaster hedge for wealth, as anything he knew, and in fact was better than gold.

He said that when the Japanese took Hong Kong in 1941, his family was transformed overnight from rich to virtually starving. With the occupation, the British economic system disappeared, and all bank deposits were frozen. The local people believed that the Japanese, with their military dominance and Greater Asian Co-Prosperity Sphere, would rule for the foreseeable future. The family owned large amounts of rental real estate in Hong Kong, but the tenants simply stopped paying rent. The family's overseas assets were intact, but there was no way of getting earnings from them. All of their sources of income dried up as the local economy reverted to barter.

As it turned out, the family survived in the early part of the war by selling its jewelry. Jewelry alone still had great purchasing power value because some Chinese girlfriends of the Japanese military desired it: they were given money and goods by the Japanese, and the Japanese bought jewelry to gain their favor. "Dumb jewels often, in their silent kind / More than quick words, do move a woman's mind," wrote Shakespeare. Neither the Japanese soldiers nor their girlfriends cared much for gold. It wasn't pretty enough.

Throughout history, conquering armies have desired sex from the women of the occupied country and some of these women have wanted jewelry, the old man said, so what happened was not unique to Hong Kong. Jewelry has also been used throughout history to beautify and to display one's rank and wealth. Jewelry also works as wealth in an environment of runaway inflation. Our studies show that gold and silver are the best inflation hedges, and since they are so much a part of jewelry, the record indicates jewelry at least maintains purchasing power during inflationary episodes. This was certainly the case in the early 1910s and in Germany during the Weimar Republic.

The international auction houses report that antique jewelry prices today are high and stable. Both Sotheby's and Christie's held auctions at St. Moritz in Switzerland this winter, and unique pieces uniformly exceeded reserve prices. Diamonds and "big rock jewelry," however, did not sell particularly well. In April, an estate auction of rings, necklaces, clips, and brooches owned by film star Paulette Goddard (who was an avid collector) exceeded estimates by 50 percent. A collection of men's formal dress jewelry, a gift from Goddard to her husband, novelist Erich Maria Remarque, was snapped up.

We haven't had much luck finding data to document the performance record of what might be called collectible jewelry. One expert described collectible antique jewelry as items that are pre-1950s; another said it had to be at least from the 1930s. Signed pieces by recognized designers, such as Art Deco pieces designed by Cartier, sell at a premium, and costume jewelry is also collectible. "The more a piece is a work of art, the better," one expert remarked. Modern jewelry must be "designed" and "in fashion" to offer value. There is no evidence as yet of Japanese buying. Bear in mind that diamonds as raw stones are not good investments, although a unique, mounted stone may be a superb investment.

In April, The Moon of Baroda, a 24-carat diamond, sold for $297,000 at Christie's. The Moon of Baroda dates back to the Gaekwads of Baroda, a family of India in the fifteenth century, and it probably decorated some magnificent décolletages, royal and otherwise, over the centuries. Marilyn Monroe used it to promote the film *Gentlemen Prefer Blondes*, in which she sang "Diamonds Are a Girl's Best Friend"—which was bad advice. All that "diamonds are forever" stuff is hype, and there is not now and never has been a shortage of diamonds. Jewelry is a girl's best friend.

Morgan Stanley Asset Allocation Model—The Works (dollar based)

Overvalued		Fairly Priced	Undervalued	
Sell	Underweight	Neutral Weight	Overweight	Buy
Japanese stocks	Industrial commodities	Silver	Real estate (Southwestern U.S.)	U.S. farmland
Real estate (Northeastern U.S.)	Antique furniture	Oil and gas properties		Antique jewelry →
	Venture capital	U.S. timberland	East Asian stocks	U.S. small growth stocks →
Modern Art	Equity index funds	U.K. Gilts	U.S. growth stocks	
Japanese real estate	Old Masters	U.S. intermediate bonds	U.S. long bond	
Impressionist art	LBO funds	Tax-exempt bonds	German bonds ←	
Baseball cards	Japanese bonds ←	Agricultural commodities	Cash →	
Trophy hotels	European stocks ←	U.S. cyclical Stocks		
	European bonds ←	Gold		
	German stocks ←	Junk bonds		
	Real estate ← (Southern & Western U.S.)	Diamonds		
		Real estate (Midwestern U.S.) ←		

FORMAT: Courtesy of Stratford Advisory Group Inc.

Section 2E:
Market Predictions

First Class on the *Titanic*

March 10, 1980

The world these days seems unusually confusing, and once again, as American financial markets fall, a shrill note of calamity and despair is heard. We think we recognize the dangers that range from a financial panic to an oil crisis and slump-flation, and we anticipate no miracle cures from policy announcements. The longer we blunder along, the greater the risk of a major financial or industrial calamity.

On the other hand, the price mechanism and the ebb and flow of the business cycle still eventually function despite a thick overlay of inflation. We expect the soaring cost of money to shortly tip our hyperextended economy into recession. Interest rates and inflation are cresting and will decline but only to levels that are historically still very high. We think the most likely case is for a stagnant, inflation-plagued economy that experiences several quarters of weakness later this year and then has a desultory recovery in 1981. Inflation and subdued growth are the two dominant characteristics of the economies of the United States and other developed nations, and it is difficult to predict when or exactly how stagflation will end. Like a person with a persistent, bad cold that has dragged on, you know eventually he will get better either because the cold gradually disappears or he is hospitalized with pneumonia. The odds still favor the former resolution.

For an owner of capital in an unstable, inflation-prone world, there is no place to hide for long. Short-term investments can shelter capital for a while from the ravages of inflation and the violence of volatile markets, but by definition one has to invest long to enhance the purchasing power of capital. Our studies conclude that American equities are still the investment medium likely to provide the best chance of capital enhancement under differing scenarios. They also are virtually the only real asset that can still be purchased at 1970 prices. The difficulty is that 17 percent short-term money is tough to compete with, and who knows what price/earnings ratio stocks should sell at in the face of such rates.

We see ourselves as travelers forced to get from here to a better but distant there in order to enhance our capital. To do so we must sail on the new *Titanic*, and the ocean is full of storms and icebergs. Unfortunately, those at the helm are indecisive Keynesians, and their vision and resolution are clouded by politics. The odds are we will make the journey without a shipwreck. However, since we are embarking on an uncertain voyage, why not go first class.

There are those who will argue that stock selection in this environment is akin to rearrangement of the seating at the captain's table on the old *Titanic*. Our sector valuation studies clearly suggest that first-class quality represents the best intrinsic value in the current market structure. We continue to recommend overweighted positions in energy, oil service, capital goods, technological growth, and smaller, emerging growth companies. We are now inclined to further broaden our emphasis to include high-quality defensive growth companies such as drugs, hospital supply, and consumer product names with total return potential of 18 to 20 percent. Interest-sensitive stocks also are becoming attractive. Always we want to own the best companies not only because they will perform superbly if we make it but also because they are the strongest swimmers in case of disaster.

"It's a Bull Market, You Know . . ."

October 11, 1982

After the stunning surge in stock prices last week, once again the natural reaction is to do some selling, to cut back positions. I continue to feel this tendency should be resisted and that it is too soon to sell anything. I say this for a couple of reasons. First, wanting to do some selling now is the sensible, easy thing to do, and almost always in the stock market the easy, sensible reaction is wrong. The hard thing in this market is going to be to sit tight and not sell the big, boring, quality stocks too soon.

Second, everyone thinks it's right to do some selling, so it must be wrong. Merrill Lynch reports that its public customers continue to be heavy net sellers and short sellers, and every businessman with whom I talked last week told me how ridiculous the surge in stock prices was, considering how lousy business conditions are. Stocks will be a sale when everyone understands why they are going up and clamors to buy them because business is improving, inflation is down, and interest rates have declined. Of course, in the meantime, there will be corrections, but for the time being my judgment is that trying to play them will not be fruitful activity. It will be easy to sell but very hard to buy back at prices sufficiently lower to make the trade worthwhile. The market will beat the tendency to sell out of people as it goes up, until finally everyone is conditioned not to sell. Then there will be a deep correction.

I have frequently mentioned Jesse Livermore's *Reminiscences of a Stock Operator* in the past, and Dennis Lynch reminded me of it again last week. In the book, there is a wise old speculator named Partridge in the office whom the other traders call the Old Turkey. Often a trader would approach the Old Turkey for advice because he is so successful. The trader would explain the situation in detail and ask whether to buy

or sell. At this particular time, the Old Turkey's answer was always the same no matter what the question. He would cock his head to one side and say, "You know, it's a
bull market," as though he were "giving the man a priceless talisman wrapped up in
a million-dollar accident insurance policy." Livermore says it took a long time for him
to understand the Old Turkey's meaning and relates an incident:

> Well, Elmer made for the old man and, without a word of apology to John
> Fanning, told Turkey, "Mr. Partridge, I have just sold my Climax Motors. My
> people say the market is entitled to a reaction and that I'll be able to buy it
> back cheaper. So you'd better do likewise. That is, if you've still got yours."
>
> Elmer looked suspiciously at the man to whom he had given the origi-
> nal tip to buy. The amateur, or gratuitous, tipster always thinks he owns the
> receiver of his tip body and soul, even before he knows how the tip is going to
> turn out.
>
> "Yes, Mr. Harwood, I still have it. Of course!" said Turkey gratefully. It was
> nice of Elmer to think of the old chap.
>
> "Well, now is the time to take your profit and get in again on the next
> dip," said Elmer, as if he had just made out the deposit slip for the old man.
> Failing to perceive enthusiastic gratitude in the beneficiary's face, Elmer went
> on: "I have just sold every share I owned!"
>
> From his voice and manner you would have conservatively estimated it at
> ten thousand shares.
>
> But Mr. Partridge shook his head regretfully and whined, "No! No! I can't
> do that!"
>
> "What?" yelled Elmer.
>
> "I simply can't!" said Mr. Partridge. He was in great trouble.
>
> "Didn't I give you the tip to buy it?"
>
> "You did, Mr. Harwood, and I am very grateful to you. Indeed, I am, sir.
> But—"
>
> "Hold on! Let me talk! And didn't that stock go up seven points in ten
> days? Didn't it?"
>
> "It did, and I am much obliged to you, my dear boy. But I couldn't think
> of selling that stock."
>
> "You couldn't?" asked Elmer, beginning to look doubtful himself. It is a
> habit with most tip givers to be tip takers.
>
> "No, I couldn't."
>
> "Why not?" And Elmer drew nearer.
>
> "Why, this is a bull market!" The old feller said it as though he had given a
> long and detailed explanation.
>
> "That's all right," said Elmer, looking angry because of his disappointment.
> "I know this is a bull market as well as you do. But you'd better slip them that
> stock of yours and buy it back on the reaction. You might as well reduce the
> cost to yourself."

"My dear boy," said old Partridge, in great distress—"my dear boy, if I sold that stock now I'd lose my position, and then where would I be?"

Elmer Harwood threw up his hands, shook his head and walked over to me to get sympathy: "Can you beat it?" he asked me in a stage whisper. "I ask you!"

I didn't say anything. So he went on: "I give him a tip on Climax Motors. He buys five hundred shares. He's got seven points' profit and I advise him to get out and buy 'em back on the reaction that's overdue even now. And what does he say when I tell him? He says that if he sells he'll lose his job. What do you know about that?"

"I beg your pardon, Mr. Harwood; I didn't say I'd lose my job," cut in old Turkey. "I said I'd lose my position. And when you are as old as I am and you've been through as many booms and panics as I have, you'll know that to lose your position is something nobody can afford; not even John D. Rockefeller. I hope the stock reacts and that you will be able to repurchase your line at a substantial concession, sir. But I myself can only trade in accordance with the experience of many years. I paid a high price for it and I don't feel like throwing away a second tuition fee. But I am as much obliged to you as if I had the money in the bank. It's a bull market, you know." And he strutted away, leaving Elmer dazed.

I think there is great wisdom in this little vignette. In my opinion, the Fed's change of policy means that until further notice we are in a bull market for long-term financial assets. The United States will now reflate, and Europe will follow us. I think it is very bullish that the Fed is at least partially deserting its obsession with the incomprehensible, seasonally adjusted Ms and instead will also be observing the general price level and economic activity for clues as to whether there is too much money or too little.

I also feel this is a bull market in which investors are going to be very quality-conscious in the first leg. In an inflationary period, quality is not an advantage. Inflation is the great equalizer. Having a high return on equity, good profit margins, and little debt and being a low-cost producer merely mean that a company has less financial and operating leverage to benefit from price increases. Being self-financing counts for very little because the banks will lend anyone as much money as he wants. Debt is an advantage.

High interest rates and inflation depress P/E multiples, and the inflationary environment also compresses price/earnings ratio differentials. This is what happened in the seventies. It got to the point where investors paid a premium for low quality and a discount for the best. But in a slow-growth, disinflationary world filled with cold sober bankers, it's another story. All the quality attributes become crucial. The relative price/earnings ratios of firms that have them rise as the quality-differential spreads widen. I won't belabor this point or the fact that quality is still undervalued compared with everything else because I have talked about it too often.

I am convinced that quality, future profit growth expectations, and relative return on equity determine the relative price/earnings ratio at which a stock will sell and that in time a rising relative return on equity will result in a rising relative multiple.

But if I'm generally right, these quality stocks still have considerable upside potential. Note that most of them still sell below their highs of the early seventies and at price/earnings ratios below those prevailing at the 1974 low. Before this present migration has run its course, we may get a minor mania going, and quality issues could sell at price/earnings ratios 30 to 60 percent above the market's multiple (they once commanded premiums of 100 to 200 percent). A few might even be valued at a ridiculous 20 times earnings.

It's a bull market, you know.

Beware the Conventional Wisdom . . .

November 27, 1984

Beware the conventional wisdom, particularly when espoused by The Press. Remember during the election campaign when the pundits were babbling about the "gender gap" and the "Ferraro factor"? Well, women gave that old sexist Ronald Reagan 57 percent of their vote, up from 47 percent in 1980. And then there was all the talk about Jesse Jackson having driven Jewish voters out of the Democratic party. Wrong again. Mondale got 66 percent of the Jewish vote, which was significantly more than Jimmy Carter and John Anderson combined got in 1980.

The so-called Eastern Establishment is generally elitist, intellectual, Liberal, and often wrong. It consists of The Great Eastern University Intelligentsia, The Press (and I mean TV as well as print), and assorted hangers-on. The Eastern Establishment was rooting for Mr. Mondale. With much hand-wringing, editorial commentators have lamented the Reagan reelection. One commented that a Reagan speech was like a violin solo in that "it was loud in spots and less loud in spots, and it had that quality of seeming to last much longer than it actually did."

The *Washington Post* (I like the stock) remarked snidely that the 1984 election proves that Lincoln was wrong; you can fool all of the people enough of the time to elect a mountebank like Reagan. James Reston of the *New York Times* (another good stock) is particularly discouraged with the American people. The attitude of the pundits seems to be that voters today are a bunch of jerks who are easily conned and not the wise peasants and stout yeomen of yore who with their inherent good sense constituted "the wisest electorate in the world"—as long as they were electing liberals.

Thus it is not surprising that The Press is now moaning about the economy and the budget deficit gridlock. "Glow to gloom, mandate to stalemate," says this morning's *New York Times*. "Is the Recovery on Its Last Legs?" asks *Business Week*. The conventional wisdom is convinced that special interest groups loaded with "complexifiers" (says the *Times*) will prevent any real tax reform and that the deficit will be bigger rather than smaller because Congress will not cut spending.

Furthermore, the informed consensus says the odds are that the economic expansion in the United States and the rest of the world is about over. Last week's *Economist* had a pessimistic piece entitled "The World Settles Down for a Hard Slog," which wondered how the 31 million unemployed in the OECD were ever going to be put to work. In my view, this generally glum consensus is pretty well reflected in financial markets, and to the extent the future is less bad than what has already been discounted, stock prices can go up.

I think the gloomy scenario should be viewed with skepticism anyway. As Morgan Stanley's economists have discussed in detail, we believe the rate of economic growth in the United States will begin to accelerate again in the first half of 1985. The budget deficit is not going to disappear, but like inflation and the OPEC surplus in the 1970s, five years from now it will not be such an overwhelming problem.

So far as the flat tax is concerned, like Harvard, the special interest groups and lobbyists "will fight to the end," but truth and justice will win. The flat tax is an idea whose time has come. Look at who's for it and who's opposed. Is the country moving toward the likes of Tip O'Neill and Senator Dole or in the direction of men like Bradley, Gephardt, and Kemp? The composition of the Congress itself has changed dramatically even since 1980. How many young Tips are there on the Democratic side who want to raise taxes and have a bigger government?

I am not saying that everything is going to come up wine and roses in 1985, but rather that the Intelligentsia have a bearish bias and no special vision or wisdom. There may be legislative gridlock for a while in Washington, but it is not preordained because the *New York Times* says so. Progress toward tax simplification and lower marginal tax rates is profoundly bullish, as are strategic arms talks with the Russians. And I don't believe the economy is going to collapse in 1985, particularly now that the Fed has started to ease.

On the other hand, I wonder if we shouldn't question the conventional wisdom that a decline in oil prices is immediately bullish. There is no question that lower oil prices will permit faster, less inflationary economic growth in the long run, but an abrupt break in oil prices in the short run could be disruptive because of its effect on the banking system. Oil prices are weakening again, and my sense is that the chances of a sharp drop and a chaotic pricing scene have increased. In other words, moderate declines in oil prices are bullish, but a break would be scary.

All in all, I'm still quality- and earnings-momentum oriented and am staying bullish. Buy sheep, sell deer.

Dear Diary: Up with Which I Have to Put

July 14, 1997

H ere is what it was like in the month of July 1997 as the great bull market roared on.

Monday: On a summer evening, the platforms at Grand Central Station do not invite casual conversation. With the parked railroad cars' cooling systems blasting even hotter air into the already stale and humid atmosphere, the heat and noise are overpowering. As I hurried to my train, I was astounded when a guy came up beside me and without preamble blurted out:

"Aren't you afraid you're missing the new era? This market is going much higher. It really is different this time." His passion stunned me. It was so un-Grand Centralish.

I stammered something about valuations being at record highs, a buying panic, and exalted sentiment levels. He would have none of it.

"You don't understand what's going on. Reversion to the mean is an obsolete, old-fashioned concept. The valuations, the returns of the past are irrelevant. They relate to a world which was half-capitalist, half-communist, and inflation-prone. Now we are in a new world that is all free enterprise, in which growth rates will be permanently higher, and which has very little inflation, so the shares of good companies' stocks are going to go up faster and sell at much higher multiples than they did in the past."

"Maybe the markets have already discounted a lot of the new era," I said lamely. "After all, the Dow has doubled in two and a half years. In local currency terms the Swedish and Spanish markets are both up more than 70 percent in the last 12 months.

Switzerland is up 50 percent year-to-date, Germany 41 percent, and the Netherlands 45 percent, not to mention Brazil up 90 percent and Russia up 130 percent."

"Acrophobia is what it's called," he said and turned away. He probably was thinking senility as well.

Tuesday: At the weekly portfolio managers' meeting, M wasn't there, so I had little intellectual support for my program of doing some selling and increasing cash and buying more Treasury bonds. The young portfolio managers think I'm crazed. They don't want to raise cash or buy bonds. Stocks always outperform bonds. Somebody said, "The index doesn't have any cash," and everyone laughed.

The clients hate cash; many won't pay us for holding it, they said. Raising cash is market timing, which is the ultimate loser's game. Not being fully invested just means you underperform. Money is coming into our funds every day, and the buyers are bullish and expect us to invest their money in stocks, not hold it in cash. Besides, they added, if your Ice scenario is correct, disinflation will continue, interest rates will keep falling, and stocks will keep climbing as the theoretical P/E ratio for the market rises.

"For a while, stocks will go up as interest rates decline," I argued, "but eventually profits will suffer. Disinflation means that the nominal growth rates of the economy and of corporate profits will fall even if real growth stays the same, because inflation will be less. You can't have it both ways. The theoretical multiple of the market will be higher, but growth will be less."

We disputed aimlessly for a while. Finally, one of them, A, a young one, says in a nice way, "Look, it's fine for you to raise cash because, after all, you're old and plenty rich. But we aren't. And if we raise cash and are wrong, our portfolios and our compensation, maybe even our jobs, are at risk."

We compromised and decided to gradually raise some cash.

Wednesday: We have a big U.S. equity account where we are responsible for implementing a style-tilt strategy. After a good year in 1996 where our value and growth managers both outperformed, we are trailing the S&P this year. The trustees have a consultant who is telling them indexing is the only way to go, they are putting pressure on the chief investment officer of the institution to index more of the total fund to the S&P, and he is suggesting to us it might be politic to move part of our portfolio into our S&P Index Plus product.

The account manager, G, wants to do it. I am opposed. My argument is that the S&P 500 is really the New Nifty Fifty, in other words, the great multinationals and big-cap growth companies that have gone to wild valuations. Buying the S&P is not a move without risk. We are in the business of money management, not politics.

The S&P is in the 90th performance percentile, says G. Fine, say I; three years from now it will be in the 25th percentile. Impossible, says she. I win this one. We will stick with our growth and value portfolios.

Thursday: I go to a dinner hosted by a famous money manager. Half the people there are over 50 and the other half are over 40. The mood ranges from cautious to bearish. Even the great stock pickers say they can't find anything new and exciting to buy. On the other hand, they are relatively fully invested, they say, simply because they are hired to own stocks, not cash. The man who runs the university endowment with the great record and who is revered for being in virtually all equity-type assets says he is selling more U.S. stocks and is uninspired about what to do with the money. The man next to me confides that his young people tell him he has been bearish and wrong for too long and is hurting the firm. He is beginning to wonder if he shouldn't retire.

The host talks, reluctantly but then eloquently. He has just seen the show *Titanic*. It's a parable for our times, he says. The *Titanic* was supposed to be unsinkable, but it sank. The captain was not on the bridge where he should have been, considering the danger of the ice fields ahead, but instead was complacently socializing with his rich passengers. The *Titanic* had watertight compartments in its bow, so that if it had hit the iceberg head-on it would not have sunk, but the inexperienced officer on the bridge did it all wrong and the ship sideswiped the iceberg, opening a fatal gash. The *Titanic* did not carry enough lifeboats for all the passengers because, first, it "couldn't sink," and second, the designers wanted the space for more first-class cabins. The SOS signals from the *Titanic* were ignored because the nearby ship's radio was turned off. And so on. One symbolic image after another. When he finished, everyone applauded.

My conclusion: I don't know many young bears or old bulls.

Friday: M and I meet the chief pension fund officer, K, of one of our biggest asset allocation accounts. We tell him we are going to sell equities in the U.S., Europe, and emerging markets, buy some more U.S. bonds, and raise some cash. He groans. This is a very bright man, and we care when he groans.

His three other asset allocation managers have also raised cash, he says. They are bearish, too. We are wrong about sentiment. In his judgment, the professionals are bearish. What is there to make the market go down?

He beats me over the head about being too cautious when my Ice scenario is clearly starting to play out. Inflation in the United States is headed toward zero to 1 percent, growth stocks will sell at unbelievable multiples, and in an era of price stability, equities will be great, better than bonds or anything else. If bonds really are going to be better than stocks, his fund is in big trouble, he says. Its guidelines do not even permit him to be overweight in bonds.

We talk about the strong dollar and Asia devaluing. Bullish for bonds and even more bullish for the great U.S. multinationals that are the New Nifty Fifty, he says. It's simple: It's a new era, and we are burdened with a lot of old-fashioned baggage. He is not happy. Why is it we are selling stocks? We had better be right.

Praise the Lord and Pass the Ammunition

October 18, 1999

I continue to believe that big-cap U.S. stocks, technology, and the Internet crowd are poised on the brink of a bear market. The U.S. Treasury bonds and high-grade tax-exempts are value, in my judgment, and will beat the S&P 500 over the next six months, but I may be early because the current inflation scare may take yields a little higher.

Will the public continue to buy the dips in the stock market? I think my plumber will buy once, maybe twice more because he has no respect for what he calls "the opinion of the alleged professionals," in other words, me.

Only when rally after rally fails, new highs are a distant memory, and the popular averages and the speculative stocks go to new lows after each rally will he capitulate. At that point, he will have to get interested in toilets again, because he will have lost all his gains and his capital and maybe then some.

As I said last week, a decline in the U.S. stock market eventually is bullish for bonds, not just because investors will flee to bonds as a safe haven but also because they will conclude that a bear market will lead to a slower economy and possibly even a recession. Although our economists disagree, I am of the view that the American economy is already slowing. As you would anticipate at this stage of the cycle, commodity prices and labor costs are rising, but as you might not expect, there is still very little pricing power, so these higher costs will be very difficult to pass on. Profit margins are fat, but they are going to get skinnier.

I also believe in the potency of self-reinforcing circles, both virtuous and vicious. Equity markets are the primal element that usually triggers such circles. Once a virtuous circle is in effect, the American boom teaches that it has been a mistake to underestimate its power and sustainability. On the other hand, the experience of Japan instructs that vicious circles have similar cascading characteristics.

Why do circles end? Because both futurists and doomsayers take a trend and extend it indefinitely, forgetting that the boom or doom factor sooner or later generates a coping mechanism, a countervailing effect. The historian Barbara Tuchman wrote: "You cannot extrapolate any series in which the human element intrudes; history, that is the human narrative, never follows, and will always fool, the scientific curve." It's a crucial insight for investors to comprehend.

Although they last a long time, both virtuous and vicious circles tend to end suddenly, often with a bolt out of the blue. Chairman Greenspan addressed this subject last week when he said: "History tells us that sharp reversals in confidence occur abruptly, most often with little advance notice. These reversals can be self-reinforcing processes that can compress sizable adjustments into a very short period."

If sustained, the break in equity markets will have secondary effects that could alter the trajectory of world economic growth. Everyone knows about the potentially pernicious wealth effect in the United States, but a less obvious consequence may be the inability to complete the huge calendar of equity financing that overhangs everywhere.

Last week a number of offerings were pulled or flopped. The U.S. high-yield market already has indigestion, but another vulnerable area may be in the emerging markets. The Koreas, Thailands, and Brazils of this world need more equity investment to generate faster growth, and they need the growth to deal with their bad-debt problems. A serious bear market in the United States reverberating around the world could abort the global economic boom that everyone seems to expect next year.

The accompanying table shows my ranking of major stock markets around the world, based on a variety of different factors. (These are my views and not necessarily Morgan Stanley Dean Witter's official position, which appears in *The Macro Navigator*.) As is apparent, the valuation factors are all quantitative, although the ranking system within a factor is relatively subjective. Five is the maximum ranking a country can get in any one category, and one is the lowest, although Hong Kong was awarded a rare zero for monetary trend, and Austria and Ireland got sixes on forward yield gap and liquidity, respectively. The measures of fundamental change are a mix of both quantitative and subjective factors, as are the technicals. Obviously, an equally weighted system such as this does not do justice to the complexities of deciding the relative attractiveness of various countries, nor do I pretend that all the relevant factors are even included. But it is a starting point for considering the problem of country allocations, which in my opinion is still the most important factor in global investment performance.

Ranking the Major Markets—A Subjective Appraisal

September 1999	United States	Swed	Ital	Switz	Den	Fin	Fra	UK	Austral	Bel	HK	Ger	Neth	Can	Nor	Jap	Spa	Austria	Ire	Sing
Valuation																				
Historical value	2	1	2	2	4	1	2	3	3	4	3	4	1	3	5	2	3	4	3	2
Price/book	1	2	4	3	4	5	1	5	3	2	3	5	2	5	5	5	4	5	2	5
Forward yield gap	1	1	2	4	2	1	2	2	2	4	1	2	3	3	3	5	3	6	5	5
Normalized PE/bond yields	1	3	3	3	2	2	1	4	5	1	3	2	2	2	5	3	3	5	4	5
Earnings revision	3	2	2	2	3	2	3	3	2	5	3	2	3	4	4	3	4	1	4	5
Earnings momentum	5	2	1	2	2	3	3	3	2	3	4	1	5	4	1	4	3	1	2	6
Value score	13	11	14	16	17	14	12	20	17	19	17	16	16	21	23	22	20	22	20	28
Fundamental change																				
Economy	4	4	3	3	3	5	4	3	4	4	3	4	5	5	2	2	5	3	5	5
Economic acceleration	1	5	3	2	3	3	3	4	4	3	3	4	3	2	3	4	2	4	5	4
Inflation/wages	2	3	4	5	4	3	5	2	4	5	5	5	4	3	3	5	3	5	3	5
Monetary trend	1	3	2	1	3	5	3	1	3	2	0	3	5	3	3	3	5	2	4	2
Fiscal policy	4	3	3	3	3	4	4	3	3	3	4	4	4	4	3	4	4	3	4	5
Policy/politics	4	4	3	3	3	4	3	3	3	3	4	4	3	4	3	3	4	4	5	4
Fundamental score	16	22	18	17	19	24	22	16	21	20	19	24	24	21	17	21	23	21	26	25
Technicals																				
Liquidity (MZM)	4	1	3	3	2	1	4	3	3	3	3	4	4	1	4	1	4	5	6	4
Sentiment	3	3	4	3	3	1	3	3	3	3	4	4	3	3	3	3	3	5	4	3
Price momentum	3	4	3	3	3	5	4	3	2	2	4	2	3	4	4	4	3	1	3	5
Technical score	10	8	10	9	8	7	11	9	8	8	11	10	10	8	11	8	10	11	13	12
Total	39	41	42	42	44	45	45	45	46	47	47	50	50	50	51	51	53	54	59	65

SOURCE: Morgan Stanley Dean Witter Estimates.

"Even Monkeys Fall from Trees"

March 6, 2000

There is still no sign of any loss of momentum in technology around the world, and as a result, growth and momentum investing are crushing value. I don't believe this can go on indefinitely, because the history of investing proves that nothing is forever and that there is an ebb and flow between investing styles. Sociologically, the fall last week of some truly great value investors is another straw in the wind that it may not be too long before the tide turns.

There are many intriguing similarities between now and the early 1970s. Then, as now, a group of stocks perceived to have exceptional growth prospects representing a new era were in intense demand, and there was extreme divergence between this elite group and the rest of the market. Then, as now, value investing was in utter disrepute after years of underperformance. In the early 1970s even the best value managers and funds lost a huge amount of business; last year $33 billion was withdrawn from large-cap value funds, while $97 billion was added to large-cap growth funds. There are many differences between the two periods as well, particularly the inflationary bias of the 1970s, but nevertheless it may be worth studying the past. As Mark Twain is supposed to have said, "History doesn't repeat itself, but it rhymes."

Small-capitalization, speculative growth stocks peaked in the middle of 1969 and began a vicious bear market, but big caps, particularly growth stocks, kept going up. In January of 1973 the S&P made its top and began to drift down, but the Nifty 50 continued to work sideways to higher until October, when they collapsed and the great secular bear market of 1973–1974 began in deadly earnest. Is it possible that a similar pattern will emerge this year, with the growth leadership being the Nasdaq instead of the Nifty 50?

Exhibit 1   Nifty 50 versus Un–Nifty 450

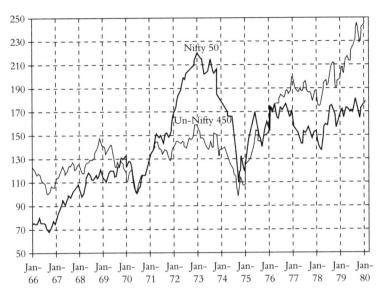

NOTE: Based on monthly performance data.
SOURCE: Sanford Bernstein Research.

We have gone back and tried to reconstruct a detailed price history of the 1966 to 1980 period, breaking the S&P 500 down into the Nifty 50 and the so-called Un-Nifty 450. Unfortunately, 15 of the 50 no longer exist, and only month-end prices are available for the rest, so it is difficult to be precise.

Exhibit 1 is our best effort, but we suspect that, based on the high-growth, speculative nature of the names that have disappeared, if we had daily information for all 50 stocks in the Nifty 50, the index as a whole would show new highs in the late summer of 1973.

Exhibit 2 graphs the relative performance of the two groups. It is a little simplistic to say that the Un-Nifty 450 represent pure value, but it is not too much of a stretch. This conclusion is confirmed by history. Even the very best value managers had extremely difficult times in the late 1960s and early 1970s. Growth dramatically beat value from 1966 until the turn in the fall of 1973. In a wonderful talk called "The Superinvestors of Graham-and-Doddsville" that was subsequently published in the *Columbia Business School Magazine*, Warren Buffett documented the vicissitudes of the great value managers during this period. Eugene Shahan later published an excellent addendum to the Buffett piece.

Buffett's thesis was that you had to persist with value investing even through multiyear stretches of underperformance. Value investors were likely to have a relatively tougher time in good years than in bad ones, and the record showed that even the best underperformed the S&P 30 to 40 percent of the time. In the long run, value would

Exhibit 2   Un–Nifty 450 Relative to Nifty 50

NOTE: Based on monthly performance data.
SOURCE: Sanford Bernstein Research.

pay off, because the "search for discrepancies between the value of a business and the price of small pieces of that business in the market eventually would close." Value investing was the rational way to run money, because growth was essentially ephemeral. True value investors are unreasonable men. G. B. Shaw said, "The reasonable man adapts himself to the world; the unreasonable one persists in trying to adapt the world to himself. Therefore all progress depends on the unreasonable man."

Of the seven great value investing firms of that time, all did very badly from 1969 to 1975 compared with growth managers, and almost all did worse than the S&P 500. Pacific Partners, the firm with the best long-term record of the seven by a wide margin, underperformed the S&P 500 for six straight years from 1970 to 1975, and for one three-year stretch was 49 percentage points behind the index. The great Charles Munger was 38 percentage points behind. Those are huge discrepancies. The article doesn't disclose how much capital was withdrawn from these firms; I leave to your imagination what their loss would have been in today's consultant-driven environment.

All the great value managers came roaring back in the second half of the decade, but Pacific had the best comeback of all. In 1976 it was up 127.8 percent versus a gain of 23.6 percent for the S&P, and in the two following years Pacific gained 108 percent, compared with 17.2 percent for the index. The point is that when style shifts, the rebounds are staggering. All the firms posted returns far in excess of the S&P for the entire cycle, which is what really matters.

Exhibit 3   Forward Yield Gaps for S&P 500 and S&P Nontech

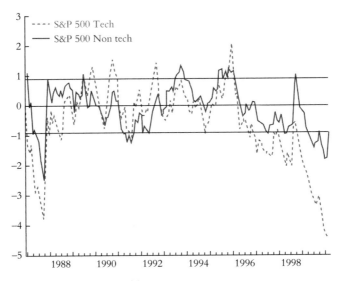

SOURCE: FactSet; I/B/E/S; DRI; MSDW Investment Management.

As Exhibit 1 shows, both indexes fell during 1974, but growth fell faster in this great bear market year. The improvement in the relative performance of value was the first sign of a change in leadership. Off the bottom in 1975, both groups had strong rallies, but growth had the biggest snapback; then came disillusioned selling into that rally. From that point, value had a tremendous run that lasted through the hangover period until the early 1980s.

Where are we now? Not too far from the point where value takes over again in relative terms, but equities in general are still expensive. Take the United States. The problem is that, as Exhibit 3 shows, the forward yield gap on nontech—though cheaper than the S&P 500 and therefore much cheaper than tech alone—is not cheap by historical standards. In fact, it is still one standard deviation expensive. Sure, nontech is cheaper than it was a year ago in absolute terms, but bond yields are 125 basis points higher, so actually nontech is not truly cheap, as Exhibit 3 shows. As for tech, the yield gap is virtually off the page.

If we focus on the MSCI Value versus Growth indexes, value is very cheap in relative terms compared with growth, in both the United States and Europe. Exhibit 4 shows the relative trailing P/E ratios of value versus growth in Europe and the United States. In both cases value is trading at the biggest P/E discount to growth since the secular bottom in 1974, and we noted earlier the outcome of that event. However, the trailing P/E ratio of MSCI value is still high, at about 18 times. Of course, the trailing P/E of growth is stratospheric at 45 times.

Exhibit 4 Value Relative to Growth: Relative Trailing P/E Ratios—United States and Europe

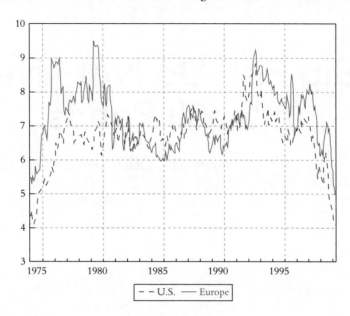

Source: MSCI.

My conclusion: Don't despair on value, and for goodness' sake don't fire value managers now and hire growth firms. In fact, the rational, brave fiduciary with a contrarian bent should be doing just the opposite. The Japanese have a proverb: "Even monkeys fall from trees." Tech and growth managers are very agile, but. . . .

Big Fish Do Not Live in Small Ponds

April 3, 2000

The traumatic events of the last few days signal that a major leadership change has occurred between the New Economy (Growth) and Old Economy (Value) groups. The issue now is whether the fall in the New Economy stocks (Nasdaq) is big enough to cause another decline in the Old Economy stocks (the S&P and EAFE) or whether the leadership transition that has already begun will continue seamlessly. My guess is that the outcome will be the former rather than the latter, because Nontech—though relatively very cheap compared to Tech—is nevertheless expensive.

I think institutional portfolios should be moving toward being half-weight TMT (technology, media, telecommunications—now 32 percent of the world) and should be preparing to redeploy cash into Old Economy groups like banks, financial service companies, and pharma.

In the chart I published several weeks ago, in "Even Monkeys Fall from Trees," forward yield gap analysis showed that tech then was about 4.5 standard deviations overvalued while nontech was 1.5 overvalued. Relative to tech, nontech was as cheap as it had ever been. Since then, interest rates have fallen further, nontech has rallied, and tech has fallen. The accompanying chart shows the levels as of March 31. Obviously, prices have moved a lot since then, but it is safe to say that values in nontech are still not compelling.

The argument for a seamless transition is that the decline in Nasdaq will cause the economy to slow and take the pressure off the Fed to keep raising rates and that bonds will therefore rally further. This combination would be bullish for equities. The counterargument is that with the speculative parts of the market falling and the animal spirits of the speculators fading, it is more likely that they will choose to hold cash while they lick their wounds rather than blithely rotate into an entirely different genre of equities. In fact, it seems to me that it all depends on whether Nasdaq erodes or collapses. And who knows? Maybe it has one more rally left in it.

The Japanese economy, the second largest in the world, has languished like a sulky, sick teenager while the rest of the world has celebrated prosperity. Thus, it would be a major event if Japan revived and joined the global boom. Presently, there are signs that, against the odds, the Japanese economy is continuing to strengthen. Imports and capital spending are strengthening, and business confidence is improving. Consumer spending is still sluggish, but it, too, should revive as summer approaches. With so much of the rest of the world enjoying strong growth, if Japan joined the parade now it might be construed as bad news, because it would add to the overheating and generate higher inflation and interest rates. The recent strength in the Baltic Freight Index confirms that world growth is, if anything, accelerating.

S&P Forward Yield Gaps: Tech versus Nontech (through March 2000)

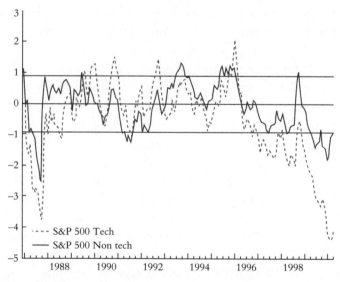

SOURCE: Factset; I/B/E/S.

However, since the end of last year, industrial commodity prices have weakened again, and both the CRB Raw Industrials and Metals Indexes look as though they have rolled over. The price of oil is down from its highs, and gold has broken again. Some argue that wage inflation is about to accelerate, but it hasn't happened yet. Thus it appears that the disinflationary/deflationary boom is continuing. It's an incredible world, and the combination of economic Fire and inflation Ice can result in stock market melt-ups. This may well be what the strength in Old Economy stocks in the United States, Europe, and Japan is foretelling.

Meanwhile, the big-cap tech stocks still seem to have the Force with them. Cisco ($77), Intel ($132), Nokia (ADR, $222), Oracle ($75), and the rest of the elite "rat pack" have recently touched new highs, and although they got beaten up along with everything else on April 4, they clearly are the best performers in the tech universe.

Elsewhere around the world, nonetheless, there are some serious cracks in the more speculative small-cap growth and OTC markets. For example, by today the Nouveau Marché, the FTSE Techmark, the German Neuer Markt, Jasdaq, the Nikkei Communications Index, and Kosdaq were all off more than 30 percent from their highs of a month ago, and the Netherlands Euro New Market, Italy New Market, and the Amex Biotech index had each fallen more than 40 percent. Hong Kong and other Asian Internet shares have lost all or most of their gains for the year. These declines are not corrections but collapses, and they are sharp enough to have singed the hairy brows of a number of the more hirsute speculators. I suspect these indexes have seen their high-water marks for the year.

It would be dangerous to postulate that this year is anything like 1973, because the economic fundamentals are totally different, even if the stock market dynamics are not. Oil prices and inflation were the transforming events of 1973 that combined with overvaluation to pop the bubble. This time, at least so far, there has been no event as cataclysmic as inflation was then. But it is intriguing to remember that in 1973, the Nifty Fifty were not alone. A further 25 to 40 other smaller growth companies were thought to be candidates for inclusion in the hallowed circle of "One Decision Stocks." As 1973 unfolded and the Nifty Fifty kept working higher even as the rest the S&P faltered, first these camp followers and then some of the lesser lights in the Nifty Fifty itself began to get roughed up. As the year progressed, the Nifty Fifty got narrower and narrower, and by late summer, only a small number of the biggest and the best were holding up. Then, of course, in late October everything plunged.

It also is interesting to remember how far these great growth stocks fell without serious earnings or product disappointments (in most cases). Polaroid and Avon both had problems, and the shares fell 90 percent and 86 percent, respectively, and ITT lost 81 percent. But nothing really awful happened to American Express, which declined 74 percent; McDonald's and Xerox, 72 percent each; GE, 60 percent; IBM, 58 percent; and Citicorp, 57 percent. The best drug stocks had falls ranging from 65 percent for American Home to 47 percent for Merck. The Nifty Fifty as a group dropped 59.81 percent, according to Ned Davis Research, and most of the damage was done in 14 to 18 months. It took 10 years on average for the shares of these great growth companies, whose earnings per share in most cases kept growing, to get back to the previous highs—and 16 years to recover when adjusted for inflation. The secondary names fared even worse, and the speculative stocks that were mostly dreams and whispers all seemed to go to $3.

My opinion continues to be that investors should be moving to a 50 percent underweight in TMT. How quickly, I don't know, but at this point they should certainly hold less than the 35 percent weight of technology in the global indexes. It is sobering to look at the history of 1973 and remember the July rally and recall how long it took for the Nifty Fifty to truly collapse.

Therefore, in view of the deflationary boom still going on, I think the proceeds from these sales should be reinvested in Old Economy stocks around the world, but particularly in Japan. The Old Economy is where the values are, and the recent agonies of the great value investors make me suspect that the bottom has been reached, certainly in terms of relative performance.

Real estate stocks almost everywhere are a sector that epitomizes value, in my judgment. In the United States, the shares of REITs are selling at 15–20 percent *discounts* to the private market value of their underlying real estate. A couple of years ago, REITs traded at a 30 percent *premium*. And LBO transactions confirm that this analysis is not imaginary. In Europe, discounts to private market value are at least that big in the United Kingdom, France, and Sweden, and they are close to 40 percent in Spain. Do these discounts guarantee performance? Of course not, but they do suggest defensive characteristics.

The commercial real estate cycle in the United States is more mature than in Europe, where the market is just now turning up, but it still has a considerable way to run, in the opinion of our people who are involved on a day-to-day basis. The yield on the Morgan Stanley REIT index is 8.3 percent, compared with 1.1 percent on the S&P 500. REIT dividends are growing at least 5 percent per annum. European and U.K. real estate shares are very cheap and have done nothing for the last year. The Morgan Stanley REIT Index has gained a paltry 4 percent in the last 12 months.

In Japan, as strategist Alex Kinmont discussed last week, there is developing evidence that commercial real estate is beginning to clear and that the bear market is over. Both prices and volume are turning up. Until last week, Japanese real estate stocks were down almost 20 percent since a year ago, in a roaring bull market. The improvement in real estate has big implications for the Japanese bank stocks, which are selling at close to their all-time relative lows. At one point, the banking sector amounted to over 30 percent of the MSCI Japan Index. It is now 8 percent. There continues to be a lot of bad news about the banks, and their mergers on first blush do not appear to be dramatic events in terms of cost-cutting and restructuring. However, the ill tidings are well known, and I sense the banks are good buys.

Section 3

THE GLOBAL VIEW

In the chatter about emerging markets, it is fashionable to focus on the new hot country that is about to be discovered. It's best of all when that country is positively menacing, with lurking, Uzi-toting teenagers and nubile girls in chadors fanatically committed to some middle-aged, potbellied Marxist sheik who still rages about the syphilis that Cortés's men spread or about the massacre by the Redcoats in some dusty village square centuries ago. These are the turnarounds that an emerging market investor dreams of.

—*Barton Biggs, July 19, 1993*

Barton Biggs is widely credited as one of the first global investment strategists and a man ahead of his time. When Biggs first started traveling internationally to seek out and write about foreign investment opportunities, the world economy was in a binary orbit dominated by two superpowers, the Soviet Union and the United States. The term *emerging markets* had yet to be coined. Countries that didn't align neatly with either NATO or the Warsaw Pact were tongue-tyingly labeled LEDCs (less economically developed countries) or, more colloquially and pejoratively, the Third World.

At the time, China barely made the list of top-10 economies. If not for Nixon's historic and unexpected trip to Beijing in 1972, most Americans would have considered the bamboo curtain an impenetrable barrier shrouding an ancient, vaguely menacing horde of Communist agrarians. Instead, Biggs saw market potential that would blast China from the muddy rice paddies into the upper troposphere as the second-largest world economy over just a few decades.

Biggs grew to have great respect for the industriousness of the Chinese people, whether on the mainland or as part of the broader global diaspora. "The astounding success of the overseas Chinese everywhere derives from a combination of hard work, utter dedication to education, willingness to adapt to the local culture and sheer brains," he wrote in 1987.

While he knew the China story was a crucial market force to be recognized, Biggs was pragmatic enough to understand the limits of his own intellectual access to their enigmatic economy. Ultimately, he concluded it was "unanalyzable." He also appreciated the peril represented by that limited knowledge for outside investors in dealing with a system that didn't play by the same rules of Western free markets. "The big risk is that one morning you wake up and they have announced that everything owned by foreigners in China has been nationalized," he wrote in 1993.

By the late 1980s, Biggs was quick to see opportunity in the creative destruction rocking the Eastern Bloc that would shift the balance of world powers and made a case for more European investment. "The Cold War era of confrontation is over, and all its institutions—NATO, the Warsaw Pact, Star Wars, John le Carré novels—are obsolete, relics, kaput," he wrote with characteristic literary flair. "It will be interesting to see which leader understands this first and exploits the opportunities and dangers of the new Europe."

He was also one of the first money managers to recognize—and visit—India for its emerging investment potential. Likening it to a young family with a growing income but a large home mortgage, Biggs compared the subcontinent to "Chicago in 1870 or Denver 25 years later, which after all weren't bad places to own equities, as long as you didn't trip over the risk premium or get nicked by a stray bullet from the weekly gunfight."

Biggs was an equal opportunist in his international assessments both culturally and economically. "It's a delightfully civilized country to visit," he remarked about Italy, "but it's barbaric economically and politically." He saw a good case for investing in South Korea despite finding the place "breathtakingly deficient in charm."

In 1993, Mexico was "an investment dream," Brazil "a nightmare," and Argentina "a magic show, in the sense that the story seems held together by threads of gossamer." Ireland had "all the charm and blarney in the world but it lacks the raw dynamism and glamour of the exploding emerging markets."

Of all the places Biggs visited that touched his mind and heart, Thailand clearly touched his soul. Some of his most eloquent and dreamy missives captured in words the beauty, majesty, and charm in the place he would call, "Camelot . . . where the sun always shines, money grows on trees, everybody smiles, and stocks seem only to go up."

"Bangkok, bisected by a swirling brown river, is a typical Asian city full of towering ornate temples, gold Buddhas, traffic jams and masses of people who, while living primitively, are not in the depressing abject poverty of an India," he wrote about his favorite "neglected market" in 1986. "You can walk anywhere without feeling threatened and even the street hustlers are affable."

Biggs was prescient in understanding the need for global diversification and the explosive growth potential of international markets—especially in the post–Cold War era. He seemed to truly enjoy immersing himself in the crush of humanity and the swirl of cultures against the common backdrop of economic value creation and then relaying those experiences back to his readership with mirth and eloquence.

The selection of dispatches collected here provides a mere glimpse into the worldview of a magnificent global strategist.

Section 3A:
China and Hong Kong

Buy Hong Kong

November 1, 1983

E ven from the middle of the harbor you could hear the throbbing roar of the city like some great economic dynamo, and the Chinese broker was lithe, articulate, but seemed a little dazed. "My family came to Hong Kong 20 years ago and we've made it big, but now I fear it's the old Beirut or late Shanghai. Our stock market is rice cheap, but maybe it's our last chance to get out with something," he said wistfully, gazing at his magnificently appointed powerboat with its crew of three. "I wonder if this boat could make it to Canada?"

Instead, I suspect it's the time to buy the Hong Kong market. According to Capital International, that market through September 30 was the poorest performer in the world this year with a decline of 31.5 percent and is down 74 percent from its all-time high of a couple of years ago. Many of the blue-chip companies are selling at five or six times next year's earnings with yields of 7 percent. The entire market sells at a 33 percent discount to stated book value—by contrast, the S&P 500 has sold at about book value at the great bottoms of the last 20 years.

Hong Kong, along with Singapore, is the classic entrepôt, and it has risen time and time again like the phoenix from the ashes, most recently after the Chinese-instigated riots of 1967 and the recession of the early seventies. The stock market is probably the most volatile in the world, so it is not for the fainthearted, but with market capitalization of $25 billion and heavy trading, it is surprisingly deep.

Now, the trauma has come from the Chinese government's hard, uncompromising stand to date in the Sino-British talks about the future of Hong Kong after 1997, when the lease expires. Not surprisingly, Hong Kong's 5.5 million residents, 98 percent of whom are Chinese with everything they have built committed to Hong Kong, view total Chinese administration as an unmitigated disaster. They worry about bureaucratic regulation of business and trading and a stifling of the atmosphere of flexibility and creativity that has made Hong Kong flourish. As one Chinese businessman commented to me: "I switched my company from manufacturing wigs to video games and I'm changing again. I can do it because here we can do anything, buy the skills, and the people are smart and want to work hard. A Mandarin bureaucracy would tie us in pigtails just as China is tied now."

When the Sino-British talks bogged down in late September, suddenly Hong Kong panicked. The HK dollar plunged to 11 cents U.S. versus close to 17 cents a year ago. The Hang Seng Index fell 22 percent in September alone. Property values collapsed, and, typical of the psychology, apartments above the fifth floor became virtually unrentable because people believed the Chinese wouldn't be able to maintain the elevators. One weekend there was a food panic, and stores were literally swept clean. Several Westerners mentioned to me that suddenly the memories of the food and anti-English riots of the past returned, and even the market for powerboats collapsed.

In addition, with the real estate and stock market decline, several Chinese banks appeared to be about to fail, and lines of anxious depositors formed as rumors abounded. The bankrupt Carrian Group's offices were raided by the police, and its chief officers arrested. The English establishment business leaders appeared unnerved, and certain prominent Chinese almost seemed to fan the flames, with one Dr. L. K. Ding commenting that "the society seemed headed for collective suicide." In late September and early October, the Westerners and wealthy Chinese who make the economy go exported massive amounts of capital, and some began thinking about where to emigrate for a new start.

However, in mid-October the government in a low-key, very British, but effective way stepped in. A failing bank was taken over, new capital from outside investors was pumped into another, interest rates were boosted to stabilize the currency, and, finally, the Hong Kong dollar was pegged at HK7.80 to the U.S. dollar. The government quietly let it be known that it has perhaps $5 billion U.S. to support the peg. Last week, with the stock market firming a little and the peg holding on its own, Hong Kong's banks lowered the prime from 16 to 15 percent and announced other rate reductions of up to four percentage points.

Moreover, there is nothing the matter with the colony's booming economy. New orders are strong, and an export-led recovery is under way. Exports to the United

States in real terms are up 16 percent so far this year, and those to China by 28 percent. Unemployment is falling, real GNP should rise over 6 percent this year, and only inflation will be a problem because of the weak currency. Hong Kong today is a dynamic manufacturing and transshipping center, with a huge pool of entrepreneurial capital, innovative management, and skilled labor serving the most dynamic markets of the world—Southeast Asia.

At the same time, China uses Hong Kong as a reexport market, so the colony plays a vital role as a free port for China, almost like a clearing house. Nobody knows how big China's investment in Hong Kong is. It includes 13 banks led by the Bank of China and dozens of trading companies. This year the Chinese government formed a major company, headed by a Mr. Wang, with the marvelous name of "The Ever Bright Industrial Company."

Meanwhile, China itself is busily encouraging outside investment from joint ventures and compensation agreements. According to an article in last week's *Economist*, the domestic development program is a flop, and so far most of the $2.7 billion has come from the entrepreneurial Hong Kong Chinese. The nation is desperately short of capital to develop everything from its offshore oil fields to domestic infrastructure, and in the next decade hundreds of billions will have to be borrowed.

Hong Kong

SOURCE: Capital International Perspective.

The Chinese are inscrutable, but destroying Hong Kong hardly seems the way to foster external investment in China. And even if they are going to take over Hong Kong lock, stock, and barrel in 1997, why not let it prosper for the next 16 years so there is more to grab when 1997 comes? Another 16 years of growth and prosperity will make it at least three times as rich a prize at no cost to China. Furthermore, the Chinese need the window and the ability to buy Western technology. The current scowls simply don't make sense unless they are meant to depress the markets to buy some cheap merchandise.

Last week, when I was in Hong Kong, the mood among businessmen and investment managers was still black. It was like the bottom of a major bear market when everyone knows all the bad news and ignores the positives. Everyone I talked to complained they had too much capital tied up in Hong Kong. Bear psychology has overwhelmed incredibly cheap valuations and dynamic growth. An awful lot of money can be made in an economy growing 6 to 7 percent a year in the next decade and a half. Singapore, which is, like Hong Kong, an entrepôt but without the political risk, has a market which sells at 27.5 times earnings. Southeast Asia is the place to be.

So anyway, I bought some Hong Kong blue-chip companies for our profit-sharing plan. Hutchinson Whampoa and Swire Pacific are major trading companies (hongs). China Light & Power is the growth utility. Buy low, sell high, and assume it's not Shanghai from the deluge.

Own Hong Kong Big

Early 1988

A week ago, I was in Hong Kong where Morgan Stanley has just opened a "full-service" office. The sun never shone the five misty, cold days I was there, but the city and its environs throb and stink like the powerful dynamos they are.

Hong Kong as an investment still looks very good to me. The economy boomed with double-digit real GNP growth in 1987, and most forecasts call for 5 percent or so gains in 1988 because of the widely anticipated worldwide slowdown and local capacity restraints. In fact, neither is proving to be a problem. Company after company—from Johnson Electric to Hutchison—spoke to us of rapidly growing order books, and the factories just keep moving further out into China to tap more cheap labor. Thus my guess is that real growth this year will be closer to 7 percent, and corporate profits will expand even more than the 15 to 20 percent now expected. Meanwhile, foreign direct investment, particularly from Japan, pours in. So far, inflation is not a worry, although a rise in the prices of oil and industrial commodities could eventually be troublesome.

The general impression I got was that the "one-person, one-vote" issue is not a big deal. People in Hong Kong are too involved in the rat race. The much-publicized brain drain is another matter. Some very valuable Chinese citizens are leaving simply because they don't trust the Communists. One successful entrepreneur told me how his family had believed the Communists when they assured businessmen everything was going to be fine when the People's Liberation Army marched into Shanghai, only to barely escape with their lives and the clothes on their back. "I'm not going to make the same mistake," he said. On the other hand, we find in our office that again the best and the brightest from across Southeast Asia want to come to work in Hong Kong because of the opportunities. After all, it's the most open, vital place in the world. A large number of well-educated, ambitious young Americans are turning up for the same reason. To some extent, one offsets the other.

The other change I sense in Hong Kong is the feeling developing among a growing minority that 1997 may be a plus rather than a minus. Obviously, one cannot bank on this theory, but if investors begin to believe Hong Kong has a future as a capitalist enclave serving as China's economic gateway to the West, it should do wonders for what companies are perceived to be worth. This view is clearly not the consensus, which still believes that the lights go out and the music stops playing in 1997.

The optimists cite Deng Xiaoping's policy of "One Country, Two Systems" for the merger of Hong Kong and China. Some such as Terence Hon Kwai and our research director, Jake van der Kamp, believe Deng's motto, implying the coexistence of two different socioeconomic systems within a single nation-state, is seen by the Chinese government as a "creative solution" to the dilemma of history that is Hong Kong. Unquestionably, China is fiercely determined to reclaim the area physically and remove the last stains of the humiliations suffered over two centuries at the hands of the great powers.

On the other hand, China needs a thriving, capitalistic, entrepreneurial Hong Kong as role model. It is China's strategic trade gateway to the world and, as a major banking center, the key to financing the growth of China. Each year China tips a little more toward a mixed economic system so that Hong Kong's value as a training center and spark plug grows. John Fell, chairman of the stock exchange, clearly believes this to be the case, and at lunch he made the interesting point that in 25 years the real threat to Hong Kong's dominance may be the rise again of Shanghai, with all its geographical and traditional advantages as the commercial focus of China. Others argue that China wants to make the merger work so a stronger case can be made for reunification with the Chinese on Taiwan. In any case, the assimilation of a capitalistic Hong Kong into a mixed mainland economy is a typically gradualist, evolutionary Chinese solution. Van der Kamp believes Hong Kong will increasingly function as a service economy for the Chinese hinterlands, providing high-technology inputs and financial, transport, and commercial services.

All this may be a pipe dream, but at least there's not a whiff of it in valuations. Our Hong Kong Index sells at 11.3 times trailing 12-month earnings to yield 4.4 percent versus 33.4 and 3.7 percent for Malaysia, 21.6 and 2.7 percent for Singapore, 34 and 2.8 percent for Taiwan, 19.0 and 1.3 percent for Korea, and 12.9 and 3.3 percent for Thailand. The Hong Kong market languishes 35 percent below its 1987 high, and the local investors I talked with still seem traumatized by the crash, the closing of the market, and the scandals. By contrast, our East Asian real estate analyst, Peter Churchouse, who everyone tells me is the best in the business, points out in a study on Asian property markets we are issuing that the real estate market in Hong Kong has behaved much better than the bourse and is now at new highs. Vacancies in the Grade "A" office market are at their lowest level in many years, rents have risen 20 percent, and prices are up 30 percent. The same is true of the residential market, both luxury and small flats. The industrial property market was booming until the crash, with prices up 48 percent year over year. It immediately sold off as people worried about order books but now has recovered again to the precrash level. Hutchison just paid up big for container port Terminal 7. The Hong Kong property stocks represent over 30 percent of the index, so either real estate operators are too bullish or equity investors are too bearish. I prefer the former alternative. Furthermore, my sense is that the formidable John Fell has transformed the stock exchange in five months from a Chinese club to a modern institution.

So I'm still very bullish on Hong Kong with an outrageous overweighting of 15 percent. All of Madhav Dhar's valuation studies show it's the most undervalued open market, considering growth prospects. Jake van der Kamp's three favorite stocks are Johnson Electric (HK$7) (emerging growth company par excellence), Hutchison (HK$8) (the classic Hong Kong trading conglomerate), and China Light (HK$18) (a 3.5 percent yield growing 20 percent annually busts everyone's model).

More on China

October 4, 1993

These notes continue my discussion of the investment case for China. I am trying to present the negatives as well as the positives. As Sam Reeves, one of the investors on our recent trip, put it, you have to take into account that the civil law that governs, the moral law that values, and the cultural law of China are all vastly different from those of the West, so China will make choices that will confound and dismay. He is disturbed that a foreigner can only lease land for 50 years, not own it. Nevertheless, he concludes that when you weigh the good and the bad and the potential, the risk is in not being invested sufficiently.

The Western press is very sanctimonious about China. You read a lot about corruption and repression, but I did not sense pervasive corruption or decadence in China as I have in other developing countries. As in all societies, I am sure there is some. China has become decentralized, and local authority has been substituted for the sluggish mandarin Communist bureaucracy that ran it so poorly. It is inevitable with so much new money, so many new projects that some local government officials are profiteering. This is a small price to pay for rapid decision making and higher living standards. Don't forget, China made virtually no progress in raising its standard of living for the first three-quarters of this century, but since then, thanks to a dose of capitalism, greed, and free markets, per capita income has doubled every seven years. I asked Gonzaga Lee, the CEO of Wharf, who was with us in Wuhan, what his experience had been. He said in his years in China he had experienced lots of very hard bargaining but no personal demands.

The *New York Times* recently ran a series of articles by Nicholas Kristof, who just completed nearly five years as Beijing bureau chief, describing the decadence of the ruling class. The stories cited everything from greedy mayors and spoiled children to

Shenzhen Securities Exchange B Shares, October 1992–September 1993

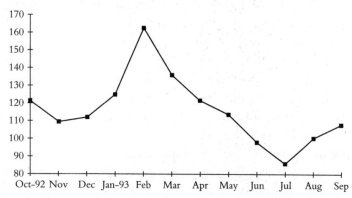

SOURCE: Morgan Stanley Research.

the food in Beijing restaurants being seasoned with opium or gold to create restaurant addiction. Though this makes for sensational journalism, I think it's mostly apocryphal. China is too dynamic to be decadent. Incidentally, the Chinese politicians we met all looked terrific. Lean, vigorous, worked the crowds—"must have had face lifts," grumbled Sig Segalas.

Those *Times* articles argue that China is more like modern Indonesia, "a nepotistic and corrupt dictatorship that presides over a booming market economy with both state and private sectors," than like the former Soviet Union or East Germany. I disagree, because although China does want to achieve the standard of living of the West without being "infected by Western political standards," its models are Singapore and Malaysia. We heard a lot about the virtues of "a democracy guided by an authoritarian single-party government." The question is, can this system work with 1.2 billion people? Singapore has less than 5 million, Malaysia less than 20 million.

Shenzhen Securities Exchange B Shares August 1992–September 1993

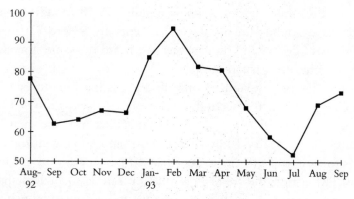

SOURCE: Morgan Stanley Research.

As I have written, enlightened dictatorship rather than coalition democracy in many ways can be best for a developing county in the takeoff stage, because hard choices and sacrifices are required. As Harrison Salisbury points out in his 1992 book, *The New Emperors: China in the Era of Mao and Deng*, Chinese thinkers traditionally have emphasized the common good rather than individual rights. This is a wonderful book about the dynastic struggles of the men and women who have created the modern China. They are truly the "new emperors" who have lived and ruled much as did their dynastic predecessors over the last 2,000 years. Jiang Qing, Mao's wife and the leader of the Gang of Four, is a personality as incredible as any of the empresses of China's past. Salisbury writes of the new emperors and their secret pleasure garden, palace mazes, intrigues, triple crosses, love affairs, and ambition—but not monetary corruption. These people are interested in power, not wealth.

Some investors worry that the death of Deng Xiaoping could knock down China-related equities 20 percent or so. I don't think so. Deng is strictly a symbolic figure. In an article in this week's Sunday *New York Times*, Kristof describes three alternative scenarios when Deng dies: the authoritarian state, the democratic state, and civil war and vast upheaval. Despite the lurid drawings of a naked woman being tortured and of terrorists blowing up a dam, Kristof concludes that the emergence of "a prosperous quasi-democracy" is the most likely outcome. Even his second choice, the authoritarian state, would look rather like South Korea or Taiwan in the 1970s, which isn't all bad. Kristof concludes as I would: "Deng's death may well accelerate and consolidate that process of rapid-fire economic development and more measured political liberalization." Necrology plays usually go up rather than down when the old guy dies. Remember Disney when Walt went?

As always happens in a developing country, real estate in the big Chinese cities is in a huge bull market. We toured Shanghai with the people from Hang Lung Development. Hong Kong has 70 million square feet of first-class office space, and another 7 million feet will be added this year. Shanghai, by the end of this year, will have 2.1 million square feet. Shanghai, not Hong Kong, eventually will be the commercial capital of the new China, so everyone wants office space. There is a tremendous shortage. Morgan Stanley's new office there will be in hotel rooms. We were told a developer can get his money back on a new building in 18 months even though land leasehold prices have doubled in the last year. Rents are $70 to $80 per square foot. Hotel room rates have doubled in the last year. We heard the same story in Wuhan. The whole city seems to be a construction site.

We talked to a lot of government officials and planners about economic growth. They suggest China is into the second decade of a 30-year growth burst similar to what Japan enjoyed from 1950 to 1980. They think that over the next decade China can sustain real GNP growth of 10 percent at worst and 10 percent inflation. The goal for next year is to slow real growth to less than 10 percent and to get inflation down to single digits. The reason the trend-line inflation rate is so high is that the public-sector companies are running big deficits that have to be funded by printing money. If privatizations come sooner than is now expected and the tax collection system begins to work better, then the deficits and inflation could be lower.

With population growth of around one-half of 1 percent annually, real GNP per capita will grow very rapidly, and the middle class, which already numbers around 100 million, will triple in five years. No other country, big or small, in the last decade has had anywhere near as rapid per capita GNP growth as China. Just for the record, remember that in the first seven months of this year, total fixed capital investment soared 70 percent from the year-earlier level.

It was apparent to us that the Chinese understand the crucial role of the equity markets in their economic growth plan. We met with the head of the Stock Exchange Executive Council, the executive director of the Shanghai Stock Exchange, and representatives from the Ministry of Finance and the Central Bank. They maintain that in the long run the distinction between A and B shares will be eliminated, along with foreign exchange controls, and that there are no plans to limit the percentage of companies that can be owned by foreigners.

They all spoke of the need to develop a mature stock market for investors, not speculators, and of the importance of better accounting standards and an educated investor class. Actually, as the Arthur Andersen man explained, Chinese accounting isn't that bad, except that depreciation is calculated on useful physical rather than economic life and there is no concept of reserving for bad debts. He also said bookkeeping standards were high and turnover of accountants was low. The listed companies tend to overstate earnings, but the big state entities are inclined to understate by setting up reserves.

I am so optimistic about China because my sense is that the Chinese know what the right thing is and they are doing it. The big risk is that one morning you wake up and they have announced that everything owned by foreigners in China has been nationalized. Such an event could be caused by either another cultural revolution or if the Chinese perceived they would gain more than they would lose by such an act. Talking about Wharf's 25 percent interest in a new power plant there, the governor of Hubei Province said that he had to treat Wharf fairly because he wanted it to invest in the next power plant and the ones after that. As for the other nightmare—a panic where for some reason more foreign money was rushing out of China than was coming in—a freeze on capital repatriation could happen. In both cases, though, the Chinese know that if they did this just once, they would pay the price for a generation.

China: "The New Emperors" and the Risk/Reward Equation

October 25, 1993

*T*he New Emperors: China in the Era of Mao and Deng by Harrison Salisbury is disturbing and fascinating. The book deepens the understanding of a naive soul like me of the complex, often cruel culture and Byzantine intrigue running through the recent history of China. Its theme is that the new emperors who drove Chiang Kai-shek from the mainland and established a peasant dynasty have lived and ruled much as their predecessors did over the last 2,000 years, although Deng is very different than Mao. "There can only be one sun in the sky and one emperor, and the people must obey and tremble." Any serious investor in China should read this book to understand better the risks and rewards of what might be called "dynastic investing."

Salisbury, who died shortly after this book was published, was a Pulitzer Prize–winning foreign correspondent for the *New York Times*, concentrating on Russia and China. He spent 20 years researching and traveling in China before writing this book and had numerous interviews with almost all the Chinese leaders and those around them. On one trip he actually retraced the 6,000-mile route of Mao's Long March of 1934–1935 as he tried to discover the origins of the new emperors.

Chairman Mao Zedong was a great revolutionary leader, but like Stalin, he was a monster, Salisbury says. No young woman was safe in his presence, and at the height of his power as the absolute ruler of China, Mao's quarters sometimes swarmed with young women who "attended the chairman in couplets, triplets, or even greater numbers." Apparently, Mao's idea of a fun weeknight at home was to go for a dip in his heated indoor pool with 10 naked girls he hadn't seen before. He had a special library filled with his collection of antique erotic books, including "hand-colored pillow books, foldout picture guides to sexual practices." All of this, Salisbury points out, is in the tradition of the emperors of China.

Mao believed in *feng shui*, a 5,000-year-old body of mystic and cabalistic knowledge which taught that by sleeping with hundreds of women, a man could prolong his life to infinity. In view of security issues, keeping this daisy chain going for the aging chairman became a serious problem for Mao's bodyguards, who had to draw heavily on young wives of junior officials and women who worked in the Foreign Ministry, Salisbury reports, and participation was not optional. Although a heavy smoker, Mao was also an exercise fanatic and in middle age every day swam an hour to an hour and a half. China quickly became populated with heated indoor pools to accommodate him.

Mao and his commanders may have become addicted to opium and codeine-based sleeping pills on the Long March, Salisbury says, because they worked all night and exhausted, fell into litters and were carried all day as the army fled across China. Without sleeping pills they could not have survived. Salisbury wonders to what extent the Long Marchers who were the subsequent leaders of China were addicted to opium. He remarks that the episodes of neurotic behavior and wild plots that cost some their lives may have been because of opium-induced delusions.

There seems to be little question that Lin Biao was a drug addict, Salisbury concludes. At one time he was Mao's designated successor, but later devised a complex, fanciful plan to blow up Mao's train and was killed when his escaping jet ran out of fuel and crashed in Mongolia. During the Cultural Revolution, one of Mao's most effective ways to break his old comrades was to deprive them of their sleeping pills, reducing them to babbling paranoia in a few weeks. Salisbury says that Mao may have had periods when he overindulged in opium and that this explains long episodes of disengagement and debauchery.

Mao's third wife was Jian Qing, a pert, boyish, ambitious young woman when she was introduced into Mao's bed by Kang Sheng, a sinister police agent. Though only in her mid-20s, she was already notorious since it was rumored she had been sold as "a pubescent slave" (whatever that means), had been a teenage prostitute, and then a second-rate actress. Jian's ambition was to make herself empress of China, and she and the Gang of Four tried to seize power when Mao died. She used the Cultural Revolution to torture and persecute those she hated and feared. As Mao's wife, she didn't seem bothered by his young girls, but she was a vicious enemy to older women she was jealous of.

She particularly disliked Wang Guangmei, wife of the president of China, Liu Shaoqi. Wang could do everything, including swimming, better than Jian. Jian got even during the Cultural Revolution, when Liu Shaoqi died of starvation and torture and Wang was broken in prison.

Chinese politics in Mao's time were probably no more devious than the Western version, but the stakes were higher. Losers ended up not going back to Peoria but dying slow, tortured deaths in prisons or literally being torn apart by street mobs.

"Divide and rule" was Mao's philosophy. He had no compunction about inflicting frightful tortures on his old comrades, some of whom had saved his life on the Long March. He also had the charming habit of calling in his intended victim for a friendly, reassuring chat just prior to denouncing him. Of course, some of his old war buddies and his own wife were busy scheming to assassinate him, so it's no wonder he was paranoid.

The Cultural Revolution is another frightening story. By1966, the Great Leap Forward, Mao's ambitious program for economic growth, had proved a disaster, resulting in famine, commercial disorganization, crop failures, depression, and the pullout of 14,000 Soviet experts. Mao knew that he and his communist policies and commune system had failed to improve the standard of living of the people and that there was danger of a counterrevolution. To save himself, to divert the people, and to destroy the opposition beginning to develop, he called for the Cultural Revolution, which devastated China even further.

Salisbury clearly believes that Deng Xiaoping is a different and much better, simpler man than Mao. Among other things, he has had only one wife and does not use drugs. Deng is pragmatic, and his favorite aphorism has been that "it does not matter whether the cat was white or black so long as it catches the mouse." Salisbury sums up the difference between the two: "Mao helped the peasants seize the land from the rich—then took it back for the communes. Mao had filled the peasants' rice bowls—then emptied them with terrible famines. Deng gave the land back to the peasants, demolished the commune structure, and watched the rice bowls overflow. He put money into people's pockets, money they earned themselves. With the Deng revolution there was no more barracks life, no more 'blue ants,' no more egalitarianism."

During the Tiananmen Square incident, Deng crushed the students as though he, too, were an emperor of China (which in fact he was). Since then he has gradually faded into old age. Today it isn't clear what will happen when he dies. "There is no mechanism in the structure of Deng's New China whereby an orderly succession can be assured," says Salisbury. China's leaders don't believe communism works, but on the other hand, democracy is a messy, inefficient form of government that China is too big for. Deng has said that with democracy, China again would become "simply a loose dish of sand." He has made clear the Far Eastern brand of free-market authoritarianism that worked in Korea, Taiwan, Indonesia, and Singapore would be China's model. An emperor is at the center of this system.

The history of China is that when the emperor dies and no one holds a clear advantage, "a time of trouble" ensues. Will it happen when Deng dies? Salisbury doesn't say. My guess is that it won't because Deng's slow fade has permitted a transition period with the emergence of "younger" (60-ish) leaders. No matter who the new emperor is, he cannot afford to turn back from the "virtuous circle" blueprint of economic growth and free markets.

No country since statistics began to be kept has had compound per capita GNP growth of 10 percent per annum for over a decade. This is an incredible improvement in the standard of living, and although human rights groups may wring their hands, the Chinese are far more prosperous and probably have more personal freedom than at any time in history.

In China last month we heard repeatedly that the people will not permit a U-turn. As for the pernicious side effects of economic growth we read so much about, Deng himself has said there would be bad things as well as good: speculation, crime, prostitution, gambling, corruption, influence peddling. They represent the price that has to be paid for the rocket journey from feudalism into the new high-tech era—a small price, Deng said, to achieve great goals.

The uncertainty of succession and the hardness of the landing of the economy are the two principal risks for an investor in China. I echo Deng. "Small risks to achieve great rewards."

How Fast Is China Really Growing?

January 24, 1994

The mania for investment in China rolls on, and I still believe the long-term story. My Hong Kong/China position is the largest commitment to any of the Asian markets in the Emerging Markets Model Portfolio. I am disconcerted, though, by the almost universal acceptance of the view that China has such potential you can't lose by putting money there. I actually get calls from salesmen whose smiles come right through the phone with direct investment schemes like "I've got shares for you in a pizza chain we're going to open in Wangsow." The sentiment indicators are flashing craziness. It's like private deals in 1970 or technology in 1983. "No thanks. Been there. Seen the movie. Knew the ending."

Now in January 1994 the China thesis is riskier than it was in September 1993, because the government has reversed itself and decided to go for growth rather than slow the pace and maneuver for a soft landing. The official data say that growth is surging and inflation is rising moderately, with the November inflation number for the cities at 21 percent and December probably higher. Real interest rates are around minus 10 percent on one-year CDs and minus 8 percent on three-year CDs. The trade deficit in 1993 soared to $12 billion, and as our Hong Kong–based economist, Michael Taylor, observes, even this figure is suspect. Whether the new tax policy and exchange-rate reforms announced January 1 by the central government will work or be accepted by the high-growth provinces remains to be seen.

All in all, the risk of overheating has increased, and the stability of the Chinese economy looks fragile. In my view, the odds of a boom-bust cycle have increased, which ain't good. Lord knows what the political consequences would be. A fascinating article last week in the *International Herald Tribune* by Christopher Lingle and Kurt Wickman, two senior fellows at the University of Singapore, raised some disturbing questions and added to my uncertainty.

The article points out that the widely accepted 10 percent annual real GNP growth number for China over the last decade is not confirmed by World Bank and IMF data, which indicate growth in the 2 to 4 percent range. It boggles the imagination, say the writers, that a huge and disparate economy like China's could outpace the growth of the smaller and much more homogeneous "miracle economies" of East Asia, particularly since government policies have accentuated regional differences.

There are glaring inconsistencies in the official data that China reports. In an essay last week, Michael Taylor pointed out that the year-end figures were even more distorted than usual, and that certain key trade series "don't triangulate." In Shanghai last September, a high Bank of China official laughed when in an informal discussion I asked him how good the government statistics were. "They are a little soft," he said. "It's a big country." Other China watchers have commented that growth may be overstated and inflation understated for political purposes. If they are, China is not the first country to do this. We now know that the growth and size data for the Soviet Union and East Germany were grossly overstated by their communist regimes.

The *Trib* article suggests that China's economy even now is not growing nearly as fast as is believed. One misleading factor, the writers suspect, is that nominal growth projections may be fairly accurate but inflation is being underestimated, so real growth is well below the 12 to 14 percent figures being bruited about. They also argue that GNP estimates are very difficult in a developing economy when previously unreported barter transactions are being converted to monetary value.

The other point they make is that the growth of the booming coastal provinces is being extrapolated for all China, when in reality these areas account for only 15 percent of the country's population. Real growth may be only 1 to 2 percent in the rural, agrarian interior where the masses live. At the same time, the inflation being generated by the high-growth provinces is imposing uncompensated price rises on the hinterland provinces and on workers in government-owned companies and the underclass in the cities. For example, food prices in certain cities jumped 40 percent late last year before the government intervened. This is the stuff of discontent and maybe even civil disorder.

These are crucial points. Our bull story on China dreamed of 1.2 billion consumers on the threshold of middle-class consumption patterns. If the rising tide of prosperity is being felt by only 200 million, the story is still huge but diminished. If the mass of the people are not sharing in the prosperity but are experiencing the inflation, however, I get more worried, because that would be a combustible situation. Tensions would rise not only between rich and poor but also between the coastal provinces and the hinterland, which could even threaten the stability of the country and cause another protest on the order of Tiananmen Square. In a way, this is what the attempt by Beijing to equalize things by taxing the coastal provinces is all about.

The two Singapore University senior fellows also argue that China's crude monetary system can be expected to go on generating boom–bust cycles, which are not conducive to sustained long-term growth. As a result of such cycles, efficient, private-sector companies are prevented from getting the credit needed to adjust their production while inefficient state firms are rescued and stocks are built up. This is not a sound way to run an economy, they argue. Of course, Zhu Rongji, China's chief economic minister, would agree, which is why he is trying to reform the banking system and the Central Bank.

In December the cost of food soared in the big cities, and the government quickly froze prices, which of course only leads to black markets. Last weekend Zhu Rongji proposed tighter controls on consumer prices and credit. He also said inflation rose sharply in December. Since November inflation was 21 percent, a 25 to 30 percent number for December is possible. Is this a dangerous rate? Who knows? I have heard stories of more discontent in China than there has been for some time, and spring is always the season for trouble from students. But what does discontent mean? There's probably more discontent among the people of the Western democracies than there has been for a long time, too, but maybe discontent is more serious in an authoritarian country.

Lingle and Wickman conclude their piece as follows: "The uneven growth that has occurred in China since 1979 points to heightened regional tensions. When combined with other centrifugal forces in such an economically disparate country, these could lead to the breakup of the Chinese state." This seems too extreme to me. In fact, to the extent real growth has been less, one could argue China is less overheated. However, if it is a case of less growth and more inflation plus severe regional disparities, that is more worrisome.

I still think China is the greatest long-term story, but rapidly growing developing countries usually have boom–bust episodes within the secular trend. After the American Civil War, many European investors correctly foresaw the growth of America but ended up losing money investing here because they bought at the top and got scared out at the bottom of the boom–bust cycles that marked the United States in the last third of the nineteenth century. Investors in China must steel themselves, prepare their minds to accept volatility.

China Tales

March 1, 1994

I was in China last week and saw much but learned little. China is truly "a riddle wrapped in an enigma." With its huge economy, helter-skelter data collection system, and Byzantine political process, it's almost impossible to have much conviction about overheating or soft landings. Contradictory signs abound. The government just reported that the cost of living in the 35 biggest cities rose 24 percent in December, yet the price of gold in China has not budged since September. The government says per capita income last year rose 10 percent in the cities and 3 percent in rural areas—impressive gains, if true. The Shenzhen and Shanghai stock exchanges have been declining listlessly for almost a year now, and no one really seems to know why. "Too many new issues" is the most common explanation. A bull market is essential, in fact the sine qua non, of China's master development plan. The Chinese must revive their stock markets to get the privatizations done and to attract the billions of overseas money they are counting on.

I am a devoted student of the words of Zhu Rongji, Vice Premier, head of the Central Bank, and economic czar, but he now talks central bank-speak and is as opaque as Alan Greenspan. Still, there is little doubt that China has opted to go for growth and "damn the inflation." As Dr. Snoh Unakul, the great Thai thinker, told me, "You must remember that when a developing economy becomes addicted to high growth, even a slowdown to levels like 6 percent that would be spectacular elsewhere can have very painful and socially destabilizing consequences."

Being in China gives you a better sense of the turmoil and change that this growth is causing. One PRC expert told me he believes 100 million people are migrating each year now from one part of China to another. Most don't have the official *hukou* permits, and in addition to being industrious and entrepreneurial, they are bringing crime, prostitution, and exploitation. They are swamping the infrastructure of the cities;

during the Chinese New Year, 50 rural migrants were crushed to death in a stampede in a city railroad station. Some provinces are trying to keep immigrants out. I saw first-hand that the border security between provinces is much tougher than at the check-points between China and Hong Kong.

Two vignettes of China may be illuminating. Last week in Shenzhen we saw long stretches of uncompleted highways tying up traffic and large numbers of half-finished office buildings and apartment houses. There were almost no construction workers in evidence, yet obviously a huge amount of money has been invested and is earning nothing. Were these signs of a new austerity move? "It's all because of the new capital gains tax," said one PRC expert, which makes no sense. Another told me that the Chinese build large projects "like ants." All the "ants" concentrate on one job at one time, take it to a certain level, and then go to the next one. The workers were simply off doing something else the day I saw Shenzhen and the unfinished toll roads. My naive reaction: possible but implausible.

One day in China last week we visited the plant in one of the new economic zones of one of the best Hong Kong manufacturing companies. There are bad factories in Shenzhen where young women from the provinces lose fingers in the machinery, ruin their eyesight squinting 12 hours a day into enlargers, or breathe silicone dust and get lung disease, but this was a good one. There are plenty of bad ones. More than 140 workers died in two factory fires in Shenzhen last year.

This factory has long rows of women with lifeless, monotony-bruised faces working 10 hours a day, 13 days in a row followed by 1 off, at 20 cents an hour. Dim fluorescent lights, gray walls, gray floors: it must be unbearably hot in the summer, and it's too noisy on the factory floor to talk even if it were permitted. The women all stand so they won't go to sleep and are between 16 and 21. We saw new workers in formation learning discipline and obedience through military close-order drill, with the drillmaster occasionally prodding with a long stick. At other factories there are beatings and severe discipline. The women live in dormitories on the grounds and eat at a company canteen. At bad factories, they sleep by their machines.

Unhappy, sullen workers? Hardly. There were lines of young women outside the gates applying for jobs, and at the lunch break the workers were smiling and gay. After five years they have earned a dowry and go home to get married. This factory in China has the lowest reject rate of any facility the company runs anywhere in the world, so they must be doing something right.

Unions are coming to China, though. There is no minimum wage. Wage rates adjusted for inflation haven't changed in five years and are set by supply and demand. The supply of young workers from the interior provinces seems limitless, so wages have remained very low even by developing country standards. Now the governments in Shenzhen and Guangdong are talking of unions, work rules, and a minimum wage, but only for foreign firms. It won't make much difference in China's competitive position as the prime manufacturing location in Asia. Not only are wages lower, but as the general manager of the factory complex said: "The Chinese worker, man or woman, is the smartest with the best dexterity and concentration of any in the world." Of course, he was an overseas Chinese himself.

After 12 days in Asia, I am struck that almost everyone is obsessed with China and that one hears a new theory every day. My conclusion: no one really knows what's going on in China because it's unanalyzable, but whatever it is, it's absolutely crucial to the Pacific Rim countries and stock markets.

A China Traveler's Tales

November 10, 1994

The Vice Minister was slim in a dark blue suit and spoke softly. He was obviously smart and sophisticated, and he wasn't trying to sell us anything. Why should he? So much investment money is coming into China that there is even talk of limiting the flow. The Minister's English was excellent, and he had a gentle smile. The four of us were having a full 12-course Chinese dinner, which for once didn't seem endless.

"We are all very proud," he was saying, "that the real per capita income of all our people—those in the countryside, too, not just in the cities—is rising about 10 percent a year. This is not 'trickle down,' where the rich get richer and the peasants stay poor, as happened at first in the Asian Tigers and now in South America. This year we deregulated agricultural prices, which has caused inflation to be higher than we would like, but on the other hand it has benefited the peasants. For social stability, this rising tide of wealth must lift all the boats. Next year, we expect inflation to be 15 percent or less, but you must remember the food weighting in the CPI is 50 percent. If you are a monetarist, you will be happy to learn M3 has been falling for four months now."

He went on to say that years of real GNP growth of 12 percent do not occur evenly across a huge economy like China's, and such growth inevitably creates distortions and infrastructure bottlenecks. Pollution is bad in the cities, he admitted, and there are power shortages. Also, the transportation system is inadequate to handle the *mang liu* (literally, "blind flow") of migration back and forth to jobs across the country. The roads are dust and ruts, and air travel is too expensive. So the people must use the railroads, and there are nowhere near enough passenger trains. Even if there were, he said, the railway system is buckling because freight traffic has doubled in the past five years. "Twice as much track is needed, but we can't do everything at once."

This *mang liu* is good, he said, but must be "observed" because it could cause social instability. There is surplus labor in the countryside, and in recent years maybe 60 million people have moved from farms to the cities. This migration has "refreshed" the supply of labor in the cities and thus kept wage increases moderate, and these workers, who now earn three times as much as they had on the farms, send money back to the countryside. Last year their remittances equaled 12 percent of Chinese farmers' total income. Some of these itinerant workers also return home and start new businesses, which contribute to rural development.

We are visiting a company whose third-floor office in a fine old building overlooks a city square by the railroad station. The huge square is crammed with people, peasant workers, most of them young, 20,000 or 50,000 men and women, who knows how many? They are waiting to buy a ticket to go home, to go to the next job, to go somewhere, but passenger trains that irregularly stop at the station are stuffed so full of people that only a few new travelers can get on. In fact, the authorities won't even sell any more tickets.

So these peasant workers have squatted maybe for days in this stinking, hot square, sleeping on the hard stone at night, waiting to jam onto a train. We can smell the stale bodies. Now they are sullen, tired, hungry, and profoundly discontented with the transportation system.

As we watch, a fistfight flares in the packed crowd from some petty squabble, perhaps line jumping. With almost spontaneous combustion, the tussle spreads like wildfire as frustration and boredom coalesce. A noise like a dull animal roar rises, and the fistfights verge into riot. Mindless, the crowd, abruptly a mob, surges toward the station and the ticket windows.

Suddenly bursting from the police station on the west side of the square, 30 policemen in green uniforms and World War I–type helmets rush into the crowd, swinging thick wooden clubs. They flail mercilessly, indiscriminately but without anger at anyone unfortunate enough to be within reach, man or woman, young or old, involved or not. Fear is palpable. Like a Roman phalanx, they blast a path toward the center of the turmoil, but abruptly the fighting stops, the violence evaporates, its energy expended. There is an eerie silence in the square, except for the moans of those who were clubbed. A command is shouted, and the police squad wheels and returns to the station house. No arrests were made that I could see.

As a riot control exercise, the maintenance of peace and domestic tranquility, it was a classic performance, no different from a bad day in Manchester, Louisville, or Paris. No riot, no sacking of a ticket office, was going to happen in the city that morning. In Shanghai the same day, a doctor who issued false sterilization certificates was hung, and a street vendor who was caught by the price police selling vegetables at above-prescribed prices was thrown into jail.

Another day on the outskirts of Shanghai we visited companies. They were very impressive. China is experiencing an industrial and technological revolution. On what had been a farm three years earlier, the plant making tinted plate glass for office buildings was huge, clean, and there were only a few white-coated technicians visible. The glass flowed like a seamless river, and the stacking and handling was all automated. The exterior was landscaped with small trees. We could have been in Michigan or France, and in fact, the company was a licensee of Pilkington.

Another visit was to the fastest-growing manufacturer of telephone equipment in the world, which controls half the entire Chinese market. It has not been privatized and is owned by the Shanghai government, with a minority stake held by a European company. The assembly and testing of electronic exchanges here is high technology. This is not Thailand, where near Chiang Mai I have seen rows of farm girls squinting through microscopes 12 hours a day in Japanese-owned factories until they are half blind at 25. Nor is it the teeming factories of Shenzhen or Indonesia, where the company's edge is pure and simple: the exploitation of low-cost labor.

There is one telephone for every 77 people in China. In the United States, it is 1.3 people to 1 telephone, in Thailand, 28.5 to 1, in Mexico, 7.6 to 1. The United States was at 77 to 1 in maybe 1915. My guess is that China will be at our ratio in 30 years, which means it will get there in less than half the time it took us. But the big difference is that the Chinese market today is 10 times as big as Western Electric's was in 1915.

In Pudong, across the river from Shanghai, the avenues are broad, and the traffic flows smoothly. This is where the fantastic new city is being built, like nothing the world has ever seen, of office buildings, plants, and residential areas. Even the electronic scale model in the development company's office left us dazzled. Twenty-five million square feet of office space will come on the market in the next three years, which compares with 4 million per year at the peak in Hong Kong. And there is even more being built in the old city across the river. Shanghai is almost bound to be the future business capital city of Asia, and Pudong will have the efficiency and infrastructure of Singapore, with the raw entrepreneurial energy of Hong Kong.

We were caught in a monumental traffic jam outside of Shanghai. A massive elevated ring road is being built, and I watched laborers break out old pavement, not with jackhammers but squatting, by hand, with stakes and mallets, one man holding the stake, the other hammering. There was no earth-moving equipment that I could see. No yellow tractors, no back-end loaders such as clutter our construction sites. Earth was being moved in sacks on men's backs. Further on, several hundred men shoveled endlessly, monotonously. The road was being built by sheer, raw sweat and muscle, just as roads had been built in China for thousands of years.

The car inched forward. Under one of the completed concrete approach ramps to the expressway, a camp had been set up. It was late afternoon, but hundreds of men slept on pallets under ragged mosquito nets. A few lounged around smoldering cooking fires, and one got up and walked a few yards to urinate against a stanchion. Our driver told us that work on the road went on all day and night with the labor gangs alternating 12-hour shifts, seven days a week. There are camps like this, some much bigger, all around Shanghai, he said almost bitterly, and these migrants account for much of the crime in the city.

We were eating some strange sticky dessert. I mentioned an article in a Japanese newspaper that argued that masses of migrant peasants had always been the historical sign of "dynastic decline and a portent of imminent changing of heaven's mandate." Maybe so, said the Minister, and the government was also mindful of the destabilizing effects of inflation. But he asked with a little smile, was there ever a time in Chinese history when a dynasty collapsed when it was raising the people's real incomes at 10 percent a year? "So we cherish our growth pace, will accept some inflation as a side effect, and will, as you say, keep muddling through."

China Cooling, Us Heating

September 27, 1993

For the last nine days, a group of investors, David Roche, and I have been in China. David and I think that the overheated Chinese economy is now beginning to cool and that the odds are it is headed for a soft landing and not a bust. This is very good news for the world, because China is an economic giant and the principal locomotive of Asia. A crash in China would reverberate across Asia, and a blowoff that resulted in political instability would have dire consequences.

We were all stunned by the enormity of China. There are 30 provincial entities within China that are as big as or bigger than most countries in Asia. Greater Shanghai, for example, is three times the size of Singapore and growing at least twice as fast. Sichuan province alone has 110 million people, which would rank it as the eighth-biggest country in the world. Thanks to Wharf Holdings, we toured Wuhan and met with the Governor of Hubei province. Greater Wuhan has a population of 10 million, and the province has 50 million people with GNP growing at 14 percent per annum. Wuhan likes to think of itself as the Chinese Chicago. The difference is that it's Chicago in about 1880.

Over the years, I have heard a lot of developing-country macro stories and a couple of times even been present at the creation of bull markets, but the China story is the best and the brightest. Sometimes you have to spend time in country to get really focused on the investment case. After eight days in China I'm tuned in, overfed, and maximum bullish.

As is well known, China has the third-largest and the fastest-growing economy in the world. Real GNP growth has been running in the 12 to 13 percent range, but by last spring there were clear signs of overheating. The money supply was compounding at an annual rate of 50 percent, industrial production was surging 25 percent year over year, and there were signs of a consumer spending spree. Property values in the cities were soaring, industrial commodity prices were rising sharply, and inflation in the cities probably was approaching 20 percent. In addition, the value of the currency was dropping rapidly, the trade account had abruptly swung from surplus to deficit, and there was a flight from bank deposits.

With memories of the late 1980s blowoff and Tiananmen Square still vivid, the leadership named Zhu Rongji, 64, vice premier and one of its most powerful figures, as head of the central bank. On March 15, I wrote that China most likely would engineer a soft landing, arguing that this time was different because it was a production-driven rather than consumption-driven boom. Nevertheless, most observers predicted the boom would end in bust, and the Shanghai and Shenzhen stock markets dived. Zhu, however, is a very tough, pragmatic guy, and he did everything from raising interest rates to imprisoning bank officials who were making unauthorized loans for speculation. This week 14 "financial embezzlers" were hung. Two increases in interest rates on deposits restored some faith in the banking system and encouraged money to return to the banking system. China has a 40 percent savings rate.

Last week we heard from a variety of official and unofficial sources that the program was working and that the economy was slowing. For example, a Hong Kong property developer in Shanghai told us he could not get bank money at any rate in China to build, the mayor of Wuhan told us there were no bank loans available anymore, and in Beijing the vice governor of the People's Bank said in perfect English, "We are out of the woods." Perhaps an even more impartial source was the IMF representative in China, who said that Zhu is doing the right things and that he was "cautiously optimistic" that a soft landing was coming. Those are strong words in IMF-speak.

The statistics out last week support this view. A month-on-month fall of 5.1 percent in industrial production was followed by another decline in August, albeit from a very high level. Retail sales in the cities are slowing from double- to single-digit gains. Cement prices are softening, and last Saturday it was reported that steel quotes had fallen 15 percent in three months. In August, bank deposits jumped 40 percent, and consumer spending slowed to around 12 percent. Capital investment was up *only* 18 percent in August from the same month in 1992; in the first six months, the annualized increase was 71 percent. In fact, Zhu himself said that inflation is still too high but at least is falling and that the objective for 1994 was single-digit inflation.

Another sign that the crisis is over can be found in the exchange rate. On the swap market, the RMB plummeted from 7 to the U.S. dollar to as low as 11.2 in June. In recent months it has rallied to around 8.8 and on Friday was at 8.2. China now has a three-tier exchange rate system, but the clear message we got was this would be changed next year. However, the elimination of exchange controls may take a little longer. It is clear the RMB is deeply undervalued, and my view is that the RMB will gradually appreciate against the dollar in the years to come.

We were also very impressed with the caliber of the people running China. We didn't get to see any of the elderly big guns but rather spent time with governors, mayors, and the people running agencies. They were smart, tough, friendly people with definite vision. For example, the heads of the Shanghai Stock Exchange and the Securities and Exchange Commission spoke of how important it was to give the individual Chinese investor time to get sophisticated. They worry that the stock market will move too fast, then crash, and that people will get hurt. The provincial politicians were pragmatic salesmen. Somehow they were under the misapprehension we were direct investors, and surprised hedge-fund managers in our group were offered tax holidays if they would only locate a plant in the province.

Nevertheless, the securities business in China is on a near-vertical growth path. Guan Jin Sheng, the president of Shanghai International Securities, told us his company's revenues in RMB were 45.6 million in 1991, 102.5 million in 1992, and an estimated 500 million this year. The company's return on equity last year was 110 percent. SIS has over 1 million active trading accounts, and the entire order-entry system is electronic. If only its shares could be owned.

It is no wonder there are already 10 million shareholders. As noted, China has a 40 percent savings rate and 50 years of accumulated savings. A taxi driver told me he saved half his earnings. The tax system rewards investing. There is no capital gains tax or tax on dividends, but the maximum individual tax rate on income reaches 60 percent. Government bonds yield around 13 percent, and short-term deposits 9 percent, with inflation running officially at 15 percent.

Both the Shanghai and Shenzhen stock markets sold off late last week on disappointment about the Olympics going to Sydney. According to Christina Ko, our China analyst, the aggregate market value of the Chinese markets is $33 billion. Between the two, there are 113 companies listed. Unfortunately, there are just 30 issues of the B shares, which can be owned by foreigners, with an aggregate value of only $1.2 billion, but there are other ways to buy China, such as the H shares, the red chips, and Hong Kong stocks. The B shares sell at around 12 times this year's forecast earnings and at a huge discount to the A shares. When foreign exchange controls are eliminated, they will probably become no different from the A shares. This is a complex subject, but Christina just published an excellent study, "Guide to the PRC Investment Jungle."

My view on Chinese equities is that, despite all the caution of the authorities, sometime in the next few years China will have the mother of all bull markets. The Chinese are great speculators, and this is the biggest, most open-ended story of all time. The wild bull markets in Hong Kong (early 1970s), Singapore (late 1970s), and Taiwan (1980s) will seem like child's play. Not only will prices rise several thousand percent, I believe, but the supply of stock outstanding will double year after year. In fact today the total equity capitalization is 208 percent larger than at the same time last year. Unfortunately, at this time it's not so easy to get money to work in pure plays.

In the meantime, I am increasing the Hong Kong–China weight in the Emerging Markets Model Portfolio to 16 percent, from 11 percent, with the additional money being allocated to a cross-section of Chinese B shares. The money comes by reducing Brazil two percentage points (although we remain fully invested there), eliminating the small, 2 percent position in Pakistan, and from cash. I'm still very bullish on Hong Kong because of China and consider the best plays to be Hang Lung Development (HK$11.60), Hopewell (HK$5.50), China Light (HK$43.50), Wharf (HK$20.60), and Hutchison (HK$22.90). I have long been partial as well to Hong Kong Telecom (HK$12.30).

Next week, less euphoria and more about the problems.

Section 3B: India

India Tilts to the Right and the Stock Market Explodes

May 14, 1985

Friedrich Hayek, a Nobel Prize economist, once described India as the ultimate example of complete failure because of too much government planning. Like everyone else, he said he shunned visiting India because its grinding poverty is so depressing. India may never be a popular tourist destination, but in the last few months its young government has proposed radically new economic policies. Although this policy shift is presently overshadowed by the fighting between Hindu and Sikh extremists, it could be of immense significance.

Since India gained its independence, its governments have followed the Fabian social model whose general assumption is that the government has first claim on a nation's assets and that the state in its wisdom should decide where to allocate those resources. Since the state is responsible for growth, incomes are to be entirely at its disposal. Government controls on business through rebates, subsidies, and high tax rates are necessary to order growth and social justice, and since the rich only become richer at the cost of the poor, high taxes on their earnings are necessary to keep the disparities within tolerable limits. The maximum individual tax rate of 68 percent is reached at a mere $8,000 of income. No matter that government bureaucracy is recognized as swollen, inefficient, and often corrupt, it is still better than the greed of business and the undisciplined waste of the people.

With this model in practice, the Indian economy has limped along with real growth of about 3 percent annually but no real progress in raising per capita income or reducing poverty and unemployment. Enterprise languished. Many of the best Indians emigrated. When Rajiv Gandhi became prime minister after his mother was assassinated, there was no reason to think this unassuming former airline pilot would do anything but follow the socialist model.

But he did. Since independence, many of India's leaders and technocrats had been educated in England, where they got a heavy dose of British socialism. Nehru himself was infatuated with the ideas of Sidney Webb and George Bernard Shaw. Rajiv Gandhi did his stint at Oxford, too, but his interests were more practical—flying and airplanes were dominant themes. I am told he is much more of a pragmatist who has seen the dead hand of government interference and too little initiative and risk taking in Indian society. Perhaps he has noted the success of supply-side policies in countries like Hong Kong and the United States, or maybe somebody read George Gilder's *Wealth and Poverty*.

Whatever its genesis, with the release of the annual budget in mid-March, the Indian government announced a classic supply-side package that included a 10-percentage-point reduction in the corporate tax rate, major cuts in individual taxes through increases in bracket thresholds and a drop in the maximum rate to 50 percent, a cut in the wealth tax, and the abolishment of death duties. The budget also forecast that the nation will run a larger deficit in fiscal 1986. The government explicitly said that the tax cuts were designed to stimulate economic growth and investment, and to curb the huge black economy. The message made it clear that the government wants to reduce its presence in the economy. The respected economist N. A. Palkhivala, long a critic of Indian economic policies, said "it is an epoch-making budget for redesigning India."

After some initial hesitation, the Indian stock market soared from 305 just before the budget's release to 335.4 by the end of March. The market was then closed for several days to calm things down on the theory that the enthusiasm would soon wane and prices would crash. Obviously, the authorities hadn't read history or Jude Wanniski's book.

The more Indian investors thought about the supply-side tax cuts and the change in direction, the more enthusiastic they became. Prices soared when the market reopened, and the authorities, still fearful, closed it down after only an hour. Regular hours are now being kept again, but the market has worked higher and now stands at 350. Furthermore, Gandhi has moved on other fronts. In mid-April, he began to fulfill his promise to reopen the economy when he removed import restrictions on 685 goods. Next, he cracked down on government corruption in the issuance of contracts and announced that most existing relationships would be reassessed, as would major orders for helicopters and a natural-gas pipeline. Gandhi clearly is his own man and has an agenda.

The Indian stock market is surprisingly large: it has over 3,700 listed companies with a market value of close to $30 billion. The principal market is in Bombay, but there are exchanges in Calcutta, Delhi, and Madras. Trading activity is intense with an annual turnover of 30 percent. However, the market is almost completely unknown in the West and is very difficult to get information on. The *Financial Times* has nothing on the Indian market. Morgan Stanley has an Indian associate who, despite connections, has found it difficult to get much information for me. We can get quotes, however, and it is interesting that Union Carbide India is trading at 19.70 rupees compared with a high of 20.10 and well above its low for the year. The Indian market has not kept pace with inflation for the last 15 years and was down 3 percent (total return) in 1982 and up only 6 percent in 1983, when markets in the rest of the world were booming. We believe the average yield in the market is around 7 percent, but we are not sure what the average price/earnings ratio is. Trading favorites include Tata Iron and Steel, Reliance Textile Industries (a textile and petrochemical conglomerate), Associated Cement, Gwalio Rayon, and Hindustan Motors.

The Indian market has not always been so obscure. In the first third of this century in the height of England's rule, the Indian market was active and closely followed in London. With independence and socialism, interest gradually evaporated. Now it may be returning. Lord knows that with 720 million people and the lowest per capita GNP in Asia, the potential is certainly there. It is too soon to say whether Prime Minister Gandhi and his ministers have the conviction and staying power to defeat the entrenched forces of the bureaucracy, but the new government and the stock market are off to a propitious start. The stakes are big enough so that it's worth watching closely.

India for the 1990s

October 23, 1989

As the OECD economies mature and valuations in their stock markets ripen, the allure of the so-called emerging markets increases, for they are the frontiers of capitalism where brave pioneer investors can find gold. The last generation, the four Asian Tigers, still nourishes price/earnings ratios of at least 20, and at one time or another all, with the exception of Korea, have sported truly stratospheric multiples. The matriculating class in Asia – Thailand, Malaysia, and Indonesia – also has seen valuations explode as institutional investors with fat little legs and beady eyes discovered them. The legs, incidentally, are for running home at the first sign of trouble, which imparts breathtaking volatility. In Europe, Portugal and Turkey may be poised for takeoff, and, of course, there are opportunities in South America, Africa, and Eastern Europe for the adventurous.

Nevertheless, my pick for the best market in the world for the 1990s is India. First, however, let me confess gross self-interest: Morgan Stanley just raised privately $156 million from institutions and individuals around the world for a closed-end fund to invest in Indian equities. That said, I didn't have to put my own money in the fund, but I did. The fund is a creature of the genius of Madhav Dhar, who conceived the idea and put us together with the State Bank of India.

India, with over 800 million people, is by far the largest democracy in the world. In the upcoming election, 75 percent of the electorate will vote compared with a pathetic 55 percent in the United States. Incidentally, none of the Tigers is anywhere near as politically mature, but being a democracy also means progress is less tidy. The Indian economy is the third largest in Asia and the eleventh largest in the world, but per capita GNP is a mere $319 versus $650 for the Philippines, $1,052 for Thailand, and $6,051 for a full-fledged NIC like Taiwan. In per capita GNP, India is where the four Tigers were 10 to 15 years ago. In other words, the economy is at the point where, with luck and skill, ignition occurs.

The four Tigers and Malaysia have had to bootstrap themselves by exporting the work of an industrious, low-cost labor force because their domestic markets were too small. Even Korea, by far the largest Tiger, has only 42 million people. The Tigers were able to post very rapid growth for a while by keeping their currency undervalued and their workers underpaid.

Eventually, however, the workforce began to get sullen and demanded its share of prosperity, and the world, seeing the swelling trade surpluses of the Tigers, forced them to let their currencies appreciate. Wages in Korea, for example, are now increasing 20 percent per annum, and the trade-weighted currency is rising roughly 15 percent. Therefore, Korea's average manufacturing wage rate of around $4 an hour is effectively compounding at 35 percent, and its competitive labor advantage is vanishing.

Korea and the other Tigers will adapt, but the glorious years of spurting, double-digit growth may be gone forever.

India is different. It has no need to export because its domestic market is so huge and has such an insatiable appetite for consumer goods. The middle class alone, with 150 million people, is equivalent to the combined populations of Germany, the United Kingdom, and France and is swelling 20 percent per year. Other interesting miscellaneous facts are that the savings rate in India is 22 percent, the country is a net exporter of food, industrial production grew 14 percent last year, inflation is slowing to 7 percent this year, and exports are a mere 5 percent of GNP.

Anyway, the India story goes like this. After independence, India was ruled by an elite that had been educated at Cambridge and Oxford as Fabian socialists. Under its influence, the Indian economy, despite its immense human resource potential, grew fitfully. The dead hand of bureaucracy and confiscatory tax rates stifled the natural entrepreneurial inclination of the Indian people. Frustrated and taxed at home, the smart people and capital migrated to other countries.

After Indira Gandhi was assassinated, her second son, an airline pilot, became prime minister. Rajiv Gandhi is a practical fellow without the socialist baggage of his predecessors, and he began a process of deregulation, liberalization, and tax reduction. The top personal rate was cut from 90 percent to 50 percent, wealth taxes were lowered, and the corporate rate was reduced to 50 percent. Suddenly, the economy revived, multinationals vied for entry, entrepreneurial activity exploded, and the outflow of brains and capital reversed. The economy was transformed, and last year real GNP growth reached 9 percent. This rate is probably not sustainable, but we believe India can average 7 percent real growth for the next decade. A senior official of the World Bank quoted in the *Financial Times* was more optimistic, saying: "There could be a sudden and explosive movement into the pattern we have seen in other countries in East Asia. India would have no difficulty in achieving an 8 to 10 percent growth rate on a sustained basis."

Tourism should be a big growth industry for India and an important foreign exchange earner. Our Byron Wien, a consummate traveler if there ever was one and a man who never stays in the same hotel twice, has just returned from a vacation in India. "The single most exciting travel experience I've ever had, and I'm going back next year," he said. This is like a new restaurant getting the top rating in the Michelin guide. Incidentally, Byron is now sorry he missed buying our fund.

An economic miracle in India would be a major event in the 1990s because, after all, this is the second-largest country in the world. India already is a regional military power, and its aspirations are large. However, although the Indian stock market boomed in 1986, when Rajiv first took over, and was strong last year, in 1989 it is barely ahead 7 percent. One big worry is the national election scheduled for late next month, with Gandhi going against his former finance minister, who was one of the original architects of the economic reform. The issues are political, and whoever wins, the basic economic policies will remain.

The Indian stock market at $30 billion is already as large as Malaysia or Singapore, but it is a mere 10 percent of GNP versus 121 percent for Singapore and 86 percent for Malaysia. It has 5,000 listed companies, of which about 150 are of substantial size, 15 million shareholders (more than the United Kingdom), and 2,113 brokerage firms. Capitalism has deep roots in India. The market is closed to foreign investors and actually has a negative correlation with the gyrations of the U.S. market. Accounting practices are conservative and derive from India's British past. Average daily trading volume is about $40 million, and the market index sells at 10 times estimated 1989 earnings and 7 times next year's forecast profits. We guess that over the next five years, 14 percent nominal GNP growth will translate into 20 percent annual advances in corporate profits. The question is what the market will sell for.

The authorities fully understand the power of permanent foreign equity, and we get the impression India will follow the so-called Korean model for developing markets. In other words, a series of offshore closed-end funds (there is already a long queue at the Ministry of Finance) will be permitted to enter the market. The expectation is that these funds will sell at a plump premium over net asset value and that Indian companies will then be able to exploit that premium and finance in the international capital market on very favorable terms. Eventually, the equity market will be opened when the world is salivating, but not until the last possible moment. No one has worked this scheme more artfully than the Koreans.

The other factor is the overseas Indians, many of whom are rich and who are permitted to own Indian stocks. I expect to see a lot of their money go back into Indian stocks once the bull phase truly begins. All things considered, my guess is that five years from now the Indian market will still be partially closed and should sell at 20 to 25 times earnings, as the Korean market does today. In "modern times" our asset return studies show emerging markets have averaged 16 percent a year, a return exceeded only by venture capital. To my mind, India has all the ingredients to be the best in the world over the next five years. If things don't work out, I think the risk is boredom.

The only way to buy India now is by purchasing The India Growth Fund ($15½) on the New York Stock Exchange or the India Fund (2l2p) in London. Both sell at about a 15 to 20 percent premium to net asset value.

Great Expectations

February 20, 1990

ndia is condemned to no specific destiny. The country to me is like a college kid—big, sprawling, strong, pulsing with energy, quick and intelligent, but also messy, often disorganized, a little wild, and sometimes unfocused. India is a smart kid, but like all kids, it does dumb things. Boundless possibilities, great expectations, it could shoot the moon, but will the country ever get its act together? I think it will and have bet money that it will, but you can't be sure.

Last month I went to India for the first time. I was there for 10 days. With Madhav Dhar, I visited companies and saw government officials, businessmen, brokers, investment managers, and bankers, but philistine that I am, I did not travel to the great sights and landscapes of India. We were principally in Bombay and Delhi, although we also visited a company in Pune. The trip to Pune, through a mountain pass on a narrow dusty road choked with trucks, featured a succession of imminent head-on collisions and was the most frightening, bone-jarring day in memory.

I was stunned by the sheer, raw size of India. Everything is gigantic and diverse. The developing countries I have had some experience with, such as Turkey, Thailand, and Malaysia, seem miniature by comparison. For example, India's middle class of 150 million reasonably affluent consumers alone, although only a fraction of the total population of over 800 million, is equal to the entire populations of Germany, France, and the United Kingdom combined. Within 20 years, India could have the biggest population of any country on the globe; it is the third largest economy in Asia and the eleventh biggest in the world.

India's stock market is large and dominated by its 13 million individual investors. The market capitalization, at $40 billion, is bigger than that of almost all the much-heralded Asian Tigers and emerging markets. It is far different from the immature stock markets of an Indonesia or the Philippines, for example. Five years ago, at a similar

231

stage in Thailand's development, I went to the stock exchange in Bangkok; it was a good-sized room with several hundred people milling around rather aimlessly. When we visited the Bombay Stock Exchange, although it was just a dull day, we could hear the roar of the 3,000 floor brokers three blocks away, and Bombay is not a quiet city. Also, Indian shareholder reporting involves far more disclosure than any other Asian market.

India's commercial markets are isolated from the rest of the world. There are virtually no imported automobiles in the country, and the cars in use are all versions of models that date back to the 1960s. These solid, stodgy, but robust machines can stand up to the brutal conditions of India's roads. The same applies to other capital equipment like elevators, for example, which seem to have come straight from the 1930s. Even the exercise equipment in the hotel gyms was antique. It was like going back in time to the early postwar era. This antiquated capital stock does not make travel easy; even rising 20 stories in an office building is a painful process, and a sweaty one as well since there is little air conditioning.

I was, however, favorably surprised by the sophistication of the businessmen and entrepreneurs we met. Many of them had been to business school, not that that proves anything. Nevertheless, my impression is that Indian managements are more professional than in many other parts of Asia. The major Indian companies we visited are big enterprises with complex lines of business employing thousands of people. Everyone seems busy in India. There's activity, motion, hustle. Sure, there are beggars and poverty, but after making my way through Grand Central Station twice a day, I didn't find India a shock.

The government officials we saw were also impressive. The deputy for the Minister of Finance began our talk by asking me whether I thought India should follow the Korean or the Thai model for developing its equity market. Economic growth, fairness, and supply-side policies were on everyone's mind. The Governor of the Central Bank said all the right things and could have been at the Bundesbank, so firm was his aversion

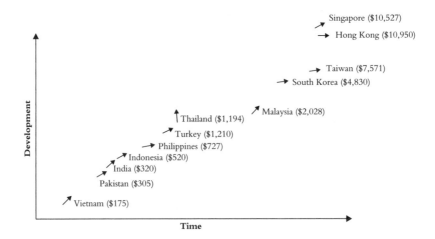

to inflation. Still, although India's public officials and politicians are of relatively high caliber, the country is a true democracy, which means it is not as efficient in dealing with special interest groups as the dictatorships, benevolent or otherwise, that generally held power during the growth acceleration stage of the four little Tigers. And India lacks the commitment to free markets, deregulation, and tax cuts that the Tigers have.

The economic outlook for India is good. Real GNP growth is likely to slow to around 5 percent in the fiscal year ending this March after a 10 percent gain in fiscal 1989. The estimate for fiscal 1991 generally seems to be 7 percent with inflation around 6 percent. For the future, agriculture, which amounts to 30 percent of the economy, should grow 2.5 to 3 percent per annum, industrial production should expand at least 10 percent a year, and the service sector should increase 7 to 8 percent. Exports are rising at a 10 percent annual rate. All in all, real GNP growth forecasts fall in the 5.5 to 7 percent range. The accompanying figure shows where we place India in the flock of Asian developing countries. The number in parentheses shows the per capita income of each country, and the arrow approximates the current growth pace of the country. Remember that India, in terms of population, is bigger than all the other countries combined.

It is clear that Indian agriculture has become much more resilient and is far less dependent on the monsoons because of modern irrigation and fertilizer. The country's savings rate is 24 percent, up from 12 percent 30 years ago. The unique aspect of India is that, unlike any other LDC with the possible exception of Indonesia, it is not dependent on exports but instead is a domestic consumption growth story. To me this means that, if it works, the growth pace will last much longer.

Right now, there is considerable uncertainty in India. First, the new government's budget is awaited with much anticipation. The new Prime Minister was the architect of tax cuts and deregulation when he was Minister of Finance, but he has talked of debt forgiveness for farmers, and his policies now that he has power are not clear. He seems a thoughtful and careful man, and most of the people I talked with seemed to hope for the best. The other problem is the incendiary agitation in Kashmir. I won't go into all the gory historical details, but India is in a difficult moral and governmental situation, and there is always the risk it could degenerate into a war with Pakistan. India would probably handily win any such conflict on the battlefield, but a military showdown is not in either country's interest.

The Indian stock market, after rising about 17 percent in 1989, has fallen about the same amount in the first six weeks of the new year. Uncertainty is weighing heavily on the market. We estimate the average stock is selling at about 10 times forecast earnings for the year that ends in March and perhaps 8 times projected March 1991 profits. With 7 percent real growth and 6 percent inflation, earnings should rise 20 to 25 percent in each of the next few years. Additional foreign funds will gradually be allowed to invest in Indian equities, and I continue to believe the market is headed toward a 20 multiple in the years to come.

India: You Have to Go There to Understand

March 27, 1995

A lot of people who haven't been there are skeptical, but for me India is still one of the best investment stories in the world. Right now, with emerging markets everywhere reeling, Indian equities 35 percent below their highs, and some disconcerting events in the last couple of weeks, it's a great time to buy. At 12 times our forecast of earnings for the year ending March 1996, the broad mass of Indian equities is as cheap as it has been for a long time. Even juicier, two of the closed-end India funds on the New York Stock Exchange (one of which is ours) can be purchased at discounts of 20 percent from net asset value, which shows how depressed sentiment is about both emerging markets and India.

India has magnificent potential, but it is also messy, complex, and frustrating, and there is one serious macro flaw, which I will discuss later. Meanwhile, the stock market is rich with intriguing investment inefficiencies, but its paper-snarled settlement procedures are intimidating, and last week the default of a single broker closed the Bombay exchange for three days and gave the market a knock when it opened on Thursday.

India is two steps forward, one back, and a cloud of hot dust. The investor in Indian equities must be steadfast in believing the long-term case and not be panicked by erratic election results, a few corrupt politicians, occasional religious massacres, and gradual rather than dynamic economic reform. In the short run, coalition democracy is perhaps the least efficient form of government for a huge, heterogeneous developing country, but in the long term it results in a lower country-risk premium.

The heat, the racket, the teeming entrepreneurial street life, the filth of a big Indian city are oppressive, but suddenly we were at the headquarters building, being ushered down quiet halls past air-conditioned rooms where uniformed employees worked on computer screens. It was like an oasis of cool tranquility after the streets. In the small auditorium, the CEO, a tall dark man in the same loose-fitting uniform spoke of ROE objectives, benchmarking, and just-in-time inventory systems. His story was simple: The Indian auto parts industry is expanding 15 percent a year, but as an efficient, low-cost producer, his company is growing 20 to 25 percent annually. The plant runs 24 hours a day six days a week; the average employee works 48 hours a week.

Then he told us how he managed the company. "We treat our employees like family. Their wages are three times the average of this area, but it's more than that. Twice a year we tell them exactly how we are doing financially. We have a subsidized company store, and we are deeply committed to self-improvement programs. Every Saturday there is a computer class, and we sponsor summer camps for their children. There is a company high school. As we grow, our workforce has expanded, but we give first call to the children of our employees. As a result, we haven't hired a nonfamily person in five years. Once a year, each employee has his 'day.' That morning, he brings his entire family to this building, where I greet him and our picture is taken. Then he and his family spend the rest of the morning touring the plant and being greeted by his fellow workers. The objective is to bond the family to the company."

Then we toured the plant. It was a huge, partially enclosed tin shed. Furnaces and welding equipment vented smoke and fumes into the air, which was foul and stifling. It was early spring, but the temperature in the shed must have been well over 100°F. The mostly middle-aged men labored doggedly, but their glances were friendly. The machinery wasn't exactly spick-and-span, but the production process moved smoothly. Quality-control exhortations were everywhere. The air in the plant was so foul I couldn't wait to get out, even into the hot sun.

This jewel of a company has a market cap of $165 million, of which 55 percent is owned by the founding families. Return on equity is around 30 percent, and although earnings are doubling every three years, the company is pretty much self-financing because the dividend payout is kept very low. The stock sells at 13 times earnings.

That's one side of the story. We saw a number of companies like this that made everything from bicycles to soap—wonderful growth stories in understandable businesses that were just approaching the takeoff stage. In Buffett's words, it's the investor's dream of great companies at great prices, but you truly have to be a long-term investor because stakes of any size are so illiquid. Broad diversification is essential.

The other side of the story is the state-owned companies. Some are jewels, some are grossly overstaffed and inefficient, but all have immense potential because India is nowhere in terms of per capita consumption of anything.

Another category might be called "abused companies," those that have been exploited by owner-managements at the expense of the public shareholders. The main reason: excessive regulation and tax laws. Until a year and a half ago, by government decree the maximum salary paid to a CEO was set at $15,000. Capital gains and income tax rates are sky high, all of which combine to persuade some less scrupulous businessmen to take their compensation in perquisites.

We visited one company that shall remain nameless but has a great consumer products business which is growing rapidly. On sales of $500 million the company had pretax profits of just $20 million and an ROE of 8 percent. Not understanding all the subtleties of India, we were baffled. The CEO seemed smart and made a virtuoso presentation. At lunch the mystery was resolved. The company had two helicopters, a G-3, an ocean-going yacht, three resort retreats in India (one of which we were at), castles in Scotland and England, a chateau in France, and who knows what else, all ostensibly for the entertainment of clients but really the private preserve of senior management.

This stock sells at eight times earnings because investors know a buccaneer when they see one. Now changes in the tax law, the need for more equity capital, and an issue of warrants to management suddenly transform an owner's motivation. India is India, and transparency is an evolving concept. The shares are another kind of opportunity.

The flaw in the macro story for India is the size of the budget deficit, which is still 6 percent of GDP, and the interest burden, which consumes half of government revenues. Otherwise, India is healthy. Last year the trade account was in balance, but there was a current account deficit that amounted to only 0.6 percent of GDP. Foreign debt at $90 billion seems to have leveled off, and only $10 billion is short-term. Interest payments are down to 11 percent of exports, and the debt service ratio is 25 percent. Indians have overseas bank accounts of at least $120 billion.

At the Finance Ministry in the magnificent government complex that the British built early in the century, with its long corridors, inner court, high ceilings, and spacious rooms, we met with Montek Singh Ahluwalia, the finance secretary. Ahluwalia's blue Hermes tie matched his turban, and this brilliant technocrat who is at the heart of the reform process lucidly explained the master plan for India.

"We want to promote reforms on the one hand, and we want to strengthen the antipoverty strategy on the other," he said. He didn't need to add that after all there is an election in 1996, and most of the voters are still very poor. He went on to say that India's economy is growing strongly, with growth of 6 to 7 percent expected for the year ending March 1996. The budget assumes inflation will slow to about 8 percent, but my worry is that financing the deficit will be inflationary and interest rates will go up.

Ahluwalia pointed out that as a percentage of GDP the deficit is declining and that the cuts in tariffs and excise duties will help reduce inflation. With output in the private sector growing 10 to 12 percent a year, tax revenues are rising at a 20 percent rate, and tax collection is being improved. Only 4 million Indians actually file tax returns. As a result, he said, the deficit will decline in both absolute and relative terms, without new taxes or spending cuts. Meanwhile, despite the exhortations of supply-siders, the maximum tax rate on ordinary income is 50 percent and on capital gains, 30 percent.

Think of India as a young family with a growing income but a big mortgage on their home. The faster their earnings grow, the easier the interest burden. They also have some family jewels (privatizations) they can sell to help pay down the mortgage. In addition, our family has some gold hidden under the mattress ($130 billion is the estimate for the country as a whole). Put another way, India is Chicago in 1870 or Denver 25 years later, which after all weren't bad places to own equities, as long as you didn't trip over the risk premium or get nicked by a stray bullet from the weekly gunfight.

Section 3C: Japan

More on Japan

October 25, 1983

Having just spent 10 days in Japan, I am now an expert eager to pontificate. I was part of a Nomura-sponsored group that visited with chief executive officers of a cross-section of Japanese companies, met with government officials, and listened to the views of private-sector intellectuals and economists. It was a very stimulating experience for a parochial investor like me.

For what it's worth, the sense I got was that the Japanese economy is beginning to do better, but even the optimists don't expect much more than 4 percent real growth over the next five years or so, which represents a considerable slowdown from the powerful secular growth rate of the past. The almost mystical combination that propelled Japan for so long—a very high savings rate, aggressive business leaders, a hard-working, disciplined work force, and a backlog of modern technology waiting to be exploited—is now fraying at the edges. The people want to spend more to live better and maybe do not want to work so hard. Japan has certainly caught up to the technological frontier, so the potential for huge returns from investment in known technologies is reduced. Infrastructure investments, like roads for all the cars, are now needed, and defense spending will be rising as a share of GNP. However, the business leaders seem as committed as ever, and I don't really see any signs that the fabled "consensus" in Japanese society is breaking down.

In other words, Japan is now becoming a mature economy approaching middle age in the country life-cycle. If you had to assign ages to economies, England is in its 60s although having a revival, and many of the European economies are in their mid- to late 50s. The United States is maybe 45, and now Japan is closing in on 40. The really rapid growth and progress comes in the squared-away, 20- and 30-year olds.

Although Japan's technological progress is formidable—and Nomura convincingly makes the case that major Japanese companies spend more of every sales dollar on research, development, and depreciation than U.S. companies do—I was interested to observe that the country does not have the venture capital–raising infrastructure that exists here. A fledgling Japanese company apparently gets its equity capital through large companies or the banks, and the founding management entrepreneurs end up with very little equity compared with our innovators. Several Japanese made this point to us and suggested that this lack of the big jackpot makes young Japanese engineers, scientists, and go-getters more inclined to work for the big companies than take a fling on their own. I think to be the leader nation on the frontier of technological innovation you have to be incenting the best with maximum monetary rewards.

We visited some wonderful companies, both large and small. Their managements made presentations that were better organized and more sophisticated in many cases than anything I have been exposed to in the United States. Their strategies for growth were on the whole better than what I hear from comparable U.S. companies, and the stories were good. The trouble is that their stocks without exception look very expensive.

Using Capital International's Index as a standard, the Japanese market is now selling at 2.2 times book value, 8.8 times cash earnings, 23.9 times reported earnings, and yields 1.4 percent. The U.S. market sells at 1.45 times book, 6.7 times cash earnings, 12.8 times reported earnings, and yields 4.4 percent. That's quite a difference. About a decade ago the relationship was just the opposite, with the United States at 18 or so times earnings and Japan at 10 or 11. Nomura argues that after adjusting for depreciation accounting differentials, inventory profits, and the difference in interest rates between the two countries, the true price/earnings ratio is 13.7 for Japan versus 14.7 for the United States. However, it requires a pretty good stretch of the old accounting imagination to get there.

All in all, I came away from Japan once again tremendously impressed with the country and its people but thinking Japanese stocks were fully priced. I also was awed by Nomura. Before each visit to a company, their analyst would brief us. Their analysts were just as good as the comparable Morgan Stanley analyst, and they spoke to us in English. After visiting the companies and seeing the hierarchy of shareholder relations people with their canned comments versus what we got talking to the top people themselves, I am convinced only Japanese analysts can cover Japanese companies in terms of change-at-the-margin analysis. We had a little incident with Fuji Photo that proved it.

In terms of being an international firm, Nomura hires 200 to 250 of the best college graduates in Japan they can find. After a few years of observing, they pick out the best 50 or so and send 20 to business school in the United States, another 10 or more to school in Europe, 3 or 4 to Cairo, a couple to China, and so on. In other words, they are building a cadre of multilingual professionals in every major market. No U.S. investment bank is even close to this kind of capability.

Japan is a great country, and Nomura's a wonderful firm with a persuasive story, but I still like U.S stocks better.

Long Trips

October 30, 1984

L ong trips, which I have been taking frequently of late, are bad for sleeping patterns but good for the perspective, and these days I need the latter more than the former.

I spent a week in Australia, which was fascinating. The country is almost exactly the size of the continental United States but has a population of only 15 million. And what an incredibly beautiful country—superb weather for outdoor living and such immense economic potential. Unfortunately, it has all the social diseases of Europe with a highly developed welfare state, militant labor unions, and old-time politicians.

The maximum personal tax rate of about 65 percent is reached at $35,000 of income, and there is maze of federal and state taxes and controls. One immigrant entrepreneur I talked with, who had built a business grossing $2 million a year, told me that once his income reaches $35,000, the government gets $47 and he takes home $1 out of his incremental earnings. He employs 30 people, but, understandably, none is interested in working overtime. If ever there was a country that could benefit from a dose of supply-side, tax-cut economics, Australia is it, and it might just happen, but that's another story.

The Capital International Index for the Australian stock market is a mere 36 percent higher than it was on January 1, 1970, but this lackluster performance masks a recent surge by Australian industrial stocks and very poor performance by the big-cap-italization, natural resource equities. Almost without exception, the businessmen, inves-tors, and brokers I talked with in Australia are discouraged about their country, cautious to bearish about their stock market, and very pessimistic about natural resource prices and companies. I suspect they're wrong on all three counts, and, with a new office in Australia, we will be following events and investments there more closely in the future.

On this trip, I was impressed by Elders and News Corp. Rupert Murdoch is an investor-businessman with an eye for value who reminds me of Larry Tisch, and News Corp. owns some premium properties around the world, has a breakup value well above the present market price of the stock, and a much lower valuation than comparable U.S. communication companies.

The Australian resource stocks, like Broken Hill and CRA, also intrigue me. They are certainly unloved and underowned by professional investors, and the people I talked with at the companies are discouraged and see no basis for improvement in raw material prices. As one said, "Even the old rule of seven years of famine and one year of prosperity doesn't work anymore." I would argue that a decline in the price of oil, if there is one, could result in a firming of other industrial commodity quotes. The huge rise in the relative price of oil in the late 1970s, which was not accommodated by a comparable expansion in the money supply, resulted in a decline in the relative price of other industrial commodities, and now the reverse should occur. The resource stocks are so depressed, it wouldn't take much of a price increase to push them up.

I was in Japan last week, where Morgan Stanley had a conference for Asian investors. Listening to the frantic patter and stories of the players in the Japanese market today is like hearing the high-tech chatter of the spring of 1983 in the United States all over again. I encountered many Japanese and English versions of "The Trigger" before he got value religion. All the sociological signs of a major top seem present. The multiples on rapidly growing stocks in Japan are madness, in my opinion. Somebody's going to get hurt.

I continue to think the Japanese market as a whole is overpriced. Almost every international portfolio in the world is overweighted in Japan, just as everyone used to be overweighted in energy and then technology. As I have written before, I believe the increase in Japan's RELATIVE economic power in the world has peaked and that the demands on Japan in terms of defense, trade, and responsibility in the world are increasing even as its population ages and it has to rebuild its social infrastructure. I also think I see some evidence of an erosion of the fabled Japanese work ethic and perhaps a few traces of self-indulgence.

I suspect Japan as a nation is about where the United States was in the late 1960s. Then the post–World War II miracle was over for us, social unrest was rising, but, most of all, the RELATIVE economic power of the United States had peaked. Not coincidentally, U.S. stocks underperformed for more than a decade starting at about the same time. At 25 times earnings, 2.3 times book value, and yielding a little over 1 percent, the Japanese stock market has already discounted a great deal of very good relative news. For the market to underperform relative to other markets, all it takes is for the news to be less good than what is already incorporated in those high valuations. However, in the short run, if the yen continues to strengthen against the dollar, the Tokyo Dow Jones may go to a new high.

My guess is that, for the next half decade, the most important decision for the global investor will be to be underweighted in Japan and overweighted in the United States.

Japan Inc. Wants a Higher Yen

1988

I am fascinated with the discipline and intensity of the Japanese. With great skill they have effected the transition from an export-oriented economy to one that is powered by domestic demand. Real GNP is growing rapidly, but inflation is nonexistent, and interest rates are the lowest in the world. They "managed" supply and demand so there was no panic in their stock market at the time prices were crashing everywhere else. The managements of their multinational companies are the best there are at developing high-quality products and running manufacturing facilities.

I have read a fair amount about the history of Japan. Just recently, I finished a superb history of the war in the Pacific and its origins called *Eagle against the Sun*, and Channel 13 has been broadcasting a long series on the events in the Pacific between 1935 and 1945. It was exciting to see in the grainy old newsreels the images of the people I had been reading about.

Even in modern times, the Japanese believed that the emperor was a god and that the race was superior because of its discipline, courage, and intelligence. Western culture and practices were considered decadent, and the conservatives abhorred their influence as perverting the purity of the culture. By the mid-1920s, Japan was suffering from an exploding population and lack of land, food, and natural resources. The Great Depression had a shattering impact, causing widespread poverty and near starvation, particularly in rural areas. It seemed an economic disease created in the West had infected Japan; and both the military and the business interests became convinced that Japan must expand into East Asia to build an empire to control the raw materials its developing industrial complex needed. The traumatic experience of the Depression was the genesis of the so-called Greater East Asia Co-Prosperity Sphere.

However, there was fierce controversy as to how this sphere of influence should be created. The business interests and the liberal political establishment believed it should be done by trade and that Japan could become a colonial power peacefully through superior organization and ability. They—as did some naval officers, particularly the great Admiral Yamamoto—recognized Japan's relative weakness compared to the U.S. and European powers. By contrast, the military, particularly the army officers, who came from rural backgrounds and were more parochial and conservative, argued that the "gaijin" would never let Japan compete on equal terms in their East Asian colonies and that an empire could only be created by conquest. They truly believed the "unconquerable Japanese spirit" would prevail in war and that "kodo," the imperial military way, would solve Japan's economic ills and purify the nation.

Throughout the 1930s, this conflict simmered in Tokyo. Ritual political assassination became commonplace, climaxing in 1936 when the extremist officers of the First Division, stationed in Tokyo, staged a coup and many ministers were murdered in their homes. Other civilian leaders barely escaped. The emperor ordered loyal army units into the capital and, after three days of fighting, the extremists surrendered. They were tried and executed along with some far-right civilians they were associated with. The army high command relentlessly exploited the fear and uneasiness caused by this attempted coup to establish its supremacy throughout the ruling establishment. The military, in effect, by crushing the extremist coup, took effective control of the government from the liberals and businessmen.

So the war in the Pacific was really about Japan's attempt to establish a commercial empire by force of arms. They were outmatched, and it failed. The military was totally discredited. Now Japan is run by the business class, and, perfectly reasonably, they are committed to acquiring the same empire by commercial means. For 40 years after the war, Japan was a builder and an exporter, and thus an undervalued currency came in handy. But now Japan is a victim of its own export success, and a new strategy of investment diaspora is required. The model should be England and its global commercial and banking empire built with an overvalued pound during the eighteenth and nineteenth centuries. Japan has superior managements and products, but it must build or buy manufacturing capacity all around the world. For this, it needs a strong, overvalued currency so it can buy producing and earning assets at a discount. As a commercial empire, it will want to dominate world banking. Again an overvalued currency, high equity valuations, and low interest rates result in a tremendous competitive advantage in funding for Japanese commercial and investment banks. Inevitably, the yen will become a, or perhaps even *the* reserve currency because Japan is the richest, most stable country. However, no empire has ever prevailed long without the ability to project military power.

Thus, my sense is that it may well suit Japan's strategic purposes to maneuver the yen to go higher and stay overvalued for years. George Soros, who is just back from

Japan, told me last week that he had had the same idea. He thinks Japanese industry has made an amazingly rapid adjustment to the rise in the yen both in terms of cutting costs and relocating plants outside of Japan. As compared to a few years ago, he senses very little political pressure in Japan to cap the rise of the yen. He expects the yen to climb further against both the dollar and now against the European currencies as well. He has covered his shorts in Japan.

What does all this mean for the Japanese stock market? Higher prices, I'm afraid. A strong yen augurs lower interest rates, so it's hard to see a crack in multiples. John Templeton commented last week at lunch that the Japanese look at their shares the way ladies look at diamonds. It's very hard to say what the value of a diamond is since its price is determined by how many buyers and sellers there are, and as long as the DeBeers syndicate can keep the supply limited, the prices keep on going up because there are a lot of ladies who want to wear diamonds. "Why do they want to wear diamonds?" asked John with a smile. "Not because the diamonds are so beautiful, but because it tells other ladies they've got a lot of money." The Japanese have the same attitude about shares. They want to be able to say they own Nippon Telephone & Telegraph, and it's irrelevant that the stock cannot provide any kind of reasonable investment return because it sells at 230 times earnings and yields 0.2 percent. My guess is that the yen and the other Asian NIC currencies will rise over the next few years against the dollar and the European currencies.

Japan Bought High
and Will Sell Low

September 30, 1991

Remember back a few years ago when there was much weeping and wailing because the Japanese were allegedly "buying America"? In the late 1980s, the Japanese did acquire such trophy properties as the "village square of New York" (Rockefeller Center), the "music machine" (CBS Records), and "America's soul" (Columbia Pictures). The final insult came when a Japanese investor bought our most famous golf course (Pebble Beach). The press and the Japan-bashers screamed that "they" would end up owning the best of us, and that laws should be passed prohibiting further acquisitions. In fact, however, the home team made some of the great sales of all time, and we should have put out the welcome mat.

In retrospect, the Japanese not only paid premium prices 10 to 25 percent over the market but also bought almost invariably at the top of the cycle. Now, with the marginal return on investment falling for many assets because supply exceeds demand and consumer income trends are weak, the resale value and the income from these investments are plunging. In some cases, the pain is evident in income statements; in others, it is still concealed in Japanese balance sheets.

In real estate, the Japanese had impeccable taste and bought trophy properties. Take New York as an example. In the late 1980s, Japanese insurance companies and banks bought outright or controlling interests in such prime properties as Rockefeller Center, Citicorp Tower, and the structure that MS&Co. inhabits, which used to be called the Exxon Building. They paid 10 to 20 percent premiums for these assets at the absolute top of the New York market. Since that time, overbuilding and rollovers have wreaked havoc on resale values and income streams. One broker told me last week that in a case he is familiar with, the Japanese purchase of a particular building only barely made sense on a discounted cash flow basis if 1992 leases could be written at $70 per square foot. Instead, today the building is scrambling for multiyear leases at $28 per square foot.

This is what is called asset deflation. Since the building may well have operating costs equivalent to $30 a square foot, this change in economics crashes the true value and cash flow for the owner, a Japanese insurance company. And the hard times are not going to end soon. No less an expert than John Reed, chairman of Citicorp, said recently that the bear market in real estate had five to seven years to run. Based on history, a new bull market may not begin for another decade.

Japanese buyers also paid up for trophy hotels, golf courses, and ski resorts. A wealthy Japanese bought the Beverly Hills Hotel and paid the equivalent of a million dollars a room, which solves to a nightly room rate of $1,000. In the late 1980s, Japanese companies bought at least four American ski resorts, including Steamboat, Stratton, and Breckenridge. The trouble is, they paid 10 times cash flow, or a 25 percent premium, just as the ski business peaked out. "Skier visits" nationwide, according to the industry's own trade association, have actually declined in the last two years.

The 90 or so golf courses the Japanese own in the United States have been another bad investment, but the real hue and cry came when a Japanese golf course developer, Minoru Isutani, bought Pebble Beach for a reported $800 million, which the experts say was $200 million too much even at the time. Now it looks like a disaster for Mr. Isutani and the Mitsubishi Trust and Banking Corp., which lent him much of the money. He needed to sell 700 private memberships for $740,000 each just to pay off the bank, but unfortunately there's a bear market in golf club memberships in Japan, and analysts say he would be lucky to get $300,000 a copy. In the United States, country club memberships are expensive, but Mr. Isutani is not finding many buyers in six digits, even for Pebble Beach.

Some otherwise astute Japanese corporations have also overpaid for American assets. Larry Tisch still speaks fondly of his sale to Sony of CBS Records for $2 billion, and in 1989 Sony paid $3.4 billion for Columbia Pictures. Since then Sony is believed to have shelled out another $1.6 billion for working capital for Columbia, and then paid $200 million for Peter Guber and Jon Peters's firm, plus $500 million to Time Warner to release them from a contract. Once the deal was done, box office traffic plunged, the corporate jets got bigger, the movies got worse, and the parties got better. So far, Tinseltown has been a financial sinkhole for the Japanese. Sony Pictures is a revolving door for talent, with Peters already history. Today Sony's stock is languishing, and the company is in dire need of cash and equity capital. Matsushita is not in such bad shape but clearly overpaid everyone involved when it acquired MCA.

This is not to say that the Japanese are stupid investors—far from it. Many of their "greenfield" industrial projects in the United States have worked out fine. But from time immemorial, foreign investors have paid up at the top and sold at the bottom, both for stocks and companies. Robert Sobel, the financial historian of Wall Street, has documented how foreign investors bought U.S. equities heavily in the years just before the bear markets or panics that began in 1792, 1837, 1857, 1873, 1893, and 1907. In each case the foreigners sold their U.S. stocks back to the locals at depressed prices in the postcrash period. Ten or 15 years later, the memory had dimmed, and a new crop of investors would begin investing again. Most recently, this cycle has appeared in prime farmland, where Europeans were big buyers at peak prices in the late 1970s. In fact, some states passed laws prohibiting foreign ownership—when instead they should have welcomed it then and be buying back the farms today.

American investors abroad follow the same flawed instincts: buy high, sell low. The point is that the locals are much better judges of their own economy and values than are overseas investors. So if history repeats itself, and it almost always does, the Japanese should be sellers of their tarnished trophies sometime in the next five years. They will then be great buys for long-term investors.

Section 3D:
Europe, Middle East, Africa

In the Eye of the Storm

November 25, 1986

T he small nations along the rim of the Arabian Gulf are holding up well in the face of austerity, terrorism, and war. Being there recently reminded me again of how fascinating the Middle East is. I like everything from the feeling of intensity and the complexity of the relationships to the strong bright light that washes every scene from the cities to the deserts.

The combined oil earnings of the six Gulf states (which account for 90 percent of government revenues) have plunged from $163 billion in 1981 to $55 billion last year, so it is not surprising that there is a recession there. The massive infrastructure construction boom throughout the Gulf is now about over. Five years ago in Kuwait, the Korean workers labored 24 hours day, but now the great national buildings are complete, and the city with its subtle blend of modern and traditional Arab architecture is striking as it lies shimmering in the blue curve of the Gulf. In Oman last weekend, the last of the great projects was completed when the sultan before 1,000 guests dedicated his $340 million university. The complex includes a $120 million teaching hospital, a mosque for 2,000 people, libraries, sports halls, residences, television studios, and formal gardens. At the peak, a workforce of 4,000 was involved in the construction.

The design of this university presented unique architectural problems, because, although admission is open, in accordance with Islamic tradition, male and female students have to be kept separate. Classes are mixed with men at the front and women at the back, but men and women must follow different paths to reach the classrooms. Thus, the university has been built with two completely separate networks of walkways connected by a system of gated and screened spiral staircases. The final effect is spectacular with delicate curved arches, minarets, and elegant cloisters and arcades.

In Saudi Arabia, spending on new cities and ports has been reduced and payments to contractors delayed. The new budget has been postponed, but it is expected that there will be a deficit of around $15 billion, which will have to be met from reserves. Official figures show that Saudi Arabia's foreign assets fell from $141 billion in 1982 to $109 billion in February 1986. True reserves, however, are believed to be around $70 billion as the $109 billion includes loans to Iraq and others that are both illiquid and more in the nature of gifts.

Kuwait is as orderly as ever. I stayed at the Regency, one of the four first-class hotels in the city, and it has got to be one of the most attractive business hotels in the world. It is right on the beach, has a superb sports complex, including four indoor and two outdoor tennis courts, and better service than even the great Southeast Asia hotels. Occupancy, however, seemed to be only around 20 percent, as the local economy is deeply depressed.

Kuwait City is only 90 miles from the focal point of the war between Iraq and Iran, and sometimes you can hear the dull boom of the guns. Nevertheless, the Kuwaitis are resolute in the face of many difficulties. The war has slowed down commerce, and oil revenues have fallen, but the government has responded to the new environment and has managed the economy and its reserves astutely. Bank of England estimates published last week in the *Far Eastern Economic Review* show the country's reserves at $80 billion, virtually unchanged from levels in the early 1980s.

Kuwait has had its share of terrorism, with an attack on the American Embassy and an assassination attempt on the life of the emir. However, Kuwaiti counterespionage work has been incredibly effective, and with one thumbprint the crucial clue, arrests were made, and the terrorists remain imprisoned despite threats. Large numbers of suspected dissidents have been deported, and what once was a rat's nest of houses in sections of the city in which they lived has been razed right down to the sand.

The Kuwaitis are true Muslims. Alcohol, drugs, graffiti, and pornography are not tolerated, and I have never seen the slightest hint of corruption. In fact, once, when one of our analysts who was talking to an investment official about Eastman Kodak presented him with a new $38 Kodak camera as a demonstration model, the official dropped it on the floor as though it were a hot potato, saying he never took gifts. Women wear Western clothes, and some are involved in business. The ruling Al Sabah family is revered, able, and lives modestly. For example, the oil minister, Sheik Ali Khalifa, is the only member of OPEC who travels without a retinue.

The stability of Kuwait is even more remarkable considering that the country has experienced one of the great speculative stock market bubbles of all time. Historically, Kuwait has had the biggest stock market in the Arab world. In fact, there have been two stock markets in Kuwait. One is the "official" market of companies doing business in Kuwait, and the other is the Gulfshare market, which consists of the stocks of companies registered mostly in Bahrain. For a variety of reasons, including the prosperity and huge excess liquidity generated by the rise in oil prices in the 1970s, a tremendous parallel bull market took place in the late 1970s. The official market soared with annual gains of 50 to 60 percent and P/Es of 50 to 100, but the real craziness took place in the Gulfshare outdoor curb exchange. During the peak year of 1981, returns of 100 to 200 percent a month were not unusual, and minuscule and phony companies developed huge market values. For example, the shares of a chicken farm in Oman sold at 300 times earnings. In fact, at the peak in early 1982, the combined market had a total capitalization of $90 billion, which at that time made it the fourth-biggest market in the world.

The lifeblood of the Gulfshare market was a forward payment system, really a leveraged variation on options. A block of stock would be sold for, say, 200 percent of the present price in return for a check dated months or even a couple of years after the transaction. Obviously, the buyer counted on being able to sell the shares for a higher sum than the check before the check came due. The seller could either hold the check or sell it at a discount. As investors reinvested the proceeds, the daisy chain compounded.

As prices soared, virtually all of Kuwait and much of the Gulf was embroiled in the mania. People literally quit their jobs to play the market full-time. One man, who three years earlier had been a clerk in the immigration department, had his own Boeing 707 and at the end had written $10 billion worth of checks on himself. I remember at the time Kuwaitis saying that their stock market was insane, but since it would continue because of the excess liquidity and one could make money, why not participate? Everyone believed the government would not let the whole system collapse, especially since in 1975 it had intervened to prevent an earlier panic. At the same time, a tremendous rise in real estate prices was occurring. All through 1980 and 1981, the wild bull market roared on as everyone got richer.

However, in early 1982 the Kuwaiti stock market weakened in spite of a doubling of the money stock in the last four months of 1981. Then in the spring and summer, the market began to fall apart. By August, checks being presented for payment were bouncing, and suddenly the panic was on. Some investors took their money and ran out of the country before the government impounded the passports of speculators. The clerk with the 707 didn't make it to the airport in time. In September, the government intervened and created a clearing house for checks. Eventually, the checks registered had a face value of $70 billion. When it was all over, the $90 billion of market value had vaporized 98 percent to less than $2 billion, which is the biggest percentage bust since John Law and the Mississippi scheme in 1721. Last week I was

Profiles of Great Speculative Bubbles

	Mexican Stocks (1978–1981)	Silver 1979–1982	New York Stocks 1926–1932	South Sea Shares 1719–1720	Mississippi Shares 1719–1721	Tulips 1634–1638
Initial price before bubble began	100 (index) (1970)	$6/ounce (early 1979)	100 (index) (July 1926)	b100/share (1719)	300 livre (early 1719)	100 florins (1634)
Peak price before crash	885 (index) Jan.1981	$48.70/ ounce (1/17/80)	216 (index) (Sept 1929)	b1,000/share (July 1720)	20,000 livre (early 1720)	6,000 florins (spring 1637)
Price after crash	218 (index) (July 1982)	$5.90/ ounce (1982)	34 (index) (June 1932)	B160/share (Dec. 1720)	200 livre (early 1721)	400 florins (Feb. 1638)
Percent decline peak to crash	73%	88%	87%	84%	99%	93%

SOURCE: Morgan Stanley Research.

told real estate prices have also plummeted by as much as 70 percent. The cumulative defaults on postdated checks and real estate have staggered the financial institutions of the Gulf, and the official Kuwait stock market is still very depressed. The Gulfshare market barely exists.

In spite of the tremendous stress that this crash imposed on the banking system and the economy, plus the drastic decline in GNP caused by lower oil production and prices, Kuwait has remained calm and stable. This tough little country in the eye of the storm survives, and with a hundred years of oil reserves it surely will prosper again.

You Gotta Own Some Germany

November 13, 1989

The opening of East Germany is an epic event, the stuff of bull markets. It reduces the risk premium for equities and bonds everywhere because it increases the chances for a period of disarmament, peace, and prosperity. The Cold War era of confrontation is over, and all its institutions—NATO, the Warsaw Pact, Star Wars, John le Carré novels—are obsolete, relics, kaput. It will be interesting to see which leader understands this first and exploits the opportunities and dangers of the new Europe. I bet on Gorby. Last week the American foreign policy establishment looked constipated as it contemplated the new Europe.

But David Roche, Madhav Dhar, and I agree that, most of all, the opening enhances the appeal of the West German stock market as the prime play on the coming boom in East Germany and Eastern Europe. We are dramatically increasing our weighting in German equities to 7 percent in global portfolios versus a 3 percent weighting in the Morgan Stanley Capital International (MSCI) index, and to 12 percent versus 5 percent in EAFE accounts. In our opinion, every equity account should be represented in Germany.

We believe de facto if not actual reunification of the two Germanies is now inevitable. No politician, no bureaucrat, no banker wants it, only the people of the two Germanies, and people power is what this revolution, this reordering, is all about. This transforms the West German equity market into a call on the emerging country market that is East Germany. David Roche estimates that the 16.6 million East Germans have real GNP per capita of $4,800 versus $13,300 for the West Germans. Incidentally, Bulgaria and Romania (where things could get very ugly) are at a mere $1,900 per head, with Poland at $2,200 and Hungary at $2,700, so there are other opportunities in Eastern Europe. Hourly wages in East Germany, including social and health benefits, are $2.00 to $3.00 an hour compared with five to six times that level in labor-short West Germany. The German Democratic Republic is an LDC or maybe at best an NIC with an incredibly well-educated, skilled, and motivated workforce. East Germany is a gray and glum country, not because of its people but because of its rulers. In fact, it has been by far the most successful of the Communist economies and has surprising technological capabilities.

These 16.6 million people with blood and cultural ties to West Germany will demand the same standard of living. Freed from a system that required labor without reward, they will now be able to work, invent, and build to get it. Of course, their wage level will rise, and as it does, so will their buying power. Domestic demand will swell. The East Germans will want cars, washing machines, VCRs, Coca-Cola, Marlboros, and better health care. West German industry, faced with labor shortages at home, will locate plants in East Germany instead of Spain, Italy, or Thailand. Workers from East Germany will cross the border to labor in West German factories. East Germany, over the next five years, could be the fastest-growing economy in the world, and we think West German and maybe Austrian stocks are the best way to play this emerging market.

The West German stock market is one of the cheapest in the world. According to MSCI, only one country index, Italy, sells at a lower multiple of trailing cash earnings than West Germany. We calculate that German stocks on average trade at about 12 times forecast 1990 earnings and 38 times cash flow, although some brokers say these numbers are even lower. Historically, German P/E ratios have averaged 15. Accounting is the most conservative in the world. For example, reported profits of Siemens (DM 560) are 27 percent understated compared with those of American Telephone & Telegraph ($44) and NTT (¥1,350,000), according to one study.

MSCI Germany Index to November 13, 1989

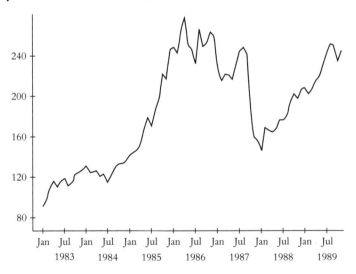

Source: Morgan Stanley Capital International.

German stocks trade at less than two times book value, even though the accountants estimate book value in Germany is understated by at least 30 percent. According to the MSCI database, the German index compared with world multiples is selling at a 41 percent discount on cash earnings, 20 percent on reported earnings, and 19 percent on book value, and it yields 50 percent more. Please remember that our studies show that cash earnings and book value are the truest comparisons and the best predictors.

The supply/demand equation is very favorable. German investment institutions typically have very low equity ratios, and I am told this will gradually but inevitably change. The stock market capitalization as a percentage of GNP is about the lowest for any developed market. I agree totally with David Roche's eloquent argument that when the frontiers of a country are being dramatically expanded, historical valuation frontiers have little relevance. Who knows what the new parameters for Germany will be. A country with a declining birth rate, a shrinking population, and labor shortages will be transformed overnight into a growth economy. All types of unanticipated and unintended consequences will arise from this dramatic transformation. Some will be bad, but investors should not forget they are dealing with a disciplined yet entrepreneurial race that is justly famous not only as warriors but also for making great commerce, inventions, and music.

The German stock market has underperformed since early October. It was one of the worst performers on the Monday following the recent Crashette in the United States. For the year to date, it is up 10 percent. Some German brokers last Friday were saying that the strength that day was an opportunity to sell because the opening to East Germany would inevitably lead to overheating of the economy and higher interest rates. German interest rates will rise, but I believe the markets will look to growth. Investors are also worried about long strikes next year, how the elections will go, the power of the Greens, and rising inflation. Other pessimists view change, even positive change, as disorder and therefore bad, which seems convoluted to me.

I think they are myopic. Investors will look over the valley. The opening to the East plain and simple means faster growth and a huge new supply of skilled, low-priced labor and vast, salivating markets. There may be some short-term dislocations, particularly if the uncertainty of the new order in Europe causes the mark to weaken against the dollar. Nevertheless, I can't imagine a central bank that is more capable than the Bundesbank of orchestrating a period of rapid growth with relatively low inflation. It is also worth noting that the big West German banks have huge hidden reserves, which they will restate to their capital accounts to support the loan growth they will now generate.

In the political cabarets of East Germany, the song of these times has been "A Waiting Country," by by **Hans-Eckardt Wenzel**. For East Germany, the waiting for the future and the golden time are now almost over, and I wouldn't wait to own German stocks. I suppose many Europeans will be more cynical and will think us naive and emotional. "The images on television are not reality. Wait," they will say, "there will be a better opportunity." We want to buy now.

Militant Fundamentalism Spoils the Middle East Story

September 13, 1993

The luminous moment, the transcendental event for emerging markets investors comes when we discover the next big winner, the potential thousand percenter, the country that has done everything wrong, where time and poverty have stood still and the peasants are dying of malnutrition while corrupt officials drive Mercedes. The thrill comes not only from the prospect of making lot of money but also from seeing a country turn and become prosperous and the people's standard of living soar. There are a lot of emerging markets investors out there restlessly roaming the world, looking for the next Peru or Poland. Everyone knows Vietnam is going to be a winner, and huge turnaround stories like Brazil and India are already recognized and on everyone's screen. We are all greedy, but Discovery, not Recognition, is the thrill.

I keep looking at the Arab Middle East for the next Discovery. Jordan has a stock market with a capitalization of $2.2 billion that is tracked by both the MSCI and IFC indexes but it is a small country and economy. Tunisia, too, has a tiny market and economy. Iraq and Iran seem farfetched prospects, although both have stock exchanges, and Saudi Arabia and Kuwait are closed and insular. Algeria, with 26 million people, is a better prospect. Per capita GNP of $2,300 puts it in the lower middle income category of developing nations, and over the last 25 years, per capita GNP (which after all is the ultimate test) has grown a very respectable 2.5 percent per year. Another candidate currently hot with investors is Morocco, with a population of almost 30 million and per capita GNP of $880. Some advocates are talking about 5 percent real growth in the future, and Moroccan equities and debt instruments have skyrocketed this year. Miles "Away" Morland of Blakeney Management has done the best work by far on the Arab markets.

The biggest potential story in the region is Egypt, with a population pushing 60 million, per capita GNP of $640, and an economy that has stumbled along for years at a growth rate barely faster than population growth. We sent a guy to Egypt recently, and he found that the big companies are generally inefficiently run and trade at three to seven times earnings and well below book value. As you would hope, the stock exchange, although old, slumbers. Like many emerging market winners, Egypt has a big tourist industry and a distinctive culture, and there are signs the government understands the policy changes that must be made to set in motion "the virtuous circle of development" and a bull market that will cause the economy to flourish.

Unfortunately, militant Islamic fundamentalism is spoiling the case for an economic miracle in the Middle East, although the PLO-Israel peace treaty could change this for the better. As I understand it, there is nothing any more threatening about Islamic fundamentalism than there is about Christian fundamentalist movements. They want a stricter adherence to the precepts of the Koran, a return to a more old-fashioned, God-fearing, religious society, and are opposed to the lewdness, decadence, and moral bankruptcy of modern life, particularly the licentiousness of the West. They also want "Islamic banking" and the prohibition of "riba," which, depending on the interpretation, is either usury or all interest (which certainly complicates banking). A reform movement within the fundamentalists led by a Syrian, Dr. Mohammad Shahur, wants to modernize the Koran. Dr. Shahur says: "We have to live in the present, not make our present in the past. We must approach our prophet as if he lived five years ago. This should determine how we look at the Koran now."

The militant fundamentalists are entirely different. They are extremists who want to kill "secularists" who have other beliefs. Throughout the Middle East, particularly in Egypt and Algeria, prominent secularists in the arts, government, and education have been targeted for death. In Algeria in July, five terrorists burst into the home of a well-known professor, Mohammed Boukhobza, tied up his daughter, and forced her to watch as they slit his throat. He was the sixth Algerian intellectual killed in the last three months.

Words like *martyrdom, jihad*, and *infidel* dominate the language of the militants, and terrorism, violence, and murder are their weapons. They are committed to using any means whatsoever to overthrow the current governments in the Middle East, which they regard as secular, corrupt, and Western-leaning. Death in battle against the enemy is the surest way to heaven. Just before he was gunned down, the army lieutenant whose squad assassinated President Sadat at the anniversary parade in front of thousands of spectators shouted: "I have killed Pharaoh. I do not fear death."

The hatred of the militants has been spawned by poverty, disease, and Arab defeats at the hands of Israel. Other factors include decades of no progress in the standard of living, high unemployment, government corruption, and extreme disparities between a rich minority and the masses. The Gulf War and the West's failure to protect Bosnia's Muslims have added fuel to the fire. The United States, of course, is despised as the embodiment of corrupt Western values.

A new, very ominous development is cross-border cooperation between Shiite and Sunni fundamentalist militants. Shiite Iran is aiding the terrorist activities of Sunni

Sudan and providing it with trade and military equipment. Iran is also assisting the Turkish Islamic Jihad group and supporting underground groups in Tunisia and Algeria. With 55 million people and a per capita income in the area of $3,200 per head, Iran is a big, rich country by Middle Eastern standards; this alliance with the Sunni militants threatens every conservative government in the Arab world.

In Algeria, over a thousand people have been killed in the past 18 months by the militants and the police. They include many writers and journalists killed by Islamic terrorists. On August 21, Kasdi Merbah, a former prime minister, was assassinated as he returned from the beach with his family. Another casualty in Algeria has been democracy. The elections of January 1992 were canceled because the fundamentalists looked as though they were going to win, and the present prime minister believes terrorism must by fought with repression. In Egypt, the more moderate fundamentalist Muslim Brotherhood that condemns violence has been denied the right to become a political party. Throughout the Middle East, the fundamentalists have good reason to doubt that they will ever assume power through elections.

Egypt may be in even worse shape, with 200 people killed in the last 18 months. The Mubarak government has tried a double-edged policy of brutally suppressing the extremists while courting Islamic centrists. It hasn't worked, and in fact there is evidence that the militants have infiltrated both the educational system and the Egyptian government. The minister of religious affairs is an avowed fundamentalist who uses his ministry to support the radicals, while the Interior Ministry baffles the same groups with police action, torture, hangings, and imprisonment. Recently, Interior Minister Hassan al-Alfi narrowly escaped assassination, although five bystanders died. The militants also have devastated Egypt's huge tourist industry, which should have earned $4 billion this year, by making random grenade attacks against tourists and shooting up tour buses. Foreign businessmen are also targets, and places they frequent have been bombed. These days Egypt is a hazardous place for an emerging markets investor to visit.

Of course, this has been true in Peru, too. In fact, sometimes the best opportunities come in countries where it is actually dangerous for investors to visit. It tends to keep the riffraff away. But this is scary stuff in the Middle East, particularly in Egypt. As noted, the militants believe they will never come to power by elections, and so violent revolution is the only course left to them. Americans, as descendants of the Great Satan, are choice targets. With millions impoverished and unemployed and with college graduates driving taxicabs, many Egyptians believe the slogan "Islam is the solution." They may not like the extremists' terrorist tactics, but they want change.

Unless governments in the Middle East move fast to create growth, narrow the disparities between rich and poor, and end the corruption, militant fundamentalism will continue to gain power, and there will be no investment story. It may be, as David Roche suspects, that the new peace treaty will cause an increase in investment flows and eventually economic growth throughout the Middle East. I'm not as optimistic, because I think these militant fundamentalists are going to continue to cause trouble, and the long-term risk is that militant fundamentalism will spread to more secular countries like Turkey, Indonesia, and Malaysia.

Section 3E: Latin America

South America for the Nineties

November 26, 1990

One of the great but risky investment opportunities of the 1990s may be in Latin American equities, thanks to the definite possibility of a turn for the better, maybe even the much better, in the fortunes of countries south of the border. Already some good money has been made in Mexico and Chile, and the next round of four-bagger emerging market stories may come not in Eastern Europe or Asia but in countries like Argentina, Venezuela, and Brazil. After huge gains in previous years, the Mexican market is up 53 percent this year, and Chile is ahead 15 percent. These results demonstrate not only the potential in South America when things begin to go right but also an auspicious lack of correlation with what is going on in the major markets of the world.

South America has many troubles. Inflation is at epidemic proportions in many countries, politics are chaotic, poverty is widespread, the foreign debt is huge, and the developing U.S. recession will damage the region's fragile economies at a crucial moment. Nevertheless, most South American countries are implementing free market

Emerging Markets GNP Percentage of Whole by Region; 1989 Nominal GNP in US$

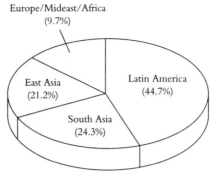

Total: US$1.9 trillion

SOURCE: Morgan Stanley Research estimates.

policies that have worked so well elsewhere: deregulation, opening the domestic economy, privatization, and reducing the size and scope of government. It doesn't really
matter whether the party in power is conservative or liberal, authoritarian or democratic; what counts are the results. The Korean and Taiwanese miracles occurred under
dictatorships; Thailand and Singapore made it as democracies. And finally, at last, South
American governments are generally doing the right thing.

There is a crucial difference from the East Asian developing countries, however.
Throughout South America, the distribution of income is more unequal than almost
anywhere else in the world. In Brazil, for example, the poorest fifth of the population
has only 2 percent of the national income while the richest fifth has 67 percent, or
33 times as much. In the successful NICs like Taiwan, Thailand, Korea, and Singapore,
the ratio of the richest to the poorest quintile is only between five and nine times.
On average in South America, the top 20 percent are 21 times richer than the poorest
20 percent; in East Asia they are only 9 times richer.

Emerging Markets Capitalization Percentage of Whole by Region; end September 1990

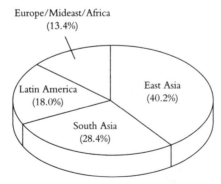

Total: US$411 billion

SOURCE: Morgan Stanley Research estimates.

According to a study by Jeffrey Sachs of Harvard University, such vast income gaps have caused social conflict to distort economic policy in the past. The political pressures and unrest stemming from these huge inequalities have compelled South American politicians from both the left and the right to repeatedly try imprudent, short-term "populist" policies such as fiscal expansion, printing money, and currency devaluation. Although at first these programs give a false bloom of health, inevitably they result in a rise in the real exchange rate, a rising trade deficit, heavy foreign borrowing, and sharp falls in real wages, output, and employment.

With each cycle of mismanagement and failure, the result has been diminished growth, higher inflation, and more political chaos.

Now, a radical approach centered on free markets is being tried by a new breed of economists and politicians. The first experiments, in Chile and then Mexico, seem to be working, and now it's the turn of Argentina, Brazil, and Venezuela. It is encouraging that despite the initial price of this approach—the dose of austerity to kill hyperinflation—the people so far still support the programs. If South America got healthy again, it would be the best possible news for the United States, because the continent with its 400 million people is our natural and biggest potential market.

Although other countries are further along and healthier, Brazil, the colossus of the south, is the big story. This is a country of 150 million people and boundless natural resources; after a decade of stagnation, it remains the eighth-largest free-market economy in the world. From 1950 to 1980, Brazil averaged real growth of almost 7 percent a year, and in the 1970s growth spurted to 8.6 percent per annum. Last August, on a visit to Brazil, I was stunned by the size and sophistication of Brazilian industry. Unfortunately, alongside this highly industrialized Brazil with a well-off middle class lives another, desperately poor country. In São Paulo, a sprawling city of 15 million people, I was appalled by the poverty and pollution.

Latin American Emerging Markets

Country	P/E Ratio 1990	Price/ Book Ratio	Yield	Number of Listed Companies	Avg. Daily Trading Value US$M	Market Cap US$B Latest	Market Cap As a % of GNP	GNP ($B) 1989	GDP per Capita (US$)
Argentina	7.0	0.4	0.5%	174	4.4	3	6%	62	1,904
Brazil	3.0	0.5	12.1%	591	19.8	25	5%	482	3,269
Mexico	10.4	1.2	2.2%	203	22.5	30	15%	201	2,381
Venezuela	6.4	0.8	0.2%	66	7.4	5.2	12%	44	2,279
Chile	5.8	1.1	7.7%	213	2.2	11.2	43%	26	2,066
Average	6.3	1.4	4.7%						
Asia*	18.1	3.5	2.7%						
MSCI World Avg.	15.3	1.8	3.1%						

*India, Indonesia, Philippines, Malaysia, Thailand, Taiwan, South Korea.
SOURCE: Morgan Stanley Research.

The excesses of the past caught up with Brazil in the last decade, and real growth has fallen to 2 percent per annum as the CPI soared above 1,000 percent. In the past, virulent hyperinflation has thwarted the efforts of each new economic plan in Brazil, but now a new government with a charismatic young president and a brain trust of young intellectuals who believe in free markets has made an impressive beginning at controlling inflation and revitalizing the economy.

This big turn for the better in South America is a highly uncertain proposition, but the other exciting part of the South American investment story is that the equity markets look very cheap. The misfortunes of the past decade are well known, and many of the owners of capital are deeply discouraged. Money has been fleeing these countries for Switzerland and the United States, and only in Mexico has the flight capital begun to come home. When it does, the effects on investment and stock market valuations can be stunning. The Mexican equity market rose 90 percent in 1988 and 71 percent in 1989, which is enough to get the attention of the most cynical expatriates.

Mexico is furthest along the path to free market capitalism, and the Mexican market now sells at about 10 times earnings, yields 2.2 percent, and is 1.2 times book value; the $30 billion market capitalization is 15 percent of Mexico's GNP. Chile has an $11 billion equity market that is at 5.8 times earnings, yields 7.7 percent, and sells at book value. Brazil, by contrast, has a $25 billion market which is a mere 5 percent of GNP, and valuations are ludicrous at 3.0 times earnings; it yields 12.1 percent and trades at 50 percent of book value. Argentina and Venezuela have smaller markets that sell at 6 to 7 times earnings. These valuations hardly seem to discount a turn for the better.

Foreign investors can participate in Brazil, Chile, and Mexico through closed-end country funds, most of which sell at discounts, or they can invest directly in local equities in Argentina and Venezuela. Brazil is closed to overseas money except through funds. We at Morgan Stanley believe in the investment growth potential of emerging markets, and our research shortly will be expanding coverage of South American and East Asian emerging markets.

No More Siestas

October 28, 1991

en days ago, before I went to Mexico, I thought that although Mexico was still on the right track as a country and an economy, its stock market seemed frothy. After my visit, I really haven't changed my view, but I was impressed with the Mexican political system and stunned by the quality of the senior government officials we met. Most were in their early 40s, had graduate degrees from the best U.S. universities, and exhibited a profound grasp of the complex dynamics of a developing country. At one time or another, I have met high government officials in a number of developing countries, but the Mexicans were the best. This changes my view about investing in Mexico in the sense that I feel the political story is even better than I had thought, so I would be a buyer sooner on weakness.

President Carlos Salinas de Gortari was the most impressive of all. The other cabinet ministers were smoother, but Salinas was deeper. I knew that he was the son of a former cabinet minister and that his family was part of the elite ruling party, the PRI. After going to school and college in Mexico, in the 1970s he earned two master's degrees and a PhD from Harvard. In between he won a silver medal at the 1971 Pan American Games as an equestrian. That medal now adorns the neck of a Steuben horse head in the president's living room at Las Pinas.

One of his classmates told me that although Salinas was hardworking, bright, and ambitious as a young guy, no one thought he was destined to be a president of Mexico, because he was not political and was so soft-spoken. He was more of a technocrat and a team player than a politician playing to the spotlight, and is almost incapable of glad-handing, this man said.

But Salinas worked his way up in the PRI and in 1988 became president after a narrow victory, amid allegations of massive vote stealing. In fact, many people in

Mexico today who think he has been a great president believe that Salinas actually finished third in that election. When he assumed office, inflation was soaring, the economy was in perpetual recession, unemployment was at least 20 percent, and Mexico staggered under a foreign debt of $85 billion. Corruption was rampant, the bloated bureaucracy stifled initiative in the huge state-owned industries, and capital and people were pouring out of Mexico. The four previous presidents were perceived as weak political figures at best and as corrupt at worst. With real per capita income down 50 percent in five years, there was a meaningful risk of a new Mexican revolution (in a country with a tradition of political violence).

In his first few months in office, Salinas used soldiers with bazookas to arrest the notorious boss of the oil workers' union, and corrupt police and federal officials were summarily fired. He moved swiftly to privatize state-owned companies, renegotiated

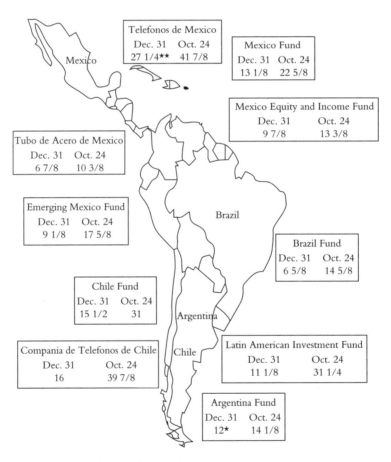

Telefonos de Mexico	
Dec. 31	Oct. 24
27 1/4**	41 7/8

Mexico Fund	
Dec. 31	Oct. 24
13 1/8	22 5/8

Mexico Equity and Income Fund	
Dec. 31	Oct. 24
9 7/8	13 3/8

Tubo de Acero de Mexico	
Dec. 31	Oct. 24
6 7/8	10 3/8

Emerging Mexico Fund	
Dec. 31	Oct. 24
9 1/8	17 5/8

Brazil Fund	
Dec. 31	Oct. 24
6 5/8	14 5/8

Chile Fund	
Dec. 31	Oct. 24
15 1/2	31

Compania de Telefonos de Chile	
Dec. 31	Oct. 24
16	39 7/8

Latin American Investment Fund	
Dec. 31	Oct. 24
11 1/8	31 1/4

Argentina Fund	
Dec. 31	Oct. 24
12*	14 1/8

*Price of initial public offering. Shares began trading October 11.
**Price of initial public offering. Shares began trading May 14.
SOURCE: *International Herald Tribune.*

the foreign debt, deregulated industries, reduced food subsidies, and cut both personal and corporate tax rates. "We have transformed Mexico from a closed society and economy to an open one," he told us. As one of the most outspoken members of the opposition, Enrique Krauze, put it: "He overcame statist taboos in a society of taboos. His economic performance has been outstanding, and in many ways, exemplary." Krauze is less complimentary about the president's progress on democratic reforms.

We spent over an hour with Salinas in his office, and then another hour with his wife. He's a balding, owlish-looking man of 43, not in the least pretentious. He was dressed in a dark suit with a striking green tie. There were not a lot of smiles. At first he seemed a little shy, but then he warmed up and spoke articulately and sometimes quite passionately in almost flawless English. The Mexican press does not like him to speak to visitors in English, but he does it anyway because it saves so much translation time.

The changes he had put into effect had been demanded by the people, Salinas said. By the late 1980s the country was beginning to spiral into both social and economic anarchy. "We could have lost Mexico," he said. Since then, he told us, inflation had fallen from 200 percent annually to 16 percent, and the public-sector deficit had declined from 16 percent of GNP to 2 percent this year; when privatizations are included, the government is in surplus. Salinas explained eloquently how a tight fiscal policy and slower money growth had set off a virtuous circle that led to faster economic growth. "No more siestas," he said with a faint smile. With much reduced tax rates—and no capital gains tax whatsoever—it's no wonder.

A little steel showed when he said that two-thirds of the Mexican people were in favor of the Free Trade Agreement, but that he was a little worried about the negative reaction in the United States. If the U.S. Congress doesn't ratify the FTA, Mexico will have to look for economic ties with Asia, particularly Japan, which would offer a lot for open access to Mexico's huge consumer market. Of course, there would be FTAs with South and Central American countries as well. Across the U.S. border, Salinas wants to export "goods, not people."

Someone asked him about the environment. Mexico City's air pollution doesn't seem to me anywhere near as bad as that in Bangkok, São Paulo, or New Delhi, but the Mexicans are very sensitive about it. Salinas pointed out that 12 million trees were planted last year around the city and that he had ordered a nearby refinery closed, which cost the government half a billion dollars a year in revenues and 6,000 jobs. Señora Salinas spoke of how crucial it was to get Mexico's birthrate down and how important education was; studies show that girls who finish high school have half the birth rate of those that don't.

Mexico still has some big problems, and a continuing U.S. recession and a possible breakdown of the FTA talks are high on the list. Another cabinet minister remarked, "In five years Mexico will be either Spain or Peru." Some argue that Mexico needs more democracy and a multiparty system. I'm not so sure. For a developing country, a reasonably benevolent, one-party government run by a bunch of smart guys may be the best solution. Tough decisions have to be made, and coalition democracies aren't usually too good at doing the right but unpopular thing. The Mexican system, in which a president can only serve one six-year term, works well with a man like Salinas, because the president in a sense is above politics and can surround himself with the best people with less worry about competition or reelection.

In any case, with a little luck and some more good leadership, in a few years Mexico will be a country of 100 million people with real economic growth of 5 to 6 percent. A burgeoning neighbor like this as part of a free trade area would be a big growth plus for the United States, just as East Germany is for West Germany. Just look at the maps. Tell your Representative to vote for the Free Trade Agreement.

Latin American Inflation Scoreboard

Country	1986	1987	1988	1989	1990	1991E
Argentina	90%	131%	343%	3,079%	2,314%	85%
Brazil	145	230	638	1,475	2,864	400
Chile	20	20	15	17	26	19
Mexico	86	132	114	20	27	18
Venezuela	12	28	30	85	41	30

SOURCE: Institute of International Finance, global finance estimates.

Global Economic Imbalance

This is the way the world looks in terms of economics . . .

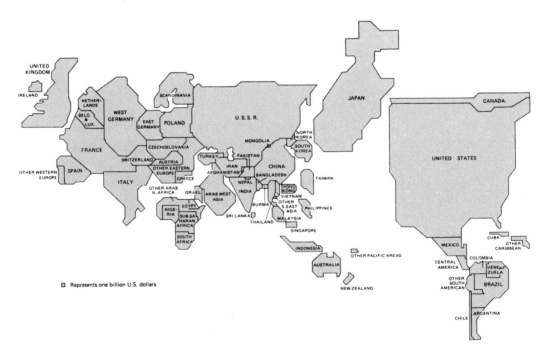

But this is the population map. The markets of the future are where the people are. Mexico, Brazil, Indonesia, China, and India stand out.

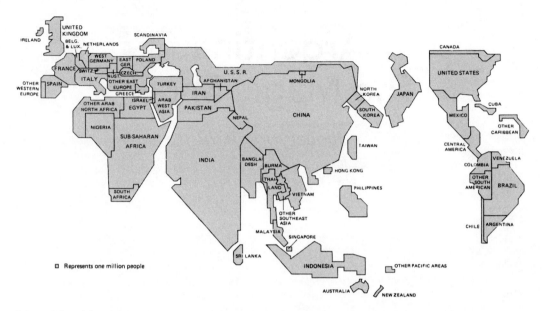

SOURCE: Adapted from Edwin O. Reischauer, *The Japanese Today,* reprinted by permission. Copyright 1988 by the President and Fellows of Harvard College.

Argentina:
The Magic Show

January 11, 1992

f Mexico is an investment dream and Brazil a nightmare, then Argentina is a magic show, in the sense that the story seems held together by threads of gossamer.

Argentina poses a very different investment dilemma from Brazil. It has already experienced the transformation from a sick economy to a healthy one. The cancer of hyperstagflation is in remission; the patient has emerged from the hospital but is still a little shaky on his pins. Argentina is also different in that it seems more European, safer, more civilized, but less dynamic. We didn't need bodyguards. Like Brazil, however, Argentina is a big, rich country with immense potential, and Argentina is *the* secondary-effect play on a turnaround in Brazil.

Argentina is also different from Brazil in that stocks aren't dirt cheap there. The great Latin American success stories of the last five years have been Mexico, Chile, and most recently Argentina. Just to put the stock markets' recognition of that success into perspective, the Chilean market since 1984 has risen 3,500 percent in U.S. dollar terms, Mexico is up 2,100 percent, and Argentina has gained 1,200 percent. Brazil, incidentally, is about unchanged over the same period. We calculate that based on 1992 earnings for companies that are profitable, Argentina sells at a multiple of 12, Brazil at 7, Chile at 14, and Mexico at 13. Price to book might be a better measure: Argentina is at 170 percent of latest book, Chile at 130 percent, and Mexico at 120 percent; Brazil trades at a 60 percent discount.

The political, economic, and social agony of Argentina from 1945—when it had the third-highest per capita income in the world—to 1990 is well known. By the beginning of 1990, a rich country that had so much going for it was suffering from both hyperinflation and a long period of economic stagnation, and it lacked an acceptable currency. Only 4 percent of the population was paying taxes, capital and brains were in despair and emigrating, and the country was on the brink of chaos. The Bolsa then sold at three times earnings, at a 60 percent discount to book, and had a capitalization of $3 billion.

Then, in January 1991, Domingo Cavallo became the finance minister. He was the perfect man in the right place at the desperately right time, and his program resulted in what seems like a miraculous transformation that ended hyperinflation overnight, generated 7 percent real GNP growth, reduced the budget deficit, and created a stable exchange rate. Today he has become the symbol of stability in Argentina, and the cross-section of businessmen, investors, economists, and ordinary people we saw spoke of him with awe and reverence. He may be that country's next president.

Mr. Cavallo's program reformed the tax system to increase revenues, made the currency convertible into the dollar, removed tariffs, eliminated price and wage indexing, and deregulated much of the economy. In the last two years, this dose of free-market economics has forced Argentine companies to restructure and reduce the layers of fat and inefficiency that had been accumulating for years. As soon as investors sensed political and social commitment to the program, the Bolsa, in typical emerging market fashion, soared, rising 360 percent in 1991, and in a mania of speculation peaked in the late spring of last year at 40 times earnings, three times book value, and with a capitalization of $20 billion. Then came a brutal correction that busted the market down by more than 50 percent before a vigorous rally began in the autumn. Still, for the full year, the MSCI Argentina index was off 39 percent. In the first week of 1993, the market rose 6 percent.

Unfortunately, Argentina is far from being out of the stagflation woods. The honeymoon is over, and the country is now faced with some hard choices. Interest rates are rising, the economy seems to be slowing, and there are congressional elections this year and a presidential election in 1994. With economic growth strong in the first flush of victory over hyperinflation, the issue of fairness among the various special-interest groups that has plagued Argentina in the past has not been a factor. But with growth slowing, that may change. The political cost of fighting inflation is definitely becoming a consideration for President Menem.

The credible commitment to a fixed exchange rate regime pegged to the dollar is at the heart of the government's program. Unfortunately, this policy increases the economy's susceptibility to external shocks and in effect forces the government to relinquish control over monetary policy. In addition, since Argentine inflation is higher than U.S. inflation, the peso is becoming increasingly overvalued, and real wages have risen dramatically. As a result, imports have soared and the merchandise trade account has gone from an $8 billion surplus to a $3 billion deficit. Argentine exporters are hurting, and even domestic manufacturers are losing market share to imports, especially from Brazil.

During our visit, I was struck by how expensive everything is. When I mentioned this to the vice minister of finance, Dr. Carlos Sanchez, he said that this was a phenomenon of Buenos Aires near the tourist hotels. However, on a side trip into the countryside hundreds of miles from Buenos Aires, I found even the local hotels, taxis, and food to be very expensive. Dr. Sanchez argued that the exchange rate was forcing Argentine industry to discipline itself to become more cost-efficient and that this restructuring would pay off in making Argentine industry very competitive internationally in the long run. For Argentina to become competitive again without peso devaluation, prices and wages will have to fall in the months to come, or output per man-hour will have to increase, he said. Productivity gains can affect the exchange rate. The government is trying to help by introducing new rules that would allow companies to hire and fire workers more easily, but in late December it failed to pass social security reform.

Of course, the current strength of the dollar exacerbates this exchange rate predicament, especially since a high percentage of the country's exports goes to Europe. Mr. Cavallo has hinted that pegging the peso to a trade-weighted basket of currencies rather than to the dollar might make sense, but every businessman and investor we talked to opposed the idea. They all maintain that the dollar peg is so symbolic that it cannot be tampered with. As one put it, "If they change the peg, the fall against the dollar won't be 10 percent; it will be 50 percent, and we will be right back where we were before."

The government is forecasting that real GNP growth will be 7 percent this year, but most other experts think 3 percent real growth is the best that can be expected. Some are more pessimistic and argue that the exchange rate peg can only be sustained if there is a period in which wages and prices actually decline under the pressure of a true recession. My guess is 3 percent real growth with 10 percent inflation, but the exchange rate will continue to be questioned.

All things considered, I'm not excited about the Argentine stock market at this level. Our weighting for Argentina in emerging market portfolios is 4 percent, versus 2.8 percent for the MSCI index and 3.3 percent for the IFC. We talked with a fair number of brokers and investors during our visit and heard a lot of stock stories. The strange thing was that I didn't hear one that was really inspiring. Apparently, the Argentines consciously understate the case for a stock, but nevertheless, most companies there didn't seem cheap. Astra (US$3.05), Baesa (US$19.50), Quilmes (Ps 7.1), and Massalin (Ps 10.10) seemed the best of the lot.

The long term is another story. Once Argentina gets by this rough patch, the future could be very bright, since there is no reason the Argentine economy couldn't average 5 to 7 percent real growth for a decade or more. Finally, Argentina would be the biggest beneficiary of strong growth in Brazil, because such a development would dry up the flood of Brazilian exports into Argentina.

Buy Mexico and Brazil

July 14, 1992

With interest rates around the world declining and the level of bearishness very high, I anticipate a summer rally in both the developed and emerging equity markets. Accordingly, I am reducing the cash position in our emerging markets model portfolio and adding to our holdings in Brazil and Mexico, both countries where, fortunately, we have been substantially underweight.

It is becoming popular to attack emerging market investing as a bubble about to be broken. "Too Late to Buy Emerging Markets?" asks *Barron's,* and of course Marc Faber says yes. I have great respect for Marc, and his life cycle theory of emerging markets contains many good sociological insights, such as identifying the stage of the stock market cycle at which a country becomes a hot tourist destination. Marc is the ultimate exotic, contrarian investor. However, his current view of the world is quite negative, so it is not surprising that he thinks many emerging markets are headed for crashes or the doldrums. I have trouble with some of his timing judgments. For example, I fail to see how he can place Japan and Indonesia together in "phase 6," the death rattle stage, when, in my view, they are at utterly different moments of economic and financial development.

As for the emerging market portfolio, I have been dramatically underweight in South America, with an allocation of 24 percent versus 47 percent for the MSCI emerging markets index, because the Latin markets seemed extended and overheated. My weighting in Brazil and Mexico had been 7 percent versus MSCI index weights of 12 percent and 23 percent, respectively, but I am now adding five percentage points to each. In the case of Brazil, the Collor corruption scandal has been the principal cause of the market's decline. Investors are worried that President Collor is a tough guy who will not resign, depriving the country of effective leadership for a couple of years, which it can ill afford. Brazil's recession and hyperinflation require action, or the country could slip into chaos and anarchy. Neither is good for P/E ratios.

My view is that Brazil is so big, has such immense potential, and is so cheap that you have to buy when the market has these sickening drops. The Brazilian stock market is incredibly volatile and has fallen about 40 percent in the last six weeks. The last few days it has rallied. The country has an active and efficient private sector with many dynamic businessmen and good managements. Commerce continues in spite of hyperinflation and political turmoil. The agreement last week with the banks under the Brady Plan is an important plus, but it has already been discounted. Eventually, Brazil will get its act together, and when it does, stocks will soar. You have to be there ahead of time. In particular, I recommend Telebras (Cr 8,440) and Usimina (Cr 2.30).

Mexico is a different situation. The Salinas program has placed the Mexican economy on a strong growth path and reduced inflation from 200 percent to a mere 13 percent. In my opinion, Mexico's financial management is as good as that of any developing country in the world. The sudden decline in *la bolsa* was caused by an abrupt 500 basis point rise in short-term rates to protect the currency and prevent the economy from overheating. Also, overseas investors began fretting about Ross Perot's views on the North American Free Trade Agreement (NAFTA). I have been cautious about the Mexican stock market because it seemed inflamed with too much nervous, speculative money. However, this correction has changed international sentiment, and suddenly everyone is bearish.

Recently, George Soros asked me, "What country is going to be the next Mexico?" "Maybe Indonesia," I replied, "or Pakistan." He smiled thinly at my naiveté. "Mexico," he said, "is going to be the next Mexico." I suspect he's right, because Mexico is still very much on track—as close as you're going to get to a sure thing. Indonesia and Pakistan have the ingredients for success, but whether they can make it is a matter for conjecture. The results of elections last Sunday in Mexico's Chihuahua and Michoacán states are further evidence of broadening support for Salinas's policies, and that is bullish.

I think NAFTA will be signed in the next few months and that the benefits are not yet discounted in Mexican stock prices. Second-quarter earnings should be good, and my guess is that short-term interest rates will begin to drift down in the near future. Inflation next year should be in the high single digits. My view continues to be that in a few years, Mexico will be a country of 100 million people with real economic growth of 5 percent, low inflation, and political stability. This profile should be worth at least 20 times earnings, and the market now sells at 11 times estimated 1992 profits. There are plenty of stocks that look attractive at current prices. We particularly like Cemex (Ps 40,100), Grupo Financiero Bancomer (Ps 5,500), Grupo Posados (Ps 1,860), and, for that matter, Telmex ($47).

To raise the money for these additions, I am spending the 5 percent cash position, reducing Portugal from 4 percent to 1 percent (MSCI index 1.3 percent), and shaving

Emerging Markets Country Allocation

	Portfolio	MSCI Index	IFC Index	Mkt Cap (US$Bil)
Latin America				
Argentina	6%	4.1%	5.4%	$28
Brazil (+5%)	12	12.4	7.7	69
Chile	1	6.8	6.1	40
Colombia	1	—	0.8	4
Mexico (+5%)	12	23.7	15.6	137
Peru	1	—	—	3
Venezuela	1	—	1.6	10
	34%	47.0%	37.2%	$291
Asia				
Hong Kong/China	10	—	—	171
Indonesia	18	1.8	1.9	10
Korea	5	10.5	13.0	97
Malaysia	8	9.9	9.6	68
Philippines	1	1.5	2.0	14
Taiwan	2	19.4	17.8	131
Thailand (−2%)	6	5.8	5.0	43
	50%	48.9%	49.3%	$534
Southern Europe, Middle East, and Africa				
Greece	0	1.5	1.8	13
Israel	1	—	—	20
Jordan	0	0.3	0.4	3
Portugal (−3%)	1	1.3	1.5	11
Turkey	5	1.1	1.2	10
Nigeria	0	—	0.2	1
Zimbabwe	0	—	0.1	1
	7%	4.2%	5.2%	$59
Subcontinent				
India	5	—	7.3	66
Pakistan	3	—	0.9	8
Sri Lanka	1	—	—	2
	9%	—	8.2%	$76
Cash (−5%)	0%			

NOTE: Totals may not add to 100 percent because of rounding.

Thailand from 8 percent to 6 percent (MSCI index 5.8 percent). Portugal has been one of the best markets in Europe this year and was actually up almost 3 percent in June. At 12 times estimated 1992 earnings, the market does not look particularly cheap, with economic growth slowing and Expo 98 a long way away. I was overweighted in Thai stocks on the assumption that it is usually right to be a buyer when there are riots in the streets. The market was up 8 percent in June, so I am cutting back a little.

Emerging Markets Data

	Cal Year P/E 1991	P/E 1992E	Price/ Book	92E P/CE	Yield	% Chg Real GNP 1992E	CPI 1992E	Five-Year Growth Trend Real GNP
Argentina	25	20	1.9	—	0.4	5	20	6
Brazil	15	8	0.4	3	1.0	1.5	600	5
Chile	22	18	2.0	—	3.4	5.7	16	4
Colombia	39	35	3.8	—	1.9	2.0	25	6
Mexico	15	11	2.6	9	1.3	3.2	13	6
Peru	15	10		—	—	−2.0	50	6
Venezuela	24	19	1.9	—	0.8	3.3	33	4
Hong Kong/ China	15	13	1.9	13	3.4	8.0	10	8
Indonesia	14	12	2.0	10	4.9	7.0	7	7
Korea	17	16	1.0	5	1.1	8.0	9	6
Malaysia	18	16	2.9	12	2.3	8.5	5	7
Philippines	13	11	2.8	10	1.5	3.0	10	5
Thailand	14	12	2.5	9	4.2	7.0	5	6
Taiwan	29	27	2.8	—	1.1	7.0	4	5
Greece	13	10	2.2	9	4.5	—	15	3
Israel	24	20	—	—	0.5	5.5	14	5
Portugal	12	11	1.1	6	3.3	2.5	10	3
Turkey	10	7	1.2	2	3.5	5.0	62	5
India	33	28	6.5	—	1.5	3.5	8	7
Pakistan	18	15	2.5	—	1.7	6	18	5
Sri Lanka	14	11	4.0	—	2.7	5.7	11	7

E = Morgan Stanley Research estimates.

Thailand has serious real estate and health problems, but stocks are quite cheap and growth is still strong. We are in the process of reassessing our position but have not completed our work.

In the accompanying market data table, the valuations are our best estimates. Who really knows what earnings are in Sri Lanka or Peru? Bear in mind that in Latin America, earnings are still extremely depressed.

Case Study: Peru

April 27, 1992

The Republic of Peru is an intriguing investment and political situation. The old saying is that it's fear and greed that dominate financial markets. In the case of Peru, it's actual physical fear. I haven't been to Peru for some years, but our area specialist who's just returned, Jay Peloski, tells me he didn't feel in any danger. Of course, he's 6′3″, 235 pounds, and played tackle for Duke.

South America's third-largest country, Peru extends from Andean ranges to sweltering Amazon rain forest and has a population of 22 million. Offshore it has the richest fishing grounds in the world; it is also blessed with abundant mineral resources, including huge reserves of copper, zinc, and oil. Yet more than half of its people live in extreme poverty. In the mid–1970s its per capita income was considerably higher than Korea's and about the same as Chile's. Then came 15 years of socialism with rising tax rates, falling tax revenues, bureaucracy, regulation, and corruption. The result was runaway inflation and a shrinking economy, and by 1990 both Chile and Korea boasted per capita income at least double that of Peru.

In late 1990 Alberto Fujimori, a Peruvian of Japanese ancestry, was elected president. He has achieved some success in cutting subsidies, opening the economy, and controlling the money supply. Inflation has fallen to around 100 percent annually, but his most ambitious plans to privatize state institutions, shrink the bloated government sector, and revive the stock market by attracting foreign investors have been blocked by the legislature. Meanwhile, the Lima stock market (because of settlement difficulties) has been effectively closed to foreign institutional investors; as a result, it's neglected, and Peruvian stocks sell for around eight times depressed earnings.

Five centuries ago at the crest of the sophisticated Incan civilization, there were as many people in the area that is now Peru as there are today, but by 1800 European diseases and Spanish enslavement had reduced the population to barely a million people. Today, half the population is crowded into 1 percent of the land in a series of river-fed oases in a narrow, 1,200-mile-long coastal desert. The country has a tradition of mismanagement, corruption is endemic at all levels of government, and extreme disparities exist between the European-descended elite and the Indian and mixed-race poor. A poet once described Peru as "a beggar sitting on a beach of gold."

For the past 10 years, a fanatical Maoist insurgency calling itself the Sendero Luminoso ("Shining Path"), or SL, has staged an unparalleled reign of terror to destabilize the country. Its stated aim is "to overwhelm Peruvian society like an Andean earthquake in order to build an orthodox Maoist state out of the rubble." The SL has ruthlessly murdered not only teachers, mayors, and policemen but also priests, foreign relief workers, left-wing politicians, trade unionists, and in fact anyone who helps Peru's poor within the framework of the state. The SL has killed 26,000 people, and the government claims to have killed 13,000 rebels. Studying this rebellion brings back memories of the early days of Vietnam and the Khmer Rouge in Cambodia.

The SL is led by a philosophy professor, Abimael Guzman, who preaches the purifying effects of violence. "Violence is a universal law with no exception. To annihilate the enemy, we have to pay a war cost, blood cost. A million people may have to die." Typically, the SL will enter and occupy a rural town with an overwhelming force. They arrest officials and businessmen (who often have exploited the people) and stage trials and public executions by stoning, strangulation, or burning. There is no mercy, ever. Once the SL is in charge, it enforces a fierce puritanical regime that punishes prostitution, homosexuality, drinking, and antisocial behavior with flogging or death. The SL also imposes rigid sanitary standards and mandatory schooling. The young are encouraged but not compelled to join the SL. "Two of the things that the SL does out there are to protect property rights and provide justice," says Hernando de Soto, an expert on the group. "These are things that the Viet Cong did, too. The Peruvian state doesn't."

The SL now controls an area that holds 20 percent of the population but grows 60 percent of the world's coca leaf (the raw material for cocaine). It raises perhaps $50 million a year—big money in rural Peru—by imposing a tax per landing on the narcos who fly into remote airstrips to buy the coca. The SL also has forced the narcos to pay peasants a higher price for their leaf. Of course, the use of drugs by the Peruvian people is punishable by death.

Violence and terror are the SL's calling card. Recently the war has moved from the countryside to the cities as the SL has infiltrated the shantytowns and slums, brutally murdering the popular and saintly mayor of Villa El Salvador, Maria Elena Moyano, who had become a symbol of grassroots opposition. At her funeral, many appeared, but few were brave enough to stay for long. On another occasion, the people of Lima awoke one morning to find dogs hanging by their necks from lamp posts as a warning. Government collaborators are beheaded, and intimidation is the weapon, just as it was in Vietnam. Recent victims have included foreign businessmen, United Nations officials, and those who help the poor. The strategy is to encircle Lima by gaining control of the shantytowns on its periphery and then "choke the city and the government." In the last few months, there have been assassinations in the best restaurants in the heart of Lima.

A few weeks ago, Fujimori imposed martial law and suspended Congress. Did he do it so the military could finally wage unrestricted war on the SL, as he says, or because he was frustrated by Congress? It's hard to say. Force alone will not defeat the SL. Peru's army is underpaid, undertrained, and underequipped. In the countryside, scared army conscripts react to the SL with brutality, torture, and rape of the peasants. Just as in Vietnam, these practices result only in more converts to the insurrection. In the long run, only rising per capita income, in other words, economic growth, will prevail.

The United States has made disapproving noises about Fujimori's countercoup, but I think we should remain open-minded. At the inflection point, disorderly developing countries sometimes need the right kind of authoritarian rule. Look at Chile and Korea, for example. Incidentally, last week a poll in Peru indicated that 75 percent of the people supported Fujimori because they agreed extreme measures were needed to deal with corruption and the SL. The Peruvian stock market, which is virtually all local money, has not declined. By contrast, the price of Peru's bank debt, which is controlled by international money, has fallen sharply and is now trading at 11¼ to 12 cents on the dollar in the secondary market.

Recently, the United States has sent Green Beret guerrilla warfare experts, and just as in Vietnam, they have become involved in the actual fighting. Last weekend, a U.S. plane on a drug interdiction mission was attacked by Peruvian jets 60 miles offshore. One crew member was killed. There are some strange things going on. Some people believe it was not a communications accident, as the Peruvians say, but a deliberate attempt to remove reconnaissance. But by whom?

In both Bolivia and Colombia, there are similar though less-developed revolutionary terrorist movements. If the SL succeeds, it would be very destabilizing for Peru's neighbors.

On the other hand, I could argue that the tide of history is against the SL. Their mindless brutality works against them, and if they assumed power, it would be years before they could attract the foreign investment capital the economy so desperately needs. In some areas, the Andean peasants have been organizing themselves into self-defense units called "rondos" to resist the SL. Thus in the long run, the SL is bound to fail. Peru is not Vietnam or Cambodia, and the guerrilla fish have to swim in a hostile environment, not the friendly sea Mao spoke of. Soon Peru will be a marvelous investment opportunity because it is the last really cheap market left in South America.

We own Peru's bank debt but not the stocks, because of the settlement difficulties and general cowardice.

Mexico Will Make It

January 25, 1993

Every time I go to Mexico I come back bullish. This time I came back bullish but not smiling. After Christmas, a group of us were there for eight days to climb the huge snow-covered volcano Popocatepetl, the sacred mountain of the Aztecs. To get ready for Popo, which at almost 18,000 feet is a serious hill, we climbed other mountains and thus saw some out-of-the-way parts of Mexico. Being in the country, talking to people, reading the local newspaper, you get a feel for what's going on, and I came back convinced that George Soros is right. For investors, Mexico will be the next Mexico—but not for a while.

The story of Mexico's miracle is well known. Without doubt, it is the best-managed developing country we follow. Carlos Salinas and his finance minister, Pedro Aspe, are in a class by themselves, and the whole team of whiz kids from Harvard and the Sorbonne, dazzling in their polish, who are running the country are first-rate. Mexican presidents are often beset with hubris in the last third of their six-year terms, and the litany of disasters of the last four presidents includes riots over electoral fraud, stock market crashes, military massacres, and peso devaluations. However, Salinas shows no evidence of that dread disease, and barring a calamity, I think he will be ranked as the greatest president of Mexico. Contrast Salinas's performance with that of many of Brazil's politicians.

Gorbachev was recently in Mexico, and as is his wont, he lectured that economic and political reform must proceed "hand in hand." But Salinas, a product of the *estabilidad monolítica*, is of the Lee Kuan Yew school of one-party benevolent authoritarianism and insists in his gentle way that economic liberalization must come first to avoid social upheaval. Russia is collapsing, and Gorbachev is out of a job, while Salinas's approval rating with the Mexican people is 80 percent, so Salinas has the better of that argument. Nevertheless, he has reformed his ruling party, the PRI, and been tough on corruption, so the old joke that "there is no distinct Mexican criminal class except the PRI" is no longer valid.

I have always liked Mexico City because it has the understated tragedy of an old-time Spanish city, with wide boulevards, chaste stone churches, and dark, mysterious public buildings on vast cobblestone squares. The anthropology museum, which annotates the history and culture of Mexico, may be the best in the world, and the pyramids of Teotihuacán, honored in their abandonment, are spectacular. I am fascinated with the brutal story of how Cortés with 500 soldiers conquered a country of 20 million that was among the most advanced in the world. Despite its reputation, Mexico City doesn't have air pollution anywhere near as bad as places like Bangkok or São Paulo, and you can walk completely safely for miles and see everything.

Anyway, one day we took a long drive west of Mexico City to climb the 15,433-foot Nevado de Toluca. At one point perhaps 100 miles from Mexico City, we drove for miles by huge modern plants of Mexican and international companies producing everything from cars to integrated circuits, mostly for export. A European businessman I talked to told me what good workers these rural Mexicans were and how his company's plant here was its lowest-cost production facility in the world. We stopped at a shopping center with a McDonald's and a huge superstore, attractively stocked with a diversity of food and merchandise. The store was jammed with prosperous-looking shoppers. Thanks to good jobs and real purchasing power, the middle class is expanding in size 10 percent annually and is a new source of growth and political stability for the country.

By contrast, another day we trained on Iztaccíhuatl, which is another big volcano. To get to it, you have to drive south through some of Mexico City's worst slums, where the sights are mountains of trash, open sewers, snot-nosed children, and cardboard shacks. But there is a positive, self-help ethic. We saw groups of men, women, and children building sewers as part of the government's popular program to provide the materials for public works, although it requires that the people actually do the labor for nothing. Still, there's a long way to go. It is estimated that 40 percent of the urban population is unemployed or underemployed, and getting enough to eat remains a serious effort for more than half of all Mexicans.

Hence, the benefits of the Mexican miracle have been unevenly distributed so far. The stock market has soared, flight capital has returned, the rich have gotten richer, and the middle class has exploded in size. However, the average worker's wage, which wasn't exalted to begin with, has declined in real value by one-third in the last decade. That was part of a policy to keep labor costs low to attract foreign investment, but many small businessmen are suffering.

Late that afternoon we drove our bus further south on a road marked as the historic Paso de Cortés, the route Cortés took on his march from the coast to Mexico City. The Paso de Cortés must not have changed much in the last 400 years. It is still a narrow dirt road that winds through small villages of dilapidated cinder block huts, each with a well-cared-for Catholic church and a dusty soccer field. Scrawny chickens run through the streets, and young women with old faces and babies on their backs work in the fields. There were few cars on the road, just men and boys with burros loaded with sticks for firewood. The fields had some thin-looking cows and scraggly crops but seemed dry and barren. The dust was everywhere. This, as Tiger's James Lyle put it, is truly subsistence agriculture. With the smell of smoke in the air and in the filtered half light of early evening, it was like a glimpse back into the Middle Ages.

But this is the same underclass that is migrating from the impoverished countryside to the slums of the cities. Eventually the system will have to offer jobs and a higher standard of living for them, or there will be another revolution. Mexico's wealth ratio is 15 to 1; in other words, the top 20 percent controls 15 times the wealth of the poorest. That's not as bad as Brazil, but it's considerably higher than Argentina and Chile, which are both at 10 to 1.

It's not going to get better right away. The government is committed to reducing inflation further and maintaining the exchange rate at all costs; it is keeping interest rates high to attract capital inflows to finance the large and widening trade deficit. The program is to trade economic growth now for capital investment and exchange rate stability that will produce faster growth later, which is fine if the underclass remains patient. So far so good, but it is essential for Salinas that NAFTA come into being and that the U.S. economy grow.

As for the stock market, Mexican equities are selling on average at 11 times this year's estimated earnings and 2.2 times book value. We calculate that the industrial sector is at 9.2 times cash earnings, which is not particularly cheap. Real GDP growth this year should be around 3 percent, and we estimate inflation will be in single digits, a remarkable achievement. The government anticipates that 1994 should begin a period of accelerating growth that will spread the prosperity without an upsurge in inflation. If all goes well, around the middle of this year investors should begin to anticipate this happy scenario. I don't think the election in 1994 will cast a wet blanket, particularly if Aspe is the PRI candidate.

So I'm bullish on Mexico now and would get very bullish as we get closer to 1994 and NAFTA or if the stock market declines again. I have a 10 percent weighting in Mexico in my emerging markets model portfolio; that's less than the 15 percent IFC index weight, but it is one of our big five country positions.

As for Popocatepetl, things didn't work out so well. On December 30, we climbed a wonderful 14,636-foot mountain called La Malinche ("the weeping woman," after Cortés's beautiful Aztec mistress), which stands alone near the town of Puebla. But Popo, the big guy, was very tough. Out of our group of 10, only one made it to the summit. We started at 2:00 A.M. on New Year's Day from the hut at 12,800 feet, but the altitude, equipment failure, Montezuma's revenge, and, most of all, the mountain took their toll.

The hard part was a long steep snow climb to the crest of the volcano. We were roped up and had on crampons, but we were breaking through the crusted snow, and each step we would sink in a couple of feet. Postholing it is called, and it is very tiring.

It was also cold and windy and very exposed. Anyway, about 9:00 A.M. at 17,200 feet, I was completely out of gas. There was still a long way to go, and I wanted to get down the brute without getting hurt. So I quit. I'm still trying to figure out why, since a half hour later I felt okay. Not making it sure takes the fun out of mountain climbing, and it wasn't a great way to start the New Year.

But Mexico will make it.

Annual Rates of Return to 1992

	Modern Times (1945–1992)		Last 10 Years		Last 5 Years		
	Annualized Return	Standard Deviation	Annualized Return	Standard Deviation	Annualized Return	Standard Deviation	1992 Return
S&P 500	11.7%	16.5%	16.2%	11.9%	15.9%	13.3%	7.6%
Small capitalization	13.5%	25.7%	11.5%	20.4%	13.6%	21.8%	23.4%
Emerging growth stocks	13.7%	27.1%	15.1%	24.9%	20.7%	22.5%	4.8%
T-bills	4.8%	3.2%	7.0%	1.8%	6.3%	1.7%	3.6%
Inflation	4.5%	3.9%	3.8%	1.2%	4.3%	1.1%	3.0%
U.S. long Treasury bonds	4.9%	9.7%	12.6%	10.1%	12.1%	5.4%	7.9%
Intermediate gov. bonds	5.8%	6.2%	11.0%	5.1%	10.2%	3.6%	6.9%
Corporate bonds	5.4%	9.8%	13.1%	8.6%	12.4%	4.9%	8.7%
Junk bonds	NA	NA	13.3%	13.0%	12.4%	17.3%	16.7%
Commercial paper	5.6%	3.6%	7.6%	1.8%	7.0%	1.9%	3.7%
U.S. farmland	9.9%	7.4%	4.3%	5.5%	8.0%	1.3%	7.0%E
Residential housing	7.3%	4.0%	4.4%	1.2%	4.1%	0.8%	4.7%E
Commercial real estate	7.6%	5.7%	5.2%	6.1%	0.9%	5.2%	−6.6%E
Venture capital	15.9%	35.4%	8.7%	29.0%	8.6%	31.7%	14.0%
Gold	4.9%	26.0%	−3.2%	14.0%	−7.3%	5.0%	−5.7%
Silver	4.2%	56.2%	−10.3%	13.3%	−11.4%	5.0%	−4.9%
Art	8.5%	15.0%	12.2%	16.7%	10.9%	22.3%	1.3%E
EAFE	12.7%	26.5%	15.5%	25.3%	1.4%	18.2%	−12.3%
Japanese stocks	15.9%	29.2%	16.2%	24.7%	−5.5%	29.7%	−21.5%
Foreign bonds	NA	NA	13.0%	14.4%	6.8%	7.6%	4.8%
Emerging market equities	16.0%	29.6%	16.3%	24.2%	15.3%	33.7%	0.8%

E = Estimate; NA = Not Available.
SOURCE: Morgan Stanley Research; Morgan Stanley Capital International.

Mexico: Virtuous or Vicious Circle?

June 1, 1993

Last week I went to a Foreign Policy Association dinner for Carlos Salinas de Gortari, the president of Mexico, and members of his cabinet. Once again I was tremendously impressed with Salinas and his associates. It isn't just that Salinas says all the right things; it's the way he handles himself, the way he responds to tough questions, the caliber of his senior ministers. Pedro Aspe may be the best finance minister around. Over the years I have met the governments of many developing countries, and I think this Mexican government is the best I have seen anywhere.

It isn't only impressionable me. All the other usually cynical, skeptical investment managers with whom I spoke after the dinner were just as impressed as I was. This is not an easy group to fool or charm, because they have built-in BS meters with little jiggly needles that are very sensitive to fiction or phoniness. Salinas wowed them. Unfortunately, Mexico's problem right now is not its leadership, but ours. The perception is growing that Clinton doesn't have the political capital to push hard for NAFTA and that the treaty is in trouble, which could be bad news for the peso.

It is very good for the United States to have a healthy, growing Mexico "exporting goods, not people," as Salinas put it. The passage of NAFTA will be very bullish for Mexico, the United States, and the world, in that order. Unfortunately, shortsighted people like Ross Perot who don't understand economics or comparative advantage are trying to scare the American people about NAFTA. Perot's quote about "a sucking sound" south of the border was pure demagoguery. In actuality, Mexico is the third-largest and most rapidly growing market for U.S. exports. Let's hope the naysayers don't succeed, because if the principle of free trade falters, it will be very bearish, not just for us but for the world.

During Salinas's administration, inflation has been reduced from over 200 percent annually to less than 10 percent, net debt has fallen from 70 percent of GDP to only 26 percent, foreign investment has surged, the stock market has boomed, and every year real GDP has exceeded population growth, so the standard of living has been steadily rising. Perhaps most important, Salinas has restored the luster and integrity of the Mexican presidency at a time when, because of past corruption, it had fallen into ill repute with the people.

There are still problems. The trade deficit is huge at 7 percent of GDP and three-quarters the size of total exports; imports are up at a 20 percent rate while exports are growing a paltry 1 percent. Reserves provide roughly five months of import cover—not particularly large relative to the potential short-term capital outflows. Also, Mexico still has too many poor people, "so growth," as Aspe put it, "is not a goal but a necessity."

Nevertheless, it is important to remember how far Mexico has come under Salinas. I believe he will be regarded as Mexico's greatest president. He has proved, as he put it, "that there is life after debt." He turned Mexico around, both morally and financially, and I think it is now on the path to becoming a major industrial power. Already the eighth-largest economy in the world, Mexico within five years should be part of G-7 (or rather G-8), and there is no question its stock market will be in EAFE. If we do something really stupid like rejecting NAFTA, it will delay but not derail Mexico's track to a prosperous future. Incidentally, Salinas has made huge progress improving Mexico's education system and its environment, despite the talk you hear from some American political and labor leaders.

Salinas is an unpretentious-looking man with piercing eyes. He works a room rather doggedly and does not radiate charisma. He doesn't smile and hug a lot the way Clinton does. When he gets up to speak, he seems almost shy and a little ill at ease. There are none of the phony gestures of big-time American backslapping, glad-handing politicians. But when he speaks, you are riveted. In a way, his diffidence gives even more impact to his message.

I was fortunate at dinner to sit next to Pedro Aspe, the finance minister and possibly the next president. Aspe has been the architect of the policies that brought liberalization, deregulation, and privatization and that opened the Mexican economy to competition. His reforms promoted exports, and in the last four years Mexico attracted $28 billion of investment; my guess is that in the four previous years, there was a net outflow of at least that much.

Aspe commented on the government's plan to amend the constitution to provide for an independent central bank responsible for maintaining the purchasing power of the peso. In effect, this government is trying to ensure that future governments won't resort to depreciating the currency, and this statement makes unlikely a devaluation in the next 18 months. Salinas and Aspe truly seem to believe a stable exchange rate is a

Mexico Stock Market and Inverse Interest Rates (to May 31, 1993)

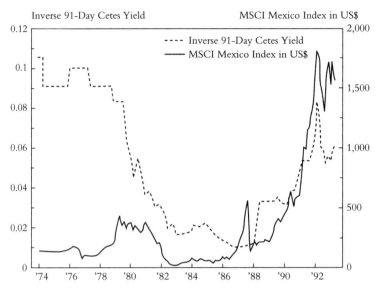

SOURCE: Morgan Stanley Research.

foundation of their policy. Aspe also noted the government's intention to issue longer-term, peso-denominated sovereign debt, which will provide a key market-based indicator of inflationary expectations. When I pressed him about the current account deficit, Aspe remarked in a nice way that it is one thing to have a current account deficit because you are importing capital goods (as Mexico is) and quite another to have a deficit because of consumer goods imports (as is the case with Argentina).

Aspe pointed out that Mexico was taking its medicine to get inflation down to single digits, so that with or without NAFTA, by 1994 the economy would be in shape for a long run of strong, noninflationary growth. Real interest rates have been kept very high in Mexico (almost 10 percent), resulting in slow growth this year and a soft stock market. I think we are still months from easing, but interest rates may be allowed to drift down a little, and the stock market may discount a policy change sooner rather than later.

If NAFTA passes, the growth path will be clearer for the United States, Canada, and Mexico.★ If it does not, I expect Mexico to lead a free-trade alliance with Canada and the rest of South America, leaving the United States out in the cold. "NAFTA and freer trade are the trend of the future," said Salinas. "NAFTA is a win-win agreement because it is job-creating, environment-improving, emigration-reducing, and wealth-enhancing. Mexico and the U.S. have had a troubled past," he went on. "This is a once-in-a-generation opportunity."

★For an excellent analysis of these issues, see *North American Free Trade*, edited by Lustig, Bosworth, and Lawrence, published by The Brookings Institution, Washington, D.C.

I couldn't agree more, and I can think of little else more bearish than our reject-ing NAFTA. What a signal that would send to the rest of Latin America, which views NAFTA as a model for expanding trade between the Americas. How can having a young consumer market of 100 million people next door to us—and one growing twice and maybe three times as fast as we are—be anything but bullish for us?

Talk at the table turned to Telmex. Some said they couldn't understand why the stock didn't act better. Aspe admitted he was puzzled. The story of rising penetra-tion, improving efficiency, and network modernization is far from over, he said, and Telmex won't need equity financing until 1996 at the earliest, so per-share earnings growth won't be diluted. In fact, Telmex just announced a $300 million buyback. The reason for the sluggishness, I guessed, is that everybody at the table already owned it; it's also a proxy for the Mexican market, which is dead in the water.

Nevertheless, to me Telmex (ADR, $48) looks like exceptional value considering secular earnings per share growth in the 15 to 20 percent range and a valuation at 9 times this year's estimated earnings and 7.5 times next year's. This makes it one of the cheapest emerging-market telephone stocks in the world. It looks good even compared to Telebras (Cr 121). Although the P/E ratios are about the same, and the investor gets more book value, lines per dollar, and earnings potential with Telebras, the regulatory and operating environment is so much better in Mexico than in Brazil.

The Mexican stock market has been lackluster since the winter of last year. A lot of American investors have bought Mexican short-term paper, Cetes. In fact, over half the Cetes outstanding are now owned by foreigners because of their attractive yield. Some smart investors are worried that more bad news about NAFTA's chances will cause foreigners to sell their Cetes and the peso. That would put pressure on the exchange rate and might even trigger a devaluation. I don't think a devaluation would be bad for the Mexican stock market, but if the government pushed up short-term rates to defend the currency, that would be negative for equities. In other words, if NAFTA appears to be losing, a vicious circle in Mexico could happen.

A happier scenario, which in fact seems the most likely, is that NAFTA passes the Congress this fall, and with a presidential election in 1994, the Mexican government eases and interest rates fall. The Mexican economy takes off on a five-year growth run, and this in turn sends the stock market into a new orbit. I can easily imagine—with a virtuous circle in effect—Mexican corporate profits doubling between 1993 and 1997 and the stock market going from 10 times earnings to multiple of 17 to 18.

Brazil: An Act of Faith

January 4, 1992

mages of Brazil: Rio . . . a hot city that lives on miles of beaches exulting in sun and nakedness in a hundred shades of brown . . . "the ass," Updike says, "the ass set off by suits of dental floss has become the symbol of Rio," but so have the pickpockets and the favelas with their teeming masses that creep ever closer to the dazzling high-rises . . . the homeless children, scavengers, ranging in packs or playing soccer all night on the floodlit sands . . . the rich have helicopters, the poor live in cardboard shacks, but no one seems hungry, just desperate.

São Paulo . . . 20 million people, the city of commerce that sprawls forever with its traffic, dead rivers, leafless trees, and choking air pollution yet vibrates with industry, hustlers, and entrepreneurs who pierce the smog of stagflation . . . Belém, 2,000 miles away at the mouth of the Amazon, with its skyscrapers that soar magically out of the great brown river, but the back streets are huts and trash, and up the river 20 miles in the green jungle you are in the sixteenth century . . . Carajás, the Brazilian highlands deep in the vast rain forest, the lungs of the world, misty in the morning, shimmering at midday, flickering with light rain all night, so rich with life and minerals, so perishable.

It's summertime, the babble of Portuguese, the people warm, friendly, energetic, so why do we need bodyguards?

. . . the country throbs to a new rhythm, not of economic growth but of music, axé, a crossbreed of samba and reggae that has South America and soon the world dancing in a voluptuous carnival, mocking the human need that is everywhere . . . watch that child with the sad, abandoned face, for—quick as a flash—she will slash your wallet pocket out of your pants.

For the first three-quarters of the twentieth century, Brazil was the fastest-growing economy in the world. There were some fabulous spurts, like the era of the "Brazilian miracle" from 1950 to 1980, when the country's real GNP grew at a compound annual rate of almost 8 percent. Then in the early 1980s Brazil hit the wall as soaring oil prices and bank debt, plus appallingly bad government, devastated the economy. For the past 12 years, the economy has stagnated while inflation skyrocketed; per capita income at

$2,000 is now 8 percent lower than it was 12 years ago, and real retail sales are down 30 percent. There has been a massive drain of capital ($80 billion is the whisper) and brains from the country, and its stock market has been the worst of all the emerging markets and by far the poorest in Latin America.

Visiting Brazil these days, you have the sense that the political system, the economy, the society itself are teetering on the brink of chaos. The social infrastructure is literally falling apart. The charismatic young president, who just a year ago glittered with promise and potential and made the world believe Brazil could be saved, has resigned, after being exposed as venal and corrupt, and once again the people are terribly disillusioned with the slick politicians in faraway Brasília. His successor, a stubborn populist, blunders time and again as markets fall and confidence erodes. The whole government sector in Brazil is out of control, with gross mismanagement of resources, overstaffing, and corruption. There is considerable political opposition to privatization because of the patronage controlled by state-owned companies. As one Brazilian said to me, "The system is biased against efficiency." Brazil's flawed constitution has spawned disproportionate representation, gerrymandering, and 30 different political parties. This truly is coalition democracy run amok. It is generally recognized that a new constitution is desperately needed, but it would take years to enact.

Only a third of Brazilians finish even secondary education, and the literacy rate is falling. Ignorance, disease, and filth stalk the dilapidated favelas. Brazil has the most extreme disparity between rich and poor of any major country in the world, with the poorest fifth of the population having just 2 percent of the national income, while the richest fifth has 67 percent, or 33 times as much. By contrast, in the emerging nations of Asia, the comparable ratio is about 5 to 1, and Mexico's is 15 to 1. It is no wonder that after a decade of falling per-capita income, the streets of Rio, São Paulo, and Belém are actually dangerous. Today the children of the wealthy have bodyguards to take them to school.

Latin American Stock Markets Appreciation in US$

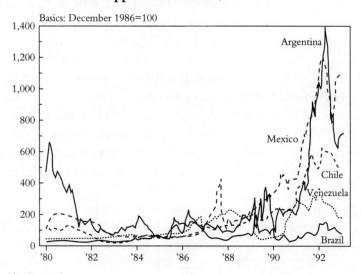

SOURCE: Morgan Stanley Research.

Meanwhile, inflation, like a cancer deep in the country's gut, grows silently in the night, sucking the life out of the economy. Hyperinflation, the black plague of paper money, may be next. Today Brazil is the most indexed economy in the history of the world. Unfortunately, inflation and indexing have become so accepted that there is no overwhelming constituency against them, except the underclass that inflation has impoverished. The indexing creates tremendous distortions, and the intellectual energy and effort required to deal with it are staggering. But the veil of money and arithmetic does create opportunities—in fact, it seems to breed entrepreneurs.

Yet Brazil is a powerhouse. With 155 million people and the eighth-largest economy in the world, the potential is so huge that as investors we have to care. By several important measures, the country is not in bad shape economically. The public sector deficit is 2 percent of GDP, the current account has a healthy surplus, and the adjusted savings rate is about 20 percent. Foreign debt is not a problem. The Brazilians are probably the best businessmen in all of South America, and their companies are highly efficient, low-cost producers by world standards. Many are big dollar earners. Accounting is good, and corporate debt as a percentage of equity is half that of Mexican or Argentine companies. The Brazilian consumer is way underborrowed as well. If the economy began to grow again, the earnings leverage of Brazilian industry would be enormous. The manufacturing sector is operating at around 70 percent of one-shift capacity, whereas in the past it has functioned at 90 percent of three-shift capacity. Retail sales per capita are a fraction of its neighbors'. There is no protected, feeble corporate sector as there is in India, for example.

In Brazil for eight days last month, we talked with 38 businessmen, economists, politicians, and investors. All were deeply discouraged by the political situation, and not one was optimistic about the intermediate outlook for either the economy or the stock market. Some had lost hope for the long term as well. "After all," one said, "Argentina had stagflation for 45 years." Stock market valuations reflect this despair. Brazilian equities sell at half to one-third of book value, two times cash flow, and seven or eight times deeply depressed earnings. Most emerging market and Latin American portfolios have meager representation in Brazil because the performance has been so bad for so long.

In my experience, this combination of both local and international pessimism, plus dirt-cheap valuations, mandates buying. If Brazil found its way and did the right things, international money would drench the $40-billion-capitalization stock market, and prices could soar 10 times in the subsequent five years. The market could easily rise 50 percent this year if the news is only less bad than the continuing disaster that already has been discounted. The problem is not that the Brazilian establishment doesn't know what the agenda should be; it's just that it can't get politically organized to implement it. The risk is that I am early and stagflation continues, the currency continues to depreciate, and the international investor loses 20 percent this year.

I would take my chances now and buy Brahma (Cr 2,100), Vale Do Rio Doce (Cr 795), Usiminas (Cr 5.65), Lojas Americanas (Cr 6,600), Aços Vallares (Cr 3,200), Souza Cruz (Cr 96,950), and Cimentos Itau (Cr 2,630).

Section 3F: East Asia

The Best-Managed Country in the World

November 22, 1983

T he Singapore stock market, at 17 times earnings, has the highest price/earnings ratio in the world, and once you've been there, it is apparent why. Singapore is the most squared-away, well-managed, fastest-growing country around, yet, except for its prime minister and its people, this city-state has no natural resources. Its only domestically produced export is orchids. However, the island of Singapore at the tip of the Malay peninsula does have a strategic location in the middle of Southeast Asia.

Singapore's real GNP growth has averaged 9 percent per annum for the last 15 years and, in the face of the world recession, has been about 7 percent in each of the last two years. Its 2,472,000 people have the fastest-growing per capita income in the world and the second-highest behind Japan in Asia. Its port is the third busiest in the world, its airline is far and away the best, and in the last decade it has, through land reclamation, expanded the island from 586 to 618 square kilometers. There is no unemployment, and, in fact, there are over 100,000 guest workers. As the *Financial Times* recently pointed out, Singapore achieved this record of growth by offering—apart from its well-developed infrastructure of airport, seaport, banking, and tele-communications—a stable government that is pro-business, pro-profits, and free of corruption, an absence of foreign exchange controls, total industrial peace (there has not been a strike since 1978), and a literate, hardworking, English-speaking labor force. In addition, it followed policies of avoiding like the plague budget and balance of payments deficits, maintaining a strong currency, and encouraging high levels of savings to use for expansion without borrowing. Singapore now has a $15 billion national fund, which is invested around the world.

The architect and father of modern Singapore is its prime minister since 1959, Lee Kuan Yew. In *Leaders*, Richard Nixon commented that Mr. Lee was one of the great leaders of our time but that his stage was small. Lee does not tolerate sloth, messiness, disorder, or dissent. In a recent speech to his people, Lee said: "In Exodus there was a passage which says 'and then there was a king that knew not Joseph.' Joseph helped the Pharaoh. The Pharaoh died, a new Pharaoh came up. He did not know Joseph. So soon there will be a generation here which will not know what I know—riots, arson, revo-lution, subversion."

Lee knows of what he speaks because he was present at the creation of modern Singapore. He studied in London and came to power as Singapore achieved independ-ence. It was a turbulent time. Not only was anticolonialism rampant, but also there was bad blood between the Indians, Chinese, and Malayans of Singapore. The communists were poised for takeover. Lee campaigned as a revolutionary pro-communist, but after he won the election in 1959, he imprisoned the communist leadership and immedi-ately reached out to the Chinese and Western elite. "This place will survive," he said, "only if it has got the will to make the grade. It's got nothing else but will and work." Later, as Singapore grew strong both economically and militarily, he remarked: "We look after ourselves because no one else will if we don't."

By our standards, Lee is a harsh disciplinarian with a streak of Victorian morality. He motivates his people to do what he thinks is best for them with financial incentives. At times he has regulated the length of men's hair and, if he could enforce it, he would tax sexual promiscuity. There are no massage parlors in Singapore, and there is little crime. The court system is efficient, the jails are unpleasant, and bad guys get hanged, sometimes publicly. Mr. Lee is a liberal in his view of the social responsibilities of the state to the people, but he considers crime and criminals antisocial. The penalty for the possession of heroin is death. A foreigner carrying drugs is in big trouble. Recently, marijuana was found on two of a group of four American teenagers whose parents were American businessmen living in Singapore. The families were told they (in other words, the entire family) had to be out of the country in 24 hours. Needless to say, Singapore does not have a drug problem.

There is very little automobile horn-blowing in Singapore because Mr. Lee considers it discourteous. Last month, campaigns were under way to motivate the people to speak Mandarin and to be more courteous. Failure to wear a seat belt when driving results in an automatic fine imposed by ladies in black who monitor the roads, and financial incentives are used to control the flow of rush-hour traffic. In Singapore there is no problem with the savings rate since by law everybody saves 23 percent of compensation, which is matched by the employer and put into a national savings fund. Mr. Lee thinks deficits are immoral.

Lee believes that Singapore must restructure its economy by "upgrading" toward high tech, producing goods with high value-added involving sophisticated skills, and expanding service activities. To motivate women as well as men to work, Singapore has a tax-incentive system that is just the opposite of ours. A husband and wife who both work are taxed at lower, not higher, rates as their incomes rise, and the career woman's role has been glamorized by the government. To avoid overpopulation, schooling priorities are given only to a family's first two children, and "streaming" occurs very early in the school system. Singapore is not for "late bloomers."

However, recently Lee was displeased to learn that Singapore's brightest women were producing an average of 1.7 children, while the least intelligent groupings were having from 2.7 to 3.5 children. Studies show that 80 percent of a person's intelligence quotient is inherited and only 20 percent is environmental, so in a recent speech Lee warned that the quality of Singapore's people and work force was being "frittered away" because bright women are not having enough children and that the result "is going to be felt . . . in one generation, in 25 years."

Although a final program has not been announced, it appears the government is leaning toward a system of financial incentives that would be based on the combined standardized test scores of husband and wife. One government official remarked to me that there was evidence that the mother was a bigger factor in the ability quotient than the father, so they might weight her score more. In other words, if a couple's combined SAT scores were at a high level, tax breaks and bonuses would be provided at an ascending rate the more children they had and vice versa for couples with low combined scores. The proposals are generating some negative reaction, but Singaporeans in general seem willing to trade some aspects of a free society for prosperity and benevolent direction.

Singapore, like everywhere else, does have problems. A hotel building boom is under way just as tourism has begun to decline, perhaps because Mr. Lee's puritanical ways make Singapore a dull port of call for high livers. As an island of prosperity in the midst of relatively poor countries with large populations, Singapore has to worry about security. "A generation's effort can be wiped out in days," says Lee, and he has modeled the country's military apparatus on those of Israel and Switzerland. Nine percent of GNP is spent on defense, and national service of 24 to 36 months for every man is followed by annual reserve training up to age 40 for enlisted men and 50 for officers. Training stresses skill and adaptability with a low emphasis on rank and hier-archy. Within days, Singapore could have 200,000 men under arms, and its standing air force of 112 aircraft is rated by far the best in Southeast Asia. Another problem is who will succeed the 60-year-old Mr. Lee.

Can this incredible little country, with its peculiar mix of free markets and regi-mented society, keep growing at around 9 percent per annum as it expects? The answer is probably yes. But is the country's stock market attractive at present lofty valuation levels? It seems rich to me, but then I never have been a high P/E buyer. Mr. Lee alone is probably worth 10 multiple points.

Korea: Fat Premiums, Thin Pickings

April 26, 1988

On my recent trip to Asia, I spent four days in Korea, which hardly makes me an expert commentator. Nevertheless, with due humility, I came away with a mixed impression. Although the country is breathtakingly deficient in charm, the case for investing in Korea is still good, albeit maturing, but what you have to pay to play is crazy.

The stunning "miracle" of the economic rise of Korea against all odds is one of the great legends of the postwar era. The modern history of the "Hermit Kingdom" is bitterly intertwined with that of Japan, climaxing in the agony of "the dark age" of Japanese occupation from 1910 to 1945. Then came the partition of the country, the attack from the North, and the inept, authoritarian government of Syngman Rhee, which lasted until 1960. By 1963, Korea had only $40 of GNP per capita, which had soared to $2,826 per capita by last year and is expected to reach $5,800 by 1992.

There is little question that Korea will continue to be one of the high-growth economies in the world. The government's latest five-year plan projects real GNP growth through 1992 at a little over 7 percent annually, after the last five years that averaged 10 percent per annum. The country's foreign debt is steadily being repaid, and its overseas assets are growing rapidly and are expected to equal the debt within four years. The plan is to reduce the growth of exports, stimulate domestic demand, and accelerate public works spending. The Korean savings rate is 36 percent, inflation is about 6 percent, and unemployment is 3 percent.

The work ethic in Korea remains exceptional: the average workweek is around 52 hours. Capitalism and an entrepreneurial mentality are deeply entrenched because they

have worked. Also, demographic trends are very favorable: the workforce is growing rapidly, and industrial wages, at around $4 an hour, are still far below the $20 of Japan and
the United States and the $8 to $10 levels of Singapore and Taiwan. Furthermore, in the
last year, the country has made great progress toward becoming a functioning democracy.

The negatives are that wages are considerably lower in even less industrialized
countries like Thailand ($4 a day), Malaysia, and Indonesia, so Korea can no longer rely
on having the lowest manufacturing costs. The Korean won may be the most undervalued currency in the world on fundamentals, and I wouldn't be surprised to see it
rise 50 percent against the dollar and most other currencies in the next three years. The
Koreans will scream and yell, but it is inevitable.

At the same time, there is considerable labor unrest because working conditions
are poor, hours are long, and the workers, emboldened by the new democracy, want
their share of prosperity. Industrial unions at the big companies are currently demanding wage increases in excess of 20 percent and shorter hours. There are strikes and
lockouts. The corporate executives I talked with dismissed the unrest as the work of
radicals, but I think it is serious and justified because labor has been exploited. The one
factory I saw was straight out of Dickens and the nineteenth century, and sensitivities
were recently jolted by a fire in a textile loft in which many women workers died at
their machines. Al Woljinower forecasts that the combination of an appreciating currency and rapidly rising wages will result in real wages in Korea equaling those in the
United States in 10 years. This means the life span of Korea's cheap labor advantage is
circumscribed. The economy is also vulnerable to external influences because exports
amount to 40 percent of GNP.

The other negative is that Korea is a high-risk country. The extreme disparities of
income are a festering sore, and there are still dissidents in jail and bad feelings from the
recent riots. Korean politics seem to focus on confrontation, manipulation, and street
demonstrations, and another round of pitched battles between students and the police
could produce another army coup. Also, the threat from North Korea, which is run by
bona fide maniacs, is real and definitely affects the psyche of South Koreans. As a result,
Korea spends a disproportionate amount of its GNP on defense.

Nevertheless, considering the good and the bad, Korea comes out with far more
pluses than minuses. Even though you know you are not early, it is definitely a market
you would want to invest in. The problem is that, for the foreigner, what you have to
pay for Korean equities is, in my view, too high. On a weighted-capitalization basis,
the Korean market sells at about 18 times latest annual earnings and yields 1.5 percent.
Korea bulls argue that the true multiple is much lower because an adjustment should
be made for the banks and construction companies, which sell at high multiples and
have large capitalizations. This seems a strange argument to me. A market is what it is,
and the reality remains that the large Korean companies sell at fairly rich multiples by
world standards.

I would still be a buyer of selected Korean stocks if I could buy them at the price
Koreans can. As is well known, however, the Korean market is closed to foreigners,

and the only vehicles available for legal foreign investment are the authorized funds, which sell at around 80 to 100 percent premiums, and four Euro-convertible bond issues, which have premiums presently ranging from 36 to 95 percent. In talking with Ministry of Finance officials, it was clear that the authorities have no intention of opening the equity market to foreign investment until it suits their purposes. Why should they? The Korean stock market is doing fine. The two reasons the market could be at least partially opened would be either a sharp decline in the market where foreign buying would be needed to avert a panic or valuations that were so excessive that the Koreans wouldn't object to selling shares to foreigners.

The attitude of the authorities is completely rational. As a developing country, Korea needs equity capital to sustain its exceptional growth. But Korea wants its companies to be owned and controlled by Koreans, not foreigners. So, like every developing country, it has to orchestrate a subtle and delicate con game whereby it creates an artificial scarcity and attracts foreign equity capital at the highest possible price. If I were the Koreans, I would do the same thing. But I am not a Korean, nor am I the World Bank, and it is my judgment that the price with the premium they are demanding of somewhere between 30 to 40 times earnings (which, incidentally, are not always conservatively reported) for quality Korean companies is excessive. Obviously, a lot of very smart people disagree with this assessment.

The Korean stock market has risen 70 percent in the last year. It barely noticed the October crash. Unlike the other Asian markets, which on a day-to-day basis key on New York and Tokyo, it has a life of its own. John Clay of Globe Finlay, a fellow with a sensitive antenna permanently on his roof, makes an interesting analogy. In 1964, the Olympic Games were in Japan, and the event signaled the reemergence of that country. The anticipation and buildup of national pride was as intense then in Japan as it is in Korea today. The Japanese stock market climaxed a long bull run the day the Games ended and plummeted 40 percent.

Camelot

January 15, 1990

I have just spent 10 days in Camelot, otherwise known as Thailand, where the sun always shines, money grows on trees, everybody smiles, and stocks seem only to go up. Admittedly, there are traffic jams and fierce air pollution, and it's frustrating when the telephones and the airline don't work too well, but overall it's a magic kingdom with a thick sheen of growth and happiness. The wealthy, the speculators, the entrepreneurs are all becoming very rich, and the prosperity is seeping down to the ordinary people, who suddenly have jobs and money to spend.

To me, Thailand right now is the most fascinating country in the world because it is the newest case study of how a nation and a culture adjust to explosive economic growth and its side effects. All things considered, the Thais with their highly flexible, pragmatic, Buddhist economic and political system are coping about as well as any country ever has.

And the pace is truly awesome. Real economic growth in 1990, for the third straight year, should be around 10 percent, making Thailand the fastest-growing economy in the world by a considerable margin. Export-driven manufacturing, which should jump another 20 percent, has been the main propellant, but tourism, construction services, and growth in domestic demand are right behind. Inflation is rising but should be a tolerable 5 percent or so, although the GNP deflator may jump close to 10 percent, which suggests some industrial overheating. Interest rates should tick up a little this year, but most of the bankers I talked with expect a rise of only 50 to 75 basis points. The currency is expected to remain stable.

The progress one sees, traveling around Thailand, is stunning. Construction is everywhere, everyone is working, there is a pervasive sense of momentum. The area around Bangkok has become clogged, so the government is promoting regional development by self-contained "industrial estates," which provide utilities, communications, security, and all facilities for business and manufacturing. Tax holidays and attached residential communities are part of the package.

The Board of Investment has, however, become much choosier about the applications it approves. Low-technology, pollution, and Japanese projects are in disfavor. The prime minister, in a candid but indiscreet moment, recently commented that he wants Thailand's second language for his children to be English, not Japanese. Japan is by far the biggest direct investor in Thailand, followed by Taiwan. In 1989, fewer but bigger projects were approved, and the high-value-added, non-Bangkok plants get sanctioned fastest.

An example of the efficiency of the entire process is a Japanese electro-ceramics plant I visited in an industrial estate near Chang Mai. The company was registered by its two Japanese parents on October 28, 1988, it received its license from the Board of Investments on November 28, construction began on December 15, and the facility was completed on August 30, 1989. Production began mid-September. This state-of-the-art but labor-intensive facility gets a 10-year tax holiday and employs skilled, motivated women workers at $2.65 a day. The women escape from the blazing heat and bending of the rice paddy and work in air-conditioned silence, although in the long run they also get eye strain and probably lung disease from inhaling alumina dust all day. Our Thai guide remarked that the plant would not be approved so quickly, if at all, today.

How long can Thailand maintain this burst of growth? Dr. Snoh Unakul, the country's visionary economic planner, tells me it is sustainable for another five years. Thailand is still early in its growth curve with per capita income a mere one-fifth of South Korea's and one-seventh of Singapore's. Two-thirds of its workforce remains involved with agriculture, and, as one measure of Thailand's immaturity, Dr. Snoh cites the 1.8 telephones per 100 people (6.8 per 100 in Bangkok) versus about 25 per 100 in the Asian Tigers.

Dr. Snoh believes wage increases will remain moderate for five years as it will take that long to absorb the country's supply of agricultural and underemployed labor. The average wage rate is around $0.75 an hour. Heavy investment in infrastructure and education are essential to sustain the growth rate beyond this initial stage. Eventually, however, there will be a wage explosion.

The Thais are beginning to worry about the side effects of growth. "Better to be NICE than a NIC" is being heard in some circles, and there is worry about forests, beaches, sewage, and particularly air pollution. The people are better fed and have more possessions, but the quality of life may have deteriorated. The traffic jams and air and noise pollution in Bangkok, Chang Mai, and elsewhere have to be experienced to be comprehended. A scratchy throat is now part of life, and it takes an hour to go three miles to a meeting.

The people who run the country are also unhappy that the new prosperity is not more evenly distributed. Phisit Pakkasem, the secretary general of the key economic policy and planning agency, told me: "Our pattern of growth in the future will have to be more conducive to redistribution. We can't wait for the natural triggers to cause trickle down through the economy." Income tax rate cuts, capital gains tax, and an inheritance tax may be ways to broaden the tax base. Dr. Phisit is also not happy with what's going on in the booming Bangkok stock market, but more about that next week.

Nevertheless, Thailand still looks awfully good. The key is still "to keep overheating within manageable proportions," as Dr. Snoh expressed it. The country now boasts a balanced budget, an expanding balance of payments surplus, and soaring reserves. Revenue from tourism is growing 20 percent per annum, and Thailand's exports increasingly are going to other Asian countries rather than to the more cyclical industrial economies. However, a recession in Japan would put a dent in Thailand's growth pattern, and a sharp rise in oil prices would intensify inflationary pressures.

The Thais also believe they are best situated to benefit from the inevitable economic explosion in Indochina. Countries like Burma, Laos, and especially Vietnam should be the Thailands of the late 1990s, and geographically and culturally, the Thais are the natural developers. Symbolically, a consortium of Thai companies is proposing a huge project to build a railroad from Vientiane to Bangkok. Already, hotel and manufacturing deals are being done with the Vietnamese, who, the Thais say, have lost none of their entrepreneurial instincts.

So it's really hard to see what could derail the Thai economic express in the first half of the 1990s. Wage explosions in Taiwan and Korea and the political turmoil in the Philippines make Thailand appear even more attractive for direct investment. The country does not have the racial animosities of Malaysia or the censorship of Singapore. There is evidence of a political backlash in the reelection by a landslide of the reform mayor in Bangkok, but the authorities are very conscious of fairness and distributing the prosperity throughout the society, so disruptive political turmoil seems unlikely.

All in all, Thailand seems as sure a bet for high growth as any economy I know. My guess is that real GNP gains will average 8 to 10 percent and that corporate profits will expand 30 percent per annum over the next five years, barring a global recession. What stock market valuation that kind of growth is worth will be my subject next week. One Thai quoted an old Urdu Indian poet to me: "Short lived is the spring in the garden of the world. Watch the brave show while it lasts."

Letter from Myanmar

March 6, 1995

Burma, or Myanmar as it is now called, could be a great investment story, maybe even better than Vietnam. I was there for five days last week, and it was fascinating although somewhat unpleasant living. Myanmar is still a police state, traveling is a difficult adventure, the food explodes in your mouth, and there isn't a gym in the country.

With huge natural resources, Myanmar in 1950 was one of the richest countries in Asia, but after 45 years of socialism and military rule it is one of the poorest (see table), ranking below even Afghanistan and Bangladesh. The amazing thing is that there are no beggars, it's dusty but not dirty, and you don't get any sense of grinding poverty, even though its GDP per capita is half of India's.

The country is still ruled by a 21-general military junta. I called on the five who run the economy, and without in anyway condoning their alleged human rights violations, I was impressed. They were interested, articulate, and had a basic understanding of the policies needed to attract foreign capital. It was clear they all realized they had to generate faster economic growth and a better standard of living, or else the people would take to the streets again.

I was told by a variety of sources the generals are not particularly corrupt. They have plenty of perks, like government cars and houses, but they are not into the money game. My five generals seemed like a nice bunch of guys and weren't fat or menacing like some others I have seen elsewhere. However, appearances can be deceiving, and their record is not good. They are disliked and feared by the common people. The generals tell the men what kind of clothes to wear, force the people to work harder, are puritanical, and are convinced they know what is best for the country.

Although Myanmar is a pariah in the West, the government's "father knows best" attitude is not repugnant to other Asian countries, particularly Singapore, Thailand, and Japan. If the West refuses to do business with or invest in Myanmar, ASEAN countries would tend to say, "All the better, we will do the whole thing ourselves." Just last week, the Thai government reaffirmed its policy of "constructive engagement," which means "do as much business as possible."

As a result, Asian money is moving in, and even more significantly, flight capital is returning. I met with members of the Ho family from Thailand, who fled Burma 30 years ago and are now investing there in hotels, an industrial park, and an office center. You have to be really bullish to come back to a country where you lost everything. Both the Japanese and the Singaporeans are active, and Hong Kong investors are very involved in the textile industry. Myanmar offers a reasonably literate workforce, stable labor relations (unions are illegal), and very low wage rates (20 percent of those in Thailand). It lacks the infrastructure of Thailand, Malaysia, or even Indonesia, but operating costs are much lower. Liberal tax incentives are also provided, with a three-year tax holiday and only 15 percent on profits thereafter.

The government is also pushing tourism. In 1994 a mere 100,000 tourists entered Myanmar, compared to 6 million each for Singapore and Thailand. Lt. General Kyaw Ba, the Minister of Tourism, told me Myanmar was going to be a "health and cultural" tourist destination, no sex, nightlife, or gambling like Thailand and Malaysia. He spoke of temples, mountaineering, trekking, and rafting. I went up country to Pagan to see the temples, and they were striking but not spectacular. Of course, once you have seen Angkor Wat, everything else is an anticlimax. My hotel in Pagan was a fly-infested, immobilized nineteenth-century river steamer, which was quaint but uncomfortable.

Yangon (previously Rangoon) is a beautiful old Asian city with broad, tree-lined boulevards and wonderful old colonial buildings. Traffic is light, and there is little air pollution. The street life is intense. Time seems to have stood still. There are no high-rises, and in fact nothing seems to have been built since the British left. I stayed at the Strand, the famous old hotel on the waterfront that has been completely restored by the Aman Group of Amanpuri fame. It is an oasis, but even so, after a few days with the generals, the heat, and no newspapers, I got bored. Myanmar may have to rethink its tourism program if it wants to attract anyone other than backpackers and schoolteachers, neither group exactly known for its free-spending ways.

One incident illustrates the time warp of Myanmar. As I sat on the ancient propeller plane for the flight to Pagan, with the locals' baggage piled in the aisle, I was shocked to see the pilot. I am old, but this pilot must have been 75 or 80. Apparently for 40 years no pilots were trained, and the people were told to ride the trains. As a result, when recently the domestic airline was started, the authorities had to find World War II–era local pilots. Incidentally, my 80-year-old pilot did fine.

Here's what the generals think they can deliver over the next five years. They expect real GDP growth of 8 to 10 percent per annum and inflation to fall from 30 percent to 10 percent. Tourist arrivals should rise from 100,000 to at least 500,000 by 2000, and a stock market is planned for 1997. Myanmar has a huge natural gas field offshore at Yadana, which will be adding $1 billion a year to a $10 billion GNP economy by 1998, and new plant openings alone could easily add five percentage points to annual GNP growth. Although the country currently has a trade deficit (because of capital equipment, not consumer goods imports), a lot of smuggling goes on because of the dual exchange rate system. The export of drugs is a major FX earner. The central government runs a deficit equal to 5 percent of GNP. Without going into all the macroanalysis details, suffice it to say that Myanmar's financial situation is somewhat shaky but not precarious.

The Thai and Singapore businessmen I spoke to indicated potential returns from direct investment in Myanmar are in the 40 percent range free of taxes. The risks are high because the generals are very unpopular, and Suu Kyi, who is still under house arrest, would unquestionably win a free election. She is a great lady, but she knows nothing about the economy and her advisers are redistributionists. Were she and they to come to power, anything could happen. Today's investors have to bet the generals can grow their way into the affections or at least tolerance of the people. Myanmar is a high-risk, high-return gamble.

Myanmar Comparison with Its Neighbors

March 1995

	Indonesia	China	India	Philippines	Thailand	Vietnam	Myanmar
Population (mm)	193.4	1,196.5	911.0	66.2	59.8	73.7	45.7
Population growth (%)	2.3	1.2	2.1	2.3	1.5	2.3	2.1
Infant mortality (per 1,000 births)	66	31	79	40	26	37	81
Life expectancy (years)	63	71	61	65	69	67	58
Literacy rate (% of population)	84.4	80.0	52.1	93.5	93.8	88.6	81.5
People per doctor	6,786	809	2,272	1,016	4,361	2,857	12,500
Calorie intake (per day)	2,750	2,703	2,243	2,452	2,316	2,233	2,448
People per television set	16.7	32.3	31.3	20.6	8.9	25.6	500.0
People per telephone	104.2	65.4	100.0	52.5	26.3	270.3	416.0
Urban population (%)	33.0	27.0	26.0	45.0	34.0	20.0	25.0
GDP growth (%) 1994	6.7	11.4	4.2	4.3	7.4	8.5	5.8
GDP-PPP per capita (US$) 1994	3,140	2,413	1,210	2,480	5,890	1,263	676
Inflation CPI (%)	9.6	27.4	9.0	7.8	5.8	11.3	30.3
Savings (% of GDP)	38	36.0	24.0	15.0	37.0	7.0	12.0
Foreign debt (US$bn)	87.8	83.7	77.0	35.3	42.7	15.4	5.3

SOURCE: *Asiaweek Magazine*; Irrawaddy Advisors Ltd.

Victory Has
a Thousand Fathers

September 3, 2002

The noisy debate about Iraq and differing views within the Bush administration has degenerated into a condition of decision incompetence. Unless there is a much more subtle agenda than I perceive, the public discussion has robbed us of any ability to achieve "surprise," which is most unfortunate, and perhaps the ability to act, which is even more serious. Military doctrine maintains that the effects of a successful surprise attack are geometrical. Clausewitz wrote that "surprise is a force multiplier." He postulated that "the combat capability of the side achieving surprise is—on the average—almost doubled." An MIT study estimated that "surprise changes the ratio of casualties in favor of the attacker from about 1:1 to 5:1."

The history of war supports this thesis. Hitler was a bad guy, but he was a master of strategic surprise. In the spring of 1940, the German and Allied forces were evenly matched in manpower, and the Allies actually had more armored vehicles than the Wehrmacht, but the Blitzkrieg achieved total operational and directional surprise and resulted in a rout. In Operation Barbarossa, the German air and mechanized forces were outnumbered in the border area three to one by the Russians, but surprise was the key element. Pearl Harbor is a dramatic case of the devastating effect of overwhelming surprise, and the 1973 Arab-Israeli war is another example of surprise and "alert fatigue."

Skeptics may well wonder if a democracy, an open society, can ever achieve strategic surprise. In this regard, it is interesting to review a successful American surprise attack that changed the course of the Korean War and saved an immense number of American lives. In June 1950 North Korea attacked the South with complete surprise, quickly taking Seoul and, with Russian armor, decimating the unprepared, demoralized ROK army. The United States quickly inserted the regular Army 24th infantry division, but it was desperately outnumbered, poorly equipped, and softened by garrison duty in Japan. Almost at once, North Korea drove the 24th and the ROK army down the peninsula, with the objective of pushing them into the sea. This "withdrawal" was fought over rough, hilly terrain in drenching rains and brutal heat. The U.S. troops were short of food, ammunition, and water, and became ravaged by dysentery. The U.S. forces suffered 30 percent casualties in the first six weeks.

Withdrawal became retreat through steep mountain passes, complicated by tens of thousands of fleeing refugees clogging the roads. The North Koreans were brutal and vicious fighters, whose special forces mingled with the refugees and used them as cover to attack the beleaguered American and ROK units. Atrocities and the torture of prisoners were common. The 24th bravely tried to make a stand on the high ground before the Kum River, and then at the ancient city of Taejon, where an intense house-to-house fight took place. On July 19, with the city in flames and many units cut off and surrounded, William Dean, the commanding general of the 24th, disappeared, last seen trying to stop a tank with his .45 pistol. The retreat south was one of the darkest, most humiliating episodes in American military history.

As the retreat continued, it became clear that General Douglas MacArthur, who had now taken command, was trading space for time. Eventually, the Korean and American troops were pushed into a defensive perimeter around Pusan at the tip of the Korean peninsula. On July 29 Mac issued a "stand or die" order. "There will be no Dunkirk, there will be no Bataan." With their backs to the sea and reinforcements and equipment beginning to arrive, the extended bridgehead held through August and the first half of September. But the North Koreans also continued to bring in fresh troops along unimpeded supply lines, and they held the high ground, which made it difficult for the ROK and U.S. troops to relieve the pressure on their 130-mile front. The fighting raged on in the brutal heat and dust at Pusan, with the armies taking heavy losses. Both sides were merciless with prisoners in the platoon-sized encounters, and U.S. morale was low. Back in the United States, impatience with the losses grew, and both Mac and President Truman knew the ROK and U.S. forces had to break out of their defensive position or lose the war.

At this point Mac (never a modest man) devised what he describes in his memoirs as a "master stroke—a turning movement deep into the flank and rear of the enemy that would sever his supply lines and encircle all his forces south of Seoul. The alternative was a frontal breakout from Pusan which could only have resulted in a protracted and expensive campaign." He chose the port city of Inchon for an amphibious landing, 200 miles north of Pusan and 20 miles west of Seoul. Once he had it, he believed he could take Seoul and "paralyze" the North's supply system, which in turn would let him "choke" the forces besieging Pusan.

Inchon had always been considered invulnerable. The port could only be approached by a narrow, winding channel that could easily be mined and would be blocked if one ship were sunk. There were no beaches at Inchon, the tides were huge (30 feet or more), and only high tide would carry landing craft up to the sea wall protecting Wolmi-do, the elevated, heavily fortified island that commanded the harbor. Two hours after high tide, landing craft would be stuck in the mud. Even when the tide was at full crest, the sea wall loomed 60 feet and was believed to be impassable, with guardhouses spaced along it. Even if the fortress were taken, the landing force would have to cross a causeway and fight house-to-house through the very heart of the city.

When Mac briefed President Truman and the Joint Chiefs on his plan, they were appalled. General Omar Bradley, no fan of Mac's, said it was the "riskiest plan he had ever heard of." Even some of Mac's own staff thought it was a 1-in-50 shot. On August 23 Mac scheduled a council of war at the Dai Ichi building in Tokyo. The president sent Averell Harriman, Secretary of the Army Frank Pace, and two of the Joint Chiefs, with instructions to play for time.

At the meeting, everyone resisted the plan as too dangerous. Inchon, the army argued, was too far to the rear of the present battle to relieve pressure on the front. The Marines worried about scaling the seawall in the very face of the garrison. The amphibious experts said landing craft would be sitting ducks in the mud flats; the Navy maintained the channel was too dangerous. Reviewing the presentations, Admiral Sherman announced: "If every possible geographical and military handicap was listed—Inchon has 'em all."

When everyone had spoken, Mac recalled, he waited a moment to collect his thoughts. "The tension rose in the room. If ever a silence was pregnant, this one was." He began by saying, "My father warned me: 'Doug, councils of war breed timidity and defeatism.'" Frank Pace years later told me that with those words the hair literally rose on the back of his head. "The very arguments you have made as to the impracticabilities involved will tend to ensure me the element of surprise," Mac went on. "For the enemy commander will reason that no one would be so brash as to make such an attempt. Surprise is the most vital element for success in war." He then went on to say that he would be at Inchon, he would make the decisions if adverse circumstances arose, and that he alone took full responsibility and would stake his reputation on the success of the operation. He concluded: "Make the wrong decision here—the fatal decision of inertia—and we will be done in Asia. I can almost hear the ticking of the second hand of destiny. We must act now or die."

There was complete silence. Nobody said anything. The force of Mac's personality and conviction was so overpowering. The attack was on. Moving expeditiously and with complete secrecy, a force of 262 ships and 70,000 men was mobilized, and on the night of September 15, 1950, the attack was launched—with total surprise. The North Koreans were so unsuspecting that even the navigation lights in the channel were on as the U.S. ships came up it. The raiding force from the 1st Marine Division reached the seawall without being detected, used grappling ropes to silently scale it, killed the sentries, and quickly captured the fortress before the enemy knew they were being attacked. Then under heavy fire, the Marines secured the causeway. Inchon was taken by nightfall, and a week later Seoul fell.

Meanwhile, the 8th Army, taking advantage of the diversion, broke out of the Pusan perimeter, and just 12 days after the landing, half the North Korean Army had been trapped in a huge pincer movement. By October 1, the U.S. and ROK forces had driven the North Koreans completely out of the South and back across the 38th parallel. It was one of the most dramatic turns of fortune in the history of war. The president and the Joint Chiefs could hardly believe the news. The country was jubilant. In his book, Mac chronicles the congratulatory messages that poured in from all over the world. (Of course, the naysayers had selective memory, recalling that they had been for the operation all along and just wanted to make "constructive suggestions.")

There are many obvious differences between the situation today with Iraq and then. One could argue that Iraq is a strategic decision, while Inchon was essentially tactical.

But the Inchon story does demonstrate the advantage of private debate within the government about strategic issues, the value of surprise, and the need for the leader to make a decision rather than play Hamlet or wait for a consensus to develop. And of course, as always it's the old story: "Victory has a thousand fathers, but defeat is an orphan."

Section 3G:
Emerging Markets Roundup

A Bigger, Faster World

June 28, 1993

am still trying to understand all the implications of the International Monetary Fund's new weightings of developing economies by purchasing power parity instead of market exchange rates. It seems to me that this revision really is a big deal, because it says that we have all been viewing the world incorrectly. Among the implications are that the world economy is bigger and growing faster, that developing countries' currencies are by and large undervalued, that the developing countries are not as poor as they are assumed to be, and that China, India, Brazil, Mexico, and Indonesia are much bigger markets than generally realized.

To briefly review the argument for PPP as the medium of conversion, the IMF's *World Economic Outlook* for 1993 points out that market FX rates may be distorted by speculative bubbles, central bank intervention, asymmetric speed of adjustment in goods and asset markets, or macroeconomic shocks. The result is that FX rates in both the short run and the long term can be biased away from PPP and thus can point to misleading conclusions.

There are many examples of the distortions that result from using market FX rates. From 1985 to 1990, Asia was the fastest-growing area of the world, but its share of world output seemed to fall from 7.9 percent to 7.2 percent. The new data show Asia now to be 18 percent of the world economy. From 1970 to 1990 China's economy grew over twice as fast as the rest of the world's, yet its exchange-rate-based weighting was smaller, because of the depreciation of the yuan. On the same basis, China's GDP last year was less than Canada's, which doesn't make sense considering that China has over 35 times as many people. Yet another example is the United States, which because of fluctuations in the value of the dollar rose from 25 percent of the world economy based on exchange rate conversion to 31 percent in 1985 and back to 25 percent in 1991.

The Balassa-Samuelson theory of systematic currency undervaluation for developing countries relates to productivity and relative price differences in the tradable and nontradable sectors. The developing countries have much larger nontradable or service sectors than do the industrial economies; because of low wages, prices are very low in foreign exchange terms. Most developing countries also have a bias toward keeping their currencies undervalued. (All one has to do is visit a developing country and see how much more one's currency buys.)

For all these reasons, the size of the world economy is understated. The IMF's PPP work argues that the big currency and size discrepancies are in the emerging Asian and African economies and not in South America. GDP per head in China, India, Indonesia, Pakistan, Bangladesh, Tanzania, Kenya, and Zimbabwe jumps at least fourfold when PPP is used, partly as a function of the currency and partly because of the structure of the economy.

Based on exchange rate weightings, the developing countries accounted for only 17 percent of the world economy in 1992. Using the new PPP weightings (which are five-year moving averages), they amount to 41 percent. Since the developing countries have 77 percent of the world's population, the old calculation suggested tremendous wealth inequality.

World Gross Domestic Product—1992

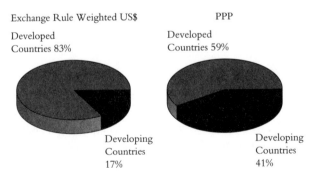

Exchange Rule Weighted US$

Developed Countries 83%

Developing Countries 17%

PPP

Developed Countries 59%

Developing Countries 41%

SOURCE: Morgan Stanley Research; IMF.

Also, world economic growth is faster. According to the IMF, the new weightings indicate that real GDP growth between 1983 and 1992 was 0.5 percent faster per year than previously believed—which is not chopped liver in a world growing at 3.5 percent per annum. In 1992, real growth was fully 1 percent faster than under the old measure. Since the IMF anticipates that the industrial countries will be able to grow only 2.5 percent per annum in the next five years—while the developing countries overall should grow 5.2 percent (our more selective emerging markets universe solves for 6.5 percent)—the theoretical future growth for the world rises from 2.9 to 3.5 percent per annum.

The second implication of the new PPP calculations is that developing country currencies are generally undervalued. According to the IMF, the only developing country with an overvalued currency on a PPP basis is Argentina. To me this conclusion

The World by PPP
GDP, US$ Billion Purchasing Power Parity

1.	United States	$5,710
2.	Japan	2,434
3.	China	2,178
4.	Germany	1,615
5.	France	1,069
6.	India	1,036
7.	Italy	994
8.	United Kingdom	936
9.	Russian Federation	835
10.	Brazil	786
11.	Mexico	613
12.	Canada	532
13.	Indonesia	525
14.	Spain	499
15.	Korea, Rep.	377
16.	Thailand	324
17.	Australia	293
18.	Turkey	292
19.	Iran, Islamic Rep.	287
20.	Netherlands	258
21.	Pakistan	241
22.	Ukraine	229
23.	Egypt, Arab Rep.	194
24.	Colombia	184
25.	Argentina	179
26.	Belgium	177
27.	Poland	174
28.	Venezuela	173
29.	Philippines	153
30.	Sweden	148

SOURCE: Morgan Stanley Research; IMF.

does not mean that the Turkish, Indonesian, and maybe even Mexican currencies may not depreciate in the short run, but it does argue that they are undervalued in the long run. This is an important point for foreign buyers of both stocks and bonds in these countries. I think it is most crucial to bonds: emerging market bonds have a high risk premium built into them because they are perceived as having substantial foreign exchange risk, when in fact for long-term investors, the wind is at their back.

The third conclusion, that the developing countries are not as poor as believed, is also important. On a PPP basis, China's GDP per head, on its 1.1 billion population, jumps from $417 to $1,895, and India's goes from $343 to $1,196. This is crucial support for our theory that for the new generation of big emerging countries, the growth story is domestic demand, not exports. As a result, the new generation is much less vulnerable to slumps or other shocks from the industrial world—especially protectionism. This makes these countries an *independent*, rather than a *dependent*, growth story.

It also proves what we have always suspected, mainly that the middle class in these countries is much bigger than the raw GDP-per-head numbers suggested. Above all, the middle class has the purchasing power. Unilever has estimated that the middle class in the developing countries is growing 5.9 percent per annum, compared with 1.1 percent in the developed world. Nearly 70 percent of China's urban households have color TVs, and 81 percent have washing machines. We estimate China's middle class at 300 million and India's at 180 million

Finally, PPP conversion rates mean that these economies are much bigger than we had thought. Of the 30 biggest economies in the world, 18 are emerging countries. Of the 18, 14 have emerging stock markets of one variety or another, and you can be sure that before long the other 4—Russia, Iran, Ukraine, and Egypt—will figure out a way to get in on the action. The World Bank uses different PPP developed by the UN's International Comparisons Program, which leads to somewhat higher numbers. Using it, China's 1992 GDP, for example, rises to $2,460 billion, which nudges it ahead of Japan, and India moves into fifth place, in front of France.

If the developing countries amount to 77 percent of the world's population and 41 percent of the global economy, and if they are growing more than twice as fast as the rest of the world and represent 8 percent of the world's equities, should you own more?

Jewel in the Portfolio

July 19, 1993

think the emerging market equities again will do better than most bourses of the industrial countries in the second half of 1993. My sense is that the money flows into developing countries for both equity and debt are very powerful. The three events that could cause trouble for the emerging markets would be an economic collapse in China, a serious bear market in the developed countries, or a big increase in protectionism.

In the chatter about emerging markets, it is fashionable to focus on the new hot country that is about to be discovered. It's best of all when that country is positively menacing, with lurking, Uzi-toting teenagers and nubile girls in chadors fanatically committed to some middle-aged, potbellied Marxist sheik who still rages about the syphilis that Cortés's men spread or about the massacre by the Redcoats in some dusty village square centuries ago. These are the turnarounds that an emerging market investor dreams of. The problem is that these markets, though glamorous, are usually too small to get serious money into.

If you are very brave and very convinced, you can do what one investor did in Peru in 1991 and acquire directly from companies large blocks of new equity. This particular guy says he knows he got cheated and lied to, and they got him back for the clean-limbed tribal chieftains that helmeted European troops tossed over precipices into scalding volcanoes in the seventeenth century, but he was a believer and wanted the exposure and didn't mind paying up. His firm made a fortune when Peruvian stocks subsequently soared, but if Abimael Guzmán, the leader of the Sendero Luminoso, hadn't been caught and the Lima Bolsa de Valores hadn't been discovered, he would have been stuck forever with totally illiquid positions.

Today, the two hottest new markets are Morocco and Poland. Both have already soared, but the few stocks available still sell at single-digit multiples. Recently, a meeting in New York on a Moroccan debt issue was packed with the cognoscenti, and last week an investment tour was in Poland, terrorizing Polish businessmen with questions that they had never imagined and complaining about the air pollution. Our man tells me that after one session the unfortunate Polish executive was actually shaking because she hadn't been able to answer a single question; nevertheless, the investors were all salivating to buy. Good luck. The market cap of Poland is $1 billion, and Morocco's is less than $1 billion. As the Antichrist in John le Carré's wonderful new book, *The Night Manager*, says, "Been there. Seen the movie. Thanks."

For big emerging market money, the highest-potential situation today in my judgment is India. The four other big plays—Brazil, China, Indonesia, and Turkey—are all fine to one degree or another, but there are no secrets, and all of them have had fabulous moves this year. As far as China is concerned, with every news magazine babbling about overheating and a crash, you have to bet on a soft landing, but there are very few stocks. India, by contrast, is down 20 percent year to date and 50 percent from its all-time high and is shrouded in a veil of misinformation and ignorance; it's also difficult to invest in.

India also has its gene-encoded colonial memory of English matrons, the colonels' wives, starched and plump, sipping tea and murmuring banalities as a continent starved. But that is its *Jewel in the Crown* past. With the fifth-biggest economy in the world, a middle class of 200 million people, and a government that is beginning to do the right things, India is a natural. Maybe even *the* natural. Where is all the new emerging market money going to go if China flops? Furthermore, with 20 million shareholders and 5,000 listed companies, India has a far more mature and sophisticated equity market than either China or Brazil. That there is some paperwork involved before a foreigner can invest directly means India is minimally owned. A Ministry of Finance official told me last week that eventually this will change, but in the meantime it is a blessing.

The Indian economy is definitely picking up and is showing strength on both the industrial and the agricultural fronts. Real GDP growth should reach 6 percent this year, and further gains to 7 to 8 percent are likely in 1994. Equally impressive, inflation is now down to close to 6 percent, and interest rates are falling. The trade account is now in surplus; exports are running 29 percent ahead of last year. The government is continuing its liberalization program and has recently issued approvals for a series of 100-percent-owned direct investment projects, including the return of Coca-Cola. Don't be distracted by episodes of sectarian violence or political scandals. They are sideshows. The main event is that India is doing the right things and is on its way. Eighteen months ago, the naysayers were writing off the Punjab; today it is calm and prospering.

Another misconception about India is that its cities are nothing but massive slums and that it is "overurbanizing," in the lexicon of the social scientist. The United Nations estimates that India's cities are growing at a rate of 6 percent annually and that Bombay and Delhi will each have more than 15 million people by the turn of the century. Of course, the UN also estimates that Mexico City will have a population of

Morgan Stanley Emerging Markets Model Portfolio

Country	Model Portfolio (%)	MSCI Global (%)	MSCI Free (%)	IFC Global (%)	IFC Investable (%)	Local MktCp ($Bil)
Argentina	3.0	3.0	4.3	2.8	5.6	18.2
Brazil	12.0	10.5	15.1	9.4	11.9	65.7
Chile	4.0	5.2	7.4	4.1	2.0	28.3
Colombia	1.0	—	—	0.8	1.5	5.4
Mexico	10.0	18.9	23.3	14.5	28.7	126.3
Peru	3.0	—	—	—	—	3.0
Venezuela	1.0	—	—	0.9	1.0	7.2
Hong Kong*	11.0	—	—	—	—	226.5
Indonesia	6.0	2.3	3.3	2.1	2.3	16.3
Korea	4.0	18.1	5.2	14.3	3.1	119.1
Malaysia	6.0–	15.4	22.0	14.5	22.6	124.7
Philippines	3.0	1.8	2.6	2.1	2.2	17.1
Taiwan	6.0	13.1	0.0	14.4	1.0	132.6
Thailand	8.0	6.4	9.1	7.3	4.5	57.8
India	8.0+	—	—	5.8	2.5	53.1
Pakistan	2.0	—	—	1.0	0.6	7.4
Sri Lanka	1.0	—	—	—	—	2.0
Greece	1.0	1.4	2.0	1.1	2.0	9.8
Israel	1.0	—	—	—	—	30.0
Poland	1.0	—	—	—	—	1.0
Portugal	2.0	1.4	2.1	1.4	1.7	10.4
Turkey	5.0	2.2	3.2	3.0	6.4	19.1
Jordan	0.0	0.3	0.5	3.0	0.3	4.3
Nigeria	0.0	—	—	0.5	—	1.1
Zimbabwe	0.0	—	—	—	—	0.6
Latin America	34	38	50	33	51	254
Asia	55	57	42	62	39	564
Eur/Mid/Afr	10	5	8	6	10	76
U.S. Cash	1.0	—	—	—	—	—
TOTAL	100	100	100	100	100	$894

*Imputed weight is 15%+. Benchmark weights as of June 30, 1993.
+/− Direction since last publication.
SOURCE: Morgan Stanley Research.

31.6 million by then and that São Paulo will reach 26 million. Cairo, Jakarta, Seoul, and Karachi will be at least as big as Bombay and Delhi.

In fact, throughout history migration to cities from the countryside has always occurred as a nation develops, because cities offer relative opportunity, a higher standard of living, and better jobs. Poets have always idealized the beauty of rural life, but it was really an endless cycle of backbreaking, monotonous labor. Furthermore, as Jeffrey G. Williamson points out in an interesting essay—"How Tough Are Times in the Third World?"—developing countries are managing "urban growth with far greater skill and resource commitment than did, say Manchester, in the 1830s."

India, for example, allocates a much higher percentage of investment to public health, housing, water supplies, and social overhead than did either England or the United States during the Industrial Revolution. Its democratically elected government is much more responsive than most and far more attentive than we were to critical inputs for the quality of life. Bombay, Delhi, and Calcutta have appalling poverty, but as Williamson says, "If we are looking for urban 'failure,' then we are more likely to find it in a nineteenth century European or American city than in Third World cities today."

As we have noted previously, the listed companies in India are growing much faster than the economy as a whole. Ignore the valuation figures published by most brokers, because they are for the Bombay index, which is dominated by seven companies. The overall market is selling at about 13 times prospective earnings for the year ending March 1994, and we anticipate future annual earnings growth of 20 percent. The India funds all have been bid up; the India Growth Fund ($16) on the New York Stock Exchange now sells at a 20 percent premium, and our India Magnum Fund ($31) is trading around net asset value. Instead, we would buy Reliance ($12¾), Hindalco (Rs 560), Grasim ($11¼), Icici (Rs 1,003), and Telco (Rs 182.50).

Section 4

CHARACTERS
AND CULTURE

This man had an ego that would fit snugly into the Temple of Dendur but he owned one of the very best long-term records in the world. He also had two Monets in his bathroom, a G-4, and his own full-time tennis pro. Treasury Secretary Rubin was said to call him from time to time. His words dropped like fat pearls of wisdom into the silence.

—*Barton Biggs, June 2, 1997*

It's probably only natural that an English major from Yale couldn't lead his entire professional life confined to dispensing rote investment advice. Barton Biggs had a trademark talent for literary narrative. It's a talent he used artfully to paint vivid portraits of the wacky characters comprising the culture of Wall Street. To read Biggs is to be let backstage at the zoo where a teeming ecosystem of strange and wonderful creatures go about their business in a fabricated, yet convincingly real, habitat.

Biggs seemed to maintain a certain bemused professional detachment when interacting with his peers and other market luminaries. He abhorred hubris, big egos, and narrowly informed opinions. But unlike today's bombastic pundits who enjoy the arms race of loud argument and caustic rebuttal, Biggs chose the subtler path of well-veiled sarcasm as a means of staying grounded.

Biggs drew caricatures to make his points. He used literary foils like Jim "The Trigger" who became the personification of whatever hot investment fad was sweeping the stampeding herd of overcaffeinated hair-trigger traders of the day. Biggs's plumber became a metaphor for the dot-com bubble when tradesmen turned into day traders overnight and picking winners was as easy as throwing a monkey wrench at a stock page.

Along the way he had more sober and thoughtful sit-downs with leaders in finance and politics alike. He got close enough to these leaders to feel their gravity without ever being captured in their orbits. He exchanged brief quips with a sitting president, spoke frequently with John Templeton, dialogued with Warren Buffett, and had lunch with Margaret Thatcher—a profound experience of "heroine worship" he reported as a "shamelessly ardent admirer."

His experiences taught him that traversing investment markets was not a path to be taken lightly. It's a lethal jungle full of threats and opportunities to either thrive or die. The price paid for success is rarely monetary, and the success is rarely permanent. The currency is mental, emotional, physical, and interpersonal.

"Market stress affects people in different ways," Biggs would relate. "Insomnia goes with the territory; the more extreme manifestations are afflictions like eating binges, irritability, migraines, stomach cramps, inability to putt, and diarrhea."

Despite the potential toll, it's clear that Biggs enjoyed the carnival ride.

Section 4A:
Lunches with Luminaries

Investment Alchemy

March 4, 1986

S ome investment managers talk as if they own only up stocks and always get the market right. In other words, they lie a lot. I found out that one guy reads the new high list when you ask him on the phone what he owns. George Soros is just the opposite. When we had lunch last week, George, in his usual suave manner, began by describing all the mistakes he had made recently.

Of course, he can afford to be self-deprecating. His offshore fund, Quantum, was up 123 percent last year from $449 million to $1.003 billion, and it has advanced another 25 percent or so in 1986. His long-term record is the best. An investment of $10,000 in Quantum at the fund's inception in 1969 after all fees would be worth $1,640,000 today versus $45,700 if invested in the S&P. The same investment made in 1955 with another international superstar, John Templeton, by the end of last year would have reached a "mere" $632,000.

George grimaces with distaste at any discussion of his wealth or compensation, but Dan Dorfman recently wrote that Soros earned between $100 million and $183 million in 1985. Obviously he had accumulated some capital previously. I figure that both in terms of performance and net worth enhancement, George is the most successful pure investment manager in history.

In spite of his wealth, there is no trace of hubris. George lives with style and class in a magnificent New York apartment and a Southampton estate, but he is not ostentatious. No jets or chauffeurs but plenty of charities. He likes good conversation and worries most about his skiing and tennis game. He's always joked that his portfolio is his mistress and that he gets nervous when anyone fools with her too much, but now he says the "mistress" is secondary to his second wife, Susan.

Soros, 55, was born in Hungary and came to the United States as a refugee in 1956. One dominant characteristic of his personality is his willingness to reverse a major position in a flash if it doesn't feel right regardless of how foolish it may make him look. It may stem from his experience during World War II, when his family was on the run from the Nazis in Hungary. George watched his father move them from one "safe" house to another strictly on feel and instinct. It didn't matter if they had just arrived and their hosts' feelings might be hurt.

George is very calm and very tough. He had a rough personal period in the early 1980s, and in 1981 his fund was off 22.8 percent because he "got carried out of the bond market not once, but twice." In 1982 he began to get redemptions, and that summer the short sellers went after his technology stock portfolio as rumors circulated there was a run on his fund. Soros was finished, said the wolves. I called him one dark day in July at the height of the storm to see if there was anything we could do, and the housekeeper in Southampton told me Mr. Soros was outside supervising the repositioning of the shrubbery with the gardeners and could not be disturbed until evening.

Basically, George is a global macro investor rather than a stock picker. Last year, for example, his performance was principally attributable to currency plays on leverage and being long bonds and foreign stocks. His U.S. stock performance was mediocre. In 1980, when Quantum rose 102 percent, he made it in British gilts and U.S. stocks.

His firm is organized with three analyst-portfolio managers who concentrate on stock selection, and when he gets interested in a particular country, he may use a local portfolio manager to run a segment. "I am totally burned out on stock selection," George says, "but the macro game fascinates me. I am not out to maximize the fund's returns anymore, but I don't resist opportunity when it appears." Now he always keeps a 20 percent liquidity reserve "in case you lose a lot in something." He characterizes himself not as a contrarian but as a contra-contrarian.

Today, George believes we are in the "bull of a lifetime" and has his equity fully invested in stocks but is not using leverage. Like me, he thinks we are in a Kondratieff wave cycle. He is now out of bonds. George has long been obsessed with the international debt crisis and believes that it is coming to a head. "What is obvious now happens," he says. "Mexico shows there are limits to austerity for debt service." He is impressed by the weakness in the dollar. "Something is happening that is not obvious, but I am not yet sure what it is." He is still in the yen but thinks the deutsche mark is the most attractive currency presently.

Performance Record

Value Date	Net Asset Value per "A" Share	Change in Net Asset Value from Preceding Year per Class "A" Share	Size of Fund	
Jan. 31, 1969	$ 41.25	—	—	
Dec. 31, 1969	53.37	+29.4%	$ 6,187,701	
Dec. 31, 1970	62.71	+17.5	9,664,069	
Dec. 31, 1971	75.45	+20.3	12,547,644	
Dec. 31, 1972	107.26	+42.2	20,181,332	
Dec. 31, 1973	116.22	+8.4	15,290,922	
Dec. 31, 1974	136.57	+17.5	18,018,835	
Dec. 31, 1975	174.23	+27.6	24,156,284	
Dec. 31, 1976	282.07	+61.9	43,885,267	
Dec. 31, 1977	369.99	+31.2	61,652,385	
Dec. 31, 1978	573.94	+55.1	103,362,566	
Dec. 31, 1979	912.90	+59.1	178,503,226	
Dec. 31, 1980	1,849.17	+102.6	381,257,160	
Dec. 31, 1981	1,426.06	−22.9	193,323,019	
Dec. 31, 1982	2,236.97	+56.9	302,854,274	
Dec. 31, 1983	2,795.05	+24.9	385,532,688	
Dec. 31, 1984	3,057.79	+9.4	448,998,187	
Dec. 31, 1985	6,760.59	+121.1	1,003,502,000	(unaudited)

Source: Company Data.

His portfolio is 60 percent U.S. stocks and 40 percent international. He considers his foreign stocks to be a currency position as well. "In Europe, the funds flow is so large and the markets are so small," he says, "that I am not inclined to tinker much with my equities presently."

George is very bullish on the Finnish stock market. It is the Korea of the north, he says, without the political risk and the investment restrictions. The people are tough (they fought the Russians to a standstill in the Winter War), disciplined, and hardworking. Finland has the best growth record in Europe (3.7 percent real GNP annually since 1978), a triple-A bond rating, and equities selling at five to six times last year's earnings. Inflation is ebbing there, the government sector is a relatively low percentage of GNP and declining, wage settlements are moderate, but interest rates are still very high. Soros expects them to fall and thinks price/earnings ratios in this undiscovered market will soar. His main position is Pohjola, the largest insurance group in Finland, which also has a huge Finnish stock portfolio and thus represents a call on the whole market. The shares sell at a 20 percent discount to market book value and at an even larger discount to true book, including real estate. Some kind of rights offering is presently under way. The market capitalization of the company is in excess of $500 million.

Soros also likes some U.K. stocks. The shares of insurance companies like General Accident, Royal Globe, and Sun Alliance look cheap, and he has been buying London International, a condom manufacturer benefiting from the AIDS scare.

Right now George is obsessed with the book, tentatively entitled *Financial Alchemy*, that he has been working on sporadically for five years. I have read parts of it, and it is the best, most profound investment book since Graham and Dodd, but it is extremely formidable to read because it is so intellectual, yet existentialist. This bothers him because he wants people to read it.

George is sometimes knocked as arrogant and ruthless, but I have never seen any of it. Since, as he puts it, he takes his portfolio with him, he can be anywhere from Aspen to London to Southampton and therefore is not the easiest call for salesmen. It sounds corny, but George is a real gentleman. He's also a real investor. Take a look at the record that follows.

Lunch with
the Global Investor

January 7, 1986

I had lunch with John Templeton on a bright, sparkling day late last week at the Lyford Cay Club. The remarkable investor, now in his early 70s, has the appearance and manner of a much younger man. He is alert, responsive to new ideas, and quick. I can detect no indication whatsoever of the garrulousness or mental dimming of old age. His intellect seems like a hard, polished jewel. During our extensive conversation, the only times his attention strayed was when his pink two-and-a-half-year-old granddaughter with the consistency and shape of a sand-covered peach hurtled by our table.

We talked about the investment management business. As a true global investor with an established organization and record, his firm's assets under management have soared from $2.5 billion a few years ago to in excess of $7 billion. The biggest problem with this growth is that his funds now have several hundred thousand shareholders, "too many of whom want to communicate directly" with the man whose name is on the door. His private account business also is booming. Incidentally, I am told John is a tough, cost-conscious businessman and that his firm is unusually well managed. It has just over 200 employees, many excellent analysts that he gives much credit to, but there is no question who squeezes the ultimate trigger.

John says he has found no correlation between size and performance, and the remarkable history in the table bears out this assertion, which is so contrary to the wisdom of the consultants. From inception to October 31, 1985, the net asset value of the Templeton Growth Fund increased 3,770 percent versus a gain in the Dow Jones Industrials of only 254 percent. A $10,000 investment is now worth $632,469. Yet, as the record shows, Templeton had some poor years (particularly when he was smaller), but the bad years—like 1957, 1963, 1967, and 1982—were inevitably followed by truly great surges of performance. After being in the 13th percentile in 1961, the 41st in 1962, and dead last in 1963, if there had been consultants then, they would have been very negative on our hero. Yet in three of the next nine years he finished first of everyone! Note also the distortion of averages. His average percentile ranking is a respectable but hardly overwhelming 67, although the 31-year record as a whole is unsurpassed.

We talked about the high valuations of investment management firms, the "rich" compensation of portfolio managers, the disenchantment of clients with performance in general, and the trend toward indexing. Wasn't there a contradiction here? I asked. Wasn't there going to be pressure on fees? Not for the true professional, John said, who was willing to take major stakes away from the indexes. He believes the Dow will reach 3,000 in the next five years, that we are in a financial asset period, and that some investment firms are selling out and cashing in too soon.

For Templeton, 1985 was not a great relative performance year. Basically, he was right in being only 3 percent in Japanese equities versus about 20 percent in the Index, but he had less than some other global funds in Europe and more in the United States, Canada, and Australia. John thinks Europe has serious endemic structural problems with its ebbing work ethic and entrepreneurial vitality. The surging European markets are now fully priced, and he does not find many values there, although he apparently likes European chemicals such as ICI and Hoechst.

Templeton's style has been to be brave and maximize his convictions. He was heavy in Europe and Canada in 1963 at the right time, 52 percent in Japan and 32 percent in governments before the 1973–1974 U.S. bear market, and overweighted in the United States for the 1983 bull surge. But John seems to say that, as he sees it now, 1986 is not a year for big bets. It may be a stock-picker's year. However, the three big Australian banks look very cheap to him, and he has very large positions in each. He also likes the Aussie dollar and Australian bonds. I tried the Singapore story on him, and although he was polite and courtly, in essence he said the stocks didn't look cheap enough yet.

John said his organization is working on investing in "emerging" markets. He took a personal flyer in Argentina that has worked out very well, and he had analysts in India recently with the idea of doing a fund. But was it worth the trouble? I asked. Yes, he said, because you get some special insights into other markets. The busy granddaughter reappeared before I could amplify this comment.

Templeton believes the endemic inflation rate in the Western world is still 8 to 9 percent. He is convinced that the American and Canadian dollars plus the Japanese yen will be strong over the next five years versus the European currencies. Purchasing-power parity losses and Eurosclerosis will work against the mark, the franc, and the pound. The currency factor is now the overriding factor in the investment equation, and John recognizes he can no longer ignore it. He told me he had searched the world for an organization that could really help him with currencies, and while he has a couple of ideas, he has more study to do.

Templeton Growth Fund, Ltd.
Study of Relative Investment Performance Based upon Wiesenberger Investment Companies Service

Calendar Year	Total Assets at 12/31	% Change in Net Asset Value per Share	Total Return S&P 500	Templeton's Performance Relative to Other Funds		
				Ranking by % Change	Number of Funds in Study	Percentile Ranking
1955	$ 7,000,000	+13.7	+31.6%	32	110	71
1956	5,600,000	−1.7	+6.6	16	117	86
1957	3,000,000	−17.2	−10.8	115	133	14
1958	4,400,000	+49.0	+43.4	11	145	92
1959	4,800,000	+14.4	+12.0	52	155	66
1960	6,200,000	+14.2	+0.5	9	160	94
1961	6,200,000	+17.8	+26.8	155	179	13
1962	5,400,000	−13.5	−8.7	115	194	41
1963	5,300,000	+5.1	+22.7	200	200	0
1964	4,200,000	+28.4	+16.4	1	207	100
1965	4,900,000	+22.0	+12.3	76	213	64
1966	4,600,000	−5.2	−10.1	102	223	54
1967	4,800,000	+13.7	+23.9	220	245	10
1968	6,200,000	+37.8	+11.1	12	210	94
1969	7,200,000	+19.6	−8.5	1	244	100
1970	6,600,000	−6.2	+4.0	169	279	39
1971	7,900,000	+21.7	+14.3	101	312	68
1972	16,900,000	+68.5	+18.9	1	325	100
1973	16,700,000	−9.9	−14.8	68	333	80
1974	13,500,000	−12.0	−26.5	65	348	81
1975	19,796,132	+37.5	+37.3	80	357	78
1976	42,844,213	+46.7	+23.6	14	361	96
1977	89,993,952	+20.3	−7.4	15	380	96
1978	195,484,228	+19.2	+6.5	48	298	84
1979	340,460,731	+26.8	+18.5	154	537	71
1980	557,514,524	+25.9	+32.5	209	544	62
1981	640,504,058	−0.2	−5.0	131	535	76
1982	681,037,671	+10.8	+21.6	493	563	12
1983	890,632,400	+32.9	+22.5	25	560	96
1984	942,765,331	+0.1	+6.2	208	598	65
1985–10/31	1,220,829,868					
					Average Percentile	67

SOURCE: Wiesenberger Investment Companies Service; Morgan Stanley Research.

Templeton's single biggest country concentration is in U.S. equities, but in his benchmark fund he's down from 65 percent in 1981 to 35 percent today because it's harder to find value. One cheap stock he owns big is Union Carbide. He agrees with me that the trend toward indexing will push up the big capitalization, multinational blue chips that are proportionally underowned. He continues to be very light in technology and doesn't own IBM in accounts I have seen.

As we talked and his wife, daughter, and grandchildren passed by and members of the Lyford Cay Club where he is a founding father greeted him, I was most struck by his insistent responsiveness to moneymaking ideas. We discussed a Singapore stock, and he was ready to give me an order. This remarkable man, who was a global investor when we were all free-agent analysts, for all the family, social, and religious demands on his time and for all his wealth, is still obsessed with being a player. The fire still burns. That we should all be so fortunate.

Vanity Fair

April 2, 1990

I hardly know Peter Lynch; obviously he's a great investor, but his recent retirement announcement proves he's also almost unique in his lack of hubris. Business hubris, in my experience, is a common affliction of the successful, and it inevitably levels its victims.

Hubris, from the Greek *hybris*, according to the dictionary means "insolence stemming from excessive pride," but it also has the connotation of wanton arrogance and contemptuous disregard for moral laws. The Greeks regarded it as a mortal sin: "He whom the gods would destroy, they first make proud." The Bible says, "Pride goeth before destruction, and an haughty spirit before a fall," and a Turkish proverb states that "God hates the proud." There is also a touch of narcissism in hubris. "I find no sweeter fat than sticks to my own bones," wrote Walt Whitman in *Song of Myself*.

Hubris and the feeling that the rules no longer apply to you have destroyed many a powerful man, and although history does not repeat itself, it rhymes, as Mark Twain put it. Napoleon overreached and was an obvious victim of a bad case of hubris. Victor Hugo said that, toward the end, "God was bored with him." Muhammad Ali, by contrast, in his more lucid moments, seemed to understand the danger of hubris, remarking: "I said I was the greatest, but I never thought I was."

What I respect about Peter Lynch's character is that he did not succumb to the hype and come to believe he was an investment genius who could still be a superstar without all the labor. He obviously believes the rules still do apply to him. In fact, if the press reports are right, he quit because he found himself working longer and harder. When he first started at Fidelity, he said, he hardly ever worked on weekends. Then he began going to the office every Saturday; recently, it became Sundays as well, and then he found himself taking work home.

Success breeds hubris, and it is not surprising that there are all kinds of business hubris. I have seen very able chief executive officers who become so self-confident, almost narcissistic, that they believe they can spend more time out of the office playing golf or whatever and still run their companies just as effectively. Inevitably, they can't, bad things happen, and they can't understand why. There is also intellectual hubris, where a leader comes to think he is infallible and that his vision is so inspired that he wants to hear only what confirms his own ideas and turns against subordinates who question or challenge him. CEOs who talk a lot and subordinates who are silent at meetings in the presence of the chief are telltale signs.

Another version of the affliction is the leader who has great personal warmth and charisma but begins to believe he can manage by charm rather than by giving his sub-ordinates tough, honest evaluations. I know of a company where the murmur in senior management circles is that the chairman will say "whatever he has to in order to get you out of his office with a smile on your face." The trouble is, now that they've fig-ured this out, the smile doesn't last very long but the distrust does.

In the investment world, hubris is everywhere, particularly in young guys. The older ones may talk cocky, but there is a deep streak of humility that the market has instilled. After a run of good decisions, an investment manager begins to believe he has what Churchill called "the seeing eye—that deep original instinct which peers through the surface of words and things—the vision which sees dimly but surely the other side of the brick wall or which follows the hunt two fields before the throng. Against this, industry, learning, scholarship, eloquence, social influence, wealth, reputation, an ordered mind, plenty of pluck, counted for less than nothing."

I've known plenty of investment managers who thought for a while that they had "the seeing eye" and believed "industry" and "an ordered mind" really weren't essential. Some succumbed to wine, women other than their wives, and song, and some just suc-cumbed, but they all faltered because the game is so demanding and the numbers are so unforgiving.

There is also institutional hubris. The Bible, in Genesis, relates the first case, in the land of Shinar, when the people in their arrogance wanted to "make us a name" and began to build a city with a huge temple, a ziggurat, whose top "may reach unto heaven." They called it "The Tower of Babel." God walked the streets of the city and was angered at the hubris of this race; He confounded them by creating a multitude of languages so they could not understand each other. Confusion reigned, and the people with their many tongues abandoned the city and the tower and scattered over the land.

A country, an army, a company, and an athletic team can become afflicted with institutional hubris. Success breeds complacency, overconfidence, and arrogance—a deadly combination. The British Empire suffered from hubris early in this century; that's what the poem "Recessional" was all about. Years ago, when everything was com-ing up roses, the New Haven Railroad, General Motors, IBM, Xerox, et al., became puffed up with hubris, and we will see how the San Francisco Forty-Niners and Joe Montana deal with it. Morgan Stanley has to guard against it also. Anyway, my hat is off to Peter Lynch for being a great investor and not coming down with the disease.

Heroine Worship

February 21, 1994

This is going to be very personal, highly subjective, embarrassingly naive, and fulsome. It's about Margaret Thatcher, of whom I am a shamelessly ardent admirer, so if that kind of impressionable reaction offends you, I apologize, and the reader should go no further.

I think Margaret Thatcher is one of the great figures of our time. I've maintained for years that if I could select from all the fascinating people of this century one or two to have a private dinner with, she would be at the very top of the list. Winston Churchill would be an intriguing companion, too, but a little huffy and formidable and inclined to get into his cups. FDR and JFK would be on the list, as would Mao. Stalin had frightful table manners plus being a murderer, and Gandhi and Woodrow Wilson would be too sanctimonious. It would be interesting to meet Hitler, but I certainly wouldn't want to have dinner with him. So it was a huge thrill to attend a small lunch that Julian Robertson, oozing charm from every pore, gave for "Margaret, the Lady Thatcher" and to sit next to her. In his gracious introduction, Julian compared her to Michael Jordan, which seemed to please her. It amazed me she knew who he was.

She exceeded my most extreme expectations. She wore a bright green dress with a gold pin on the lapel, and her hair still has that light reddish glow. She looked trim, fresh, and terrific. I have been reading her book* in which she relates that she had trained herself over the years to sleep only four hours a night. I was tempted to ask her if that was still her practice and how she could still look so rested, but that seemed a little brash. She was friendly, alert, very interested, and very nice. But there was none of the backslapping, first-name phoniness that so many of our politicians affect. On the

---

*Margaret Thatcher, *The Downing Street Years* (New York: HarperCollins, 1993).

327

other hand, you could see that she not only didn't suffer fools gladly, she didn't really suffer them at all. At one point, someone asked how it felt to be a woman prime minister. "I don't know," she said. "I've never experienced the alternative."

Lady Thatcher arrived at Tiger early and was asked if she wanted to see the art collection. Politely she replied that she would prefer to visit the trading room, where she asked where "the Cable is trading" (traders' slang for the dollar/pound exchange rate) and what oil and "the Footsie" were doing. It was the Monday after the Fed raised rates 25 basis points, and she expressed surprise at the reaction of markets around the world. At another point she remarked that "a central bank can either manage the exchange rate or the domestic money supply, but not both at the same time." Many central bankers still have not grasped that verity.

At lunch she talked easily about the world. Her language sparkles, and the thought process is straight-line, rational, and perfectly clear. There is no equivocating or BS. She commented that she had recently spent a considerable amount of time with Prime Minister Hosokawa of Japan and that she was most favorably impressed. "He is much more open and flexible than the old breed of Japanese politicians and he may make a real difference." She was not optimistic about the near future in South Africa. "The ANC still doesn't understand economic reality," she said. I didn't argue. In fact, when that piercing gaze got turned on you, you didn't feel much like arguing. Even the usually irrepressible Byron Wien questioned, then wilted.

She then went on to say that the Western democracies must be careful not to cut their defense spending too much. The world is not safer than it used to be. Russia and China are still expansionist powers, and there are many rogue players. The democracies must have the capability to project power, and their leaders must be confident that the means are there. At the time of the Falklands and the Kuwait invasions, she could act with confidence that her decisions could be backed up with military power. If the president of the United States does not have that confidence, it would be a very destabilizing thing for the world.

She said the rise of endless meetings of heads of state and functionaries in the world is a mixed blessing at best because nothing comes out of them but talk and press releases, and they tend to result in the hard decisions being postponed. The inaction on Bosnia was an example of this, whereas the prompt response to the invasion of Kuwait was the result of action, not meetings.

Incidentally, in her book (which is wonderful because it is so much in character), she damns George Bush with faint praise as a "decent, honest, patriotic American" and then says: "But he had never had to think through his beliefs and fight for them when they were hopelessly unfashionable as Ronald Reagan and I had to do. This means that much of his time now was taken up with reaching for answers to problems which to me came quite spontaneously, because they sprang from my basic convictions." Later she says, "I learned that I had to defer to him in conversation and not to stint the praise." She likes Reagan, and the operative adjectives for him are "warmth, charm, complete lack of affectation, buoyant, self-confident." There is a wonderful picture in the book of Mrs. T speaking at the White House and Reagan gazing raptly at her. Reagan's inscription: "Dear Margaret, As you can see I agree with every word you are saying. I always do. Warmest friendship. Sincerely, Ron."

Lady Thatcher also lectured us in a nice way that it was a great mistake for America to become a two-language nation. All the immigrants who had come here for hundreds of years had learned English, and it was a great bonding force, both cultural and patriotic, for a country to have a common language. If we let ourselves drift away from that to become a two-language nation, it would be divisive and debilitating in the long run. We must not let it happen, she said.

She also told us we must be careful that we did not let the press tyrannize and dominate our political process. She felt that the press was hounding good people from public life and discouraging others from entering government. The rise of investigative journalism began with Watergate and had now gone too far. The press in many cases was intoxicated with its power to conduct witch hunts. Unfortunately, she didn't answer my question as to what the solution was.

But the real passion came when she spoke of the IRA. "There is no excuse for the IRA's reign of terror. They are terrorists and not freedom fighters or an army." She recounted the British government's efforts to conduct elections and deal with them. "My policy toward Northern Ireland was always and above all about upholding democracy and the law." She spoke with great emotion of the long line of terrorist acts and cowardly assassinations—from the Mountbatten murder to the Hyde and Regent Park bombs to the murder of her own private secretary and the attempts to blow her up.

Finally she talked of her foundation and answered a variety of questions. Incidentally, her book is a great read, although you want to pick your spots as it goes 900 pages. The chapters on the Falklands war are particularly fascinating, and the story of her overthrow is poignant. I also liked the chapter entitled "Over the Shop," which describes her modus operandi as prime minister. It all reads just the way she talks, and I see no evidence in the acknowledgments that she had someone write it for her. She wouldn't. It is both candid and personal, and you get a real feel for the character of this remarkable woman. At the end she writes: "Being prime minister is a lonely job. In a sense, it ought to be: you cannot lead from the crowd. But with Dennis there I was never alone. What a man. What a husband. What a friend."

Poker Games on the *Titanic* and Sir John

November 6, 1995

Last week at our Lyford Cay conference, we had a session on technology. I think technology stocks are in a manic, blowoff phase, but there weren't many voices agreeing with me. That particular meeting happened to be last Thursday evening, which was the day technology exploded to the upside.

By contrast, the bulls spoke with great conviction and eloquence about the parabolic potential of the new technologies, particularly the Internet. They argued the world was on the threshold of the greatest technology revolution of all time that would change the way people live, more than the automobile or the telephone, and that as investors you had to be there or your investment survival was in doubt. One of the most passionate advocates even said that this time, valuations don't matter; buy the concept. That's dangerous talk, but someone else chimed in with the hypothetical question of what investors should pay for something that is growing 1 percent a day like the Internet.

The history of our Lyford Cay conferences for some reason has been that if you get 50 of the best investors in the world in the same room for three days, the most assertive consensus is often wrong. This rule doesn't always work, because some years there has been no consensus at all, but it's held true often enough to be significant.

In 1982 everyone loved oil service stocks, and bonds were "certificates of confiscation" in 1983. In November 1987 George Soros talked, and everyone was scared and bearish. In November 1990 the best speculators in the world were convinced the U.S. banks were bankrupt, and that Citicorp was a short at 10. In 1991 biotech was going to change the world, and you had to own the stocks. In 1993 it was emerging markets, and last year Mexico was going to be the next Mexico, if you know what I mean.

The point is that, by definition, the extreme of a market in a concept has to be the point of maximum conviction when its advocates have total confidence and are willing to say ridiculous things. After the meeting last week, George Kelly and Mary Meeker, the two analysts who presented, were surrounded by adoring fans, asking for their favorite stocks. The fact that I got roughed up at our technology session is, in a way, reassuring.

In my opinion, people buying technology stocks today are speculators, not investors. Attempting to identify the best technology stocks will be like being one of the winners of the last poker games on the *Titanic*. There won't be enough room in the lifeboats when the loudspeaker says, "Abandon ship."

Sir John Templeton sat in on our conference, and a couple of us had dinner with him the night before the conference began. He is now fully retired from his firm and spends his time on his foundation activities and running his own money. His wife died last year after a long illness, but John still lives at the Lyford Cay Club in his white, old-style Southern mansion overlooking the golf course.

John is incredible. He is as alert and perceptive as ever; his face is unlined and smooth and his eyes are clear. He speaks precisely and carefully. At dinner he drinks nonalcoholic beer, and every day he "water-walks" half a mile, using both his arms and legs, in about four feet of water in the ocean.

He told me he still travels about one-third of the year and in fact had just returned from a long trip to Asia. He found this particular trip (sponsored by an organization that shall remain nameless) a little disappointing because it featured too many cocktail parties and not enough intellectual substance. John is still an active acquirer of knowledge. One of the great things about being a professional investor is that even after you are retired, by actively managing your own money, you can stay active and be involved.

John has farmed out some of his money. He always asks me for my ideas on new hedge funds run by smart young guys, but I sense he is most comfortable with the battle-tested, veteran investors who run the great partnerships. He said he is not in the least concerned about paying them 20 percent of the profits, because he wants the best, and what he cares about is performance after the carry.

He says he is still looking for individual stock values anywhere he can find them in the world. He thinks some of the best bargains are in riskier places like Mexico, India, and particularly Russia. There are so many more analysts at work in the developed markets than 10 or 20 years ago that it is harder to find overlooked cheap stocks.

John has always been a bull and a believer that the pace of change was accelerating, but a year or so ago, he grew relatively cautious (for him), saying that he was having trouble finding values. Now he seems very optimistic about economic growth around the world and about equities.

He points out that it is very exciting that almost 2 billion people have gone from being communists to capitalists in the last decade. A revolution occurred in the Soviet Union and Eastern Europe, but against all odds it was virtually bloodless. China has become the fastest-growing country in the world, and although everything isn't perfect there, China is managing its affairs better than almost anyone would have thought.

He went on to point out that over half of all the scientists and technologists who have ever lived are alive and working today, which means innovation and change are accelerating. Nevertheless, he said specifically that he agrees with me that technology stocks are crazy and have discounted growth well into the 21st century.

I asked John about his allocation between stocks and bonds for his foundation. John is a conservative but aggressive investor, and I thought that considering the income requirements for grants from the foundation and the levels of real interest rates, he would be something like 60 percent stocks, 40 percent bonds. Instead, he said he has 80 percent of the corpus invested in stocks and 20 percent in bonds, and the 20 percent is in fixed income only until he can find more good stocks. Long-term bonds are short-term investments, and equities are the place to be.

Part of this is because of his bright view of the future, and part because he thinks inflation is the way of the modern world. Politicians in democracies are always going to take the easy course of spending more than they should, so that inflation is going to run in the 4 to 6 percent range over the next 20 years, with occasional ups and downs. Stocks are inflation hedges, and in fact good companies are inflation beneficiaries. Bonds will suffer and will be lucky to earn their coupons.

Another interesting comment John made was that it might have been better for Canada if the secessionists had won, because then the issue would have been settled. With its deficits and debt, Quebec may be a negative rather than a plus for the rest of Canada. However, higher inflation should help Canada, because it is a market dominated by resource companies.

Section 4B:
Jim the Trigger

The Summer of 83

June 27, 1983

C*orrection: In this wonderful Age of Automation, we find our trusty word processors some-times let us down. Because a line in Barton Biggs's comment in this week's* Investment Perspectives *was dropped by an insubordinate machine, we have reproduced the article below. We apologize to Mr. Biggs and to our readers for this blooper.*

What's it like in the summer of 1983? Well, a little bittersweet. It's having breakfast with a portfolio manager from the West Coast named Jim the Trigger and, amid the white napery, the blue house china, and the sparkling silverware, having the coffee suddenly taste sour because you realize you're not on the investment frontier with the real men hunting Indians but are just an old fogey. I've known Jim for some years. They call him "the Trigger," like in "hair trigger" because he reacts so quickly to a story.

The Trigger's career has experienced a few undulations. His aggressive growth fund was up 60 percent in 1980 when his portfolio was loaded with "whisper" stocks like the small oil exploration companies and drillers with names such as "Three Guys and Rig Inc." Then 1981 came, and oil went overnight from being black gold to just another commodity. That year Jim's fund was down 50 percent. He almost lost his job, he told me, and he got no bonus, and his salary was cut. Things weren't much better last year as he missed the bottom, but now the market is in heat again and it's nothing but up stocks, endless blue skies, and a little fine red wine in the office after the close to savor the triumphs of the day.

Jim showed me his portfolio. Forty stocks, and I had only vaguely heard of a couple. I started talking. The market had gone too far, too fast. It was ahead of the fundamentals at least temporarily. The world had unfinished business to deal with in the LDC debt. I told him small, aggressive growth stocks had never been so overvalued relative to big-cap, quality stocks, and I could prove it. There was trouble ahead, and it was time to own quality. IBM would outperform any portfolio of 20 to 30 small technology stocks over the next year.

Jim's eyes always have the faraway, spaced-out look of someone who buys stocks on the telephone and looks them up later, but now they were positively glazed over. With boredom. Not disagreement—just pure, unadulterated boredom. He started talking. Concept technology is the place to be. Real technology is too specific, too much like a commodity with its price-cutting and obsolescence, but the conceptual stuff is ethereal, ephemeral, and there are no disappointments to bust stock prices because everything soars on hope and imagination. Besides, sometimes a black box worked. Digisonics had a microportable computer printer that could fit in your pocket, and it would earn $0.20 a share this year and $1.00 next. With the stock at 40, management was going to raise its estimate to $1.50. He grinned. Just like the old days, the earnings estimates follow stock prices up.

Had I looked at Datalabs? What was a company worth whose earnings doubled each year? The guy that just started Electrobion is so smart he designed a microbit when he was seven and has never played in a losing TV game. You had to go with winners. He was buying people, technology, and companies, Jim the Trigger said, not stocks. Stocks were for dummies; companies were for entrepreneurs who make serious money. How could I say owning Telephone, IBM, and GE was adding value to a portfolio? His fund was starting to buy private placements of letter stock in companies that were about to go public. That was being creative, adding value. "We just bought one," he told me, "Bioelectronics, that will be so hot it can go public in six months without an underwriter."

"The new-issue market is fabulous," the Trigger said. He figured he could add 5 to 10 percentage points of performance a year to his portfolio's total return through trading hot issues. The new arrangement where you agreed with the underwriters to buy 10,000 in the aftermarket if they gave you 10,000 on the offering guaranteed that prices would go up.

"Doesn't it mean that if the stock goes down you lose twice as much?" I asked.

"How can it go down," he said, "when there's always more buyers? You can't lose the way it is this time."

Halfway through the breakfast, I realized we had nothing to say to each other. It's like we operate in different worlds. Jim thought my worries about debt levels, protectionism, and the deficit simply were irrelevant, and he had no interest in my stocks, which he considered boring, too big, too dull, and too high quality to outperform. He would never own them.

Conversely, I had no interest in the small companies that he wanted to tell me about. I had never heard of them, they had already quadrupled, and they all sold at 100 times trailing 12-month earnings but at only 30 times hoped-for next year's earnings. Besides, I probably couldn't understand why what they did was different, and how can you own what you don't understand? I knew I would never buy any of them. When people say "you can't lose" with that invincible tone of voice, a little bell starts ringing faintly but insistently like an unanswered telephone in the back of my head.

Our salesman who was along was no help either. "Bill gave me some great ones," Jim the Trigger said, smiling at salesman Bill. "Good," I said, pleased that at least our research was relevant. "Absolutely," the Trigger went on. "Unisound, Analistics, and Tachnicalics all came from him." Salesman Bill, who was, by his own admission, wiped out personally in the mini–bear market of 1978, smiled smugly from the depths of his new Paul Stuart special order suit complete with darts.

"All three were better than triples in my own account."

"Where did you hear about them?" I asked, trying not to sound bitter. "Certainly not from our analysts."

"No, of course not. I keep my ear to the ground."

"Well, at least you didn't get them from your barber," I remarked. Bill looked hurt. Based on what I know about good old Bill, "the ground" tends to be the varnished floors of midtown watering spots, but it's clear those locations have been a more relevant research source than our 33rd floor.

Jim the Trigger is a good fellow, and I like him even if he does think that he's one of the three or four people in America that God speaks to about the stock market. The real trouble is we are in different businesses and right now his is better than mine, so I'm jealous. But, constitutionally, I can't play Jim's game.

"How much are you up year to date?" the Trigger asked, trying to make polite conversation. I told him we were ahead about 22 percent for the year, which is about what the S&P 500 is up year-to-date.

A brief smile flickered across his face, which is certainly not careworn. "I'm up 45 percent, and I want to make it 50 percent by half-time. This could be a three-digit year if I can just stay with the Mo and the flow."

"Fifty to 22 at half-time, that's some lead," said our jolly Bill getting back at me for the barber crack. "What will the score be at the end of the game?" If I'd told them, they wouldn't have believed me anyway.

The Trigger Comes Back for Lunch

December 13, 1983

Jim the Trigger was back in town last week, and we had lunch at one of those dark, expensive French restaurants where the waiters have sensitive, aristocratic faces. We didn't lunch at Morgan Stanley because the Trigger had added a stewardess who was into sipping icy Stolichnaya vodka laced with bitters and looking bored. The salesman who was with us last time, flush with success, had left the firm to start his own venture capital fund.

As you may remember, the Trigger and I had breakfast in late June when the new-issue, technology stock market was "young and easy under the apple boughs about the lilting house and happy as the grass was green." In those days, the Trigger, "golden in the heydays of eyes, and honored among wagons . . . was prince of the apple towns, green and carefree, famous among the barns about the happy yard in the sun that is young once only, time let him play and be golden in the mercy of his means." At mid-year, to my chagrin, the Trigger's aggressive emerging growth stock portfolio was up 45 percent compared with my meager 22 percent and 23 percent for the S&P, and the Trigger was "honored among foxes and pheasants by the gay house under the new made clouds and happy as the heart was long." Now with a month to go in this year's game I'm ahead 21 percent to 18 percent, and the stodgy old S&P is beating us both.

The Trigger is and always has been a player, and his strength and weakness is that he has no memory. He always comes back to the hot-stock game, and in the past he has always gone over the cliff. "And nothing I cared, at my sky blue trades, that time allows in all his tuneful turnings so few and such morning songs before the children green and golden follow him out of grace."

Now the Trigger was talking while drinking some Stolichnaya himself. "We have fallen on evil times," he said. "Today I had to go to a meeting at some club down on Wall Street for Synergistic Technologies. It's down from 30 to 8 and its luggable, desktop microprocessor is overweight so the buyers are getting tennis elbow carrying it and some are suing, but the worst thing is that it turns out the management was making its money selling tax shelters on wooden windmills that were phonies. The IRS got them. Anyway, all the guys own Synergistic, but you hate to be seen at the meeting of a loser, and we were all trying to sneak in late so we wouldn't be recognized by the brethren. The trouble was that everyone had the same idea, and the men's room was jammed with the best and the brightest. Every stall was locked with guys reading the *Wall Street Journal* and trying to wait out the pack so they could sit in the back row.

"It's almost a disaster a day now, when a few months ago it was a disaster a week. The office called this morning to tell me the president of Applied Digitalogics was in the paper in San Francisco today for writing a bad check for $10,000 to a dog clothing store. Apparently he and his new girlfriend are into buying beautiful clothes for their dogs. The trouble is that the market is so sensitive that this kind of news will knock Digitalogics down 10 points today. We own 200,000 shares."

The Trigger shook his head. "Frigging dog clothes are now killing me. I can't believe it. The infinite variety of disappointments. It's no use being fast anymore because first of all every young kid punk running money is fast, too, and secondly they always open the busted ones down the max. It's pathetic, everyone, the market makers, the analysts, the salesmen, are so skeptical and cynical now. There's been a loss of imagination, no one believes in the magic of a good story these days." The Trigger grimaced over the Stolichnaya at the stewardess, who for the first time showed a flicker of interest. "This whole thing is getting to me," he said. "Last summer I could bench-press the world; now I'm too depressed to even work out."

He asked me what I thought about the emerging growth athletes. I told him I think we're due for a rally, but it would be a rally in a bear market. The good ones with intact fundamentals will race back to their highs of last summer, and a handful will go on from there. The busted ones will go up a lot but not to where they were and then will die again. Relative and absolute multiples on the athletes are still too high. Dennis Sherva's work shows that the relative multiple on his index is down from 2.2 times the S&P to 1.9, and the best companies, the Olympians, are still at 30 times next year's hoped-for earnings. As a class, emerging growth stocks will be lackluster relative performers in the second, quality leg, which I think is about to begin.

In addition, I said the world is going venture-capital technology mad. The Japanese now understand the gap in their financial system and have created a new over-the-counter market so small entrepreneurial companies can finance. Venture capital technology funds are being created in Germany and other parts of Europe, and in the United States the mania is still in full swing. All this is marvelous for future economic growth and productivity, but it means further acceleration of the pace of change, shorter product life cycles, and inevitably lower returns and more risk for technology investors and the existing companies.

The Trigger shook his head. There was too much money still coming to the boutique investment management firms that only buy emerging growth stocks, he said. Money from the public, money from abroad, and most of all, money from the pension fund plan sponsors. It is just a correction in a bull market, and before long it will be young and easy and shining again, and he would climb one more blessed time to "the high fields." He is still buying the good ones, the hurt ones, and the new ones—the smaller the better, because small caps go up the most. The next top will be the big one with real garbage, moon balls, and wild speculation. "I'll have a billion dollars under management by then," he said.

But how was he ever going to get out of even part of a billion dollars of illiquid stock in small companies, I asked. Wasn't he going to go over the cliff again? Lord Keynes, a great investor-speculator as well as economist, once wrote: "The game of professional investment is intolerably boring and overexacting to anyone who is entirely exempt from the gambling instinct whilst he who has it must pay to this propensity the appropriate toll." How was the Trigger going to avoid paying the toll to the witch of Wall Street?

For the first time all day, the Trigger smiled. "I've got that figured out this time," he said. "No more cliffs, no more toll. This time at the top I'm going to sell my firm and all those fully invested, overpriced portfolios to some bank or insurance company for 10 times fees, and then I'm going to live happily ever after on Fern Hill."

"With me and the Nautilus equipment," said the stewardess.

U3 or "Many Shall Be Restored That Are Now Fallen and . . ."

September 11, 1984

My old acquaintance, Jim the Trigger, was back in town last week. The Trigger and I and an institutional salesman who subsequently left Morgan Stanley for some West Coast boutique that later disappeared first had lunch in June of 1983 when the Trigger was soaring on the high-tech growth wave. In mid-December of last year, I saw the Trigger again, and at that time he was traveling with a stewardess, some portfolio melancholia, and a lot of iced Stolichnaya vodka, but he still believed the high-tech emerging growth stocks were going to come back.

However, last week I found out it was a different story. The Trigger told me he and a couple of other guys have started a new firm called "U3." "For our investment style, the three U's," said the Trigger. "We only buy the undervalued, unloved, and under-owned. We were thinking about calling our firm GraBuf, you know for Ben Graham and Warren Buffett, but that seemed a little obvious. One of my partners liked the name Value Associates, but I convinced them that U3 would appeal more to the consultants. We even have a firm motto from Horace, an old Roman you've probably never heard of who was a major poet and a minor speculator. 'Many shall be restored that now are fallen and many shall fall that now are in honor.' Ben Graham put it on the first page of *Security Analysis*, which is our new bible."

I remarked that I thought he had always been a growth-oriented investor. "No more," said the Trigger. "I'm through with growth and earnings momentum. It hasn't worked recently. My portfolios died horrible deaths earlier this year, and even the survivors that had the earnings gains collapsed. The better the earnings momentum, the worse the action. The market is brutally efficient; it discounts earnings momentum so that's a loser's game. Value is still a winner's game. Book value, cash, net quick assets, free cash flow, all that stuff. Balance sheets instead of income statements.

"Value is the wave of the future, and it's going great. You don't have to worry about earnings surprises; our stocks all have lousy earnings. It's just reading the numbers and waiting for some LBO or acquisition crazy to take you out. Besides, the consultants are all looking for disciplined, value-oriented managers with formulas. When we make presentations, I carry a copy of Graham's *Security Analysis* with me. I gave it to my three-year-old to play with to make it look thumbed."

I asked him if the emerging growth stocks were dead. The Trigger nodded. "I think so. They've just had a rally, but it's a rally in a bear market. There's too much technology, too many entrepreneurs and venture capitalists. Nobody cares about growth and earnings momentum anymore. I hear there is going to be an asset value conference this year, and I bet it will outdraw the H&Q conference."

What was his formula, I asked. "Just what the name says," was the answer. "We buy stocks that on our valuation screen come out as being undervalued in terms of book value, unloved as indicated by a low price/earnings ratio, and underowned by institutional investors. Once in a while, you get into one that deserves to be undervalued and it goes bankrupt, but that just shows you're in the game. Like an injury in football.

"The real problem is that now a lot of people are doing it, so it's hard to find cheap stocks that are really institutionally unloved, but the routine sounds good anyway, and the clients and consultants love it. We also throw in what we call the 'fat man factor,' which is that we try to find companies with overweight chief executive officers because we figure they're more likely to be lazy, complacent types, running loaded laggards. We just have a secretary go through the annual reports looking for CEOs with fat faces. Our other rule is that half of the portfolio has to be made up of single-digit priced stocks because they have the potential to become double digits, and at worst they can only go to zip."

I must have looked skeptical, because the Trigger said almost apologetically: "Yeah, I know it sounds boring, but it sells in consultantland. And from a business viewpoint, this is the efficient way to do it. We run our screen on a PC using the S&P tapes. We don't need to spend any commissions buying research, so we execute through Autranet, which pays for all our office overhead, including the secretary and the PC, with soft dollars. The firm's going to have unbelievable profit margins. It's much better than the old days when we used commissions for research and actually made company calls. You can't make a field trip to check book value."

How was everything else, I asked. The Trigger smiled. "The stewardess is gone—she didn't respond well to bear markets—and I'm back with my wife. I've given up drinking and the fitness center and am playing golf again. Back to the old values. No more modern art in the office, just an American flag behind my desk and *Security Analysis* on it."

The Trigger Finds an Arb

February 20, 1985

My old friend Jim the Trigger is back in town. As you may remember, the Trigger closed his high-tech boutique last fall and joined a value investing firm called U3, which stands for Undervalued, Unloved, and Underowned. Jim always has been a relative strength player with lightning reactions, which is why we call him The Trigger, and his strength and weakness is that he has no memory or sense of history and thus travels unencumbered by the baggage of experience.

"Hey," said The Trigger, "risk arbitrage is money falling out of the trees like leaves in October. And there's no risk if you're smart and quick and talk to the right guys. I gotta get into it. Come see Peter the Great with me. We're going to do something with him."

Obviously I'd heard of Peter the Great, as he is one of the top "arbs" in town, and the story of his rise on raw brains from a Cleveland blue-collar background is well known. The mere rumor that he was buying could set executive paunches and putters quivering from Shinnecock to the Los Angeles Country Club.

The reception room at Peter the Great's office suite had a huge oriental rug and fine antique furniture. "Peter is obsessed with getting into Blind Brook, and he has this idea that merchant banking is classy," said The Trigger. "He's got a couple of phony Englishmen at rolltop desks in the other room, but it's just a front." On the paneled walls were framed annual report covers, which I recognized as defunct companies that had been acquired or put in play by Peter. One of the husky young Englishmen in the reception room took our coats. "Former commandos," The Trigger whispered. "Ever since Peter read that Yamani has British commandos as bodyguards, he's had some, too. Very big on the cloak-and-dagger stuff. Code names, disguises, secure telephones. It's like you're in the CIA."

As we waited, The Trigger told me more about Peter. "Tough, competitive guy. He's an edge player. Was a wrestler in high school and he would chew garlic so he would smell horrible, which might just slow the other guy down for a second. He's the only 45-year-old I know who still cheats at tennis. Compulsive about using time and redundancy. Always tries to do at least two things at once. Has an exercycle built into his limo so he can work out, read, listen to music, and get driven to work all at the same time. Claims he only sleeps about two hours a night. Runs a sweatshop here. Half his analysts burn out and end up in communes in Oregon."

One of the commandos took us into Peter's office, a huge room with a panoramic view and a massive structure in the middle, which was half desk, half control center. There was no chair, but there was an exercycle by the desk and a set of gold-colored weights in one corner. Peter himself was a lean, deeply tanned man, coatless, but beautifully dressed with bright red suspenders.

"Welcome to *Battlestar Galactica*," he said, gesturing at the console, built into which were numerous screens flashing prices in different colors. "Any kind of unusual market activity is displayed in color," he told us, "but look at this here." The lower screens were divided into 20 sections, and on each a researcher or trader could be seen. Peter showed us how he could talk direct to any one of them or put one's face directly up on the big screen. He spoke quickly and in bursts of words. They can't get away from me and they can't see me unless I want 'em to, and I even have a system where I can deliver a low-voltage shock, but I've only used it on my kids when they worked here last summer and on one guy who picked his nose redundantly on my time. Discipline and self-control are the keys to this business."

A phone rang. "Orient Express from the field. Sir," a voice said. Peter picked up the phone and jumped on the exercycle and began to pedal furiously. We could hear snatches of the conversation, which seemed to involve whether somebody's wife was having an affair. Abruptly Peter hung up. "When these corporate preppies try to block me, they'd better be ready to go to war," he shouted, panting from the exercycle. "My guys can dig up anything, and I'll use it. The chairman's wife is fooling around with a tennis pro," he said disgustedly, "and they think they're going to get away with trying to crown jewel me? What is this? The Yale-Harvard game? That crud won't be able to go to Blind Brook when I get through with him. I'll kill 'em."

The Trigger loved it. "Go get 'em, Peter. That's why you're so great. How can they say arbitrage is parasitic and produces nothing when you're doing creative stuff like this? Big companies shouldn't be run by clowns whose wives go for short-pants tennis pros. Greenmail, golden parachutes, and poison pills are the essence of the market economy at work. You're changing the nature of capitalism. You may even get the Nobel Prize."

Peter nodded. "We are also breaking new ground with LBOs and junk bond financing. Why shouldn't a thrift institution own some high-yielding junk? *BusinessWeek* is going to do a cover story on risk arbitrage. Incidentally, I don't believe in diversification. I don't like people equally or wines equally so why build a portfolio

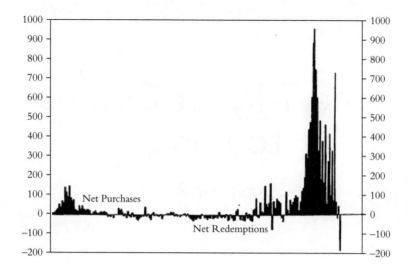

equally. Own monster positions of the stocks you really like or else you're only practic-ing. It's all greed versus fear, but getting nervous is a misallocation of energy.

"My master is my purse. Everything's for sale except my kids and maybe my wife. I'm a business nymphomaniac. He who has the most money when he dies, wins. But I want to do some good in the world, too, and get to be a trustee of the Ford Foundation. I give a lot to charity—like I'm very interested in religious studies and I'm funding scholarships on reincarnation. They're trying to find out who I'm coming back as next time so I can leave my money to myself. Did you mean the Nobel Prize for economics or peace?"

"Either one," said The Trigger enthusiastically. "Peter, you're great, you've got the best business in the world. The spreads will be fat forever. I'm going to be in it with you so I can get rich too!"

The Trigger Comes to Lunch

December 9, 1991

I had lunch last week with Jim the Trigger, a money manager I've known in good times and in bad, and 1991 has been a boomer for Jim. Last week he was positively oozing hubris from every pore. Incidentally, we call him "the Trigger"—as in "hair trigger"—because he reacts so quickly to a story. Jim's not much younger than I am, but he made me feel like an old fogey incapable of shooting fast and stalking the big game with the real hunters.

The Trigger's career has experienced a few undulations, which I have chronicled in the past. In the early 1980s his aggressive growth fund was loaded with "whisper" stocks like the small exploration companies and drillers with names such as Three Guys and a Rig, Inc. He was up 65 percent in 1980, but then in 1981 oil went overnight from being black gold to just another commodity, and the Trigger's fund was down 50 percent. He almost lost his job, as I remember it, but in 1982 and 1983 he came back and shot the lights out with the small tech and emerging growth stocks, "the athletes" as he called them then.

Subsequently, when the athletes died horrible deaths and the moon balls crashed, the Trigger actually did get fired, but he has a great sense of the game and always gravitates toward relative strength. He spent the second half of the 1980s with an investment firm called U3, for Undervalued, Unloved, and Underowned, which also did risk arbitrage. But at lunch last week he told me: "Value sucks and Ben Graham was a loser. Buying cheap stocks on book value analysis is for small-minded accountants. I never once got an adrenaline rush the way I do now from an up stock or panicking the shorts."

344

So the Trigger is back as an aggressive growth stock investor with his own hedge fund, and it's full of biotech, medical technology, software, and Mexico. "I'm like Michael Jordan hitting a string of 30-foot jump shots," he grinned. He showed me his portfolio, and of the 40 stocks I had only vaguely heard of a couple.

"You're too skeptical and you're getting old," he said. "You gotta get with it. Get yourself a kid. Kids don't have scars or memories. When the market is in heat in frontier areas, experience is a big negative. My kids specialize in triples. We have our own fitness center with Nautilus equipment, and we all lift weights together. I feel like I can bench-press the world."

I started talking. I was cautious. The economy was lousy; there was too much debt and too little leadership from Washington. A lot of stocks and even some countries like Mexico had doubled and tripled. The crack in November was a warning of things to come. Biotech was marvelous, but there were too many companies, too much easy money, and expectations were way ahead of the fundamentals. The stocks were rallying back toward their highs, but it could be a trap. It was time to take some money off the table.

The Trigger's eyes always have the faraway, spaced-out look of someone who buys stocks on the telephone and looks them up later, but now they were positively glazed over. With boredom. Not disagreement—just pure, unadulterated boredom. He started talking. Fundamentals were irrelevant in biotech and medical technology. His kids had proved that biotechs with negative net worth and no earnings performed best. Concept companies where you could dream a little were the place to be. Real companies making money with actual products were dangerous, because they were analyzable and could be valued. There could be earnings disappointments, product failures, or competitive developments that would bust a stock, but the conceptual stuff is ethereal and ephemeral. By definition there are no disappointments on hope and imagination, just soaring stock prices.

As for the market, the Trigger now believed he was much better off staying fully invested and concentrating on stocks. Sure, there were a few guys who were good at timing markets and currencies, but they were wrecks with insomnia and ulcers. Was it true that one of Jones's guys had his Reuters beeper surgically implanted to get an edge? Forget that November market crack baloney. The biotechs were in a bull market that would last for years, and cracks were gifts for buyers.

He babbled on. Biotechnology was changing the world, and you had to be there. He had just bought a private placement in Centagon, which has a new anticoagulant that sells for $23,000 a copy. Wasn't that expensive? I asked. He looked at me with disgust. "I figure it cost us around $25,000 for each Iraqi soldier we killed in the Gulf War. Are you telling me we aren't going to spend the same amount of money on the chance that it could save an American life? With a market cap of $1.5 billion and sales of $10 million, Centagon is a little rich, short-term, but this is a product that will be as huge as Band-Aids."

The Trigger is also very high on South America. He argued this was a story as big as biotech. "You like Telefonos de Mexico?" I asked. His smile was condescending.

"Everyone knows that Baby Bell in diapers stuff," he said. "Mexico has been picked over pretty good. I want to get out on the curve. I hear Manolovici was in Bogotá last week, and some guys were in recently saying that when the Shining Path takes Peru, it will do a Korea." (North or South? I muttered to myself.)

The big growth stocks, especially the drugs, were okay, too, he said, because they epitomized the ultimate virtuous circle. New drugs make people live longer, so there are more old people who need more health care and have to buy more drugs so the drug companies can raise prices, and then the circle stalls again. Glaxo, Merck, Pfizer, Johnson & Johnson—they are all 20 to 25 percent growers. I asked how huge companies with market capitalizations approaching $40 billion, like Coke and Walmart, could keep compounding at that rate. Didn't they have 10-year charts that were parabolic?

He shook his head in disgust. "It's a new era of very slow economic growth and disinflation, and growth stocks are the only place to be," he said. "The cyclicals are for the senile. As interest rates come down, the prices of long-duration financial assets fly. And incidentally, I don't believe in diversification. I don't like people equally or wines equally, so why should I build a portfolio equally? Own monster positions in the groups and stocks you really like, or else you're only practicing.

"The new issue market is a slam dunk," the Trigger chattered on, almost compulsively. "One of my kids has got perfect taste." He figured he could add 10 percentage points a year to his portfolio's performance through flipping hot issues. The new arrangement—where you agreed with the underwriters to buy 50,000 in the aftermarket if they gave you 50,000 on the offering—guaranteed that prices would go up initially.

"Doesn't that mean that if the IPO goes sour, you can lose twice as much?" I asked. "Syndicate guys were doing these one-for-one deals in 1983, too."

"How can the price go down when there are always more buyers?" he replied. "You can't lose the way it is this time."

Halfway through lunch, I realized we had nothing to say to each other. It's as if we operate in different worlds. The Trigger thought my worries about debt, pricing power, and the deficit were irrelevant, and my concerns about the economy actually made him more bullish on his growth stocks.

Conversely, I had no interest in the small biotech and illiquid South American stocks he wanted to tell me about. I had never heard of them, they had already quadrupled, and if they had profits (and many didn't), they sold at 100 times trailing 12-month earnings but at only 30 times hoped-for 1993 earnings. Besides, I couldn't understand what they did or if the science made sense, and how could you own what you don't understand? When people say, "You can't lose" with that invincible tone of voice, a little bell starts ringing, faintly but insistently, like an unanswered telephone in the back of my head.

Investment Life
Its Own Self

February 22, 1993

Jim the Trigger is an investment manager I've known for years, and he's my weather vane, my sentiment indicator, the way *BusinessWeek* covers or the *Fortune* list of the most admired companies. You see, Jim is called "the Trigger" (as in "hair trigger") because he's fast on the investment draw. But in life, and in his career, Jim's so fast he's always late, because by the time he's somewhere, attracted by the high returns, it's nowhere; the mania, the game is over. The theory of reflexivity is what Soros calls it, or investment life its own self.

Jim is a beautiful friend. He's always there if he needs you. He's getting older now, although he still looks perfect and blow-dried, as though he just set a new Big East hair spray record. As I have chronicled, Jim the wunderkind started his own hedge fund in 1972 and got killed in the secular bear market of 1973–1974. The pattern has tended to repeat itself as our hero got involved in an energy fund in the late 1970s, ran a high-tech mutual fund in 1983, did risk arbitrage and LBOs in the late 1980s, and in 1991 founded a partnership to invest in drug and biotech stocks. Somehow he missed the commodity fund craziness. But Jim always lands on his feet, even if his clients don't.

Anyway, last week the Trigger told me he was now a "macro" player. Macros, in case you don't know, are a new breed, a superrace of global warriors, sprung directly from the investment loins of the modern titan, George Soros. Macros trade asset categories, derivatives, volatility, options, and currencies using huge leverage. Things with names like new, exotic candies, such as opals, curls, and knobs (knockout options), that you need a PhD in math to understand. "Stock selection sucks; it's a loser's game like Charley Ellis says," the Trigger told me. "It's for old-timers with small minds and

347

no imagination. Macro is the big time, it's baroque, it's like being a quarterback in the NFL.

"Everybody wins in macro," said the Trigger, almost shouting with excitement. "You ever heard of a macro loser except for some crazy Indonesian or Midwestern bank that read charts upside down and was short the mark? And as for getting seriously rich, it's better, faster, cleaner than LBOs or commodity funds. The big macro guys make $50 to $100 million a year, collect Remingtons, own G-3s, and have big houses with long driveways in Aspen. If you weren't up at least 35 percent in 92, your name was Bubba. I was up 45 percent, but that was trash compared with the big guys."

The Trigger rambled on about how the macros ruled the world. Hadn't they knocked off the tough old Bank of England? They were the new vigilantes. No government, no central bank, no currency could stand up against them when the posse rode. If the macros didn't like a country's economic policies, they took the finance minister and lynched him, and maybe the prime minister, too.

"You know," said the Trigger, "I want to be like George when I grow up. I want to be Robin Hood, too, and take money from rich governments and make the world better by giving it to the Eastern Europeans. Being a macro player you have to think big-time. My own self, I'd like to be minister of finance or head of the central bank of some South American country and go to the World Bank meetings in Washington talking fancy and getting some serious insights from those guys whose family trees don't fork."

The Trigger has always played golf, but back when he was a stock-picker, he also played tennis. "A loser's game," he says now. "All the really big macro guys play golf. Golf is a macro, big-picture game that requires nerves, courage, vision, just like macro investing. Grace under pressure, that's how Hemingway describes courage. Like golf.

"Just spent a week at Leadbetter's. Nothing but private lessons with the man. I'm hitting the ball good just like I'm hitting on currencies. Last week, playing with big Dan at Augusta, I smoked a low draw that streaked out like a missile under the radar for 200 yards and then began to climb with a little tailback. Got me a birdie with that one," he was saying now. "Anyone who has held a useless two iron under water and drowned the mean son of a bitch wants to get a birdie at Augusta."

The Trigger went on to say how he was never out of contact with the markets, even at Augusta, even asleep. He has a special Reuters Body Beeper that is programmed for his positions. If there is an event or a price breakout, the Beeper gives its master a gentle nudge, like an electronic love pat. If he doesn't call control in three minutes, it nudges him again, harder. The Trigger, who is coming to the end of a poetic third marriage, says it works like an aphrodisiac, too. Last time he had a toothpick in his mouth when the wedding picture was taken.

The Trigger was reminiscing, expansively: "I've learned a lot in the last year as I got richer and smarter. First, value investing doesn't work. Second, never average down. Ben Graham was a loser. Always average up. Go with the flow and the mo. The tape had higher SAT scores than you did."

We talked about how the Trigger was invested. "There's a bunch of layups out there right now," he said. "There's so much dumb, slow money around just asking to get picked off. My view is the world is in a slow-growth, deflationary cycle. Inflation is dead! My big positions are that I'm long the dollar, short the mark, short the U.S. consumer stock index. I'm loaded with options on one-year German paper, own the Hang Seng contract, short volatility, and own Japanese export blue chips, own Italian and French bonds, and have written calls against gold. I got money in Peru and Vietnam, too. And of course, I got it all on big leverage."

"What happens with all that leverage if your longs go down and your shorts go up?" I politely asked. "That could happen for a day or two," he replied, "but I'm so quick and our positions are diversified and hedged so they can only nick me; they can't hurt me."

Frankly, I wonder. Although the Trigger's portfolio is diversified and hedged, it is all based on one investment scenario. If, God forbid, that forecast is wrong, his shorts will go up, and most of his longs will go down. Furthermore, since many of the other macro players have a similar view of the world and have the same positions on, and since they are "quick," too, as they all race to reverse their positions, their losses will be magnified.

After the Trigger left, I decided macro investing is an accident waiting to happen. The returns have simply been too fat for too long, and there are too many guys like the Trigger coming into the game. Fast and late, as usual. The risk is that they will probably wreck the game for the expert practitioners, too. Up until recently, there were maybe only a dozen or so really smart macro players in the game who truly knew what they were doing, but today there are probably 50 or 60 or maybe even 100 new guys thrashing around, following the smart guys, creating huge clouds of dust, and churning up the fairway, so it's much harder for even the great players to hit off it.

Unlike the energy, high-tech, or biotech fads, where the excesses were in the valuations and everybody got killed together, the good macro guys probably will escape relatively unscathed but with lower returns, while late arrivals like the Trigger will get carried out. In this sense, the macro fad is more like venture capital in the mid-1980s or LBOs in 1990.

Anyway, as I said earlier, it's just investment life its own self, and we've seen it all before.

A Country of His Own

January 13, 1994

last saw Jim the Trigger about a year ago. At that time he was a macro player with his own brand-spanking-new global hedge fund. "Global macro is the big time," he told me then. "It's baroque, it's like being a quarterback in the NFL." Jim has had some bad breaks on timing; he's so quick that he's always late, if that makes any sense. But creating new investment management firms to exploit what's hot is a tough game, like investment life its own self.

However, macro has lost its charm for the Trigger. "It's a jungle out there in macro now," he told me at lunch. "There are so many macro players and momentum investors they're bumping into each other. There must be a couple hundred new hedge funds run by guys who think they're boy George Soroses playing macro. And then there are the rogue central banks from Third World countries trying to trade currencies (because they think they have an edge) that stumble into you. Some of these new guys are so green they can get you confused with their stupidity. And they can hurt you. I got crunched hurtfully between an Asian central bank and some rookie hedge fund guy on his first macro trip. But it was just bad karma."

So there he was, tanned and rested despite his bruises, so I asked him what he was up to. The Trigger has always had a great nose for the latest craziness. "Hey, forget macro. I'm out there where the sky meets the sea," he told me. "My face bronzed by unknown suns, my tongue twisted by strange dialects. I'm an emerging markets guy now.

"This emerging markets game is easier than macro; it's bigger and will last longer than biotech or technology," he told me. "Dummies with phony accents and striped shirts with white collars who think Turkey borders Malaysia have portfolios that were up 70 percent last year. It's redemption, too. You can get rich while being out there with the World Bank and the Ford Foundation easing the pain of all those poor, starving people in the Third World with rickets and AIDS. The white man's burden and all that kind of thing. This one may get me to heaven. But then maybe it won't, since I got a new twist."

"So you've got your own firm?" I asked. "Guess again," he said. "You're going to do a closed-end fund?" "Better than that," he replied. "Much more effervescent than that. I'm going to start my own country."

I must have looked confused because he went on. "What are the two biggest crazinesses? IPOs and emerging markets. Put them together and you've got the potential for a really big score. Did you read the story in the *Times* about the football player and his IPO? I mean the guy is going to the Hall of Fame, but still this is wild. He buys $5,000 of stock in this company he and another guy create, and presto! It's worth $10 million after the first day of trading.

"This is a company that operates out of the guy's house, has $36,000 in sales, no products to speak of, sports a market cap of over $15 million. Plus the football player is paid a salary of $145,000, gets $600 a month as an automobile allowance, and 7.5 percent of the company's profits *before* taxes and interest payments. His contract requires him to work at least a backbreaking 15 hours a week. But the guy I love is the president who got the football player and his mother to loan the company $730,000 to get it going in the first place. That's the guy I want to model.

"Anyway, it got me thinking. If smart guys can create a company out of repackaged Gatorade and make some serious money, with all this emerging markets craziness, why can't I start a new country and mint what Gerry Goodman calls supermoney? So that's what a bunch of us are going to do. Give these emerging market moonies what they want—an undiscovered, cheap country with a great big fat virtuous circle like a halo around its head to plow their billions mindlessly into. These guys are wild to find fresh stories. They babble about it in their presentations; they'll buy anything in a new country that's fresh and hot."

The Trigger went on to tell me how he and his group had bought this "big old island off the coast of Brazil that's nothing but swamp land and mosquitoes—which is good." The idea was to create a new Third World country called "Going" and then "IPO it."

"As in *going* up or *going* to grow, or *going* places," said the Trigger. "We've got a bunch of concepts going," he went on happily, his voice rising. "It will be like Singapore, a benevolent dictatorship, and it will be all free markets, a supply-sider's dream. We got the specs: 50 percent savings rate, law and order, completely open economy, deregulation, a negative corporate tax rate . . ."

"How's that work?" I asked.

"If a company makes money, the government pays it money instead of taking money from it. You see, we the promoters of Going will be we the people, the government of Going. We own all the stock in the companies we create, and we sell shares to emerging markets investors as privatizations. Going will have a complete developing-country menu of stocks: a telecom, banks, the power company, a couple of cement names, retailers, and of course a few brokers for the aggressive guys."

This was big stuff, even for the Trigger. "What I'm thinking of," he went on, "is that the market will be real cheap at first—five, six times earnings, discount to book, high yield, like Thailand in 1984, but we will engineer a much longer market cycle because we won't let valuations get too high even when stock prices go through the roof."

"How will you do that?" I asked.

"Earnings will rise almost as fast as stock prices, but I'm not quite sure how yet. Maybe we'll do it through cross-holdings or some kind of unconventional accounting, but we'll do something."

"But won't the investors figure it out?" I asked. "After all, it's a fraud."

"Come on," he said, "it's not much different than what's already going on with IPOs right in the big old sophisticated USA, with the SEC's blessing. Even old-time value investors are closing their eyes and playing the IPO market. As long as guys are making money, they don't care."

"But there's nothing on your island now," I said. "It won't work." "Aw hell," said Trigger, "have some imagination. We'll have an office with a bunch of smart guys with some creative writing skills and insect repellent to answer the faxes and issue pompous press releases. They'll have a great time. It will be like running their own country."

"But what happens when the emerging markets portfolio managers want to come visit the country and see the companies?"

"Get real," said the Trigger. "You don't think these guys actually visit most of the exotic countries, do you? Who's actually been to Peru or Pakistan or Morocco? They only go to the big fashionable ones that have five-star hotels with French restaurants and health clubs. That doesn't stop them from pouring their clients' money into the latest flavor of the week. If some jerk gets insistent, we can keep people away by letting it be known we have the scariest airport in the world. No one goes to Nigeria because of the horror stories about chaos at the Lagos airport, but Going will be worse. If that doesn't work, a little terrorist activity is usually good for the P/E ratio, and it keeps the investment managers away. Just look at how well Peru has done, and nobody would dream of going there."

I shook my head. "But how are you going to end the scam and get out rich—and alive?" I asked.

"When the whole emerging markets bubble gets pricked, we'll just disappear without even an oil slick. You don't really believe all this emerging market BS, do you? The developing countries will only follow trickle-down, stock-market-capitalism policies as long they benefit. Some day, when for whatever reason more foreign money starts going out of a country than is coming in, when the local stock market is going down instead of up, and the magic doesn't work anymore, a mob will burn the stock exchange, hang all the local big hands, and all the investor-friendly policies will get repealed overnight. Capitalism will be out, socialist populism back in, all the companies get nationalized without compensation by the new government for the good of the people, and no one, including the foreign investors, can take any money out of the country. Just like what happened to the banks in the 1980s, the utilities in the 1930s (remember Brazilian Power and Shanghai Light?), or for that matter, Barings, the Sixth Great Power, in the 1880s. Nothing new."

He laughed. "We'll stage a revolution in Going: Indian peasants from the jungle with AK-47s, the city sacked, the prime minister and his girlfriends shot by firing squad at dawn. It'll be Going, going, gone. And we disappear into the sunset with a fortune to live happily ever after."

Talking Technology with Jim the Trigger

September 6, 1995

J im the Trigger came through New York last week on the road show for his new technology fund wearing a big grin. That smile goes with him everywhere—he sleeps in it and even hand washes it for freshness on weekends because sometimes it gets a little ragged. It got frayed subsequent to our last chat in January 1994, when the Trigger was immersed in emerging markets and in fact was starting a country of his own.

But knowing Jim, that big, beaming grin means he has got something good going, and it's always worthwhile to pay attention, because Jim is nothing but quick. In fact he's so quick he's always late—if that makes any sense—because by the time he is somewhere, attracted by the high returns, it's nowhere; the mania, the game is over. But the Trigger always lands on his feet, even if his clients don't.

This makes him a great sentiment indicator, like *Business Week* covers. Jim has been late to most of the great investment parties of our generation: he ran an energy fund in the late 1970s, started a high-tech fund in 1983, did risk arb and LBOs in the late 1980s, in 1991 founded a partnership to invest in drug and biotech stocks, and then got involved with emerging markets in mid-1993. "I've always had a great nose for craziness," he says, "and craziness is where it's at."

HIM: Investing in technology now is the investment magic of this era. The pace of change and progress is exponential, and this cycle is going to last well into the next century. You cynical old guys are just bitter because you all sold your Intel too soon and you don't have the imagination to grasp cyber life.

354

Memory and a fixation with value are a liability, not an asset, because this time it really is different.

ME: That's what you always say. About once every 10 or 15 years, the technology movie gets replayed. Just like this time, it starts sane with real companies that are growing and have low P/Es. Technology stocks are difficult to analyze, and nobody really understands their products, so they are particularly susceptible to manias. As prices soar and the speculation spreads to smaller, highly speculative companies, the IPOs get crazier, the whisper stories dominate the market, and finally the bust comes. Every bubble has a solid fundamental basis, but stock market expectations get way ahead of economic reality, and prices get so inflated they have to crash.

HIM: This is the biggest, the best one I've ever seen. Much bigger than biotech, and much more real than emerging markets, which is smoke and mirrors. Technology, the information networks are changing the way the world lives. This is the new Industrial Revolution, as important as the discovery of electricity or the development of the telephone. Bill Gates is Thomas Edison and Alexander Graham Bell. The difference between then and now is that the speed of change is much faster, so investors can make more money quicker than ever before. It's like an old-time gold rush.

ME: Only the early birds got rich, and everybody else came back from the Yukon broke. I agree that technology, as always, is dynamic and that some very exciting things are happening in the real world. Whether cyber life is going to have the same effect on humanity as electricity or the telephone is doubtful. But in the stock market world, prices have already discounted the hereafter. There's nothing unusual about this. Marc Faber points out that the same thing happened with railroad stocks early in the century, and it's occurred three times with technology: the late 1950s, the early 1970s, and then a big one in 1981–1983. The technology breakthroughs were for real, but the stocks got way ahead of reality and subsequently crashed.

HIM: Baloney. It's a new world. Like the analysts say: strengthening secular demand patterns colliding with systemic capacity shortfalls set the stage for continual upside earnings surprises, perpetually higher multiples, and ongoing price momentum. Semiconductors will continue to drive the underlying functionality of end equipment and as a result will grow faster than the end markets themselves for these products. A growth rate of 20 percent per annum in units for the next decade is probably low. The smart guys believe the semiconductor cycle is repealed for good. There's going to be a shortage of almost all technology into the next century.

ME: People said the same things the last three times, too. Worldwide semiconductor capacity is exploding and will increase 25 percent in the next year— which is even faster than demand is growing. South Korea's semiconductor exports will exceed $20 billion by year-end. The capacity to build computers is increasing at a 20 percent rate. PCs are on the verge of having the demand cycle of TVs or calculators. As for the bleeding-edge high-tech stuff, because the pace of change is accelerating, product life cycles are foreshortened, and manufacturing capacity becomes obsolete faster. These trends are very positive for the rate of technological progress but not so wonderful for the actual companies involved, whose products and capacity that were state-of-the-art last year are obsolete this year.

HIM: You are getting senile. As Nicholas Negroponte points out, the population of the Internet is now increasing at 10 percent per month, which means that by 2003 the total number of Internet users will exceed the population of the world. How can you not want to be involved in that kind of growth? What kind of P/E should a stock sell at whose earnings are doubling every year?

ME: Who knows? But I do know technology companies are not true growth stocks. They have to spend so much of their operating earnings on developing new products to replace their existing ones and then on new capacity to build those products that they have a low return on equity and virtually no free cash flow with which to pay dividends or buy back their stock. The S&P 500 technology sector has a 10-year ROE of 11.4 percent versus an ROE of 22.5 percent for consumer nondurables and health care and 13.5 percent for the S&P Industrials as a whole. The S&P technology sector yields 0.6 percent, and traditional growth stocks 2.4 percent, or a little less than the S&P 500. In the long run, logically, relative P/Es gravitate toward relative ROEs, yet the 48 technology issues in the S&P sell at 23.9 times earnings, while the 61 consumer issues at 20.3 times.

HIM: Are you saying that those stodgy old consumer product companies with single-digit unit growth rates are attractive?

ME: No, I'm not, because they aren't cheap, either. But at least they have the characteristics of true growth companies in that dividends keep rising and they continue to buy back stock to shrink their capitalizations. Technology companies don't have the free cash to do either, and in fact, they have to raise more equity from time to time. They are a lot like the airlines, and I don't think you should pay a lot more for them as a group. We calculate that Applied Materials ($113), for example, is selling at over 100 times its free cash flow and Cisco ($70) at 73 times. Texas Instruments ($80) is a free-cash-flow-deficit company. Even Intel ($65) is at 20 times, and its capital spending has been compounding at 41 percent a year.

HIM: Irrelevant. Analysts don't even bother to forecast cash flow for technology companies. Microsoft's free cash flow is expected to increase 35 percent in 1996 and 27 percent in 1997.

ME: Of course, there are always exceptions. Microsoft ($95) is a great company, but is it worth $55 billion, 12 times book, and 9.4 times sales? As a private businessman, would you buy the stream of earnings that is Oracle ($44) at 22 times book or Cisco at 9 times sales and 14 times book? Some of the smaller stuff is even crazier. Putting money into technology at the right time may be smart speculation, but it's not investing. To use the old analogy, these are trading sardines, not eating sardines.

HIM: Who cares? I'm buying stocks, not companies, and the price momentum dynamics are awesome. One week in July, all the net money going into mutual funds in the United States went into technology. The flow of venture capital money is also soaring. For example, Venture One, a venture capital research company, reports that in just one segment, Internet, the venture capital money will be in excess of $200 million this year as compared to $42 million last year.

ME: Too much money chasing too few good deals is not bullish for investors, although it may be good for America and the dollar. It just means more competition and faster change. And at some point, accelerating change becomes parasitic. Today's leaders, the Intels and the Microsofts, get consumed by newer killer companies, just as Transitron in the 60s, Scientific Data Systems in the 70s, and Wang in the 80s got eaten alive.

HIM: This cycle is different, and the flows are much bigger and self-sustaining. Do you realize that in three weeks in July, new money coming into technology funds amounted to 10 percent of their assets? One fund, Seligman Communications, took in $300 million in two weeks. These are technology funds. They have to invest the new money in technology stocks. How can prices do anything but go up? And as the stocks go up and the funds' NAVs rise, they attract even more money.

ME: Sounds like a Ponzi scheme, but you are right as long as the money keeps coming in. But isn't all this new money coming into open-end funds, and isn't the history that it can rush out just as fast as it flows in? Then instead of driving up prices, it will drive them down, just like what has happened every time since the Dutch got disenchanted with tulips. And the bear market that will follow will be secular, lasting years, not cyclical.

HIM: Ponzi was a smart guy, and he understood momentum. Look, you gotta own up stocks, and the more they are up, the more buyers they attract. Big moves attract short sellers, which we then run in.

Section 5

TRAVELOGUES

Frankly, writing travelogues is a little embarrassing but some people say they're the best thing I do, which is even more embarrassing.

—*Barton Biggs, September 18, 1989*

"We all need an utter cultural change every so often to blow out the dust and debris," wrote Biggs in 1980. Despite a near-crushing global travel schedule over the next few decades, Barton Biggs had real-life adventures away from the grind of investments that became legendary missives among his more routine market repertoire. He called them, "highly discretionary reading: a pure, self-centered travelogue with no redeeming business virtues."

Whether it was a safari in Kenya or personally summiting famous world peaks from the Matterhorn to Mont Blanc, Kilimanjaro, or Rainier, Biggs managed to impart the experience in a style worthy of Jon Krakauer. Biggs seemed to absorb his adventures with a sense of boyish wonderment and came away from them clearly refreshed in body and mind. They also serve to demonstrate a life well lived surrounded by family and friends, fully living in the world, not just watching from the sidelines.

They may not have had much business virtue, but literary virtue? You be the judge.

Africa

September 8, 1980

We went on a safari in Kenya, and I recommend it for the soul and the psyche, but also because it is a totally different experience. We all need an utter cultural change every so often to blow out the dust and debris, and Africa and the animals are, in my opinion, the ultimate catharsis. It is as though your mind runs transported on a fresh, deep track totally away from the stock market, analysts, and buy-sell decisions. The teenagers and children along also were enthralled.

Africa is a long way away, and safaris aren't cheap, but it will leave you and your family with something different to remember when all those vacations at Vail and the beach have blurred with the years to sameness. In other words, the trip is worth the added money, but don't wait too long because economic and social change is rapid in East Africa, and no one can predict how long the animals and the land will be left wild. No shooting of animals is allowed in Kenya, although big game hunting is allowed in Tanzania.

Kenya lies along the equator, but the game reserves are mostly in the broad highlands at altitudes of 3,000 to 7,000 feet. The landscape is like nothing I have ever seen. As Isak Dinesen once said, there is no fat on it, no luxuriance, it is Africa distilled up through 6,000 feet, like the strong and refined essence of a continent. The colors are very clear but dry and burnt like fine, burnished old pottery, yet where a river winds, there are dyes of deep rich greens from the wide branching mimosa trees.

The air in these equatorial highlands is as cool and fresh as water. There is very little humidity. You feel as though you are living up in the sky where you can breathe deeply yet move lightly. The days are bright and clean with a strong sun, but as soon as it plunges below the horizon (as it does abruptly at that latitude), the air is delightfully cool. With night comes the sweet, pungent scent of mimosa wood fires, the spice of the

African night, and the deep black tapestry of stars and moon, with a profusion of great white sailing clouds.

The views are immensely wide. At one point, for three days in Masi Mara we were at a camp that fronted on a broad plain with a circling river that stretched to the great vault of the sky on the horizon. Across this vast expanse of grass and vegetation flowed, in ever-changing patterns, migrations of zebras and wildebeests, herds of elephants and buffalo, giraffes, antelopes, and occasional predators—mostly lions. The plain was like watching the ocean, only infinitely more intriguing because it was alive. At night, the babble of the animals was like the low roar of the surf, except for the sudden trumpet of an elephant or the roar of a lion, which would set off frantic braying by the wildebeests, and lying in your tent you could sense the intense movement all around you.

Into this incredible drama you venture either walking, led by a guide with an ancient gun, or by safari car. When walking you do not see the exotic game, but the excitement of being on the same ground with the animals is immense. Their sheer size is awesome. Giraffes are as tall as medium-sized trees, and their jerky but somehow graceful lope reaches speeds of 40 miles per hour. It is like watching not a herd of animals but a family of long-stemmed, gigantic speckled flowers moving through the bush. An elephant weighs five to seven tons. Once I saw one in the low woods behind our camp pacing along, oblivious to the small trees, as though he had an appointment at the other end of the world.

Another time we experienced real fear walking across that plain when we seemed caught between a herd of migrating wildebeests, protected on the flanks by their bulls, and a group of African buffalo. These dark and massive ironlike animals with mighty, horizontally swung horns are regarded as extremely dangerous by the natives because of their irascible, aggressive disposition. Several of this group rose and sullenly stared at us, but we changed course, and they did not charge. Later we rounded a bend in the river to the astonishing sight of some 30 huge hippos and their babies, the "river horse" of the ancients, blowing and blubbering in the muddy water.

From the safari vans with their open tops, you can range across the bush and through the gullies. Incredibly, the animals have little reaction to the vans, although many would savage a man. It takes a lot of bumpy, dusty riding, but the sights are spectacular. A lion, royal even at work, dragging with her jaws a 300-pound wildebeest she has just killed back through the grass to her mate. The deep affection between a mother lion and her cubs as they play, the sinewy grace of a leopard draped like a vine in a tree, a band of elephants standing in a circle paying their respects as though at a funeral, by touching either with foot or trunk the body of a dead elder with an occasional trumpet of grief. Other groups saw the even more dramatic drama of the kill, which apparently is not gory but instead has a raw beauty and timelessness of its own.

But many of the sights are not dramatic, and the excitement comes because they are like reflections in a forest pool of things that have been happening for 50 centuries. A giant warthog, fat and self-important, his plump wife, and three young pigs bustle by on an outing for all the world like an overweight, middle-class family . . . a mother rhino shows her baby how to roll in the waterhole mud to keep cool on a hot day . . . two ostriches mate with much fanfare and flourish and then hurry off in opposite directions . . . the gymnastics of a group of baboons. These are the mundane but exquisite sights of Africa, the land, and the animals, and you feel there is no present or future, only the past happening over and over again. Believe me, I am no naturalist or nature lover, and I detest the smell and atmosphere of zoos, but the contrast between a zoo and Africa is like comparing a crowded, chlorinated swimming pool to the vast freshness of the ocean.

Kenya itself is a wonderful country. Democracy and capitalism are flourishing in Kenya, which is politically stable and has had a decade of 9 percent annual real GNP growth. Kenya is probably America's best friend in Africa, direct investment is pouring in, and some even talk of Kenya becoming the Switzerland of Africa.

However, like all non-oil-producing LDCs, the latest round of oil price increases has thrown the balance of trade into deficit, and rigid currency controls keep the Kenya shilling pegged above its free market value. Another problem is Kenya's volatile and irascible neighbors—Ethiopia, Uganda, Tanzania, and Somalia. The United States in its infinite wisdom is currently supplying arms to Somalia, an unstable country with territorial ambitions, which makes you wonder if Washington has a coherent policy for East Africa.

We ended up our safari at a tent camp on the Indian Ocean that had unpretentious accommodations but the finest food, beach, and service of any resort I've ever stayed at in the world. It was located in a pine cove in the center of a 12-mile crescent of deserted beach, which in turn was flanked by high dunes that were filled with flowering beach vegetation and masses of birds. Depending on the tide, the ocean was as calm as a millpond yet at high water had surging surf. At low tide, the beach itself was very firm, and you could walk for miles without seeing a soul. The fishing and snorkeling are superb.

But the food was the thing. It is cooked on an open wood fire in metal boxes with coals heaped on top of them and is delivered on the run from the kitchen tent to the dining tent by two grinning waiters. The owner's English wife oversees the native cooks, and the menu features an eclectic international cuisine superbly prepared and always served with marvelous sauces that were somehow both strong yet subtle. Specialties included fresh fish, homemade bread and ice cream, pasta dishes, and trifles.

Other points that come to mind: the food on the safari itself was generally good (with lots of fresh vegetables and fruits) even in the safari camps. Since the country is justly famous for its coffee growing, the black, strong brew you get everywhere will spoil your taste for our bland domestic variety. On the other hand, the water is absolutely awful, the roads are rough and dusty, and the trip to and from Kenya is very long. My advice is to fly third class, but do your safari first class. If you want any help, let me know.

The Idaho High Country

October 14, 1986

Ernest Hemingway always said Idaho was the loveliest place in the world, and, discouraged and dissolute, he picked Ketchum to blow his brains out one morning a quarter of a century ago. I've run, biked, and hiked in a lot of different places in other countries with big reputations for scenery, but after a week this summer in the starkly beautiful Idaho "high country," I have to agree with Hemingway. The land can be as dry and hot as a forest fire or as wet as a beaver's belly, but it is always wilderness and invariably beautiful. The people are hang-loose, homespun Westerners, and all conversations seem to start with a friendly "Where you folks from?"

We were principally in the Sun Valley area and the Stanley basin. The terrain is spectacular. In the Sun Valley bowl, the foothills are very round with velvet green sagebrush covers. In other places, the hills are almost bald and come in different shades of brown and green. They seem to reflect the colors of the arching sky, which is pink in the morning, deep blue during the day, and then gold at sunset. There are always dark blue islands of ponderosa and lodgepole pines on the northern slopes where there is more moisture, and the meadows running up to the hills are filled with flowers with wonderful names like Indian paintbrush. The Sun Valley area, which runs for a hundred miles, is bisected by fast, clear streams (Silver Creek is the most famous) that provide some of the finest trout fishing in the world.

Ketchum is an interesting, sophisticated town with several fine restaurants and, of course, the Sun Valley Lodge, which is world class. As a town, Ketchum is "new West," but it has been developed with great care, and there is not a hint of honky-tonk. The town fathers won't even let McDonald's have a store there, and in the fall the cattle are still driven down the main street past the bookstores and the boutiques with designer clothes. You can rent a good bike in Ketchum and get on a flat road and ride at speed, breathing that marvelous pure air, for a couple of hours through one of the most spectacular valleys anywhere. One morning on a ride I saw deer, elk, several hawks, an eagle, a bear, and maybe five cars in three hours. You felt like you were flying. It was exhilarating.

Across the Galena Pass where the explorers and settlers trekked is the Stanley Basin, an Alpine valley that is higher and more lush and rimmed by the jagged, tough-looking Sawtooth Mountains with patches of snow on them even in August. This is truly an Acadian primeval wilderness, with the "old West" town of Stanley having a permanent population of 98, and one night from the Idaho Rocky Mountain Ranch on a hill you could see the thunderstorms building in the peaks from what must have been 100 miles away, and when darkness finally came there was only one other light in that huge, luminous starry night. There are inexpensive inns like the Redfish Lake Lodge in the area, though, and the ranch mentioned is rustic and has a fine dining room. But the evening view from the front porch across that magnificent expanse with some cold beer after having covered a lot of miles is the best of all.

In the Stanley Basin there are vast sprawling pastures with grazing cows, and the aspens are a lighter silver green. You drive to the Sawtooth National Recreation Area and then backpack in. Some people set up base camps and hike by the day. There is no litter or sign of people anywhere. These areas seem almost totally unpopulated simply because they are so vast and you have to work hard physically to get in. Money or an American Express Card won't do it. We hiked one day four hours up into rough country, reaching maybe 10,000 feet, and struggled to get across a vast expanse of multicolored granite boulders left by an ancient glacier; but then we were rewarded by the sight of a snowmelt-fed turquoise crystal lake rimmed by meadows splashed with the yellow, orange, and purple of Alpine flowers. The lake was breathtakingly cold, but what a place to camp.

There are no trail signs as in Switzerland, and you have to find your own campsites, but you get that unique feeling of the real wilderness thing and what it must have been like to come across this immense country. The variety of the hiking experiences is dazzling. Another day we hiked 10 miles on trails smelling of pine to find a waterfall that cascades down from one of the high peaks in the Sawtooth. And so it goes on and on. I'd love to take a shot at climbing one of those mountain peaks, but it wouldn't be easy.

River trips are another way to experience the wilderness, and we did that one summer going down the Middle Fork of the Salmon. They are particularly good if you've got children who are either too young to hike or not inclined. With the guides doing most of the rowing and all the cooking, it's an extended Victorian picnic in the West, and our children still maintain it was the best trip we ever took. The Middle Fork flows for more than 100 miles with over 300 rapids, dropping 3,000 feet through steep brooding granite canyons, surging, crashing swift and loud but still clear, through narrow gorges, and running across broad stretches with meadows on either side. There are also some lovely guest ranches on the Salmon River.

The autumn in Idaho is spectacular. The elaborate, many-branched cottonwoods turn yellow, and the aspens flow down the hillsides in bright avalanches of shimmering gold. Unfortunately, fall is hunting season, which is not my thing. In winter, both the downhill and cross-country skiing are excellent. The landscape is still spectacular although more austere, and what winter takes away in color, it gives back in intricate design.

The Idaho high country makes you feel as though you're climbing up to the rooftop and are walking on the ridge of the continent. The price is right, too. Like they say, it doesn't get any better.

Making a New High on Your Own Time

September 19, 1988

T his is highly discretionary reading: a pure, self-centered travelogue with no redeeming business virtues. That said, in August I was part of a group of 14 friends ranging in age from 20 to 55, men and women, that had, corny as it sounds, a wonderful bonding experience training for and climbing Mont Blanc.

The Mont Blanc Massif is a complex, magnificent range of peaks, bowls, and plateaus of rock, ice, and snow, the summit of which, Mont Blanc itself, at 15,771 feet, is the highest point in Western Europe. This great white mountain dominates the green Chamonix Valley and, on some days, can be seen from as far away as Geneva. In fact, so perfectly visible is the mountain that the first successful ascent in 1785 was followed by telescope from Chamonix.

Mont Blanc has always cast a spell. Accounts of the "Monts Maudits" (Cursed Mountains), with "glaciers" that consumed men and where witches celebrated their Sabbath, have drawn tourists to Chamonix for centuries. The great 800-foot-thick glacier, La Mer de Glace, creeps inexorably and thus disgorges, years later, objects and the preserved, elongated bodies of people trapped in its coils. It was long believed no man could live through the night on the upper reaches of the mountain, and Mont Blanc is infamous for its treacherous weather.

On a clear, deep-blue Alpine day, the mountain crests glisten in the sunlight with pristine beauty, and the glaciers glide elegantly down into the green forests. Then, Mont Blanc is a lovely woman nonchalantly basking in the sun. In grayer light with a wind blowing, however, she is suddenly cold and forbidding, a deadly witch. The crevasses and icy couloirs vein her face like scars. The weather and snow conditions in the Alps change much more quickly than in the United States. Climbing Mont Blanc in good weather is a long, strenuous, athletic voyage of discovery. In bad weather, it is a hard struggle; in mist, it is alarming, and, in a storm, it can be very dangerous. Each year, about 20 climbers die on the mountain, but almost all have attempted the ascent without guides. Nevertheless, storms, rockslides, and avalanches are a threat even to the professionals.

Climbing Mont Blanc is what big-time mountaineers dismiss as "a snow slog." However, it does require some basic Alpine skills such as the use of the ice axe to break a fall on a snowfield, attaching crampons (basically spikes) to boots so one can walk securely on steep snow- or ice-covered slopes, and roping procedures. None of us had any familiarity with these techniques. Snow slog or not, you should be in good aerobic shape, and most of our group trained several months ahead of the climb. However, the only conditioning of one of the successful climbers consisted of cutting his lawn with his mountain boots on.

In Chamonix, we stayed in the Mont Blanc Hotel, which has been there forever and was just what it should have been, with simple rooms, an elegant dining room with excellent food, a fine garden with tables and a view of the mountain where one can drink beer at the end of day, and an interesting cast of employees and guests that was French life its own self. Chamonix is small and surprisingly unspoiled. We saw very few Americans.

The first two days, we hiked without guides to acclimatize ourselves to the altitude. We took long climbs through *Sound of Music* meadows soaked with bright wildflowers and up high slopes in clear, sweet air. Lunch in the mountain huts was wonderful— omelets and raclettes. On the third day, we began our serious training with guides. The guides at Mont Blanc are an elite corps with a cemetery and a long and proud tradition. They are serious men. We drank beer in the hotel garden with ours, but, on the mountain, they speak and you do. There is no discussion.

That third day, we practiced with our crampons on La Mer de Glace, climbing across crevasses and around holes, but the training was cut short by a drenching rainstorm. The following day, we took the cog railway to a high mountain valley on the other side of Chamonix. After a hike in, we went through an ice axe arrest drill on a steep but short slope. Unfortunately, one of the group propelled himself too enthusiastically and fell hard, breaking four ribs. Then, we learned rope climbing up steep, snow-covered slopes, followed by a traverse of a cliff on a rock ledge where there was a big drop. The trick is to keep going and not look down. People who thought they were acrophobic discovered they weren't when they had to move. We had lunch sitting in the snow and sun looking down over the whole valley, and then there was the long trek back.

The fifth day was very tough. We took the big Aiguille du Midi cable car up to 11,500 feet, shouldered our packs, put on our crampons, and roped up, with each group consisting of two members of our party and one guide. We were still getting used to our crampons and the altitude; the slopes were sheer, and the ledges, narrow. The steep climb to one of the secondary peaks, Mont Blanc du Tacul, at 13,800 feet, was long and tiring. There was a lot of falling in deep snow but no injuries. Once as we were trekking across the plateau, behind us and off our trail, a great ledge of snow and ice broke off and thundered down. By the end of the day, we were exhausted. The garden of the hotel looked awfully good in the twilight, and we began to wonder if we had bitten off more than we could chew.

We had planned to have one more day of training and conditioning, which would have made a big difference in everyone's confidence. Unfortunately, we had to begin the climb on the sixth day because reservations at the overnight hut on the mountain were only available for the next night. The following morning, the climb began. From Eagles Nest, we hiked three hours and 3,000 vertical feet up a rough trail of broken rock and dirt to the Tete Rosse Hut. The hut was crowded, and there was much talk about the weather. After lunch we roped up and crossed a long snowfield where there had been rockfalls and then began the long, scrambling traverse up a 3,000-foot cliff by a series of steep, narrow, rocky ledges. It was a somewhat frightening but exhilarating afternoon because you actually had your hands on the rocks of the mountain, and it was very athletic in that you used your arms as well as your legs. The Gouter Hut is perched at the top of this immense ridge, and you feel as though you are on the roof of Europe.

We got to the hut about six in the afternoon, had a dinner of sorts, drank some wine, and watched the sun go down. The Gouter Hut, at 12,500 feet, leaves a good deal to be desired. Getting to the latrine, which dangled on a ledge, required courage, and using it needed a strong stomach. Rest consisted of lying like sardines on mattresses. I was next to a gentlemen of unknown nationality who must have subsisted solely on garlic. When the lights went on at 2:00 A.M., we were glad to go.

The night was clear and moonlit. As we hiked with crampons up the immense fields of hard snow, the glow of Geneva in the far distance was clearly visible. Ahead, the lights of other climbers flickered against the dim white mass of the mountain. We climbed steadily and crossed the broad saddle of the Col du Dome, but the pace was easy and not particularly fatiguing. However, just before dawn, my feet were very cold, and the wind picked up. After about three hours, we traversed a steep ridge passing the Vallot Hut at 14,330 feet, which is the last refuge. The final three hours to the summit were tougher in that we were going up steep, narrow trails across ridgelines with long, sharply sloping snowfields on either side. Sometimes, the utter splendor of the views and the mountain was distracting, but with crampons on, ice axe in hand, and roped to a partner and your guide, there was not a sense of great peril. We reached the summit, which is a broad snow ridge, at about 8:00 A.M., and you could see from the other great Alpine peaks in Switzerland to half of Italy. The elation of finally making it was indescribable.

The descent was exhausting. The scenery is magnificent, but by this time you are satiated, and the only views you want are of a bathtub and a beer bottle. Besides, by then your legs ache, your pack is heavy, your boots are wet, and your feet hurt. Particularly at the end, when we had to pick our way carefully across the crevasses and ice holes of the glacier, the journey seemed interminable. We finally got back to the hotel at about five in the evening. It had been a grueling day and a half. That night after a fine dinner, we drank some old port in the hotel garden and looked at the mountain glistening in the moonlight. It was all worth it.

Stretching
the Mid-Life Envelope

September 18, 1989

F rankly, writing travelogues is little embarrassing, but some people say they're the best thing I do, which is even more embarrassing. Anyway, here goes one more, which may be the last.

In recent years, a group of us have been doing family mountain climbs: Kilimanjaro two years ago, Mont Blanc last summer, and Mount Rainier in Washington this August. The party this year included nine "old people," ranging in age from 39 to 56, and seven "kids," from 18 to 25. There were 5 women and 11 men. Everyone went into the episode in good physical shape, although unbeknownst to me at the time, I had acquired Lyme disease the week before from an elite Sun Valley tick while trekking the pristine Idaho hills behind Julian Robertson. Our experience of trips like this is that, after some initial reluctance, the kids really like them and have a considerably easier time than the old people. On this climb, all the young ones made the summit, whereas, for a variety of reasons, not all of the adults did.

Mount Rainier, the Queen of the Cascades, is, at 14,410 feet, the highest perpetually snow-clad peak with the largest single glacial system in the lower 48 states. The experts say it is by far the most demanding endurance climb. Of course, Mount McKinley in Alaska, because of its greater height and northern location, is in another league. With guides, the proper equipment, and a little training, Rainier, like Mont Blanc, can be climbed by fit amateurs.

The mountain is about two hours south of Seattle and only 45 miles from the blue waters of Puget Sound. It is a glacier-covered dormant volcano that reaches into the upper atmosphere and disturbs the great moist tides of Pacific air flowing east. The resulting encounter creates prodigious snowfalls and spectacular cloud halos. In the surrounding foothills, only a few minor rock peaks rise to slightly more than 6,000 feet, so Rainier with its mist-shrouded summit is an awesome landmark of the Pacific Northwest. The mountain is part of the 978-square-mile national park, which also features old-growth forests of giant Douglas fir, red cedars, and western hemlocks, some of which soar over 200 feet above mossy, fern-draped valley floors abundant with red and blue huckleberries. The lush opulence of this primeval wilderness provides a stunning contrast to the glacial austerity of the upper mountain. The park is not crowded and is meticulously cared for. Littering is virtually a capital offense.

The best place to stay is the Paradise Inn, which is at 5,000 feet and fronts the meadows, forests, and awesome south face of the mountain itself. The inn is a massive old wooden building with simple rooms and a huge, vaulted dining room that offers large amounts of plain American food. Whole families can gorge in the morning for the price of one continental breakfast at the Regency Hotel in New York. There are also a couple of good rustic restaurants at the entrance to the park.

To get acclimatized, we hiked on our own for three days in the foothills above Paradise, which are a mosaic of tree "islands" and sub-Alpine meadows. These meadows are a soft, sparkling carpet of flowers with wonderful names like sky blue lupine, white avalanche lilies, yellow glacier lilies, magenta paintbrush, and golden marsh marigolds. There are elk, black-tailed deer, mountain goats, and legions of unafraid hoary marmots. We hiked to waterfalls, caves, and panoramas in what should have been spectacular scenery. Unfortunately, we hit an unusual spell of mist and light rain that reduced visibility, so we saw only fog-shrouded snatches of the great vistas until the last day. We also spent one day at the snow- and ice-climbing school where the guides teach you what you have to know to climb the mountain.

The guides of Rainier Mountaineering are probably the best in the world. Most of them are professional mountaineers (not a lucrative activity, incidentally), and this is the way they stay in shape for the big stuff. Several of them are among the handful of Americans to have climbed Everest. They were superb with our group. Any amateur who attempts this dangerous climb without a guide is nuts. The glaciers, crevasses, and cliffs of the mountain are demanding, and the weather and avalanches can be treacherous. Rainier does not have anything like the traffic that Mont Blanc does, but nevertheless, a lot of people have perished on it.

On the fifth day, we left the guide house next to the inn at about 10 in the morning carrying packs that contained food for two days, water, sleeping bags, and heavy clothing plus crampons, ice axes, and ski poles. We hiked two hours up through the meadows to Pebble Creek and then three more up the Nisqually Glacier past Moon Rock to Camp Muir. It was a hard slog up the snowfields with the heavy packs, but by early afternoon, it began to get very beautiful as the mists blew off the sheer white cliffs of the summit towering above us. Below us was a sea of fluffy clouds, but we could clearly see the tops of Mount Adams and Mount St. Helens, and in the far distance Mount Hood poking through.

Camp Muir, which is the legendary base camp for summit climbs, is at 10,000 feet and consists of a couple of bunkhouses on a rock ledge. We arrived around 4 P.M., arranged our gear for the next day's ascent, and watched the night smudge the mountain as we ate dinner. The bunk house was cramped and cold, and only the young slept. Shortly after 1 A.M., we formed into rope teams and left Camp Muir carrying lighter packs and wearing crampons. For several hours, we hiked up the steep snowfields of the Cowlitz Glacier, past Cadaver Gap, and around 4 A.M., the narrow ledges illuminated only by our head lamps, we began to traverse the steep shale rock cliff that is called Disappointment Cleaver because so many climbers quit after experiencing it. It ends in a steep snowfield, which we crested just as the sun was rising. Exhausted, we stopped here even though it was windy and very cold, with a breathtaking view of what seemed like the whole Northwest spread below us and the long, sharp angles of the steep snowfields and glaciers of Rainier above us, a deep pink in the early morning light.

From this point it took about four hours of hard climbing over crevasses to reach the summit. We had perfect weather, but it was still a long cardiovascular slog with your pack tugging at your back. The summit is actually a crater about a third of a mile wide, and the older climbers collapsed in the warmth of the sun while the kids raced around. We started down around 11 A.M., and as always, getting down was worse than going up. The snowfields were slippery in the hot sun, and several of us, including yours truly, took falls. We were roped and carried ice axes up so we couldn't plummet off the mountain, but it still was unnerving as we could have fallen into a crevasse. In addition, there is always worry about an avalanche if the day is warm. The last scary part was the climb down Disappointment Cleaver; in daylight you could see the drops that fortunately were obscured on the way up. Even the young ones were spent by the time we reached Camp Muir. Then we still had to reload our packs and stagger two and a half hours more on jelly legs back down to Paradise Inn. We arrived about 7 P.M., for an elapsed travel time of about 33 hours, most of which was spent hiking at altitude with packs.

There's no high like the coming-off-the-mountain high. It lasts for days. We drank some beer that night, and the next morning was a clear day, and the mountain was there looking at us as we left, and it was all worth it. Why do I do it? It's an adventure. Some of the dangers and uncertainties have been removed, but you can still get a sense of wonder, feel fear, find great beauty, and to some extent experience the real meaning of self-reliance. Stretching the mid-life envelope, as they say. Anyway, it sure takes your mind off the stock market.

Japanese Landscapes

September 9, 1991

For the first time in quite a while, our floor brokers in Tokyo report real buyers in Japanese equities besides the gaijin and the index arbs. An awful lot of sleazy news has been absorbed, and the broker rebate scandal seems to have been fully discounted. Many traders are still bearish, based on both valuation and the very negative supply/demand imbalance.

Nevertheless, the hard investment facts are that the yield on the 10-year government bond has fallen 15 basis points in the past week. At 6.27 percent, it is almost 90 basis points below its year-end level. But the Nikkei index is still down 5 percent, even though based on cash earnings Japanese blue-chip industrial companies are as cheap as comparable U.S. companies, and the Nikkei's price/book premium to the U.S. market has shrunk (see the chart). My view continues to be that Tokyo stocks are poised to rally, but a new Mount Fuji bull market is years away.

Our economist in Tokyo, Noboru Kawai, believes that the Bank of Japan last week signaled a bias toward ease by reducing the gap between the overnight call rate and the official discount rate. Dutifully, several banks cut the short-term prime rate by 25 basis points. Kawai says the Tankan survey released last week indicates that the Japanese economy's "downshift is well under control," with real growth slowing toward 3 percent but no recession. Thus from the BOJ's point of view, he argues, there is no immediate need for another ODR cut unless the stock market falls sharply again or the yen becomes too strong, perhaps if the Fed were to ease again. The latter seems most likely. Euroyen interest rates are rich—just under 7 percent—and hot money may begin flowing back into the yen.

Just for fun I have been reading about the history of Japan from 1880 until 1940. The political stuff is fascinating, matched by the economic history of the time.

I am struck by how insular and feudal—yet instinctively capitalistic and financially sophisticated—the Japanese were during this period. It is interesting that a little over 60 years ago (there's that two-generation thing again) there was a banking panic in Japan. Five zaibatsu ruled Japanese business then: the four that still exist today—Mitsui, Mitsubishi, Sumitomo, Yasuda—plus a fifth, Suzuki.

The Suzuki conglomerate in Kobe was ruled by its matriarch, Yone Suzuki, who the *New York Times* in 1922 said was the richest woman in the world. She was very intelligent, strikingly beautiful, ambitious, and strong-willed, but manipulative. By the mid-1920s she controlled 65 companies, her trading company had overtaken Mitsui to become the largest, and her manufacturing interests were threatening the other zaibatsu. Hubris and leverage were her undoing. Unwilling to raise equity outside the family to finance the group's expansion, she relied on bank borrowing from two major banks. In 1926 she took control of one of them, the Bank of Kobe, thinking this ensured her access to credit.

Flourishing in Japan at the time was Bushido, a relativistic code of honor and aggression in which brutality was sanctioned as a means to an end. Both politics and business were played for keeps. Between 1912 and 1932, five prime ministers and at least a dozen cabinet ministers were assassinated. By 1925, Yone Suzuki was seriously bothering the other zaibatsu, and they felt dishonored by being bested by a woman. An elaborate trap was laid for her. The Bank of Kobe and her other principal bank had secretly relied for funding on term loans from the Mitsui and Mitsubishi banks. Suzuki either ignored this fact or believed that the other zaibatsu would continue to support her banks, and piled leverage on leverage as she bought businesses and expanded. Mitsui and Mitsubishi let her get extremely extended and then suddenly, with no warning, called the bank loans. There was a run by depositors on the Bank of Kobe, which they may have engineered; the two Suzuki banks failed; and the Suzuki dominoes began to fall. The whole thing reads like a chapter out of *Shogun*.

There was a hitch: the resulting panic threatened to engulf the nation as an indiscriminate run on banks across Japan began. It got so bad that there was even a run on the so-called Peers Bank, which held the emperor's personal wealth and was one of the largest banks. This spurred the government to act, and bank-reform legislation was raced through the Diet, restoring confidence in the banking system. It was too late for Yone Suzuki and her empire, which had gone bust. The big four, however, emerged from the panic much stronger, with their deposits doubled and controlling one-third of the banking system. But the Japanese economy remained stagnant until 1933, perhaps laying the social groundwork for Japanese militarism and the expansion into Southeast Asia.

The last weekend in June, I climbed Mount Fuji with a group from our Tokyo office plus Chris Wood, the brilliant Tokyo correspondent of the *Economist*. The sacred mountain is open to the public from July 1 until the end of August, and each summer 50,000 to 100,000 Japanese make the ritual climb. By filing an application with the local police, you can go on the mountain at other times. We were literally the only climbers on June 28, and the mountain was clean and fresh. However, I am told that climbing Fuji during the season is a wonderfully Japanese experience for gaijin.

Fuji may be the most beautiful mountain in the world. The elegant simplicity of its contour, sweeping up in the graceful shape of an inverted fan, is symbolic of the quest for serenity and perfection. The volcano mountain floats between heaven and earth, neither rock nor cloud but a cone of crystallized sky suspended above Japan. The views from the mountain through episodes of mist across the delicate Japanese landscape of blue lakes, dark green woods, and the soft browns of the rice fields are straight from one of those exquisite Japanese prints.

We arrived at the gate at 6,500 feet about three in the afternoon after a two-hour bus ride from Tokyo. Carrying light packs, we walked upward for a little over three hours to a simple inn at 9,100 feet. The mountain itself is volcanic ash and rock. The trail is a succession of 99 switchbacks, and the climb becomes quite steep and aerobic as you approach the summit, but it is never in any sense technical. You could easily do it in jogging shoes, though low hiking boots are better because of the loose scree. Any reasonably fit person—or nonfit but extremely determined person—can climb Fuji, although it may take a while.

We reached our inn at around six-thirty in the evening and climbed another 700 feet or so before dinner. You really feel as though you are on the roof of Japan, with the dark green of Japan spread out below and the lights of Tokyo in the far distance. The innkeepers cooked a typically Japanese meal, which we ate squatting on mats, drinking Kirin beer and talking. About 10 we lay down on futons in a large bunk room and slept fitfully till about 1 in the morning. Then we were off, because by tradition you must reach the summit before dawn. The final ascent took about three and a half hours and was over scree. As we climbed, it became colder and windier. We were literally alone on the mountain.

Down from Mount Fuji, Japan Price/Book Relative to U.S. Price/Book

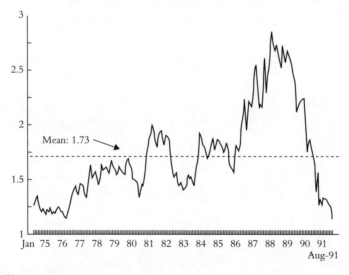

NOTE: 1.13 on 8/30/91.
SOURCE: Morgan Stanley Research.

The summit itself at dawn was exciting. Fuji is a big mountain, a real volcano with a plug, and the walk around the circumference of the crater takes at least 45 minutes and involves some rock scrambling. When we got there, at a little before five, the wind was fierce and a rain squall came through. Fred Miller, editor of this publication, put it best. Standing on the summit, buffeted by the wind and mist, watching the sun come up over the mass of Japan, he said, "This is the most exhilaration I've felt in a long time." I can imagine that at noon on a perfect summer day, it must be an incredible spot.

However, we had an afternoon plane to catch, and we started down shortly after six. There was a quick breakfast at the inn, and then we were descending again. If it took us about six hours to get up Mount Fuji, it took less than half that to get down. We were back in Tokyo by noon. As the old Japanese proverb has it, "A wise man climbs Mount Fuji once; a fool climbs Mount Fuji twice." Nevertheless, I wouldn't mind doing it again sometime.

The Snows of Kilimanjaro

February 26, 1987

Kilimanjaro is a snow-covered mountain 19,710 feet high, and it is said to be the highest mountain in Africa. Its western summit is called the Masai "Ngaje Nagai," the House of God. Close to the western summit is the dried and frozen carcass of a leopard. No one has explained what the leopard was seeking at that altitude.

—*Ernest Hemingway*

Competitive investment management is an intense, grinding profession, and its aficionados often suffer from "burnout" and "lockbrain." The first malady speaks for itself and is usually fatal to a career. The second describes the condition where you have argued your investment thesis so often that unwittingly your mind closes to other views. It is a subtle disease that is very dangerous to the health of your clients' portfolios.

Vacation is the best antidote for both maladies. Unfortunately, in modern times, most vacation destinations are within easy range of the telephone and the *Wall Street Journal*. A change of venue is refreshing and good for family life, but when you are calling the trading room three times a day and are irritable until you've seen the New York papers, your mind has not exactly disengaged from the battle for investment survival. Until it does, no intellectual capital is being restored.

The career-extending, performance-enhancing vacations are the ones where you are, first of all, out of market information range and, second and equally important, utterly absorbed in an enterprise. People are different. Byron Wien is going to China this fall to steep himself in its culture, which will do the trick for him. I would expire from boredom fishing a Nova Scotia trout stream, but for some it works. To each his own, but don't kid yourself that another two weeks at the beach or skiing is rewinding your head.

In August, I had a vacation that detached my mind from the market. Seven of us (five from my family and two close friends) went to Tanzania in East Africa and climbed Mount Kilimanjaro, the tallest mountain in Africa with a crest higher than any peak in the midcontinental United States or the entire continent of Europe. We spent seven days and six nights on the mountain and hiked about 70 miles.

Kilimanjaro is the highest free-standing mountain in the world, rearing in splendid isolation, a solitary volcanic massif, from the rich African plain. The mountain and its legends have long fascinated me. The local Chaga people believed it to be the home of an angry god who punished anyone who dared to climb it. When the first missionary to see Kilimanjaro in 1848 reported back to the Royal Geological Society that there was a mountain within three degrees of the equator capped with snow, he was ridiculed as a lunatic. All the early climbing expeditions failed, and it was not until 1889 that the summit was reached.

Thus, Kilimanjaro is the cradle of many mysteries, always intriguing. When you are on the mountain, it becomes an obsession, looming above you, shrouded with clouds or glistening in the moonlight. The climb itself is sunlight and green hills, cool water, and the yellow warmth of bright mornings. Yet, the mountain is also as cold and ruthless as any sea, more uncompromising than its own deserts. Its weather is fickle and without temperance in either its harshness or its favors. The mountain yields nothing but offers much to people of all races. And it is dangerous to those who do not respect it. While we were there, two men who were very careless died in separate incidents.

Kilimanjaro is the only one of the "Seven Summits" that requires no previous mountaineering experience or rock-climbing skills. It is just one long, extremely tough hike that any reasonably fit person can manage. After all, the four adults in our group ranging in age from 54 to 46 all made the peak. You do have to be determined, however. Age adjusted, I would rank the week we spent on the mountain right up there with my first weeks at Marine Officers Candidate School or at the Ranger program.

Another unique aspect of the climb is that, in its course, you pass through all the climatic zones of the earth. Commencing in the red earth and rich green equatorial African countryside full of animals and people, you first ascend into a lush, tangled tropical rain forest, almost a jungle, filled with warthogs, monkeys, and birdsongs. The initial hut camp is here, close to the Manundi crater at 9,000 feet. Next, you hike for six hours through Alpine meadows, giant heather trees, tumbling streams, rolling hills, and great sweeping panoramas of Africa to the second camp at 12,335 feet. We intentionally lingered two extra days at this camp to acclimatize and to explore back into the sparse moors and wild country of the saddle between the two great peaks of the mountain.

In the next stage, you hike up to an Alpine desert, like the long waves of the southern ocean, strewn from the volcanic eruption an eon ago that created the mountain with stark boulders like massive modern art creations. Flanked by the twin looming peaks of the summit, it seemed the plains of the moon. The weather is a real factor at this altitude, and for us a golden day suddenly became a hail storm. The third hut is at 15,520 feet, and from there to the summit, you are climbing steeply in near-arctic conditions.

The final ascent begins at two in the morning, when the footing is firm. By this time, you are tired, cold, and suffering from the altitude, but the spectacle of the Mawenzi summit looming magically in the moonlight across from you, with all Africa stretched below, is exhilarating. The Kibo summit, the crest of the continent, is reached around daybreak, and the warm equatorial sun is like a shot of pure whiskey. From there, you look into the crater and at the glacier that caps the mountain. The view seems the most spectacular in the world. After that climb, you need some tonic. We all found the last six hours as taxing an aerobic exercise as we had ever experienced.

We got to the mountain by flying to Amsterdam and then taking the once-a-week direct KLM flight to Kilimanjaro airport, two hours from the mountain. We stayed in a marvelous, antique hotel straight from *Out of Africa*, run with iron hands by two old European women. In the quaint dining room where every table has a small brass vase with a few wild flowers, the guests talk obsessively in many languages of Kilimanjaro. There is a sense of apprehension but also the easy camaraderie of strangers thrown together in a great adventure.

Tanzania very wisely has made the mountain area into a national park and charges $150 a head for admission, so there are no riffraff or day-trippers on the mountain. You can pitch tents or stay in the crude A-frame huts at the three camps. To climb without guides and porters is insanity, but a few hardy souls do it and pay a heavy price above 15,000 feet, where the atmosphere contains less than half the oxygen available at sea level. Our party was supported by 12 porters, three assistant guides, and a head guide. The total cost for our entire group on the mountain, including food, lodging, and tips for the entourage, was $40 per day for each of the seven of us.

The guides and porters are of Africa itself and are an important part of the experience. Africa has its own slow, inexorable pulse, and the blood of its people is as venerable and chaste as truth. Our Chagas were strong and proud, dirty and friendly, but never obsequious. They were full of the chatter and laughter of free men but are of a tribe that observes with equal respect the soft voice and the hardened hand. They carried heavy loads at high altitudes as though it were nothing, and they nursed some of our party in the final ascent with a gentle sweetness. They told us little, but often they looked deep into our eyes to gauge how we were holding up.

The darker side of the story is that Tanzania is truly a Third World country (even in the cities, electricity is only on for four hours a day) in which travel is a nerve-racking adventure. On the mountain, you're on your own. There is no medical care; the huts are primitive, and the sanitary conditions, horrible. Weather can make the climb even more demanding, and, in fact, we hit a very bad patch. Sleeping can be difficult because of the altitude, and don't think when you get down the mountain your discomforts are over. You'll be lucky to get seven days' grime off in a lukewarm bath. Nevertheless, despite a week of chicken, potatoes, and gruel cooked over wood fires and drinking stream water, none of our group ever had even a queasy stomach. Before we left New York, however, our arms were heavy with inoculations.

At the end of a strenuous day, I like a warm shower, cold beer, good food, and a soft bed. I'm not into roughing it or masochism, but Kilimanjaro was worth it. I hardly ever even wondered about the stock market. If anyone wants to experience Kilimanjaro, give me a call.

Pitfalls in Tokyo, Sand Traps in Colorado

August 31, 1992

My guess is that in the weeks to come the rally in the Japanese stock market will carry the Nikkei toward 20,000 on the back of high hopes for the government's rescue package. As I said last week, the consensus has to get bullish again before the next leg down in Tokyo comes. Already, the commentators are saying that while government intervention may not work elsewhere, Japan is different—a rescue package will save the economy, the banks, and the stock market, and isn't it marvelous the way the government and the Big Four have combined to rout the evil gaijin short sellers.

My view is that the winds of disinflation and change are blowing so hard in Japan that the stimulus package will be a minor event, although it will forestall a systemic failure. The banks, the stock market, and the real estate speculators still have to finish paying the proverbial piper for their previous sins. After all, we calculate that the Nikkei at 20,000 would be at 56 times March 1993 earnings and 50 times March 1994's. I believe that Japanese bonds are a buy but that stocks have not made the final bottom, which will come amid general despair and capitulation. Finance ministers don't cause bear markets to end; people and time do.

The story of exorbitant Japanese investment in U.S. office buildings, hotels, and golf courses is well known, but this summer I ran into an odd twist of it. In south-central Colorado, just below the Continental Divide, there is a great Alpine valley that is 100 miles long and about 60 miles wide. To the east of this sweeping valley are the jagged snow-topped summits of the Sangre de Cristo Mountains; to the west are the San Juans with their blue-green foothills of fir trees. For six months a year, melting snow from these two mountain ranges transforms the valley floor from a desert into fertile, brown-green meadows with groves of ruler-straight aspens and cottonwoods. In summer the grasslands are lush with wildflowers, meadowlarks, and grasshoppers, and they tell me that in the fall everything from the cottonwoods to the hay turns gold, glittering under a blue-yellow sky.

The fusion of desert and mountain lets you see forever. It is a land of big thunderstorms with curtains of rain you can smell miles away, big sunsets that linger until they break your heart, and clear air with the perfume of juniper trees. The roads are few and straight, the ranches huge, and there aren't many people. The land and the mountains have enthralled dreamers for 15 centuries and are steeped in history. First came the Indians—the Utes, the Navajos, and the Comanches—then the Spanish conquistadors, and finally the gold prospectors and settlers. In 1874 when the first Americans struggled to the summit of 14,345-foot Blanca Peak (which I intend to do next time), they were astounded to find a stone breastwork on the summit. The Utes, believing it to be a sacred mountain, had been there maybe half a millennium before them.

At the valley's eastern edge, there is an incredible sight: vast hills of sand towering as much as 800 feet over the plain, some of the highest dunes on earth, made from sand blown across the desert valley by the winds until the rock wall of the mountains traps and funnels it. The sand sings mystically in the wind, and the whole formation—over 50 square miles—is shaped by the wind into ripples, transverse ridges, and sweeping perfect curves. The area is preserved as the Great Sand Dunes National Park, and the visitor fords a shallow river and then wanders in the dunes. It is paradise for children, particularly since there are legends of disappearing herds of sheep, enchanted buffalo, and missing wagon trains. There are good backpacking and hiking in the park as well, or you can climb a mountain.

But the story that intrigues me is not about nature but commerce. Five years ago, I am told, four Japanese businessmen saw the valley. They had a dream, too: Buy vast tracks of ranchland cheap, build hotels and three golf courses, and lay down a long runway that could be used by 747s flying direct from Tokyo. Their idea apparently was to package charter flights, golf vacations, the Great Sand Dunes, and duty-free shopping. They bought the Zapata Ranch with 100,000 acres five miles from the national park, but then something happened.

The fairy tale the locals tell is that one of the Japanese, Hisayoshi Ota, had a spiritual experience when he looked deep into the black, enigmatic eyes of a wild bison; he fell in love with the vast, sprawling valley and bought out the other three businessmen in order to save it. Whatever his motives, Ota has saved the ranch, at least so far, renaming it the Great Sand Dunes Country Club and Inn. He stocked it with 2,000 bison and converted the original rough-hewn log buildings into an inn with 15 rustic but luxurious rooms at $150 a night. You eat outdoors on simple wood tables, but the food is superb and reasonably priced. The chef is an Egyptian straight from the Ritz in Paris. There is a swimming pool and exercise center, but the real gem is the golf course.

The course is two years old but has a mature look and feel because it was designed around the existing towering cottonwoods and follows the Zapata creek and the ancient irrigation canals that crisscross the ranch. The views from the tees on the front nine are of the sand dunes and the Sangre de Cristo Mountains; on the back nine, you are hitting directly into a panorama of the Rockies, particularly the big guy, Mount Blanca.

The fairways are thick bluegrass, and the greens of bent grass are in superb shape. From the blue tees, the distance is 6,816 yards, par 72 with the front nine 3,757 yards, par 37. The rough is high and tough. From the red tees, the course is 5,840 yards. The women's par is also 72. The great thing is that the course is empty and informal. You can walk or ride, and there are no tee times. There are also some unusual historical touches. For example, on the 10th fairway, a noose dangles from a cottonwood tree where a horse thief had been summarily hanged. Green fees are a hefty $25, carts cost $10.

The inn is going to add a few more rooms this winter because, thanks to a good review in the *New York Times* travel section, occupancy picked up this summer. Even so, Mr. Ota must be losing a fortune. There are an awful lot of people working on the ranch and the golf course and mighty few players. Bison herds can't come cheap. It's hard to believe he doesn't have something else in mind, but for the time being it is very special. Getting there isn't half the fun—it's a three-and-a-half-hour drive from either Denver or Santa Fe.

Section 6

BOOKS AND LETTERS

Receiving information is the lifeblood of the investment manager, and reading is the most efficient way to imbibe it.

—*Barton Biggs, May 5, 1987*

Where did Barton Biggs draw his knowledge and inspiration? The same way he imparted it. Through the written word.

Biggs was a voracious, albeit disciplined reader. Before the days of Google searches, video clips, and CNBC, Biggs consumed information through a system of short-term periodicals, analyst reports, investment books, biographies, and historical accounts of world events. By his own reckoning, he read or at least scanned "literally hundreds of investment books, many of them apocalyptic, most of them worthless."

The best he lists here, along with his personal reading plan. Some are obscure—or at least were until Biggs touted them in some of his periodic book review columns. Of course, there are old classics like Graham and Dodd, as well as some new classics like Schwager's *Market Wizards* and Bernstein's *Capital Ideas*. The list alone is like viewing a wireframe model of Biggs's investment mind and intellectual makeup.

Think of it as Biggs's best iTunes playlist. A beginning investor, or even an old hand, will find something of value—even if some titles seem outdated at first glance. Good music, like clear thinking and good writing, endures through the ages.

Section 6A:
Book Reviews

"Groupthink" and What to Do about It

May 14, 1984

I have written about that deadly scourge "groupthink" before, but I just finished reading a new book (*Groupthink*, by Yale psychology professor Irving Janis, who originally identified the phenomenon) that has some remarkable insights. The book's analysis is so significant and startling that I think anyone who is a member of a decision-making committee should read it. The best defense against this intellectual cancer is awareness of it. In my opinion, almost every investment policy committee, including our own, is plagued to one extent or another by the ailment.

Janis describes groupthink in clinical language as a "mode of thinking that people engage in when they are deeply involved in a cohesive in-group, when the members' striving for unanimity overrides their motivation to realistically appraise alternative mental efficiency and reality testing . . . a marked distortion in information processing that results from in-group pressures." Bad judgment, lack of vigilance, and excessive risk taking are forms of temporary derangement to which decision-making groups of

387

intelligent people are susceptible. As Nietzsche said, madness is the exception in individuals but the rule in groups.

Janis is not talking about a noncohesive, politically oriented group or a leader/dictator-manipulated group. Groupthink occurs even when the leader does not try to get the group to tell him what he wants to hear, but sincerely asks for opinions, and even when the group members are intelligent, motivated, and are not sycophants afraid to speak their minds.

The book discusses major international events as case studies of committees working both positively and negatively. The good ones include the Cuban Missile Crisis and the creation of the Marshall Plan, and the bad ones are the Bay of Pigs, Pearl Harbor, U.S. troops in North Korea, escalation in Vietnam, the *Mayaguez* incident, and Watergate. The analysis of the leadership and the decision-making process in these examples is fascinating; however, investment policy committees would be an equally fertile source of groupthink case studies. Reading about the National Security Council meeting of November 9, 1950, when U.S. troops were overextended and exposed in North Korea with a Chinese offensive imminent, the wishful thinking of Dean Acheson, George Marshall, President Truman, and General MacArthur—each of whom was hoping for one more victory—is so similar to the deliberations of an investment committee too fully invested in a bear market as to be spooky.

There are quite a few symptoms of groupthink, and any one group will manifest only some of them. Groups that are insulated by position, whose members come from common backgrounds, and who are experiencing high stress from external threats are particularly susceptible to groupthink. Remember that the more prestigious membership in the group is, the better the group gets along, and the more the members socialize with each other, the more important a place in the group becomes and the more likely it is that groupthink will occur. In fact, a group of friends that party together, as did the Kennedy and Johnson groups, is particularly susceptible to groupthink. This is because individual members are unwilling to risk group disapproval or ostracism by dissent because continuing to be a member means so much to each of them.

Without going into a lot of detail on each groupthink symptom, and noting that the bracketed comments are mine, not Janis's, the symptoms are:

1. Collective rationalizations of shared illusions generally believed. ["It's just another correction in a bull market."]
2. Crude, negative stereotypes of out-groups. ["The bears are a bunch of losers and idiots." "Valuation models are for impractical academics."]
3. Shared belief in the inherent morality of the group. [More applicable to government and corporate policy decision making.]
4. Illusion of invulnerability to dangers arising from a risky course of action. ["We've hung in there before when things looked bad and it's worked. Something good will happen." Combat units and athletic teams may benefit from shared illusions about their power and luck, but policy-making committees do not.]

5. Illusion of unanimity and suppression of personal doubts. ["Everyone else on the committee thinks it's just a correction, so I must be wrong to be worried, and, besides, if I told them, they'd think I was chicken."]

6. Subtle group pressure on dissenters. ["I used to think Joe was a good, smart investor, but now it looks like he's losing his nerve."]

7. Self-appointed "mindguards" who protect the group from thoughts that might damage their confidence in their policy. ["There's no point in having that crazy bear technician in."]

8. Docility fostered by suave, previously successful leadership. [Janis cites President Kennedy in the Bay of Pigs decision as a classic example of this. The group believed Kennedy was a born winner, and he managed the meetings to encourage consensus with his viewpoint.]

9. Free-floating conversation in group meetings. [This is a sign of a disorganized decision-making process and is characterized by general, unstructured discussion of issues.]

10. Lack of standard risk analysis using methodical procedures. [I don't agree with Janis completely on this one. He thinks there should be formal study of alternatives, objectives, risk-reward analysis, and contingency plans. I question whether these factors can be quantified, but consideration of them is probably a good discipline.]

In the course of the case studies and in the text itself, a series of prescriptions for avoiding groupthink become evident based on what has worked. However, because each group is different, the proper mix of the prescriptions is an art, not a science, and some of the remedies that follow are mine, not Janis's:

1. The leader must establish a group norm that gives the highest priority to critical appraisal. There must be intellectual suspicion amid the personal trust. The members of the group must feel confident of their acceptance in the group and sure that their standing and compensation will not be jeopardized by their making critical or contrary arguments.

2. The leader must be initially impartial and use his influence to encourage hard-headed debate and praise critical evaluators. Later, he must demonstrate that he can be influenced by those who disagree with him and not be overly directive. Sometimes, the leader should let the group meet without him to encourage freer talk.

3. The core group should form several independent policy planning and evaluation groups of subordinates, each under a different leader, to report back to the core group. This mitigates insulation and gridlock in the core group and exposes it to divergent opinions.

4. While policy is being debated, the core group should from time to time divide into two or more subgroups and then return to report separately. This gets the group out of what may be a stultified meeting format.

5. Each member of the policy group should discuss, periodically, the group's deliberations with trusted associates outside the group and report their reaction.

6. Outside experts or nonmember colleagues should be invited to meetings and encouraged to challenge the views of the core members. Here, again, the objective is divergent opinions.

7. At every meeting, at least one member should be assigned the role of devil's advocate to challenge the consensus. Bobby Kennedy was a vehement, bruising, but effective devil's advocate at the Bay of Pigs meetings. The leader must be careful not to "domesticate" his devil's advocate, as President Johnson did. Psychodramatic role-playing may be another way to accomplish the same objective.

8. The group itself should not be too homogeneous in terms of business experience, social background, and shared beliefs. If possible, there should be some contentious, contrary members who are maybe even a little obnoxious, but they must be respected and secure.

9. The leader must make sure the group does not suffer from "information overload." History shows that too much data results in fatigue and reduced mental efficiency, which in turn leads to groupthink.

10. After reaching a preliminary decision about policy, the group should hold a "second-chance" meeting at which members are expected to express their residual doubts and the group has a chance to rethink its decision. In ancient times, Herodotus and Tacitus report, these second-chance meetings were mandatory in certain cultures, and the decision would always be reconsidered under the influence of wine.

History suggests that harmonious meetings may be a warning of groupthink or complacency and that agitation, unpleasant arguments, and some stress are good signs. The Cuban Missile Crisis meetings, for example, were full of turmoil and even shouting, whereas earlier the same group got along fine while serenely planning the Bay of Pigs invasion.

Some of the most successful investment management firms have the most contentious, agitated meetings, but the committee members are secure in their standing as moneymakers. Janis emphasizes the importance of the leader in creating the group culture, but it is equally apparent that the group members must *work* at being open-minded and open-mouthed.

As you read the book, even though there is nothing in it about business or investment management, you discover habits and practices that you immediately know you and your group are guilty of. The investment management business uses groups to make policy to such an extent that any techniques that can sharpen the perspective of the decision-making process is of immense value, and, as I said at the beginning, sensitivity to the threat of groupthink is the best antidote. This book should be required reading.

Captain Money and the Golden Girl Ponzi

October 8, 1985

The generic phrase "Ponzi scheme" derives from one Charles Ponzi, an immigrant Italian dishwasher in Boston, who 60 years ago conceived of a creative but preposterous postal-stamp buying plan that produced large, theoretical profits on the money employed. Of course, he just told people that was what he was doing. The money was not invested in anything, and the early participants were paid off with funds raised from later investors.

Thus the modern Ponzi pattern was created, with the continuance of a scam dependent on maintaining credibility through the apparent affluence, respectability, and investment mystique of the promoter and the recruitment of new investors. As the investment pyramid expands, however, larger and larger amounts of fresh money are needed to meet redemptions, and eventually every Ponzi scheme collapses.

Nevertheless, new ones sprout up and flourish because of gullibility and greed. There are literally thousands of schemes in existence around the world at any given time; recently, the FBI estimated there were at least 200 under way in Los Angeles alone. Some are chain letters and pyramid clubs, and others are large marketing businesses that depend for their success on selling dealerships or franchises in a product rather than the product itself. But the biggest and most successful have been investment schemes of one type or another. Basically, ESM was a Ponzi, and in my more cynical moments, the LDC loans and certain famous bankers who say there can be no risk in sovereign credit lending have certain Ponzi characteristics.

In a new book, *Captain Money and the Golden Girl*, Donald Bauder chronicles the history of J. David & Company, the glitziest, biggest Ponzi scam of modern times. The writing is undistinguished, but the story is so incredible that the book, although some-thing of a potboiler, is worth reading just to refurbish your store of skepticism. The principal characters extend the imagination. Captain Money is Jerry Dominelli, a short, plump, bespectacled introvert in his late 30s who had washed out of the Marine Corps and was a mediocre broker for Bache. The Golden Girl is Nancy Hoover, a tall, statu-esque, vivacious blond who was also a broker in a San Diego Bache office. As they say in southern California, neither of them was "too tightly wrapped." In fact, they used to sit in their joint office with their bare toes touching.

The moment of conception of the scam is fuzzy, but it is known that Dominelli began to claim great success in commodity trading to impress Nancy Hoover. He fabricated a record by trading several small accounts on different sides of positions and then using the one that worked. Maybe the scam evolved from there, but he and Nancy (they were both married at the time) became lovers, and there must have been an interesting romantic moment when she discovered his record was a fraud. Anyway, Dominelli formed J. David & Company and did the trading, with Hoover selling and running the office, which was located in a dank space under a Mexican restaurant.

Hoover initially raised small amounts—$3,000 to $5,000—from individuals for her lover to trade in gold, foreign exchange, and financial futures. She sold on the basis of Dominelli's record, which, as concocted, was impressive to say the least but unaudited. Compound annual returns of 30 to 40 percent were "virtually assured" through the brilliance and trading systems of the eccentric genius Dominelli. Investors—many of them sophisticated, some celebrities—flocked greedily as the word got around. Very few did any serious checking, but those who did found the claims in the sales brochure were either false or unsubstantiated. The suckers ignored them.

Little J. David & Company became an overnight success. Some well-timed pub-licity in a book helped. Soon there were many employees and millions of dollars in the pools. The office was moved to a fancy building in downtown La Jolla, and over a million dollars was spent on lush redecorating with thick carpets, antique furniture, and original art. Later, another building next door was purchased and rebuilt with custom-designed wood floors and ceilings, accordion window shutters of mahogany, private elevators and entrances, a library, ornate dining rooms, and gold-plated fixtures in the bathrooms. Everything was first class, including the firm's professional associa-tions with the large Los Angeles law firm of Rogers & Wells and the accounting firm of Laventhol & Horwath.

There were also plenty of whirling computers and trading equipment with a vari-ety of electronic analysis systems. The secretaries were all voluptuous, and a salesforce comprised of beautiful people and former athletes that received high payout com-missions was hired. The introverted Dominelli seemed to live vicariously through the dynamic Hoover as her role in the San Diego community blossomed. For years, macho men and beautiful women had scorned him, but now his Nancy manipulated such people and he was their guru. As for Nancy, she fulfilled her fantasy of power and influence.

In 1981 the pools were moved to an offshore bank in Montserrat, which Dominelli bought for $40,000. The bank was a shell—nothing more than a name—but it enabled J. David to operate unregulated in the foreign exchange market and also to provide its investors with tax-free status. Montserrat's laws conveniently forbid audits, so investors got no confirmations—only an unaudited monthly statement of the gain in their accounts. Dominelli claimed that details would permit others to learn his trading techniques.

Captain Money and the Golden Girl reveled in the glamorous fast-lane, southern California style, spending immense amounts of money on jewels, clothes, foreign cars (Dominelli at one time owned 30), estates, horses, and two airplanes. The Golden Girl quickly parlayed success and a willingness to pick up checks into associations with San Diego's most prominent and richest citizens, many of whom became investors. She ostentatiously supported local charities and poured money into the political campaign of a future mayor of San Diego. Their generosity to employees was legendary. All this contributed to the aura of wealth, glamour, and respectability that was essential to the continuance of the scam. If anyone got nosey or made disparaging comments, Dominelli's lawyer would gently hint of a lawsuit.

As time progressed, suspicions were aroused. For one thing, the J. David office became increasingly disorganized, and some investors began to wonder how Captain Money could wander around most of the day oblivious to the foreign exchange markets he was supposed to be ravishing. For another, foreign exchange traders around the world had never heard of J. David and never saw the firm on the other side of trades. Then England refused to grant the firm a license to do business in the United Kingdom. People began to note that Captain Money and the Golden Girl kept no records and carried huge amounts of cash with which they paid for everything.

Between 1979 and 1984, over $200 million was taken in from a celebrity-studded cast of investors mesmerized by promises of 30 to 40 percent tax-free returns. It appears over a quarter of it went for personal spending sprees by Dominelli and Hoover (the Golden Girl would spend $70,000 in an afternoon of shopping). Another 25 percent or so went into lavish commissions, salaries, and office fixtures, and Dominelli probably lost a lot of the remainder before he quit trading, which he was really lousy at. Poor commercial investments also consumed some, and the rest just disappeared. All the evidence suggests that in the last three or four years very little if any trading was ever done.

In December 1983, Captain Money's behavior became increasingly bizarre, and some checks bounced simply because of careless management and not because of a liquidity shortage. There was talk of losses (which was ridiculous since there was no trading), and redemptions began to increase. Initially, the problem was dealt with by paying out those who were most insistent and by reporting spectacular monthly returns. January 1984 returns were up 7 percent. The firm's year-end party at the elegant Hotel Del Coronado was more extravagant than usual, as the golden couple continued their pursuit of life on the edge. Commission payouts to the salesforce were raised in early 1984, but soon some of the salesmen and insiders began withdrawing their own funds. Suddenly, the run began in earnest, and J. David collapsed. The lawyers went after Captain Money and the Golden Girl, but they hadn't stashed anything away. They were broke. The spree was over. There was nothing left except the furniture and the antiques.

Dominelli tried to get away but was caught and brought back in handcuffs. In jail he suffered a stroke. Hoover is out on bail. She and the former mayor of San Diego have been indicted for perjury and conspiracy for funneling $357,000 into his election campaign. Of course, the irony of the whole thing is that if Dominelli had invested the money in Treasury bonds at 10 percent and at least pretended he was trading, the scam could have gone on for years. Instead, the two spent and dissipated the money and at the end put on such an outrageous show it was as though they had some subliminal drive to be exposed. Adversity has proved that the two opposites, Captain Money and the Golden Girl, truly loved each other. The problem is that most of the investors' $200 million is gone. Caveat Emptor.

The Alchemy of Finance

July 8, 1987

This is a personal, unquestionably biased review of the book *The Alchemy of Finance* written by George Soros and published by Simon & Schuster. I'm prejudiced because I like George a lot and I believe (and, for that matter, the record proves) he's the best pure investor ever. George is a true alchemist who instead of trying, like his medieval predecessors, to transmute magically the baser metals into gold, transmutes events into profits. In my opinion, he is probably the finest analyst of the world in our time, and now, beyond having made himself several hundred million dollars, he wants intellectual impact.

In the introduction, George says that the book is not meant to be a guide to getting rich in the stock market. "I am using my experiences in the financial markets to develop an approach to the study of historical processes in general and the present historical moments in particular." He goes on to write that "I would value it much more highly than any business success if I could contribute to an understanding of the world in which we live, or better yet, if I could help to preserve the economic and political system that has allowed me to flourish as a participant." Best of all, he means it.

So it's no surprise that I think *The Alchemy of Finance* is a seminal investment book right along with Graham and Dodd's *Security Analysis* and Lefèvre's *Reminiscences of a Stock Operator*. It is not self-promotion because George recounts how often he is wrong, nor is it an intellectual tour de force full of big words and sentences that run on into the next time zone. Instead, it presents a dialectic of analysis just as *Security Analysis* defined the value-investing case. The book espouses the theory of reflexivity, which is the philosophical model from which he views the world. But more than that, reflexivity gives one the tools to understand the "shoelace theory of history," booms and busts, and essentially how the world works. I think the book should be read, underlined, and thought about page by page, concept by idea. But the only way to understand this book is to spend substantial time on it.

That said, the book is not easy or fun reading. As George says in the introduction, it is a "difficult and dense book." It will not make time in an airport waiting room go quickly, nor will it divert you on a day when your longs went down and your shorts went up. It is a very serious, profound book. Jerry Goodman and Marty Sosnoff wrote superb books about the money game that were aimed at the millions of practicing investors. They were designed to entertain and enlighten. George's book was written for the maybe 500 serious, intellectual, professional investors; for the academics; and for the people who run the world because George thinks his insights can help them run it better.

I can assure you that the book will not be a commercial success—not that George cares. The tragedy is that it may not get the intellectual attention and acclaim it deserves. In talking with people who have read the book, I find that some professional investors with an intellectual and philosophical bent are absorbed by it. Others, who when all is said and done run money more by ear, want to read it because of George's reputation but can't stay with it. "After a couple of chapters, I decided to wait for the movie version" was one reaction. Intelligent people who are not investment professionals find it heavy going and discard it before extracting the serious meat.

Unfortunately, the academics and the economists in the think tanks whom George really wants to read the book so that reflexivity can have a hearing are such snobs that they won't deign to because he doesn't have a PhD and because he is a rich Wall Street speculator who they think by definition can't be a serious thinker. In fact, the book argues that the conventional wisdom of classical economics, Keynes, and the monetarists about markets and economics are "based on a fundamental misconception." In this sense, the book is radical and breaks new ground. Since the book in effect obsoletes all their training and accumulated knowledge, you can be sure that the academic establishment will continue to ignore it. At a recent meeting sponsored by a prominent think tank to discuss the book, virtually none of the economists present had even bothered to read it so there was no dialogue. This was frustrating for George and stupid of the institution since with his generosity he could have healed their finances for eternity.

Reading *Alchemy* is like climbing a mountain. While you're doing it, it's demanding and exhausting work, but it's uplifting and the view from the top is magnificent. But the reader should be under no illusion that he is going to find 10 new ways to make money in the stock market. Instead, if you really work hard at it, you will get a feeling of how the model functions, your ability to understand human events will be deepened, and you may get a glimpse of how George "reads the mind of the market."

The book is 349 pages long and has five parts. The first deals with the concept of reflexivity and its application to the stock market. George argues that the theories of equilibrium and of efficient markets are dead wrong and asserts that market valuations are always distorted. Moreover, the distortions can affect underlying values. Stock prices are not merely passive reflections; they are active ingredients in a process in which both stock prices and the fortune of the companies whose stocks are traded are determined. As he puts it "the stock market is generally believed to anticipate recessions; it would be more correct to say that it can help to precipitate them." At another point he writes that reflexive interaction is "like shooting at a target when the act of shooting moves the target." In one chapter, Soros makes the point that reflexivity and expectations are even more important in the foreign exchange markets than in the stock market.

In the second section of the book, George writes about reflexivity from the perspective of recent events. He explains his theory of vicious and virtuous circles and Reagan's "Imperial Circle." Then he proceeds into the third section, which is a 14-month real-time diary he kept of his thoughts, analysis, and reactions as he ran his billion-dollar fund. I found it fascinating, although I wish he had linked it better to his basic theory of reflexivity. As an investor, George is incredibly flexible and willing to change his mind if the markets appear to be going against him. One of his great strengths is that he has no pride of position. Does this come from reflexivity or observing his father change safe houses on intuition when the Gestapo was chasing his family in Budapest during World War II?

Part IV of the book evaluates the results of the real-time experiment and explores the scope of alchemy and the social sciences. In the last section, George muses about the problems of today and presents his proposals for a world central bank and an international currency. In the epilogue, George writes with some emotion of his own search for meaning and happiness. This final revelation, his self-exposure, shows the depth and intensity of his commitment to this work. What more can I say.

I Wish
We Didn't Have to Play
for George Steinbrenner

December 20, 1988

Jerry Goodman, alias Adam Smith, has written a new book called *The Roaring '80s*. Jerry's TV program is fresh and intelligent, and some years ago he authored two of the best, most profound books ever written on "The Money Game." The new one is not in the same class, but Jerry writes with such flair and wit that it's still fun to read. One part of the book, though, got me thinking.

Goodman describes a long talk with Warren Buffett. Of course, Buffett has now become The Investment Folk Hero of modern times, up there in the Hall of Fame with Lord Keynes and Ben Graham. He also is everybody's All American because, in this day of greedy, get-rich-quick yuppies and conspicuous LBO consumption, he still lives in the same old house in the same old town, even though he's amassed $2 billion and he buys stocks in the old-fashioned, value way.

As usual, most of what Buffett says makes a lot of sense. He talks some about passing on wealth to children. The analogy he makes is to food stamps. Everyone agrees that giving out food stamps is debilitating because the recipients don't bestir themselves, which causes the cycle to repeat itself. However, according to Buffett, people miss the point that giving wealth to children is like giving them a lifetime supply of food stamps. Buffett once said that, as much as he loves his children, he wouldn't leave anything to them. Jerry interviewed Buffett's daughter, and she doesn't seem too enthusiastic about that idea. Her kitchen apparently needs remodeling.

Now, Buffett admits he is not that draconian. "I think kids should have enough money to be able to do what they want to do, to learn what they want to do, but not enough money to do nothing." This makes a lot of sense. The gift of some freedom and time to enable young people to figure out what they want to do can be priceless if it's not abused. You always think your children will be different and won't be spoiled by money, but the odds are very much against you. Rags to riches to rags in three or four generations is about as immutable a law of human nature as there is.

The part of the discussion that lodged in my craw, however, was when Buffett said to Goodman: "In the securities business you're a batter in a game in which there are no called strikes. They can throw you General Motors at forty and you don't have to swing. They can throw you IBM at one-twenty and you don't have to swing. They have to keep pitching but you don't have to swing. So if you're patient, the odds are with you. You can wait until you get one right where you want it." What Buffett wants is a "good business at a good price" or an ordinary business at a very good price.

"You might not swing for six months," Jerry said to him. "You might not swing for two years," answered Buffett. Well, that's fine for Buffett to say, but he's not in the same investment business that most of us are. We don't have the luxury of letting pitch after pitch go by. We have to swing. The umpires who are the consultants and the clients call strikes on us and post the score every quarter. If we don't put some good numbers on the scoreboard, the owner takes us out of the game. It's as though we all play for a demanding, irrational owner like George Steinbrenner who only cares about what you did for him yesterday. However, it's even worse for us than it is for the Yankees. We have to compete not only with the other batters but also with a hitting machine called Index Fund who plays for practically nothing.

The irony is that most of us run our own accounts as Buffett recommends. We don't worry about what decile our own account is in for the quarter or how we are doing versus the S&P. We don't have to swing. As long as our patience and discipline hold out, we can wait for a fat one. Incidentally, although what Buffett calls "The Great Investors of Graham and Doddsville" have consistently beaten the market over the long run, there have been "short" runs of three or four consecutive years when even the best value investors have underperformed. Today, if you lag the market for three or four years straight, you had better start checking if there are any hardware stores for sale in Vermont.

So, whose fault is it that we don't invest for our clients in the way Buffett invests? I think it's a vicious circle in which the clients, the consultants, and we money managers are all to blame. The clients want performance because the portfolio or the pension plan is a profit center, and they put pressure on the administrator. Yet, they lament out of the other side of their mouths that they can't run their companies properly because money managers are so oriented to quarterly earnings. Investment managers complain about the short-term horizon of clients yet buy and sell stocks with hair triggers. The consultants just pour gasoline on the fire. Everybody blames everybody else, but the process is circular.

So, with that diatribe off my chest at year-end, where are we? In my opinion, the breakout from this long trading range will come on the upside, so I think you have to own stocks now. It's too pat to say that bonds have to move before equities do. Peace, Perestroika, central banks obsessed with inflation, and moderate economic growth are all very bullish for stocks. Expectations about Gorbachev, Bush, inflation, interest rates, and profits are very low, and cash positions are very high. I think the dollar is completing the second part of a major double bottom.

The most attractive markets are those in the United States and Hong Kong. In the United States, I would buy cyclicals like the paper, chemical, technology, and machinery groups because the 1989 earnings of those companies are going to be considerably better than expected and because their dividends are about to go up a lot. I would also buy medium- and large-capitalization high-growth stocks like Merck ($58), Walmart ($31), Eli Lilly ($89), IBM ($122), Compaq Computer ($58), Abbott Laboratories ($47), Sallie Mae ($77), and Waste Management ($41). As we have documented ad nauseam, true growth stocks, both large and small, are as cheap as they have been in years. For almost five years, value has done better than growth, but my guess is that it's a new ball game and it's time to swing for growth.

Noise and Babble

May 19, 2003

Probably the biggest intellectual problem an investor has to wrestle with is the barrage of noise and babble. Noise is extraneous, short-term information that is random and basically irrelevant to investment decision making. Babble is the chatter and opinions of the well-meaning, attractive fools who abound. The serious investor's monumental task is to distill this overwhelming mass of information and opinion into knowledge and then to extract investment meaning from it. Meaning presumably leads to wisdom, which should translate into performance—which is the only thing that matters. It's nice and even superficially impressive to be well informed, but in the long run the client world doesn't care how well informed you are. It cares about numbers. Managing the information deluge and separating out the noise have become more difficult because in the Internet era there is so much more information and opinion readily available. Yet babble has always been there.

Nearly 70 years ago, at the very beginning of the so-called information explosion, that somber soul T. S. Eliot asked metaphorically: "Where is the knowledge we have lost in information?" Maybe he should have added: "Where is the information we have lost in the haystack of data and opinion?" And the trouble is, most data are noise, and most opinions, no matter how articulate, are babble.

Noise and babble can be very hazardous to your investment health, and there is a massive amount of it being disseminated, often with the best of intentions. In *Fooled by Randomness*,* one of Nassim Nicholas Taleb's major themes is that the wise man listens for meaning, but the fool gets only the noise. The ancient poet Philostratus said:

---

*Nassim Nicolas Taleb, *Fooled by Randomness* (New York: Texere LLC, 2001).

"For the gods perceive things in the future, ordinary people things in the present, but the wise perceive things about to happen."

I don't know Taleb. The dust jacket of the book says he is the founder of Empirica Capital, "a crisis hunting hedge fund firm," whatever that is. *Fooled by Randomness* is a serious, intellectually sophisticated book, well worth reading carefully. At times, the book is almost condescending, as though the author had discovered the holy grail of investing. There ain't no holy grail, and the book's cosmopolitan tone can be somewhat off-putting. Nevertheless, there are some great insights.

At one point he explains the difference between noise and meaning with this example. Suppose there is an excellent investor who can earn a return of 15 percent in excess of Treasury bills with 10 percent per annum volatility. Standard deviation analysis means that out of 100 sample paths, about 68 will fall between plus 25 percent and plus 5 percent and that 95 paths will be between plus 35 percent and negative 5 percent. In effect, this investor has a 93 percent probability of generating an excess return in any one year. However, as the time scale shortens, the probability of outperformance declines drastically, as shown in the table:

Probability of Making Money
Comparative Absolute Valuations

Scale	Probability
One year	93%
One quarter	77
One month	67
One day	54
One hour	51.3
One minute	50.17

This is standard Monte Carlo simulator stuff. Taleb's important insight, however, is that almost all investors experience more pain and anguish from losses than they do pleasure from gains. The agony is greater than the ecstasy. I don't know why this is true, but it is. Maybe it's because the investment business breeds insecurity.

But to the extent that the investor is focused on the daily or even minute-by-minute performance of his or her portfolio, as the table shows, the time of pain is inadvertently increased and the time of pleasure reduced. And this is a particularly bad trade-off, since moments of pain are more poignant than the times of pleasure. The problem is (and Taleb doesn't say this) that investment pain leads to anxiety, which in turn can cause investors to make bad decisions. In other words, continual performance monitoring is not good for your mental health even though contemporary portfolio management systems and their suppliers strenuously promote it. In fact, Taleb argues, you will probably be a better (and happier) investor if you only deal with monthly or maybe even annual statements.

Most investors think they are rational, but in fact they are prone to drown in randomness and to incur emotional torture from short-term performance swings. Taleb says: "When I see an investor monitoring his portfolio with live prices on his cellular telephone or his Palm Pilot, I smile and smile." In other words, turn off the Bloomberg. When an investor focuses on short time increments, he or she is observing the variability of the portfolio, not the returns—in short, being "fooled by randomness." Our emotions are not designed to understand this key point, but as investors we need to come to grips with our emotional liabilities. It's not easy.

Taleb says he does it by denying himself access to information except in rare circumstances. "I prefer to read poetry," he says. "I am aware of my need to ruminate on park benches and in cafés away from information, but I can only do so if I am somewhat deprived of it." He maintains that it is better to read the *Economist* from cover to cover than the *Wall Street Journal* every morning, both from the standpoint of frequency and the massive gap in intellectual content. "My sole advantage in life," he writes, "is that I know some of my weaknesses, mostly that I am incapable of taming my emotions facing news and incapable of seeing performance with a clear head."

This is also a time management issue. You can't read everything and talk to everybody. There simply is not enough time. As far as babble is concerned, you must be disciplined and control how you spend your time. You can't let others control it for you, which often happens in the office environment of a big investment management company. Keep your office door closed to discourage casual chatters. Don't answer your phone. Don't be compulsive about reading every piece of trash that lands on your screen. To avoid frivolous chitchat, one of the best investors in the world requires that his analysts communicate with him by e-mail. He said he found it too difficult to get them out of his office if he let them communicate with him face-to-face. He couldn't be rude to his own analysts. On the other hand, he is completely comfortable cutting off loquacious phone conversations with a curt "thank you." He is right. You must be rational by managing your time and not allowing others to waste it. Your client doesn't care if the salesman from X likes you or not.

Of course, what it all comes down to is converting knowledge into wisdom and then into vision—"a seeing eye." As Philostratus wrote, "the wise perceive things about to happen." Investors have to fertilize their minds with meaning and wisdom as best they can, so they can perceive things about to happen. This is the "seeing eye" that Churchill describes in this wonderful passage about David Lloyd George, the maverick prime minister, possessed of a perceptive mind.* Cultivate your seeing eye. All the really great investors have one.

The offspring of the Welsh village whose whole youth had been rebellion against the aristocracy, who had skipped indignant out of the path of the local

---

*Keynes described Lloyd George as follows: "How can I convey to the reader who does not know him any just impression of this extraordinary figure of our time, this siren, this goat-footed bard, this half human visitor to our age from the hag ridden magic and enchanted woods of Celtic antiquity."

Tory magnate driving his four-in-hand, and revenged himself at night upon that magnate's rabbits, had a priceless gift. It was the very gift which the products of Eton and Balliol had always lacked—the one blessing denied them by their fairy godmothers, the one without which all other gifts are so frightfully cheapened. He had the "seeing eye."

He had that deep original instinct which peers through the surface of words and things—the vision which sees dimly but surely the other side of the brick wall or which follows the hunt two fields before the throng. Against this, industry, learning, scholarship, eloquence, social influence, wealth, reputation, an ordered mind, plenty of pluck counted for less than nothing.

Section 6B:
Biggs's Reading List

Too Much to Read

May 5, 1987

Receiving information is the lifeblood of the investment manager, and reading is the most efficient way to imbibe it. Each day great stacks of paper arrive that we all compulsively paw at, but the objective of processing information is making wise investment judgments, not reading for reading's sake or even just acquiring knowledge. Sometimes I let getting through my inbox dominate me so that I literally lack time to think. I become so obsessed with sorting and discarding the junk that I end up carrying the "good stuff" I have set aside to read carefully back and forth from home in the bottom of my briefcase. Processing the pile and having a clean desk can become a compulsion that hurts rather than helps.

In other words, as investment managers we must control our reading, rather than let it control us, by being disciplined and discriminating. I need original judgment insights that deepen my understanding of the investment environment, an industry, or a company and specific new information at the margin. Change at the margin is what moves stocks and markets. Ninety percent of the written material I receive each day is worthless to me because either it repeats what I already know or it's irrelevant. The problem is that I can't winnow out the 10 percent without glancing at the rest, and no secretary, no matter how smart, can do this for you. Incidentally, the same time-management dilemma exists in controlling whom you talk with and for how long, but that's another subject.

In any case, here's how I try to deal with the reading problem. First, I quickly scan the summary of the industry and company reports I get to see if there is a chance of an insight or information at the margin. If something fresh whets my appetite, I read on. But as soon as it gets stale, into the trash the report goes. It is far better to err in throwing too much away than to risk getting bogged down. The odds are very low of finding anything new in one more 20-page report on, say, GE. I believe you must limit the number of firms whose research you receive and review, and I think the good research is from the best firms, but delicacy stills my tongue on the specifics. One aside, however. I find Bernstein's strategy and company analysis, though sometimes wrong, uniquely original and stimulating.

Every day I read without fail the *New York Times*, the *Wall Street Journal*, and the *Financial Times*. The last is indispensable if you are going to invest internationally, as the other two simply don't cover foreign business news. The *Washington Post* has a lot of good stuff, but I just can't get to it.

As for periodicals, I read each week the *Economist* and the *Far Eastern Economic Review* carefully. I look over the table of contents of *BusinessWeek*, *Tokyo Business Today*, *Aviation Week*, *Asia Week*, *Fortune*, *Foreign Affairs*, the *National Review*, *Barron's*, *Public Interest*, the *Asian Wall Street Journal Weekly*, *Forbes*, and *World Press Review* and read articles selectively. I do read the *Institutional Investor* and *Pensions and Investments Age* thoroughly and look at *Intermarket* to remind myself that I am completely out of the wild world of options, hedging, and investment math. I read *Time* and *Insight* rapidly from cover to cover each week. Magazines are important sources of information, but you have to treat them with disrespect.

Newsletters can add value. I get *Petroleum Intelligence Weekly*, *Middle East Economic Report*, *Grant's Interest Rate Letter*, Polyeconomics's and Smick-Medley's material. Incidentally, Polyeconomics's monthly publication *Recommended Reading*, which reprints the best articles from all over, is a lifesaver. I glance at the *Bank Credit Analyst*.

There are too many economists, and they can confuse you. I read only the good ones—our guys, Ed Hyman, Morgan Guaranty's *World Financial Markets*, and Laffer. Polyeconomics can be intriguing sometimes. Technicians can be dangerous, so I listen only to Bob Farrell, John Mendelson, and Rick Eakle. Strategists are a dime a dozen, and I read only Byron Wien, Mike Sherman, Steve Einhorn, Elaine Garzarelli, and Jim Moltz for the U.S. market.

Ray DeVoe does some interesting pieces but is long-winded, and I like the Gartner Group's work on technology. On the international side, Hoffman of AIG, Geneva's Bank Scandinave En Suisse, Hoare Govett's *Weekly World Review*, and Kleinwort Grieveson's country analysis are the class of the field. I don't find the big, comprehensive monthly or quarterly reviews to be helpful.

On specific countries, Nomura and Nikko are good on Japan, Schroeder Munchmeyer Hengst on Germany, Sung Hung Kai on Hong Kong, and Sassoon on Singapore. Vickers de Costa is excellent on all the Asian markets. In Europe, there are several good research brokers in most of the markets.

Obviously, I don't see all the research and publications in the world. Rather than be irritated if I didn't mention your publication, assume I don't receive it. Besides, this is just one bigot's opinion.

"Books, We Know, Are a Substantial World . . ."

November 25, 2002

I published this list 10 years ago, and I keep getting requests to update it, so here it is in all its infamy. Reading books about investing does two things for you. First, as investors, we are only the limited product of our own experiences and therefore vulnerable unless we read and assimilate the accumulated wisdom of the great ones. Second, as it says on the façade of the Library of Congress: *Those who have not studied the past are condemned to repeat it.* Economic and particularly financial history definitely tends to repeat itself. I have two long shelves of the best books I have read that relate one way or another to investing. Since investing is about everything, my books relate to diverse subjects ranging from history to psychology. In no particular order here is my list, with star rankings from 1 to 5. The whole exercise is completely subjective. Readability counts.

Groupthink★★★★★. Irving L. Janis. Houghton Mifflin, 1982. (The best book ever written on the complexities and pitfalls of group decision making, which is what an investment management firm is all about.)

The Alchemy of Finance★★★. George Soros. Simon & Schuster, 1987. (The master is complex, dense, but superb. His best book.)

Panic on Wall Street★★★. Robert Sobel. Macmillan, 1978. (The definitive study of American panics.)

Manias, Panics, and Crashes★★★★. Charles P. Kindleberger. Basic Books, 1988. (The best scholarly analysis of the species.)

Reminiscences of a Stock Operator★★★★★. Edwin Lefèvre. George H. Doran Company, 1923; reissued by John Wiley & Sons, 1994. (The classic work about intuitive trading. No investor's education is complete without reading it.)

The Money Game*****. Adam Smith. Random House, 1967. (Nobody writes like Gerry. Full of wisdom. It's a pleasure to read.)

The Roaring '80s***. Adam Smith. Summit Books, 1988. (More Gerry; if you get addicted, *Supermoney* is good, too.)

Contrarian Investment Strategy***. David Dreman. Random House, 1979. (A classic on why and how to be contrary.)

The Battle for Investment Survival*. Gerald Loeb. Random House, 1957. (One great idea. Put all your eggs in one basket and stare at that basket.)

The Great Crash, 1929***. John Kenneth Galbraith. Houghton Mifflin, 1961. (Good study of the Crash.)

Instincts of the Herd in Peace and War**. W. Trotter. Macmillan, 1908; reissued by T. Fisher Unwin, 1919. (Dense, insightful analysis of gregariousness and suggestibility.)

Duveen***. S. N. Behnnan. Harmony Books, 1978. (Fascinating biography of the great dealer and a wonderful history of the art market and its fads.)

Investment Policy**. Charles D. Ellis. Dow Jones-Irwin, 1985. (All of Charlie's books have great insights, especially this one and *Institutional Investing****.)

The Way the World Works**. Jude Wanniski. Touchstone, 1978. (I'm prejudiced because I believe, but this is the supply-side Old Testament.)

Wealth and Poverty**. George Gilder. Basic Books, 1981. (The New Testament of supply side.)

Growth Opportunities in Common Stock**. Winthrop Knowlton. Harper & Row, 1965. (This book and *Shaking the Money Tree**, with John Furth, are both superb on growth stock investing.)

The Elliott Wave Principle*. A. Frost and R. Prechter. New Classic Library, 1978. (Important to understand Fibonacci et al.)

The Great Depression of 1990*. Ran Batra. Venus Books, 1985. (We are condemned to repeat the mistakes not of our fathers but of our grandfathers.)

Technical Analysis of Stock Trends**. Edwards and Magee. Magee, 1966. (The manual on technical analysis.)

The Intelligent Investor***. Benjamin Graham. Harper, 1949. *Security Analysis*****. Graham and Dodd. Harper, 1951. (The bibles of value investing.)

The Long Wave in Economic Life**. J. J. Van Duijn. Allen & Unwire, 1983. (Best book I know of on cycles, which is what investing is all about.)

Confessions of an Advertising Man***. David Ogilvy. Atheneum, 1964. (Wonderful treatise on how to sell consumer products, written with wit and wisdom.)

Green Monday**. Michael M. Thomas. Simon & Schuster, 1980. (The best stock market novel ever written.)

Classics I and Classics II*****. Edited by Charles D. Ellis. Dow Jones-Irwin, 1989 and 1991. (Both collections are great browsing.)

Chaos**. James Gleick. Penguin Books, 1987. (Important to understand chaos theory.)

Investing with the Best*. Claude N. Rosenberg Jr. Wiley, 1986. (Excellent on how to manage your investment manager.)

Managing Investment Portfolios★★. Maugham and Tuttle. Warren, Gorham & Lamont, 1983. (Good stuff, but heavy going.)

Extraordinary Popular Delusions and the Madness of Crowds★★★★. Charles Mackay, 1841; reissued by Metro Books, 2002. (The ancient classic but still should be read.)

The Speculator★★. Jordan A. Schwam. Chapel Hill, NC, 1981. (Superb biography of Baruch. Note how he would from time to time retreat from the market.)

Capital Ideas★★. Peter Bernstein. Free Press, 1992. (History of the ideas that shaped modern finance. Peter sometimes is too intellectual for me.)

Devil Take the Hindmost★★★. Edward Chancellor. Farrar, Strauss, & Giroux, 1999. (Erudite, articulate history of manias and panics over the ages.)

Pioneering Portfolio Management★★★★. David F. Swensen. Free Press, 2000. (The best book ever about managing a large endowment portfolio.)

Stocks for the Long Run★★★★. Jeremy Siegel. McGraw-Hill, 3rd ed., 2002. (Absolutely crammed with fascinating information and analysis.)

The Trouble with Prosperity★★. James Grant. Times Books, 1996. (Jim writes beautifully, and all his books are great reads, although invariably bearish.)

Gold and Iron★★. Fritz Stern. Vintage, 1979. (Absorbing history of Bismarck and Bleichroeder, Europe in the nineteenth century, and capital preservation.)

Markets, Mobs, & Mayhem★★★. Robert Menschel. John Wiley & Sons, 2002. ("A modern look at the madness of crowds" and the most recent addition to my list.)

The Innovator's Dilemma★. Clayton Christensen. Harvard Business School Press, 1997. (Breakthrough idea of why new technologies cause great firms to fail.)

Valuing Wall Street★★★. Andrew Smithers and Stephen Wright. McGraw-Hill, 2000. (The rationale of the q ratio by Smithers, a brilliant analytical mind.)

The Myths of Inflation and Investing★★. Steven C. Leuthold. Crain Books, 1980. (Updated for deflation; consistent, extensive studies; not light reading.)